THE BUILDINGS OF ENGLAND

JOINT EDITORS: NIKOLAUS PEVSNER
AND JUDY NAIRN

DERBYSHIRE

NIKOLAUS PEVSNER
REVISED BY ELIZABETH WILLIAMSON

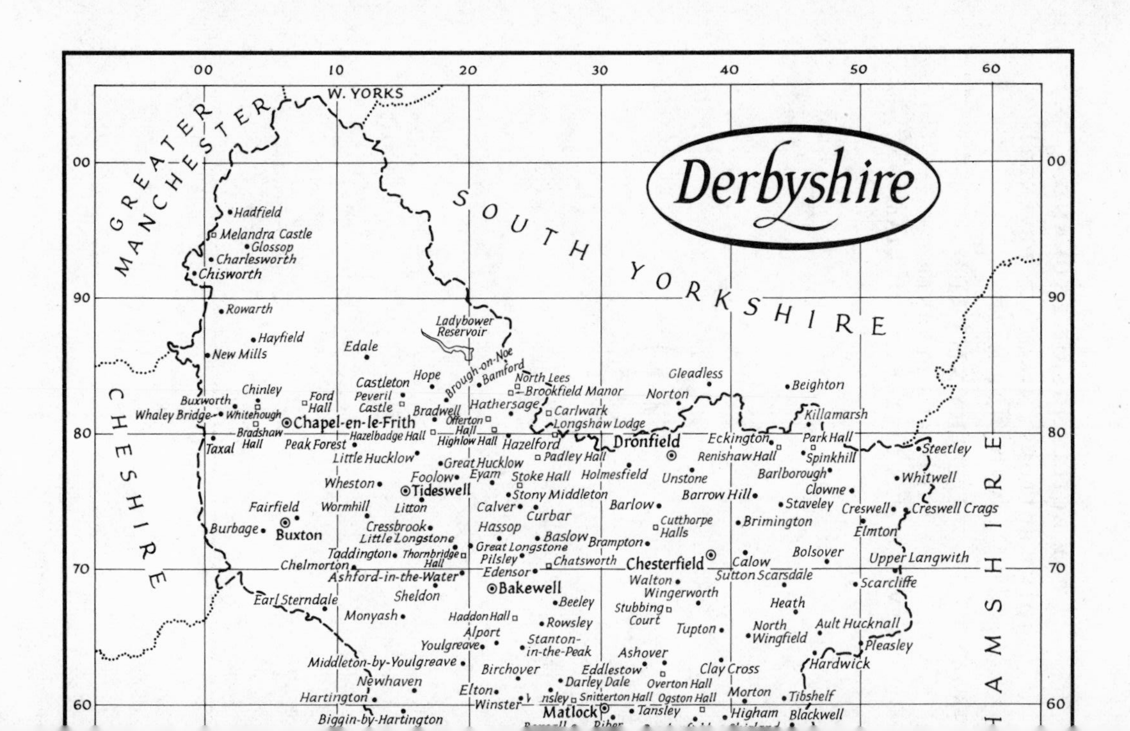
Derbyshire
GREATER MANCHESTER
W. YORKS
SOUTH YORKSHIRE
CHESHIRE
Hadfield
Melandra Castle
Glossop
Charlesworth
Chisworth
Rowarth
Hayfield
New Mills
Edale
Ladybower Reservoir
Brough-on-Noe
Bamford
North Lees
Brookfield Manor
Gleadless
Beighton
Norton
Chinley
Buxworth
Whaley Bridge
Whitehough
Ford Hall
Chapel-en-le-Frith
Castleton
Peveril Castle
Hope
Bradwell
Hathersage
Carlwark
Longshaw Lodge
Offerton Hall
Bradshaw Hall
Hazelbadge Hall
Highlow Hall
Hazelford
Dronfield
Eckington
Killamarsh
Park Hall
Renishaw Hall
Spinkhill
Steetley
Taxal
Peak Forest
Little Hucklow
Great Hucklow
Padley Hall
Holmesfield
Unstone
Barlborough
Whitwell
Wheston
Foolow
Eyam
Stoke Hall
Tideswell
Stony Middleton
Barrow Hill
Clowne
Fairfield
Wormhill
Litton
Calver
Curbar
Barlow
Staveley
Creswell
Creswell Crags
Cutthorpe Halls
Brimington
Burbage
Buxton
Cressbrook
Little Longstone
Hassop
Baslow
Elmton
Brampton
Bolsover
Taddington
Thornbridge Hall
Great Longstone
Pilsley
Chatsworth
Chesterfield
Calow
Upper Langwith
Chelmorton
Ashford-in-the-Water
Edensor
Walton
Sutton Scarsdale
Scarcliffe
Bakewell
Sheldon
Wingerworth
Earl Sterndale
Beeley
Stubbing Court
Heath
Monyash
Haddon Hall
Rowsley
Tupton
North Wingfield
Ault Hucknall
Alport
Stanton-in-the-Peak
Youlgreave
Ashover
Pleasley
Middleton-by-Youlgreave
Birchover
Eddlestow
Clay Cross
Hardwick
Newhaven
Darley Dale
Overton Hall
Elton
Snitterton Hall
Ogston Hall
Morton
Tibshelf
Hartington
Winster
Matlock
Tansley
Higham
Blackwell
Biggin-by-Hartington
00
10
20
30
40
50
60
90
80
70

STAFFORDSHIRE
LEICESTERSHIRE
NOTT
Thorpe
Bentley
Hognaston
Kirk Ireton
Heage
Ripley
Codnor
Kniveton
Atlow
Idridgehay
Mapleton
Biggin-by-Hulland
Belper
Loscoe
Heanor
Ashbourne
Bradley
Hulland
Turnditch
Hazelwood
Denby
Clifton
Kilburn Hall
Shipley
Milford
Holbrook
Smalley
Cotmanhay
Osmaston
Snelston
Muggington
Duffield
Horsley
Stainsby House
Edlaston
Ednaston
Little Eaton
Ilkeston
Norbury
Shirley
Kedleston
West Hallam
Brailsford
Morley
Yeaveley
Quarndon
Stanley
Kirk Hallam
Breadsall
Marston Montgomery
Kirk Langley
Locko Park
Dale Abbey
Cubley
Longford
Mackworth
Hopwell Hall
Stanton-by-Dale
DERBY
Sandiacre
Boylestone
Trusley
Radburne
Ockbrook
Risley
Somersal Herbert
Barton Blount
Doveridge
Dalbury
Borrowash
Breaston
Draycott
Long Eaton
Sudbury
Church Broughton
Sutton-on-the-Hill
Elvaston
Aston
Etwall
Sawley
Scropton
Hilton
Findern
Barrow-upon-Trent
Wilne
Shardlow
Marston-on-Dove
Willington
Aston-upon-Trent
Swarkeston
Eggington
Twyford
Weston-upon-Trent
Repton
Stanton-by-Bridge
Foremark
Ingleby
Kings Newton
Newton Solney
Melbourne
Brizlincote Hall
Ticknall
Bretby Park
Calke
Hartshorne
Church Gresley
Swadlincote
Smisby
Walton-upon-Trent
Woodville
Caldwell
Rosliston
Catton Hall
Overseal
Coton-in-the-Elms
Netherseal
Lullington
N
0
5 miles
H. A. Shelley
50
40
30
20
10
00
60

THE BUILDINGS OF ENGLAND

Derbyshire

BY

NIKOLAUS PEVSNER

★

REVISED BY

ELIZABETH WILLIAMSON

PENGUIN BOOKS

Penguin Books Ltd, Harmondsworth, Middlesex, England
Penguin Books, 625 Madison Avenue, New York, New York 10022, U.S.A.
Penguin Books Australia Ltd, Ringwood, Victoria, Australia
Penguin Books Canada Ltd, 2801 John Street, Markham, Ontario, Canada L3R 1B4
Penguin Books (N.Z.) Ltd, 182–190 Wairau Road, Auckland 10, New Zealand

—

First published 1953
Second edition 1978

—

ISBN 0 14 071008 6

—

—

Made and printed in Great Britain
by Butler & Tanner Ltd, Frome and London
Set in Monophoto Plantin

TO THE MEMORY OF MONKSDALE

CONTENTS

Map References

★

The numbers printed in italic type in the margin against the place names in the gazetteer of the book indicate the position of the place in question on the index map (pages 2–3), which is divided into sections by the 10-kilometre reference lines of the National Grid. The reference given here omits the two initial letters (formerly numbers) which in a full grid reference refer to the 100-kilometre squares into which the country is divided. The first two numbers indicate the *western* boundary, and the last two the *southern* boundary, of the 10-kilometre square in which the place in question is situated. For example, Long Eaton (reference 4030) will be found in the 10-kilometre square bounded by grid lines 40 and 50 on the *west* and 30 and 40 on the *south*; Hathersage (reference 2080) in the square bounded by grid lines 20 and 30 on the *west* and 80 and 90 on the *south.*

The map contains all those places, whether towns, villages, or isolated buildings, which are the subject of separate entries in the text.

FOREWORD TO THE FIRST EDITION

BY NIKOLAUS PEVSNER

The preparation of the data on which this book is based lay in the experienced hands of Dr Schapire, the compilation of the notes on prehistory and Roman antiquities in those of Mr Jon Manchip White. I am grateful to both of them for what they have done for this book. In addition I have had the valuable help of the Derby Central Library and the Derbyshire County Library, where both Mr E. Osborne and Mr Keith Mantell have taken great interest in my research. Moreover, the Ministry of Housing and Local Government, who have a statutory duty to draw up lists of buildings of architectural or historic interest, have with their customary kindness allowed me access to unpublished lists and much other information collected by the Chief Investigator of the Ministry and his staff (here abridged MHLG).* *The National Buildings Record‡ made it possible for me to use their photograph collection and for this I am indebted to Mr Cecil Farthing and Mrs Mary Parry. I have also to thank Mr H. S. Goodhart-Rendel for permission to use his manuscript card index of Victorian churches (marked here* GR) *and Sir Thomas Kendrick for permission to use his card index of Victorian stained glass (marked here* TK).

I have had to write to many rectors and vicars and have received much kindness from them. Some have gone to a great deal of trouble to satisfy my requests for specified information. The same is true of owners of houses. Here also everybody, with hardly any exception, has been most obliging both in showing me their houses and in answering questions. In return I wish to make it quite clear to readers of this Foreword that houses must not be supposed to be open to the public because they are mentioned or even described in this book.

In connexion with individual places I owe a special debt of gratitude to Mr Francis Thompson the Librarian and Keeper of Collections at Chatsworth, Colonel and Mrs Sandeman at Meynell Langley, Colonel R. B. Turbutt of Ogston Hall, the Reverend A. Hopkins, rector of Kirk Langley, Sir Osbert Sitwell, and Mr F. Ward of Torquay.

* Now Department of the Environment and abridged DOE.
‡ Now National Monuments Record (NMR).

FOREWORD TO THE SECOND EDITION

BY ELIZABETH WILLIAMSON

During the twenty-three years that have elapsed between the publication of the first edition of this book and the revision of it, changes to the county have been neither geographically nor architecturally dramatic. There have been some minor boundary changes in which Derbyshire lost Stapenhill and Winshill to Staffordshire, Beighton and Gleadless to Sheffield, and gained Tintwhistle from Cheshire, but apart from the deletion of Stapenhill from the text these do not affect this volume. Another administrative change, which has necessitated alterations to the gazetteer, is the incorporation of several villages in the Borough (now City) of Derby and in the Borough of Chesterfield. Several individual buildings have also been transferred to more appropriate places in the text. Major architectural changes, both positive and negative, have been recorded. The most notable new buildings are mentioned in the Postscript to the Introduction (**p. 46**), but the negative changes can be summarized here. Destruction has been concentrated at Derby, where the character and cohesion of the centre has been completely altered by the replacement of large numbers of* C18 *houses in the centre with a multi-lane road. As a traffic scheme this road is said to be a triumph; as townscape it is a disaster. Another notable loss at Derby is the important group of Nonconformist churches described on* *p. 173**. Chesterfield has also lost one or two buildings but has been reprieved from comprehensive redevelopment. In most other towns almost nothing of interest has disappeared.*

The rural scene remains largely unchanged. The smaller halls and manor houses are usually unspoilt working farmhouses. Most villages, except in the NE *near Sheffield, have escaped becoming prettified dormitories of large towns. The major change in the suburbs and countryside has been the total or partial demolition of many large country houses, including one or two of national interest. Eight have completely gone: Hopwell Hall (1720); Etwall Hall (early* C18*); Darley Abbey (early* C18 *and 1785, Joseph Pickford); Markeaton Hall*

* Allestree, Alvaston, Boulton, Chaddesden, Chellaston, Darley Abbey, Little Chester, Littleover, Mickleover, Normanton, Osmaston-by-Derby, and Spondon, all described individually in the first edition, are now within the City of Derby. Likewise Newbold, New Brampton, and Whittington, which previously had separate entries, are now in Chesterfield.

(1755); Egginton Hall (the Wyatts, 1782–3); Stainsby House (late C18 and C19)*; Snelston Hall (L. N. Cottingham, 1827–8); Osmaston Manor (H. I. Stevens, 1846–9). The core of Alfreton Hall (Francis Smith of Warwick, 1724–5) and most of Wheston Hall* (C18) *have also been pulled down. Altogether sixteen such houses have been completely or partly demolished since 1920.**

There has been compensation in the number of buildings carefully restored, notably Derby Cathedral, Norbury Manor, Radburne Hall, and Sudbury Hall. Part of the Crescent at Buxton and the Manor House at Dronfield have been restored and converted into libraries by the County Council. Although there has been a rapid growth of interest in industrial archaeology in the last twenty years and much research has been done on nationally important sites such as Cromford, Belper, and Milford, there unfortunately have been many losses – the most outstanding the demolition of Strutt's mills at Belper and Milford – but Calver Mill has been successfully restored, and the successor to John Lombe's silk mill at Derby has found new life as a museum of industrial archaeology. Several of the railway stations on closed lines have been re-used as workshops or as parts of small factories, and the windmill at Heage has been repaired by the County Council.

The main alteration to the text however has been the correction of factual errors and the addition of much new information from both published and unpublished sources.

The revision of this volume would have been almost impossible and certainly far less enjoyable without the co-operation of so many people both within and outside the county. First I must thank Mr Roger Evans, formerly Historic Buildings Adviser to the County Planning Department, who placed copious notes about the county at my disposal. His name or initials in the text denote his contributions, but he gave much other help in drawing my attention to buildings omitted from the first edition, in bringing perambulations up to date, and in providing cross-references which have been incorporated in the text. His assistant, Mr Robert Hawkins, undertook the revision of entries concerning industrial archaeology. Prehistoric and Roman entries, as well as the corresponding part of the Introduction, are by Mr Malcolm Todd, who was assisted by Mrs Priestly. I am grateful to Mr R. Kenning (County Architect) for information about the work of his department, and to Mr J. O. L. Brass, Director of Planning,

* Derwent Hall (C17), Wingerworth Hall (early C18, possibly by Francis Smith), Chaddesden Hall (C18), Drakelowe Hall (C18), Doveridge Hall (Edward Stevens, 1756–61), and Glossop Hall (*c.* 1850) were demolished before 1953.

Derby Borough Council, Mr T. Knuckey, Planning Officer of Chesterfield Borough Council, Mr Maurice Brennan, Director of Planning, Borough of High Peak, and Mr A. S. Martin of Erewash District Council for answering my extensive queries. I have also received a great deal of help from archivists and librarians, namely Miss Joan Sinar, County Archivist, Miss Rosemary Meredith, Archivist, Sheffield City Libraries, Miss Jane Isaac of Lichfield Joint Record Offices, Mr P. Gratton, County Librarian, Mr D. Inger of Chesterfield Central Library, Mr L. Greaves of Derby and South Derbyshire Area Library, Mr F. Atkins of Sheffield City Libraries, and the area, district, or branch libraries at Alfreton (Miss J. Marriot), Ashbourne (Mr K. B. Dadge), Belper (Mrs J. A. Coates), Buxton (Mr I. E. Burton), Heanor (Mrs F. Long), Ilkeston (Mr C. G. Browne), and Long Eaton (Mr P. A. Langham). In addition I received information from Mr Maxwell Craven and Mr Brian Waters of Derby Museum and help from Miss Beadsmoore, Mr Castledine, Mr Hughes, and Mr and Mrs M. Mallender of the Derbyshire Archaeological Society. Thanks are also due to all those people in the county who have generously contributed information about their special interests or localities, in particular Mr C. R. Allcock (Bakewell), Mr C. G. Cutts (Thornbridge Hall), Mr John Harnan (Ockbrook church), Mr D. G. Edwards (Wingerworth), Mr Keith Reedman (Long Eaton), Mr P. M. Robinson (Ilkeston), Mr G. Turbutt (Ogston), Mr H. J. Wain (Bretby), Mr J. E. Wright (Bolsover church), and last but not least Mr Edward Saunders, who not only provided me with information about Robert Bakewell and Joseph Pickford (indicated in the text by ES*), but also took me to visit many buildings. The officers of local societies gave me information on behalf of their members: Mr E. R. Meek and Mr J. T. Brighton (Bakewell Historical Society), Mrs J. Pilkington (Belper Civic Society), Mrs F. C. Robson (Belper Historical Society), Mrs W. L. Hope (Chesterfield Civic Society and Chesterfield Heritage Society), Mr D. K. Clareborough (Old Dronfield Society), Mr D. M. Soul (Duffield Community Association), Mr D. W. Haughton (Glossop Civic Action Group), Mr P. Senior and Mr J. M. Woolman (Hallamshire Historic Buildings Society), Mr A. R. W. Hobbs (Melbourne Civic Society), and Mrs Jan Knebel (Whaley Bridge Amenity Society).*

I am indebted to all the incumbents, owners of houses, headmasters, principals of colleges, directors of business concerns, and hospital secretaries who spared some of their valuable time to answer my questions. Mr T. Wragg completely revised the description of Chatsworth, Mr G. Hughes-Hartman rewrote that about Locko Park, and Mr Leslie Harris kindly provided many new facts about Kedleston from *his research. Mr Edward Hubbard wrote the accounts of Burton Closes, Bakewell and Brocksford Hall, Doveridge. Mr Anthony Blackwall (Blackwall House), Mr Stapleton-Martin (Norbury), Major J. W. Chandos-Pole (Radburne), and Mr Reresby Sitwell (Renishaw), all gave me new and detailed information about their homes. With regard to other individual places I must thank the National Trust and Dr Mark Girouard for allowing me to use the text of an unpublished guide book about Hardwick Hall, Dr M. Thompson for permitting me to use material from his unpublished paper* about South Wingfield, Mr P. Faulkner and Dr Girouard for checking my text on Bolsover, Dr H. M. Taylor for reading my entry about St Wystan, Repton, Dr C. A. R. Radford for reading that about the excavations at St Alkmund, Derby, and Mr John Hodgson for expounding the complicated building history of Sudbury Hall. Many corrections and additions have been sent since the first edition was published by Mr Alec Clifton-Taylor, Mr H. M. Colvin, Mr F. N. Fisher, Dr Andor Gomme, Mr Ivan Hall, Mr R. Hartley, Mr R. Hubbuck, Mr S. Jones, Mr R. Innes-Smith, Mr J. Lewis, Mr D. M. Palliser, Mr S. Rigold, Mr J. M. Robinson, Mr G. Spain, Mr Christopher Wilson, and Mr R. B. Wragg, to all of whom I am grateful. Mr Paul Joyce provided me with information about G. E. Street, Mr Peter Leach with information about James Paine, Mr Mervyn Miller with information about Parker & Unwin, Mr Anthony Quiney with information about J. L. Pearson, Mr Keith Reedman with information about Gorman & Ross, and Mr Andrew Saint with information about Eden Nesfield and Norman Shaw. Mr Alec Clifton-Taylor kindly revised the part of the introduction about building materials. Mr David Durant supplied details from his research into Bess of Hardwick's life, and Mr C. Stell* (CS) *a list of Nonconformist places of worship. Mr James Barron Wright and Mr Thomas Cocke visited many places to seek out or to check new information. The county map and the plans of the environs of Chesterfield and Derby were drawn by Mr H. A. Shelley. Mr John Kilday redrew the plan of Bolsover Castle and Mr Ian Stewart those of Chatsworth and Haddon Hall. Miss Linell McCurry gave much valuable secretarial help.*

In the following gazetteer, as in all the other volumes, information ought to be as complete as space permits for churches prior to 1830, and for town houses, manor houses, and country houses of more than local interest. Movable furnishings in houses are not described, but

* This has since appeared in *Problems in Economic and Social Archaeology* (ed. G. de G. Sieveking, I. H. Longworth, and K. E. Wilson), 1976.

church furnishings of before 1830 are, with the exception in most cases of bells, chests, royal arms, hatchments, altar tables, and plain fonts. Small Anglo-Saxon and Anglo-Danish fragments and coffin lids with foliated crosses are included only where they are of special interest, post-Reformation brasses and plate dating from after 1830 are mentioned only rarely. Village crosses are omitted where only a plain base or stump of shaft survives. As for churches, chapels, and secular buildings erected after 1830, examples of architectural value or significance in the light of architectural history have been selected. A note is necessary on how all the alterations to the first edition have been incorporated. Minor factual corrections or additions have been made without comment. For more extensive changes the source of information has been indicated. Other additions, unless they are in brackets, are the result of my own visits.

Finally I thank Mrs Bridget Cherry for her guidance and help throughout and Sir Nikolaus Pevsner for all his advice. Once again corrections and additions will be welcome.

INTRODUCTION

DERBYSHIRE is a county of contrasts: flat and uneventful country towards Nottinghamshire, rolling towards Leicestershire, and the forbidding grandeur of the High Peak towards Cheshire; hedges between fields in the south, rough stone walls in the north, brick cottages in the south, stone cottages in the north-west, agriculture in the south, pasture and bare moors in the north; industry in four distinct areas: the NE towards Yorkshire with Staveley, Eckington, Bolsover, etc., the NW towards Cheshire with Whaley Bridge, New Mills, Glossop, etc., the E towards Nottinghamshire with Ilkeston, Long Eaton, etc., and the S towards Leicestershire with Church Gresley, Swadlincote, etc. These industrial regions lie all along the margins of the county. The centre, especially N of a line from Ashbourne to Belper, is all country rightly popular with tourists: Dovedale, Derwent Dale, Miller's Dale, the Hope Valley, Matlock, Buxton, the High Peak. Tourists come for scenery of many varied attractions, less for architecture.*

1
2,3

Indeed Derbyshire has only two large towns: Derby, with a population of 217,930, and Chesterfield, with a small centre but far-spreading suburbs. None of the industrial towns is unremittingly ugly, and those in the NW, like New Mills and Whaley Bridge, have a distinctive blend of urban and rural atmospheres. The small towns and villages in the centre of the county, being far enough away from any large town to escape 'improvement' by the commuter, remain almost completely unspoilt. The county does not possess a cathedral (All Saints, Derby, was raised to cathedral status only in 1927), nor a large abbey in picturesque ruins, nor many parish churches as spectacular as those of East Anglia, the Nene Valley or the South West. But instead of grand churches there are grand houses: Haddon, Hardwick, Bolsover, Sudbury, Chatsworth, Kedleston; and these, especially since they have all been made accessible to the public, are what both the layman and the expert think of when Derbyshire is mentioned. The architectural historian will derive more enlightenment from domestic than from ecclesiastical architecture, and, it must be added, not only from the major mansions but also from a large number of manor

* And have done so it seems ever since 1680, when Cotton published *The Wonders of the Peak*.

houses (such as Tissington and Riber) and farmhouses, in the aggregate highly interesting. Far more of such houses are preserved in the N than in the S, because the rougher climate of the Peak prevented C18 and C19 prosperity which, in the S, destroyed more of value than it replaced. Or is this impression deceptive? Is it due to the fact that the brick house of the C18 in the S has less to arrest the eye than the gabled stone house of the N?

The dividing line between brick (and, before brick became popular, timber-framing) and stone runs roughly from W to E a few miles N of Derby.* It has its reasons in the geological structure of the county, which is relatively straightforward. There are limestones in two areas only: Carboniferous in what roughly corresponds to the southern portion of the Peak District National Park, from Matlock, Bakewell, and Eyam westwards to the Staffordshire border, with Wirksworth, Tissington, and Buxton on the periphery; and Permian (Magnesian) in the north-eastern spur of the county beyond Bolsover, to the E of the coal areas. Everywhere else there is sandstone, Carboniferous N of a line drawn from Ashbourne to Ilkeston, and mainly Triassic (New Red) to the S of this. The former comprises Millstone Grit in the N of the county and down the centre to the E of the Carboniferous limestone, together with a small area around Melbourne in the S. To the E of the Grit is the stone of the Coal Measures, from Dronfield to Ilkeston, with another pocket on the Leicestershire border around Swadlincote. Most of the New Red sandstone is Keuper, but there is a narrow strip of Bunter just S of Ashbourne and a small patch S of Foremark.

Although there is a dearth of specialized literature on the building stones of the past in Derbyshire (as in most English counties), their use accords with the geological pattern. In the NE the sandy, honey-coloured Magnesian limestone predominates, and on the high lands between Wirksworth and Buxton the light grey Carboniferous limestone is much in evidence. Around Derby and Ashbourne there is Bunter sandstone, and farther N plenty of gritstone and sandstone from the Coal Measures. Happily many buildings in this part of the county still retain their massive roofs of graded sandstone slabs. In the S the Keuper Marl yields clays well suited to the manufacture of bricks and tiles. The county has been an important source of supply for several other builders' materials. The so-called Derbyshire marbles are in fact Carboniferous limestones which will take a high polish. The best known

* We owe the revision of the paragraphs on building materials to Mr Alec Clifton-Taylor.

among these is Hopton Wood, but 'Derby Black', from Ashford and Little Longstone near Bakewell, was also popular at one time. In their polished state, however, they can only be employed internally, e.g. for paving, cladding, and chimneypieces, and they are no longer quarried. Alabaster is another Derbyshire material with similar qualities and limitations and was important through three centuries as a material for monuments. Derbyshire long remained the most important county in England for lead, which originated in mines close to Wirksworth, Matlock, Bakewell, and Hope.

Now for PREHISTORY.* The upland landscapes of Derbyshire contain a rich and varied record of man's dealings with his environment over many centuries. But these remains are not yet eloquent about their history and their wider significance, for with notable exceptions relatively little systematic field-work has been carried out. The county has, it is true, produced large quantities of archaeological material, particularly Bronze Age pottery and a fine series of Anglo-Saxon metal objects, but the bulk of these finds results from indifferent field-work. In the middle decades of the C19 Thomas Bateman, an energetic and inquiring antiquarian from Middleton-by-Youlgreave, investigated a large number of field monuments in the limestone area, paying particular attention to burial mounds of various dates. Though useful, and by no means ill-recorded by the standards of its day, Bateman's work was carried out with a speed which bordered on abandon. Many of the sites investigated by him could with profit be re-examined, as has recently been shown in certain cases.

The earliest traces of human activity occur in limestone caves in several localities, notably in the Manifold and Dove valleys, in Dowel Dale, Cressbrook Dale, and in Creswell Crags, on the Nottinghamshire border. These caves offered shelter, for longer or shorter periods of time, to hunters of the Upper Palaeolithic culture as they followed game on its seasonal migration to pastures in the Pennine hills. Deposits in the caves represent use by Palaeolithic and Mesolithic hunters over lengthy periods within the time bracket 15,000 and 3,000 B.C., but these are centuries when the pattern and basis of human life changed in no significant way, except when the climate or environment intervened. The most informative of the excavations have been those conducted, with varying degrees of expertise, in Creswell Crags, from which one of the most important of the British Upper Palaeolithic cultures, the Creswellian, takes its name. For the Palaeolithic hunters large

* The account of the Prehistoric and Roman periods is by Mr Malcolm Todd.

animals (reindeer, giant deer, woolly rhinoceros, and the mammoth) were common, but by no means exclusive, game.

The flint and bone implements from these rich deposits are very similar to the material assemblages from caves in the Cheddar Gorge, Somerset, and to the products of other industries in the Low Countries, northern France, and Germany, a fact which helps somewhat with the dating of the Derbyshire sites. These continental links suggest that the main occupation of the caves occurred between 12,000 and 7,000 B.C. Recent radio-carbon dates give a little more precision. Two for Robin Hood's Cave are centred on 8,500 B.C., and others have dated a cave at South Anston (in near-by south Yorkshire) at 8,000 B.C.

Changes in climate in the Late Boreal period (7,000 to 5,500 B.C.) brought about changes in the physical environment of the Derbyshire uplands and thus in the livelihood of their hunter-gatherer population. The kinds of game found in the area probably became fewer. Now red deer and smaller animals may have provided most of the diet, with variety provided by fish, fruit, and plants.

The transition in the uplands from a hunter-gatherer economy to one based upon agriculture was probably a prolonged and gradual process. The Neolithic phase of Derbyshire's prehistory is chiefly notable for the remains of several chambered tombs, designed for collective burials, almost all of them situated on the central limestone plateau. A group of four lie in the S (Minning Low, Stoney Low, Green Low, and Harborough Rocks) and a further three to the N (Five Wells, Bole Hill, and Ringham Low). Early excavation and subsequent stone robbing has damaged all these to some extent, and one (Bole Hill) has been completely destroyed. The evidence for their date is therefore not impressive, but they seem likely to belong to the period 2,500 to 2,000 B.C. Settlement sites of the Neolithic are as yet very imperfectly known, but slowly information is being accumulated, particularly from the limestone areas. On Elton Common, for instance, a settlement lay below the crest of a ridge at about 1,000 ft, and another lay near by at Astonhill near Minning Low. Several of the limestone caves, for example Dowel Cave at Earl Sterndale, were also occupied in this phase. The Beaker phase of the Late Neolithic and Early Bronze Age is also well represented in the limestone country and on its fringes, as well as in the Trent Valley, where settlements have been examined at Willington. The pottery of this period reveals links with Yorkshire and northern England rather than with the Midlands or East Anglia.

The most striking field monument of these centuries is the fine henge at Arbor Low, built probably about or shortly after 2,000 B.C. Though its central stone settings are now recumbent or even removed, this is visually a most dramatic ritual site, perhaps more dramatic today than in the time of its use, when there was a fair amount of forest cover on these rounded limestone hills. Another henge, the Bull Ring, lies near Doveholes and has similar overall dimensions to those of Arbor Low, but it has been intruded upon by quarrying and damaged by stone robbing.

The Middle and Later Bronze Age is best known from the abundant remains of its funerary monuments. Large numbers of these exist on the limestone plateau and the gritstone edges to the E and W. Remarkable groups of barrows, cairns, and earth circles exist at Stanton Moor, Ramsley Moor, and, before erosion by agriculture, Beeley Moor and Eyam Moor. Clearly there was a considerable increase in the population of the region during the Middle Bronze Age, perhaps due to drier climatic conditions which made the gritstone uplands more attractive to settlers. Certainly the evidence from vegetational studies indicates that woodland clearance was being pursued at the time, and both herbaceous and heath environments were being created. The period 1,300 to 1,100 B.C. seems to have been of particular importance in this respect. Unfortunately, few settlement sites of the Bronze Age have yet been examined. The settlement at Swine Sty, near Baslow, a group of circular huts within an enclosure bank, is the best excavated example to date.

Of settlement in the latest division of prehistory, conventionally known as the Iron Age, little is known outside the hill-forts. With the exception of the most impressive, Mam Tor near Castleton, these forts are rather small enclosures, only a few acres in extent, and their surviving defences and gate-openings are not exceptionally massive. The best preserved are Mam Tor, the promontory fort of Fin Cop near Ashford-in-the-Water, Combs Moss near Chapel-en-le-Frith, Castle Ring near Youlgreave, and the Carlwark near Hathersage. The history of the forts has yet to be worked out. Mam Tor was occupied as early as the Late Bronze Age, but the hill-top defences are considerably later. The evidence of pottery suggests an occupation which continued as late as the C1 A.D. and which presumably ended with Roman seizure of the Peak District. The other forts have produced little evidence for their dating and the material culture of their inhabitants. A small amount of pottery from Castle Ring suggests cultural links with the Iron Age communities of Yorkshire rather than with the Trent basin. Other forms of settlement must have existed but await discovery. The group of hut-circles and enclosures on Chee Tor near Blackwell may date from the Iron Age, but they have not yet been excavated. Settlement in the Trent valley and in the S of the county appears to be similar in broad characteristics to that which prevailed in the adjacent counties, being based on single homesteads engaged in mixed farming.

The history of the ROMAN PERIOD in Derbyshire is, as yet, the history of the occupying power, so far as this can be reconstructed from the Roman auxiliary forts established in the hill-country of the southernmost Brigantes. The earliest traces of a Roman garrison yet recorded in the county are to be found at the large and still imperfectly known fort at Strutts Park in the northern suburbs of Derby. This work dates from the reign of Nero, its foundation being probably *c.* A.D. 55–60. The occupation was brief, for in the period immediately following A.D. 71 Roman troops advanced into the Pennines and garrisoned the entire area. Apart from the need to hold down the inhabitants of this difficult terrain, Derbyshire offered accessible lead and silver deposits to the invaders, and it was not long before these resources were being tapped.

The principal garrisons which held the largely pastoralist hillmen in check lay at Little Chester (Derventio) just N of Derby, Brough-on-Noe (Navio) near the junction of the valleys Hope and Edale, and Melandra Castle (Ardotalia) W of the Dark Peak near Glossop. All three forts were founded in the period of the Flavian emperors, most probably during the provincial governorship of Julius Agricola (A.D. 78–85), under whose direction the great advance into northern Britain was made. These late C1 garrisons were housed in timber-built quarters protected by earthwork defences; at Brough and Melandra rebuilding in stone took place early in the C2. It now seems probable that army units remained at Brough and Little Chester throughout much of the C2 and probably well into the C3; at Melandra, however, there is no evidence for military occupation after about 150.

Further information on military occupation for this region is steadily accumulating. A late C1 fort is probably to be sought on the high ground at Silverlands, Buxton, where Samian pottery of this period has long been known. Another fort dating from the late C1 and early C2 has recently been located beneath the centre of modern Chesterfield and a little information gained as to its internal arrangement. At Pentrich near Alfreton, another small fort appears to lie beneath the better known small earthwork set close to Ryknield Street. Nor does this necessarily exhaust the tale. A fort-site at or near Bakewell would make good sense on grounds of spacing between known forts, and it is notable that a military inscription was long ago discovered here. Another military site might be predicted in the Wirksworth area amid the formerly rich silver/lead veins or rakes of that district.

The essential complement to the fort garrisons was a system of roads linking them, thus opening up this broken landscape. The lineaments of the road system, which presumably dates back to an origin in the later C1, are tolerably clear on the ground today, although some points of detail remain to be clarified. The main N–S route in this area of the southern Pennines was Ryknield Street, running through the eastern hills and linking the Trent Valley with the Don. An important E–W road was that which ran to the S of the Dark Peak from Templeborough, near Rotherham, through Brough-on-Noe to Buxton. From Brough itself a clearly defined route led on NW to Melandra Castle and thence to Manchester and the western Pennines. Buxton appears to have been a major crossroads, for it too was linked with Manchester, and this road passed on to the SE towards Little Chester, although its course near the last-named site has not yet been clearly traced. Little Chester too was an important nodal point in the road-system. Ryknield Street passed through here and on southward to Wall. To the W, a road led to Rocester and ultimately to the Cheshire plain. Another road led SE to the Trent at Sawley and may have joined the Fosse Way at some point in south Nottinghamshire. Within the framework of these major routes, others may well be sought. A road along the Derwent Valley, for example, approximately on the line of the present A6 through Matlock and Bakewell, is a distinct possibility, although no real evidence has yet been secured for it.

Civilian settlement of the Roman period has attracted little attention from the excavator. The closest approximation to a Roman town in the county was the spa at Buxton (Aquae Arnemetiae), but the layout and history of the place is as yet undiscovered. Several of the forts, especially Little Chester and Brough-on-Noe, possessed extra-mural villages or *vici*. Villas are as yet unrecorded, even in such areas as the Trent and lower Derwent valleys which might have been expected to contain them. In the limestone and gritstone hills, the known settlements of pastoralists resemble those of other Pennine regions. Two industrial concerns merit attention: pottery-making and the extraction of lead and silver.

Major potteries existed in the Hazelwood and Holbrook area, producing a durable, hard-fired ware (commonly termed Derbyshire Ware) from the C2 to the C4. Another centre lay at Little Chester, though its period of operation seems to have been confined to the early C2. Of wider significance, the veins of galena, yielding silver and lead, were exploited from the late C1 onward, at first under direct military supervision, later under the charge of a company of lessees, the *socii Lutudarenses*. The centre of their operations, *Lutudarum*, is not certainly located but probably lay in the Wirksworth area, where there was a considerable concentration of veins near the surface.

After the withdrawal of the Romans the county seems to have remained for more than a century in the hands of the Britons. The ANGLO-SAXONS gradually moved in during the later C6. They were Mercians, and so Derbyshire became part of the kingdom of Mercia, and Repton (Hrewpandum) the capital of South Mercia under King Peada. A number of SAXON CROSSES of Mercian character dating from *c.* 800 onwards have been found; 22 the best of this early group are at Bakewell and Eyam. Their style depends on the C7 art of Northumberland. The remarkable panel 21 from a stone coffin with scenes from the life of Christ at Wirksworth also belongs to *c.* 800. It is one of the leading examples of figure sculpture of its date in the country. Later Saxon crosses are of two types: panelled with interlace decoration (Hope, Norbury, Bakewell from Two Dales, Blackwell) and cylindrical (Brailsford). They seem to date from the C11, the latter dependent on such superior north country examples as Gosforth of the late C10. SAXON ARCHITECTURE is best represented at Repton, where a straight-headed chancel with the typical thin lesenes of the period, fragmentary indications of transepts and crossing, and 4 the famous crypt survive. The columns have thin spiral bands around and support primitive domical valuts. The date is controversial. As a vaulted crypt with columns Repton is unique in Anglo-Saxon architecture, but represents a type familiar in France and Germany.

The Danes gave Derby its name and established the shire. Derby, Nottingham, Lincoln, Stamford, and Leicester were the five principal towns of the Midlands. Reconquest by the Saxons took place in the early C10. The NORMANS quickly incorporated the county in their administrative system. William granted lands chiefly to William Peverel and Henry de Ferrers. William Peverel 50 had Peveril Castle, built to guard the mining of the Hope Valley, and Bolsover in the NE of the county. Henry de Ferrers built Tutbury (just across the Staffordshire border) and Duffield. The keep at Duffield, the foundations of which are known from excavations, was larger than any other Norman CASTLE in England save Colchester and London. Peveril Castle is by far the best preserved and visually the most rewarding castle in the county. Of the C12 Horsley Castle only a fragment remains. Most of it was destroyed by quarrying in the C18.

Of Norman CHURCHES the first rank is held by Melbourne and Steetley. Melbourne is the unique example of a mere parish church with such cathedral motifs as a two-tower W front, and a wall-passage at clerestory level. It has the unusual feature of an open gallery towards the nave between the towers and the even more unusual feature of an originally two-storeyed chancel. All the detail is robust to the verge of brutality. The tall, very narrowly placed circular arcade piers with their stilted arches are specially impressive. Norman arcade piers in Derbyshire are without exception circular (e.g. Youlgreave). Capitals vary according to their date in the same way as in other parts of the country. Arches develop from a completely unmoulded section to one-stepped, one-stepped-one-chamfered, and finally double-chamfered sections. Keeling of circular piers appears already in the transitional stage between Norman and Early English (Barlborough, Youlgreave, Whitwell). Only one Norman church other than Melbourne was intended to be on so large a scale: Bakewell, where a two-tower front was projected and begun, probably before 1100, and then a towerless C12 façade erected instead. Otherwise Norman remains belong to smaller churches, and Steetley, by far the most sumptuous example in the county of C12 decoration, is in size no more than a chapel. It consists of nave, lower and narrower chancel, and yet lower and narrower apse, the only Norman apse in Derbyshire. The arches between the various parts, the S portal, and the exterior of the apse are all lavishly adorned. Why such a display should have been made just at Steetley has never been explained. Minor Early Norman elements survive at Ault Hucknall and Wingerworth. Doorways, tympana, W towers are too frequent to be discussed here in detail. Sandiacre may be mentioned for its doorway and windows; Hognaston, Parwich, and Ault Hucknall for their tympana; Bradbourne for its W tower. Whitwell has its Norman clerestory preserved. Most Norman FONTS are plain. Amongst those decorated the most interesting is that at Ashover, because it is of lead and was made no doubt locally. It has figures in blank arcades. Similar arcades on stone fonts exist at Hognaston and Eyam, interlaced arches at Ockbrook, Kirk Hallam, and Somersal Herbert, interlaced rings and zigzag at Church Broughton, leaf decoration at Chesterfield, incised animals at 24 Tissington. The font at Youlgreave has an unusual projecting side stoup.

Of the comparatively few MONASTIC FOUNDATIONS of Derbyshire little is left. The Austin Canons had Gresley (early C12), Darley Abbey (1154), Repton (1172), and Breadsall (well before 12 1260), the Premonstratensian Canons Dale Abbey (*c.* 1200), the Knights Hospitallers Yeaveley (Stydd Hall, *c.* 1190) and Barrow-on-Trent (Arleston House, C13).* Of the Cluniac St James at Derby, the Benedictine Kingsmead Nunnery at Derby, the Dominican Friary at Derby, and the unique Lazarite preceptory at Locko nothing survives. Chief clerical landowners in the country were the Derbyshire houses, but the abbeys and priories of Burton-on-Trent in Staffordshire, Lenton in Notts, Dunstable in Beds, and Basingwerke in Flintshire also had property.

The EARLY ENGLISH style appears in Derbyshire at Ash- 10 bourne, where the chancel was dedicated in 1241. The dedication plate, of brass, survives. With its twin lancet windows in each bay (very similar to the chancel at Southwell begun in 1234) it gives one a safe starting point for the dating of an uncommonly ambitious group of later C13 churches on the same cruciform plan as 9 adopted at Ashbourne. They are Chesterfield, Bakewell, Tideswell, Wirksworth (begun *c.* 1272), and also Darley Dale, Hartington, Kedleston, and Monyash. Ashbourne, Bakewell, and Chesterfield are further enlarged by E transept aisles, a motif also present *c.* 1225–50 at Lichfield Cathedral. To the same group belongs the spacious chancel of Doveridge. It is very instructive 13 to compare the details of piers, arches, windows, etc., in this group. They give a clear and fairly complete picture of the architectural development during the years in which they were designed. For windows Derbyshire in the late C13 clearly favoured the type with two lancet lights and a pierced spandrel and the three-light type with intersected tracery. They were apparently carried on into the C14. A spectacular Geometrical window must 12 originally have existed at Dale Abbey. Only the barest indications of its former tracery remain. Pier shapes are, as in other parts of the country, of greater variety than in any other period. They are mostly developed from the quatrefoil section by the addition of shafts and also by keeling and filleting. The many possibilities

* Beauchief (Premonstratensian, *c.* 1175) was in Derbyshire until 1933. It is now in Sheffield.

can best be studied amongst the remains of Repton Priory and at Ashbourne, but also at Wirksworth, Hartington, Tideswell, Bakewell, etc. Weston-upon-Trent has simple circular piers, unusually tall and slim, endowing this relatively small church with remarkable nobility. The best E.E. W towers are at Breadsall and Eckington. They combine elegance with concision, as no earlier or later towers do. In this they clearly represent the same spirit as the window tracery of the mid and later C13. 11

It is specially illuminating to watch how, about 1300, heralding the intricacies and capriciousness of the DECORATED style, tracery forms begin to abandon the Geometrical clarity and logicality of circles with inscribed trefoils or quatrefoils. Such minor demonstrations of caprice can be studied in the Ashbourne transept, the Hartington S transept, Whitwell chancel, and at Dronfield. Mature Dec tracery is not particularly interesting in Derbyshire. Little of the flights of fancy occur that one is used to in East Anglia, Lincolnshire, Yorkshire, and the neighbouring counties. Reticulated tracery is usual and remains so until after the middle of the century (Spondon (Derby), rebuilt after 1340);* flowing tracery is rare and comparatively simple, and also still in fashion *c.* 1360 and later (Spondon, Sandiacre, Chaddesden (Derby), Tideswell, Taddington). So-called Kentish tracery is to be found at Sandiacre and Chaddesden. The chancels of these churches belong to the most important monuments of the C14 in Derbyshire. As in Notts (Hawton, Sibthorpe, Woodborough, etc.) wealthy and pious men were especially inclined to devote their means to the enlargement and embellishment of the chancels, and the dimensions and the lightness and airiness of the best in Derbyshire are indeed splendid. They are Norbury probably built *c.* 1300–7, Sandiacre built by Bishop Norbury of Lichfield *c.* 1342–7, Chaddesden built by Henry Chaddesden, Archdeacon of Leicester, *c.* 1357, Tideswell built by John Foljambe † 1383 *c.* 1360–80 as the end of a truly spectacular rebuilding of the whole church from *c.* 1320 onwards, and finally Taddington of about the same date, probably influenced by Tideswell.‡ The large parish church of Chesterfield also must have been entirely rebuilt during these years. It possesses the remarkable anomaly (from the English point of view) of a transept chapel ending in a polygonal apse. The N and S windows at Tideswell and Taddington are 15 14 16 17

* It also occurs in straight-headed windows, e.g. at Breadsall.

‡ Chaddesden is much more villagey in character than the others in this group. Dronfield should be added to the list despite the mutilation of the E window (Christopher Wilson).

straight-headed, the tracery motifs at Tideswell and Norbury oddly conservative, i.e. neither Perp nor Dec, but rather developed from simple quatrefoil and pointed trefoil and quatrefoil motifs. A peculiar variety of such tracery occurs at North Wingfield and Whitwell.

Of CHURCH FURNISHINGS the earliest screens belong to this age and their tracery is as elementarily geometrical as that just 27 referred to. They are the stone screen of Ilkeston and the timber screen of Kirk Langley, both early C14. At Tideswell (as also at Sawley) a stone screen appears in an unusual position, immediately behind the altar and a short distance W of the E wall, probably to divide off a narrow sacristy space. The earliest stained glass in the county is at Ashbourne, Dalbury, and then (C14) Cubley. The earliest wall paintings are at Wingerworth (late C12), Dale Abbey (*c.* 1300), and Melbourne (C14). A fine piece of sculpture 23 of the late C13 is the Nativity at Bolsover. Bakewell font, adorned with figures, is the best C14 font in the county, Ashbourne the best of the C13. A special Derbyshire curiosity of the C14 is stone book-rests built into chancel N walls. They occur at Chaddesden (Derby), Crich, Etwall, Mickleover, (Derby), Spondon (Derby), and Taddington.

One more architectural feature must be referred to: the C14 SPIRES. The dating of spires is hazardous. There is little historical evidence to go by. Plain and rather broad broach-spires apparently come before the slimmer spires starting recessed behind the battlements of towers. The latter is the more typical Derbyshire form (also typical of W Notts). Examples of the former are Baslow, Brampton, Breaston, Hope, Ockbrook, Rosliston, and Taddington. Examples of the latter are too numerous to be listed. In neither case are more than very occasional dates recorded. The earliest may be late C13, the majority early C14 (Repton completed 16 1340). The biggest Perp TOWERS have no spires: Tideswell of 18 *c.* 1380, Youlgreave, and All Saints Derby of the early C16. Derby with its tall four-light bell-openings and big decorated battlements and pinnacles is the most ornate. On the whole Perp towers in the county are not specially interesting. Tall bell-openings are rare. One group of towers has eight instead of four pinnacles (cf. Notts, especially St Mary Nottingham). Tideswell and Youlgreave (also Elvaston, Barlborough, and four or five others) belong to it.

The tower of Tideswell is the earliest dated document of the PERPENDICULAR style in Derbyshire. Until then probably Dec forms were still in use. The earliest dated Perp window is the E window at Ashbourne put in between 1392 and 1399.* The late C14 and C15 being a time of high commercial prosperity for the towns and villages of England, churches of the Perp style are in many parts of the country especially splendid and numerous. Derbyshire is disappointing in this respect. All Saints Derby was replaced by *Gibbs*'s church in the C18, and no other is comparable with Long Melford or King's Lynn or Newark or Grantham or Chipping Campden or Tiverton or so many others. Even such details as tracery lack interest. The huge many-panelled windows so typical of ambitious Perp church architecture are rare; piers are not specially inventive in their shapes, capitals are only rarely decorated (Beighton, Hathersage, Mugginton), and roofs are almost exclusively of the simplest types (nice but also simple tracery above the beams at Tideswell, Ault Hucknall, North Wingfield). A group of tunnel-vaulted porches with transverse arches may be singled out (Ault Hucknall, Brampton, Upper Langwith, North Wingfield, Shirland, Stanton-by-Dale, and Wilne; cf. more in Notts), also two porches vaulted otherwise (Denby, Tideswell) and finally a group of windows with straight-sided arches (Repton, Elvaston, Killamarsh).

Exactly the same scarcity of really good work is to be found in late medieval CHURCH FURNISHINGS. Both rood screens and parclose screens have been carefully listed by Aymer Vallance, but not one of them is up to East Anglian or Devon standards. The majority have one-light divisions (e.g. Ashbourne, Bakewell, Chaddesden (Derby), Darley Dale, Elvaston, Fenny Bentley 1519). Those with two-light divisions are at Ashover *c.* 1518 and Fenny Bentley, with three- and four-light divisions at Chesterfield 1475 and *c.* 1500. In the original rood screen at Chesterfield (now in St Katharine's Chapel) and at Fenny Bentley the groining for the loft is preserved. The only surviving loft is that at Wingerworth, not resting on a screen but attached to the E wall of the Norman nave. The low screen at Chelmorton is stone and embattled. Stall ends (Chaddesden), bench ends, and misericords (Bakewell, Tideswell) are so scanty that no summing up is necessary. The same applies to fonts and sculpture. The best stained glass is that from Dale Abbey now at Morley. It is dated 1482. The glass at Norbury is C14. At Ashbourne, Caldwell, and Eggington are some fragments of *c.* 1400, at Ault Hucknall is a Christ Crucified of 1527. The earliest church plate in the county is the C15 censer at Upper Langwith and the patens of Hartshorne,

26

* Tracery motifs which appear Dec occur as late as South Wingfield Manor, i.e. *c.* 1440–50.

29 Shirley and Dronfield. At Haddon Hall in the chapel there are some delightful C15 wall paintings, figure work as well as a kind of *mille fleurs* pattern.

CHURCH MONUMENTS are on the whole less disappointing. There is, it is true, only one outstanding example of the C13 and
33 the early C14, i.e. the early C13 effigy of a woman in Scarcliffe church. Also interesting are the stone slab to Matilda le Caus † 1224 at Brampton and the oddly sunk heads in quatrefoils of a knight and his lady in the floor of Kedleston church. They belong to a grave slab sunk beneath the church and according to their style belong to the late C13. Directly ALABASTER became a fashionable material for monuments, the importance of Derbyshire increased. The best quarry, Chellaston (Derby), was in the county. At first alabaster seems to have been used only for very special clients, the effigies of Edward II, John of Eltham, Archbishop Stratford at Canterbury, Bishop Edington at Winchester, etc. And indeed the earliest alabaster in Derbyshire is perhaps the best, certainly as good as any later. It is the delightful small
34 wall-monument of 1385 at Bakewell to Sir Godfrey Foljambe † 1377 and his wife, with erect demi-figures under an arch of fanciful shape, lively and very delicately wrought. Mr Gardner worked out that amongst 342 alabaster monuments listed in all English counties only Yorkshire possesses more than Derbyshire, and Yorkshire is six times the size of Derbyshire. Yorkshire has 34, Derbyshire 29, Nottinghamshire 20, Lincolnshire (again a very big county) 20. So Derbyshire and Notts are the centre not only of the trade but also of the clientele. The best alabaster tombs
36–8 in Derbyshire are at Norbury, Youlgreave, and Ashbourne. They have recumbent effigies or incised slabs and, against the walls of the tomb-chest, standing angels, or saints, or members of the family in panels or under little canopies. Ashbourne, Bakewell, and Chesterfield contain particularly rich assemblies of medieval and post-medieval monuments. The fashion for alabaster went out about the middle of the C17. Specially noteworthy later medieval stone effigies on tomb-chests are at Radburne and Ash-
39 over. The best is the latest: Katherine Babington † 1543 at Morley. The earliest brass is of 1399 (Dronfield), the best in the county
35 is perhaps that of Robert Eyre at Hathersage † 1459.

The great families for which these monuments were made, the Vernons at Bakewell, Cokaynes at Ashbourne, the Fitzherberts, Foljambes, Eyres, and so on were also the builders of the CASTLES and MANOR HOUSES of Derbyshire. And while none of the churches in the county is of more than regional interest (except perhaps Ashbourne), the domestic architecture of the C14 to C18 of Derbyshire could not be left out of any history of English architecture. For the MIDDLE AGES the chief relics are Haddon Hall 51 and South Wingfield Manor, the latter built by Lord Treasurer 52 Cromwell whose chief residence was Tattershall Castle. Both are large and both are fortified, though domestic features have precedence; also both are built round two courtyards. But Haddon has the advantage of an unbroken tradition over centuries and the ensuing illusion of still being completely lived in, whereas Wingfield is a ruin. Wingfield, on the other hand, is the outcome of no more than twenty years, and thus possesses a rare unity of style. At Haddon the gate tower, some masonry, and part of the chapel prove that the Norman predecessor of the house was of the same size. The hall with its offices and the Chamber Block 53 are C14, much of the chapel and the other apartments is C15 and early C16, and yet more is Elizabethan and Jacobean. The total 54 visual effect of the large grey embattled complex of buildings in its green setting is unparalleled in England. South Wingfield was all built between 1440 and 1456, the most ambitious surviving structure of its date in the country. The hall and the large state rooms by its side are on a truly regal scale.

Codnor Castle, of which only the scantiest ruins are left, was on nearly the same scale (length 150 ft). Other military remains are few and not important: gatehouse Mackworth Castle *c.* 1500, and remains of two fortified manor houses, i.e. a tower at Cherry Orchard Farm, Fenny Bentley, and the Elizabethan and older ruins of Eastwood Hall, Ashover. Of domestic architecture the most interesting (though minor) remains are of a large C14 and C15 manor house at Padley, the hall-house of *c.* 1250 to *c.* 1305 at Norbury Manor, and the W range (built *c.* 1500) of Ogston Hall. Prior Overton's tower and study at Repton (*c.* 1440) are one of the best pieces of early brick architecture in England. Inside are fine carved beams with ornamental bosses, similar to those at Haddon, which also has notably complete interiors, with a screen of *c.* 1450 in the hall, a unique number of fitments in the kitchens, good ceilings of *c.* 1500 in the solar and the earl's apartments, and an original painted ceiling in the parlour.

The earliest appearance of the Italian RENAISSANCE style in Derbyshire is connected with Haddon. It is in some panelling in the parlour, dated 1545 and exceptional because an example of 54 dated Renaissance panelling of before 1550. Of CHURCH MONUMENTS that to Sir John Port, the founder of Repton School, at Etwall, is still Gothic, although he died as late as 1557; that to

40 Anthony Lowe † 1555 at Wirksworth is entirely in the new taste, complete with putti and Corinthian pilasters flanking the back plate. The type of the alabaster tomb with or without mourners also remained acceptable as late as the excellent and cosmopolitan 41 in detail Foljambe Monument † 1585 at Chesterfield, and even later, † 1598 (West Hallam), † 1632 (Thorpe), † 1656 (Morley). The Pursglove brass at Tideswell † 1579 is also still medieval in composition, but this was possibly because Bishop Pursglove was a well known 'Popish' conservative.

Similarly in CHURCH ARCHITECTURE the Gothic style was not given up until after the Restoration. The church of Carsington, allegedly 're-edified' in 1648, is purely Perp. The church at Risley dates from 1593 to 1632 and is equally medieval, though its two-light and intersected three-light windows are now round-arched. The Willoughby Chapel at Wilne of 1622 is specially not-30 able for its contemporary fittings, tiles, and stained glass, the latter probably a rare example by the *Van Linges* of London. The Frecheville Chapel at Staveley also has fine C17 stained glass by *Gyles* of York. Even the church at Foremark which was built in 1662 shows its late date only in a certain exterior symmetry and some ornamental details.

Elizabethan and pre-classical C17 CHURCH FURNISHINGS are not frequent, and not of special quality, except perhaps the Jacobean pulpits of fine workmanship at Chesterfield and Dronfield. Otherwise there are the fitments in the chapel at Haddon Hall and in All Saints Dale Abbey, the family pew in the parish church at Elvaston, the pulpits at Sawley (1636) and Foremark (*c.* 1662), the seats in the Port Chapel at Etwall, and pews at Hope, Castleton, and Tideswell with parts dating from 1587 to 1690. As for PLATE, of the twenty-eight cups, ten with paten covers, from the most prolific Elizabethan years (1565–70), the only dated examples are at Findern, Wilne, and Taddington. There are a number of good C17 domestic cups dating from 1601 at Kedleston (the best example) to 1678 at Somersal Herbert. The sets of plate given in 1641 by Lady Frances Kniveton to Kirk Langley, Kniveton, Mugginton, and Osmaston have chalices of the Gothic shape preferred by the High Church party. C16 and C17 wall paintings survive at Eyam and Bradbourne.

All this does not amount to much. MONUMENTS, on the other hand, once again the true reflection of the state of domestic architecture, are many, and some of the highest quality available in England. The most usual Elizabethan type, as in all counties, is that with husband and wife kneeling opposite each other separated by a prayer-desk. The children kneel below in a kind of 'predella' (Bakewell † 1584 and † 1623, Chesterfield probably of the 1590s, Youlgreave † 1613, Tissington † 1619 and † 1643, etc.). The best monuments appear only towards the end of Elizabeth's reign and between her death and the 1630s. They begin with the Godfrey Foljambe Monument † 1594 at Chesterfield with its uncommonly 42 good allegorical figures, and the exquisite and mysterious anonymous Foljambe memorial put up by the same member of the 41 family. The shrouded figure on this, completely bundled up so that no face appears, is repeated in two effigies at Fenny Bentley 43 on a tomb to an ancestor, Thomas Beresford, who had died over a century before in 1473. All the other monuments of interest are later than 1600. Some are of the familiar type with effigy or effigies under an arch flanked by columns (Sudbury † 1600, Bess of Hardwick's tomb in Derby Cathedral, finished before 1601 to a *Smythson* design, Bakewell † 1623, Wilne † 1622). Others are more original, especially the singular, rather naive Bradshaw Monument without effigies at Duffield of 1600, the elaborate Cavendish 44 Monument at Edensor of *c.* 1616–25, the Sleigh Monument † 1634 at Sutton-on-the-Hill which has, instead of an effigy, a big black stone coffin realistically carved down to the handles, and the very Italian (although the source of the design is Flemish) and thus decidedly novel monument to the wife of the first Earl 46 of Devonshire of 1627 at Ault Hucknall. Here the new art connected with Inigo Jones and Nicholas Stone begins in Derbyshire.

In the great houses of the ELIZABETHAN AND JACOBEAN AGE SCULPTURE also appears. The Venus Fountain at Bolsover (slightly later: *c.* 1628) shows how bad it can be, the Diana at Chatsworth and the relief with the Muses at Hardwick what inter- 65 nationally good quality could be obtained, perhaps by purchases abroad.

As for these HOUSES themselves there is a rare wealth of them in Derbyshire, ranging from the small manor house to the splendours of Hardwick. On the whole many more survive in the N than in the S of the county owing to the greater recent prosperity of the S. The earliest of the grand ELIZABETHAN MANSIONS does not survive, the Chatsworth of Bess of Hardwick, begun in 1552 and incorporated to some extent in the first Duke of Devonshire's country palace. When she first began to build at Hardwick for herself, Bess was much older. She began by remodelling the existing old mansion and then, aged about 70, began a new one 59 close to the old. Her hard, able, proud character seems reflected in its uncompromising rectangularity, its regular pattern of

61 extremely large mullioned and transomed windows, and the somewhat coarse grandeur of the decoration inside. How much 63, 64 more sensitive in its proportions and details is the Long Gallery at 62 Haddon than the Gallery and Great Chamber at Hardwick. Bess's State Rooms are unusual in being on the top floor of the house, duplicated by a suite on the second floor, and reached by a dramatic staircase.* Hardwick belongs to a group of clearly defined Late Elizabethan houses, connected with the *Smythson* family of mason-architects which starts in the Midlands with *Robert Smythson*'s Wollaton, Notts, of 1580 and includes houses built by the Shrewsburys and their circle at Worksop, Notts 60 (demolished), Barlborough (1583–4), and Hardwick. All have their square compact plans (and some details) in common. Hardwick has the Great Hall in a position axial to the entrance, quite contrary to medieval and earlier Tudor custom (although it was in this position in Hardwick Old Hall); the centralized hall, high basement, and projecting corner towers amongst other things the house shares with Wollaton. There are other houses of this tall 66 compact 'Smythson' type in Derbyshire: North Lees, a Late Elizabethan tower house whose various owners were apparently connected with the Shrewsburys, and the later unfinished Weston Hall of *c.* 1630, H-plan but very tall and regular. Then there is 68 the so-called Keep at Bolsover, begun in 1612, probably by *Robert Smythson*, and continued by his son *John*, who with his son, *Huntingdon*, is buried in Bolsover church. Robert himself lies buried at Wollaton. At Bolsover as at Wollaton there is a romantic atti- 70, 71 tude of a self-conscious continuation or rather revival of medieval precedent, especially evident in the interior with its vaulted rooms.

One more large house must be mentioned, Longford Hall, whose projecting Tudor chimneys give one an idea of what the house must have been like before the Georgian and later alterations. But just as rewarding as these large houses are the more modest Elizabethan and Jacobean ones. There is a bewildering variety of them and they do not fall into easily defined groups. There is very little timber-framed building, and what there is is 56 mostly confined to the S of the country. Somersal Herbert (*c.* 1564) is easily the best timber-framed house, extremely pretty and fanci-

* The state rooms in Elizabethan Chatsworth were also 'skied', but without a duplicate suite below. Here such planning was more understandable as the fall of the ground reduced the ground floor to a basement on the E side. There was a duplicate suite at Hardwick Old Hall, and the state rooms both here and at Worksop were on the top floor.

ful in the West Country manner. Other well-preserved examples are at Hilton and Idridgehay, the latter showing signs of having been an open hall-house. Neither are there many C16 and C17 brick buildings. The other houses which must be listed here are all of stone. We start with Hazelbadge Hall of 1549, still with horizontal many-mullioned windows with pointed tops to the individual lights. The same window shapes also still appear at Offerton Hall and Stanton Woodhouse. This latter detail was soon to disappear, but the low horizontal mullioned window itself remained current in the county right down to the C18. Typically Elizabethan with some stout classical decoration are Snitterton, a real gem, and Aston Hall of 1578. For the early C17 the prize should probably go to Tissington Hall and Padley Hall, but there are more houses than can here be mentioned: Hartington Hall of 1613, Bradshaw Hall of 1620, Holme Hall, Bakewell, of 1626, Old Hall Farm, Youlgreave, of 1630, Riber Manor House of 1633, Renishaw in its H-shaped original core, the earliest parts of Brookhill Hall, the tower-like Cutthorpe Manor, and so on. To these must be added the Ashbourne Grammar School founded 1585 as an outstanding example of scholastic architecture of the age (more ambitious, for example, than Harrow),* the Jacobean House at Derby of 1677 as a late but typical ambitious town house,‡ and two examples from that little investigated field of Elizabethan and Jacobean architecture, the plaisance: the stand or hunting tower at Chatsworth and the odd so-called grandstand at Swarkeston.

55 57 58 67

The style of the MANOR HOUSE AND FARMHOUSE remained essentially Tudor to an astonishingly late date, and it is well worth referring to the gazetteer to study the minor changes by which later buildings betray the time when they were really built. Here is a list, not even complete as far as this volume goes and with no detailed enumeration. Almshouses, Ashbourne, 1640 and 1669; Old Hall, Hadfield, 1646; Youlgreave Old Hall 1650 or 1656; The Peacock, Rowsley, 1652; § Sacheverell Almshouses, Morley, 1656; Hallowes, Dronfield, 1657; Offerton Hall 1658; Ogston Hall 1659; Little Hucklow 1661; Long Lee, Rowarth, 1663; Stanton Old Hall 1667; Elton 1668; Tupton Hall 1671; Derwent Hall (destroyed 1944) 1672; Eyam Hall 1672–6 (one of

73

* Some of the windows have even here arched tops to the individual lights.

‡ The date could read 1611, and there is a long tradition that it was the first brick house in Derby (brickyards began there *c.* 1600), but the architectural evidence suggests that 1677 is right.

§ The semicircular pediment here appears again at Elton in 1668, Buxton Old Hall in 1670, and Rose Hill, Dronfield, in 1719.

the best); Old House Hotel, Newbold, Chesterfield, 1678; Seven 74 Stars Inn, Derby, 1680; Almshouses, Etwall, 1681; Wheatsheaf House, Matlock, 1681; Old Hall Cottages, Fairfield, 1687; Newton Old Hall, Blackwell, 1690; Bath House, Bakewell, 1697; Wormhill Hall 1697 (bigger than most of the others); houses at Elton 1717; Rose Hill, Dronfield, 1719; Clergy House, Litton, 1723; Spalden Almshouses, Ashbourne, 1723–4; Slack Hall 1727; Netherseal Hall 1751 (date-stone possibly moved from elsewhere); Hammerton Hall, Litton, 1768. All these have the predominance of the mullioned window in common, mostly still horizontal. Straight gables are also still the custom. Broadly speaking the development can be watched in terms of a more and more symmetrical placing of the windows, the introduction of string-courses and the attachment of the windows to them, and occasionally in the admission of doorways or applied decoration more classical than the windows and gables would make one expect. Some mostly undated late C17 and early C18 buildings are slightly more advanced, combining mullion-and-transom cross windows with other classical features such as balustraded parapets: e.g. Duffield Hall; Bagshaw Hall, Bakewell, 1684; the Manor House, the Hall, and Chiverton House of 1719, all at Dronfield; the Laundry, Melbourne Hall; and the upper storey of the Market Hall, Winster.

The INTERIORS of these late C16, C17, and early C18 houses do not survive intact. The best plasterwork, at Cartledge Hall, Holmesfield, came from the demolished Greenhill Hall in Sheffield and belongs to a group of ceilings in this area that includes those at Renishaw and Brampton Manor House. There is also good late C16 plasterwork at North Lees. No panelling, fireplaces, or staircases are worthy of individual note.

We must now try to trace the coming of the new Italian motifs and of what corresponds in Derbyshire to the revolutionary classical buildings of Inigo Jones in London. Nothing so noble and restrained exists in Derbyshire. Here the style appears instead in a less disciplined, also less knowledgeable, more Baroque form, partly indebted to Serlio, Rubens, and other architectural pattern books, and partly still to Jacobean motifs, e.g. in the retention of window tracery and the playful, curly Baroque gables popular in monuments earlier than in architecture proper. The first 68 example of this style is seen at Bolsover, in the Keep, where one window surround is a misunderstood copy of Inigo Jones's Arundel Gateway seen by *John Smythson* in London in 1618, the fireplaces are quotations from Serlio, and some of the wall paintings are Mannerist in style, and in the lavish later buildings, now in ruins. In the latter insistence on heavy rustication is also characteristic. The Bolsover state rooms and Derby County Hall of *c.* 1660 are comparable in style to Samuel Marsh's Nottingham Castle (1674) across the border.* Sudbury Hall must be mentioned here. Whenever it was begun (in 1613 or *c.* 1665), it was completed *c.* 1670 in a relatively restrained metropolitan style, obviously influenced by houses of the Coleshill type in its hipped roof, central lantern, and panelled chimneys. The frontispiece by *Sir William Wilson* is of distinctly Baroque character.‡ Sudbury also contains the most splendid interiors of the date in Derbyshire and probably among the best in the country. There is a marked difference between *Wilson*'s fireplace and the local plasterer *Samuel Mansfield*'s ceilings, which are both Jonesian in style, and the richer, more advanced decoration (e.g. the staircase balustrade composed of acanthus scrolls) by *Pierce*, *Bradbury*, *Pettifer*, and *Grinling Gibbons* from London. They herald the developments at Chatsworth.

72

75

76

Only with Chatsworth, built from 1687 to 1707, does Derbyshire reappear on the truly national stage. The work first of *Talman* and then of *Archer* is among the essential documents of the English style of *c.* 1700, closely related to Hampton Court, where Talman was Comptroller of Works from 1689 onwards. Of the contemporary treatment of the grounds the grand Cascade and *Archer*'s Cascade House remain.§ For the interiors a team of artists was called in, partly of London reputation, like the painters *Verrio*, *Laguerre* (who also painted at Sudbury), and *Thornhill*, *Cibber* the sculptor, *Tijou* the smith, and partly local men of an artistry unquestionably equal to theirs. That applies certainly to *Samuel Watson*, the sculptor and carver at Chatsworth, who had worked at Sudbury.

77–9

80

The grand style of Chatsworth was emulated in the EIGHTEENTH CENTURY at Calke Abbey of 1703, a surprisingly little known large mansion, and then turned more Baroque at *Smith* of Warwick's Sutton Scarsdale of 1724 (now a ruin) and at Locko Park built *c.* 1725. Examples of the comfortable medium-size country house begin before 1700 with Holbrook Hall of 1681. The early C18 Ingleby Toft, Catton Hall of 1741 by *William Smith*

83

* The only other public building of note in the later C17 is the small Market Hall at Winster.

‡ It seems possible that Wilson also worked for Bentley Hall, Cubley.

§ There were even more important formal gardens of the C17 at Bretby, the Earl of Chesterfield's mansion, demolished in the C18.

the younger, and Radburne Hall, begun in 1739 and also probably by *William Smith*, represent a type of brick house with a restrained exterior and occasionally with a more ambitious interior. Longstone Hall (1747), Parwich Hall (1747), and Sycamore Farm, Hopton, are early examples of this type of brick-faced Georgian house in a stone area. A livelier, earlier variety on a smaller scale appears in the pretty Latin House of 1706 at Risley and the almshouses at Mapleton of 1727. Brizlincote Hall of 1707 and Hopton Hall of *c.* 1790 are both crowned by giant segmental pediments, a Baroque feature which might have appealed to so wilful an architect as Archer. Strict Palladianism makes its entry with the remodelling of the E front of Melbourne Hall by *William Smith* in 1744, and reaches its most complete form in 1759–61 at Foremark by *David Hiorns* and at Kedleston, which was begun in 1759 by *Brettingham*, continued by *Paine*, and completed by *Robert Adam* (1760–1780s).* In his grand entrance hall Adam keeps to Paine's or Brettingham's original scheme and thus achieves a splendour of giant Derbyshire alabaster columns rare in his *œuvre*. The decoration of the state rooms at Kedleston is rightly among the most famous of its date in the country.‡ Palladian taste on a more modest scale can be seen at Stoke Hall of 1757, with some features characteristic of *Paine*, at St Helen's House, Derby, and at the small but grand Ashford Hall, a late example of *c.* 1785.

82 84 85 86, 87 88

Prosperous C18 TOWN HOUSES are most numerous at Wirksworth, Duffield, Ashbourne, and in Friar Gate, Derby, where an evolution of styles can easily be followed. No. 44 Friar Gate, with fine proportions and neo-classical details, is the house of *Joseph Pickford* and is a good example of that provincial architect's style.§ Similar in style and also possibly by *Pickford* are the Mansion at Ashbourne, remodelled in 1754–6, Long Eaton Hall, and Draycott House. Derby Assembly Rooms, the only fine example of an C18 PUBLIC BUILDING, lost its Adam-style plasterwork when it was gutted by fire in 1964. Its elegant stone façade has been moved to Crich.

90 89

Special mention should be made here of SPAS. Derbyshire has two spas of totally different character. Buxton was developed in the late C18 under the auspices of the Duke of Devonshire. Its

* One of the most conventional examples of Palladianism, Doveridge Hall of 1769 by *Edward Stevens*, was demolished in 1934.

‡ The most important post-Adam house, Egginton Hall of 1782–3 by the *Wyatts*, has been demolished.

§ His chief work in Derbyshire, at Ogston Hall and Darley Abbey, can no longer be seen, as the former was altered in the C19, the latter demolished in 1962.

C18 buildings, especially the Bath-inspired Crescent and the Riding School by *Carr*, are impressive, and its streets to some extent are planned. Its C19 Pavilion Gardens, and the Park, were the responsibility of the seventh Duke's gardener, *Paxton*, the thermal establishments of his architect *Henry Currey*. Matlock Bath grew up about the same time along the Derwent gorge and is dominated by the magnificent landscape that inspired the many Strawberry Hill Gothick villas on the hill above and the Alpine railway station. The chief building of its railway age prosperity, Smedley's Hydro, is over a mile away at Matlock Bank. Bakewell's harmonious character too owes much to its short period as a spa *c.* 1800 under the Duke of Rutland. 91

In ECCLESIASTICAL ARCHITECTURE of the period between the Restoration and the end of the Georgian era the county is not rich, but it possesses at least one example up to the standard and the scale of the most ambitious in London: *James Gibbs*'s rebuilding of All Saints Derby of 1723–5. It is with its characteristic window shapes and interior arrangement at once recognizable as the work of the architect of St Martin-in-the-Fields in London, but it achieves an added elegance by the delicious wrought-iron chancel screen, the work of the ingenious local blacksmith *Robert Bakewell*. He and *Watson* show how very much alive the provinces still were at this time. Bakewell's artistry in IRONWORK can also be admired at Derby in the gates at the W end of the cathedral, in the Silk Mill gates outside the Library, and also in gates at Ashbourne, Etwall, Foremark, and Longford.* His earliest known work is the lovely Arbour of 1706–11 at Melbourne Hall. These GARDENS, incidentally, are an authentic design by *London & Wise*, the Royal Gardeners, of 1699 (i.e. just before landscape gardening began). The grounds of Kedleston, with their many classical garden buildings by *Adam*, are the finest example of landscape gardening in Derbyshire, but the exquisite scaled-down landscape park and gardener's cottage at Ashford Hall should be noted. 19 28 81

Other C18 CHURCHES need no more than a passing mention: Trusley of 1713, a modest brick building, Mapleton with its dome and lantern on the W tower, the little Halter Devil Chapel near Mugginton of 1723, the modernization of the larger churches of Chapel-en-le-Frith (1731–3) and Eckington, the interesting octagonal church of Stony Middleton of 1759, and so on to St John

* Gates by *Bakewell* have been removed from the county. Those from Wingerworth Hall are at Penshurst, Kent, those from Wirksworth Hall at Park Hall, near Ludlow, Salop (ES).

at Buxton of 1811 with its heavy Tuscan portico, *Ireland*'s even heavier Tuscan portico at Hassop 1816–18, St Matthew at Hayfield 1818, by *Moses Wood*, St John Evangelist Derby by *Goodwin*, 1828, and Hartshorne of 1835, with their cast-iron tracery, and Hulland of 1838 with its completely surviving furnishings. A complete set of furnishings of *c.* 1700 survives at Kedleston. Of other post-Restoration FURNISHINGS it is sufficient to mention the mid-C17 stalls in a Continental style at Church Gresley, the late C17 wooden font and pulpit at Locko, *Bakewell*'s font cover of 1716 in St Werburgh, Derby, the screen and communion rails, possibly also by *Bakewell*, at Borrowash, the wrought-iron reredos at Alvaston (Derby), the delightful candelabrum at Chesterfield of *c.* 1760, and the baluster fonts at Breaston, Litton, Kedleston, and Willington. There are handsome altar rails at Eckington. Also worth mentioning are a number of CHURCH MONUMENTS. The number is small compared with, for instance, the Home Counties, and the great London names appear only here and there. In the N of the county there are hardly any monuments of note later than *c.* 1650. The exception is that NE corner where the Sitwell tombs at Eckington † 1658 and † 1667 herald the new style to come; where *Gibbs* himself designed the Cavendish Monument of 1727 at Bolsover, and where two more provincial monuments of 1673 and † 1734 remain at Brampton near Chesterfield. The only series of expensive family memorials is at Kedleston, and there also the earliest two, † 1686 and † 1727, are relatively modest. Of 1683 is the Pole monument at Radburne by *Gibbons*; it has no effigy. Grander are some monuments of the C18 and especially that at Kedleston of 1765 by *Rysbrack* (designed by *Adam*). *Rysbrack* also did one monument in All Saints Derby († 1760), *Roubiliac* another († 1735), and *Nollekens* († 1793) yet another. *Chantrey*, a Derbyshire man, was commissioned to do one in All Saints (1822) and one in St Werburgh (1832). A bust of 1820 by him is in the County Hall. To return to the late C17, the earliest of the four monuments at Kedleston is similar to that of 1673 at Brampton, and one † 1662 at Morley. A type characteristic of the late C17 has no effigy and as its centre an urn (Sudbury † 1675, Staveley † 1682, Radburne 1683, Wilne † 1688). Early C18 monuments not yet mentioned are at Morley † 1714 (a very Baroque composition of several urns), Newton Solney, erected 1734, and at Calke † 1741 and Alfreton † 1792, both of excellent workmanship, the former attributed to *Cheere* by Gunnis, the latter by the *Fishers* of York. A monument of 1764 at Pentrich is signed *A.B.*, a bust † 1786 at Hayfield is signed by *Bacon*. The

47
48

Penelope Boothby Monument at Ashbourne by *Banks* (1793) with the sleeping child is amongst the most popular of its age. *Canova* did a monument for Elvaston († 1829) and *Sir Richard Westmacott* monuments † 1805, 1823, and 1824 for Ockbrook as well as one † 1830 for All Saints Derby and one † 1835 for Belper. The usual and often very elegant late C18 and early C19 tablets with urns, in flat relief with mourning allegorical figures, are hardly ever signed in Derbyshire.* Nor do we know the names of the rustic craftsmen who did the slate headstones in churchyards in the S of the county.

49

NONCONFORMIST places of worship are, needless to say, very much more modest than those of the established Church. By far the most interesting is the Moravian Settlement of 1750–2 at Ockbrook with its handsome chapel in the centre of the main range of buildings. Chesterfield has the Elder Yard Chapel of 1694, with a classical façade, but the chapel of 1711 at Chapel Milton, Chinley, still has two storeys of mullioned windows. A grander scale was achieved only with the now demolished Methodist chapel in King Street, Derby, of 1841, which had Greek Doric columns, and was continued with the Methodist church of 1870 in Saltergate, Chesterfield. Parallel is the increase in scale in Roman Catholic architecture; cf. the churches at Hassop (1816–18) and at Glossop (1836).

So on to a summary of NINETEENTH-CENTURY architecture. Of VICTORIAN CHURCHES hardly anything need be said. There are no major works in the county by the top echelon of Victorian architects. St Mary (R.C.), Derby, begun in 1838 is one of *Pugin*'s earliest churches, still a rather thin Perp in style. St Alkmund, which originally faced it, was another typical example of Early Victorian design. It was by *H. I. Stevens* of Derby, who did much work in the county and beyond its boundaries, never cheap-looking and never in bad taste. Characteristic also of the first years of the Queen is a passing fashion for Norman imitation. This is represented in Derbyshire by Wensley 1841–3, Woodville 1846 by *Stevens*, Little Eaton 1851, and Rowsley 1856 by *Salvin Junior*. *Butterfield* built the church of Bamford (1856–60) in a local idiom, and restored Hathersage (1849–52), Heath (1882–6), Monyash (1884–7), and Ault Hucknall (1885–8). Specially sensitive restorations are by *Shaw* at Youlgreave 1869–70, Great Longstone 1873, and Upper Langwith 1877, and

* Two signatures that do recur are those of *White Watson*, the descendant of Samuel Watson, and *Joseph Hall* of Derby. Their products are not outstanding.

by *Pearson* at Steetley 1880, and Whitwell 1885–6, where he also designed the vicarage. In 1868 *Street* largely rebuilt Long Eaton church in a rather dull way. *Sir Gilbert Scott* was responsible for St Andrew, Derby (1866, now demolished), and Edensor village church (1867). The most prolific local architects responsible for many restorations and churches of an economical kind are *S. Rollinson* of Chesterfield and *F. J. Robinson* of Derby, whose masterpiece is St Luke, Derby.* Of Victorian CHURCH FURNISHINGS [31] only the early *Morris & Co.* stained glass (1860s) at Darley Dale [32] and the unusual set of plate at Buxton by *Edward Barnard & Sons*, 1839, need singling out.

The GOTHIC REVIVAL in DOMESTIC ARCHITECTURE [93] began with Arkwright's Willersley Castle at Cromford in 1789–90.‡ The architect of this mansion was *William Thomas*. Its style [94] was followed by the large addition to Renishaw carried out by the Sheffield architect *Badger* between 1793 and 1808, castellated, with fine classical interiors,§ and continues at Elvaston Castle, designed by *James Wyatt*, who died in 1813, but not begun until 1817 by *Walker*, a pupil of Thomas Leverton. The E façade was added in 1830–40 by *Cottingham*, whose specially picturesque Snelston Hall of 1827 has been demolished. Slightly earlier is Bladon Castle at Newton Solney, built as an eyecatcher in this style and transformed into a house in 1801–3, possibly by *Sir Jeffry* [95] *Wyatville*, who also provided the design in 1812–13 for Bretby, a big castellated Gothic mansion on a hill. The fashion finishes with a flourish in Riber Castle of 1862–8, the folly-residence of Mr Smedley, founder of the Matlock Hydro. It also occurs in a number of smaller houses, such as Sutton Hall of *c.* 1820, the early C19 Upper and Lower Towers at Matlock Bath, and later in the additions to Brookfield Manor of 1870. *Wyatville* appears in a different, Italian mood with his extensions of 1820–37 to Chatsworth [77] for the sixth Duke of Devonshire, i.e. the new N wing with its big belvedere. As important were *Paxton*'s improvements to the grounds in the 1830s and 40s. His Great Conservatory (1836–40), which had such a profound influence on subsequent iron and glass structures, was alas demolished in 1920. *Paxton* also designed a number of gate lodges and ESTATE BUILDINGS on the Duke's estates at Baslow, Beeley, Pilsley, and with Loudon's former

* And from outside the county *T. C. Hine* of Nottingham.

† On a smaller scale it is seen before 1751 in the deercote at Sudbury and [92] in a fireplace of *c.* 1750 at Tissington Hall.

§ The Oakes at Norton (now in Sheffield), remodelled in 1827, has a dining room almost identical with that at Renishaw.

draughtsman, *John Robertson*, at Edensor. Edensor is a pre-Victorian conception: the artificially picturesque village of cottages in many selected styles, made solid, durable, more archaeologically correct, and thereby more Victorian. It dates mainly from 1838–42 and thus is preceded both by *Wyatville*'s convincingly half-timbered Buxton gate lodge of 1837 at Baslow, and by *Cottingham*'s earlier and more typically picturesque estate buildings at Snelston, where the *cottage orné* is contrasted with a severe Tudor. The estate villages of the Harpur-Crewes of Calke (Ticknall), of the Turbutts of Ogston (Higham), and the Vernons of Sudbury are much more modest. The most varied and interesting C19 GARDENS were created at Elvaston by *William Barron* between 1830 and 1850, and include fine landscaping, topiary, a lake and grottoes, and Moorish garden buildings. Renishaw has a number of Reptonian garden buildings, both Gothick and rustic. Victorian Tudor appears at Burton Closes, Bakewell, at *Scott*'s Alton Manor in 1846, and at *Stevens*'s Callow Hall, Mapleton, in 1852. Stevens had used the style at Osmaston Manor (now demolished) in 1846–7 for a grander display. With *Nesfield*'s Lea Wood near Dethick (1874–7) we see the return to intimate scale, pretty detail, and much variety of materials and treatment in the Domestic Revival. The county possesses *Nesfield*'s first work, the model farm of 1860 at Shipley Park, and his most complete surviving interior (1872–4) at the otherwise undistinguished Bank Hall, Chapel-en-le-Frith. Only fragments of the once elaborate *Pugin* interiors at Burton Closes survive.

96

There are no important PUBLIC BUILDINGS in Derbyshire, even in Derby and Chesterfield, the only two sizeable towns. Derby's most remarkable C19 commercial building was perhaps the Trijunct Station by *Francis Thompson*, 1839–40, of which only a small part survives. (For other stations see pp. 50—1.)

The first half of the TWENTIETH CENTURY needs little space in this brief survey. There is nothing of national note in the county, except *Lutyens*'s Queen-Anne-style country house, Ednaston Manor, for W. G. Player. Of regional importance are the sound and sensitive churches of *P. H. Currey*, an architect worthy of being better known. With *C. C. Thompson* he produced at Buxton in 1915 one particularly well-detailed church, the furnishings very close to those by the Northern Art Workers Guild to which Raymond Unwin and Barry Parker belonged. Also of 1915 is the delightful hillside chapel of St John at Matlock by *Sir Guy Dawber*. It is perhaps worth mentioning that *Parker & Unwin* were both born and began their careers in Derbyshire,

20

Unwin as a mining engineer with the Staveley Iron & Coal Company for whom he designed miners' housing and amenities, before joining Parker in practice at Buxton from 1896 to 1906. Their buildings in Derbyshire include one of their best early houses (Greenmoor, Buxton, 1897–1900), a major public building in Edwardian Free Style (Rockside Hydro, Matlock Bank, 1901–7), and a complete Arts and Crafts house (The Homestead, Chesterfield, 1903–5). Contemporary with these are the buildings at Long Eaton by *Gorman & Ross*, whose distinctive brand of the Domestic Revival style shows Glasgow-school or Continental leanings.* Also of interest are some of the schools. From before World War II are those of *G. H. Widdows*, County Architect between *c.* 1910 and 1936, enlightened in plan, with covered ways and large windows and always interesting in their motifs, Tudor-Baroque at Chesterfield and Long Eaton, stripped classical at Ilkeston. After 1945 the *County Architect's Department* under *F. Hamer Crossley* began a series of schools built of light steel on a standard grid and faced with brick (e.g. Infants and Secondary School, Littleover (Derby); Longmoor Primary School, Long Eaton; Alvaston and Boulton Junior School (Derby); Shelton Lock Primary School, Allenton (Derby); and Charnock Hall Junior School, Gleadless (now in Sheffield)), which takes us up to 1953.

POSTSCRIPT TO THE INTRODUCTION (1978)

BY ELIZABETH WILLIAMSON

ALTHOUGH it is over twenty years since the first edition was published, little need be said about the buildings erected since then. The county has no New Towns or major housing developments, no university, and almost no high-rise buildings. The comprehensive development plan for the centre of Chesterfield by *Bernard Engle & Partners* was shelved in 1975, partly because of the economic climate and partly because of growing public resistance to this type of development. Derby has the rather unimpressive Civic Centre by *Casson, Conder & Partners*, ‡ but there

* Keith Reedman has given us details about *Gorman & Ross*, who first appeared in Long Eaton in 1900. Their output was small but their range wide, from semis to factories. Gorman, a local man, was appointed architect to the civil authorities in Penang in 1905–6. Ross, apparently not the creative partner, became a fruit farmer in Australia.

‡ Unfinished at the time of writing.

are imposing buildings on the outskirts of the city by *Fry, Drew & Partners* (1961–8) for Rolls Royce. The only really novel building in the county,* using a new system of construction, is SAPA Ltd's plant at Tibshelf by *Foster Associates*, 1972–3. For school building Derbyshire, together with Nottinghamshire and Leicestershire, became in 1956 one of the first counties to adopt the CLASP system, now used for most schools in the county. Its full potential is used to create a village-like atmosphere at Tupton Hall School, 1965–9 by *George Grey & Partners*, whose tiny but very carefully detailed branch library at Duffield should also be mentioned. *Gelsthorpe & Savidge*'s swimming pool at Ilkeston (1967–72) is a rare but quite tame example of 1960s brutalism. A major project which has no significance in the history of recent architecture is *Sebastian Comper*'s extension of 1967–72 to Derby Cathedral. In the cathedral is recent stained glass by *Ceri Richards*, and there is some by *Reyntiens* in *Montague Associates*' unusual chapel at Ednaston. At Chesterfield is sculpture by *Barbara Hepworth*. Finally a note should be made of the effect of the Peak Park Planning Board's policy, approved in 1959, on building in the National Park. Its ruling that buildings should harmonize in design and colour with the gabled limestone and gritstone buildings of the area has produced no imaginative interpretation. The stone extensions to Lady Manners School at Bakewell with pitched roofs of various kinds is a typical solution.

100

INDUSTRIAL ARCHAEOLOGY

BY BOB HAWKINS

ALTHOUGH much emphasis is placed on the importance of the textile factories of Derbyshire, and the achievements of early factory masters such as Arkwright and Strutt, these buildings can give an unbalanced view of the industrial pedigree of the county. Some would argue that the most impressive monuments are to be found below ground, in the many miles of tunnels, soughs, shafts, and levels excavated in the search for mineral wealth. Only occasionally do the monuments of the lead industry, for example, by means of the chimneys, engine houses, and associated buildings of a site such as the Magpie Mine complex near Sheldon, give an indication of the intensity of the activity associated

* Except that is the Olivetti building at Derby (*Edward Cullinan Architects*, 1970–1) also with an expandable format.

with the extraction and processing of the lead ore from the limestone, an activity which must have given the lead-working areas of the limestone uplands a distinctive architectural character. The same may be said of the extraction of coal and limestone, for the headstocks, winding engine houses, and coke ovens to be seen in the eastern part of Derbyshire, and the numerous limekilns associated with the stone quarries from Crich to Dove Holes, seem less telling monuments to those activities than do the holes from which the coal and stone were extracted, or the spoil heaps which accompanied their wresting from the ground.

However, it was the textile trade, and not the extractive industries, which was to be the medium for the most important contribution made within the county towards the development of distinctive industrial building forms. Some of Defoe's earliest remarks concerning Derby, as he approached the town from Nottinghamshire, relate to 'a curiosity in trade worth observing', namely the Silk Mill erected by John Lombe in 1717 to the north of the town, on an island in the Derwent whence it drew its power. Despite Defoe's scepticism as to 'whether it answers the expense or not', the impact of the Silk Mill was enormous, and it was recognized by contemporaries as a remarkable building, not only in terms of its size, but also for the intricacy of its machinery. The Strutts were later to acknowledge the influence of Lombe's concept of the textile factory upon the later mill developments, even to the point of affecting the organization of the mill work.

During the nineteenth century, the textile factory became a common feature throughout the county, from New Mills to Sandiacre, Pleasley Vale to Ashbourne. The building form showed little departure from Lombe's original concept of the multi-storeyed functional block, punctured by many window openings, and visually there is little to distinguish the C18 mills of the Derwent Valley from the much later examples at Glossop, or the huge tenement lace factories built around the close of the century at Draycott, Sandiacre, and Long Eaton. Towers, chimneys, cupolas, and stair-turrets add some embellishment to these essentially workmanlike structures, and rarely does one find buildings of true architectural merit, such as William Newton's Cressbrook Mill of 1814 with its balanced proportions, or the sterner Calver Mill of 1803–4.

99

However, it is not in architectural terms that the significance of the Derbyshire mills may be assessed, but in their contribution to the social and economic development of the factory system of manufacture, and in the advances made by *William Strutt*, Jedediah's son, in the development of metal framing as a means of constructing industrial buildings, and of fire-proofing techniques to protect vulnerable cotton mills.

Around Arkwright's mills at Cromford and the Strutt Mills at Belper and Milford were implanted communities which were the earliest form of the factory-based community, which, together with the pit villages of the coalfields, are still the most emotive symbols of the social effects of industrialization. Dwellings built for mill operatives by Arkwright at North Street, Cromford, by Nightingale at Lea Bridge, by Strutt at Long Row, Belper, and Hopping Mill, Milford, and Evans at Darley Abbey (Derby), all of which survive, are more than the industrial form of the tied cottage; they represent an enlightened, if self-interested approach to the need to provide adequate planned housing as an inducement for potential employees. These early terraces were superior to contemporary agricultural dwellings and set a standard for industrial housing rarely surpassed by C18 housing of similar type. 97

The houses being built at Milford and Belper in the early 1790s reflected the expansion of industrial activity within the two settlements at the time. Between 1793 and 1804, the Strutts built a remarkable series of mills in which William, Jedediah's eldest son, developed ideas concerning fireproofing and metal framing as applied to textile mills, culminating in 1804 in the construction of the North Mill at Belper, a building described by Skempton and Johnson as 'the fitting culmination to a decade of experiment and development in which the multi-storey fireproof building was created, and attained its final stage of perfection'. In the Derby Mill of 1793, the Milford Warehouse begun in the same year, and in the West Mill, Belper, of 1795, William Strutt used brick arches, supported by timber beams propped with cast-iron columns, themselves linked with wrought-iron tie rods to support a building which could withstand the ravages of fire far more effectively than conventional timber-framed structures. The use of an upper-floor ceiling constructed of hollow pots gave an added measure of protection to the most vulnerable part of the mill building, the roof trusses. The Derby Mill was the first multi-storeyed fireproof building, but in 1804, Strutt, who was familiar with the work of William Bage, the builder of the first iron-framed building at Shrewsbury, in 1797, used iron beams and roof trusses in the construction of the North Mill, which became the first multi-storeyed, fireproof metal-framed building to be erected, thus constituting a major advance in the history of building construction. Sadly, since the publication of the first edition of this volume, the majority of the Strutt Mills at Milford and Belper have been demolished, with the North Mill as the sole survivor, dwarfed and partially concealed by the East Mill of 1912.

The mill communities were but the first of a series of major changes in the Derbyshire landscape, the most extensive being brought about by the transportation systems demanded and sometimes financed by the entrepreneurs like Arkwright, in order to link sometimes isolated industries with wider markets. The engineers of the canal companies, and later the railways, had to contend with a county of considerable topographical variety, whilst driving their routeways through Derbyshire. Monuments such as *Jessop*'s aqueduct at Lea Wood, carrying the Cromford Canal across the Derwent, are indicative of the boldness with which the canal engineers met these physical challenges. The areas where canals met or terminated were transformed; the village of Bugsworth (now Buxworth) near Whaley Bridge was dwarfed by the complex of canal basins and arms, tramways, limekilns, warehouses, and bridges which comprised the terminal basin of the Peak Forest Canal, and at Shardlow, s of Derby, there developed on the Trent and Mersey Canal and remains the now rare example of the inland canal port, with its dependent settlement directed almost entirely to the needs of the waterway and its users.

The waterways were eclipsed in Derbyshire, as elsewhere, by the railway companies, whose ambitions and impact varied considerably. The great viaducts, such as the brick arches of Monsal Dale which so horrified Ruskin, and the latticed wrought-iron work of Bennerley Viaduct which spans the Erewash Valley near Ilkeston are not only notable examples of engineering, but testimonials to a change in scale. The canals were small, and generally modest and subdued: the railways reflected the exuberant self-confidence of the mid-Victorians, and their apparent wish to make their achievements obvious. Despite their brashness, the contribution of the railways was considerable, with the architecture of the stations contrasting with the feats of engineering. *Francis Thompson*'s involvement with the Midland Railway was fortunate, resulting in minor masterpieces such as the now neglected South Wingfield station; and *Joseph Paxton* contributed to the architecture of the railways at Rowsley and Matlock stations, as did his son-in-law *Stokes* at the delightful French château-style station and house at Cromford. The bridges carrying the Midland line northwards along the Derwent Valley are generally beautifully constructed, the group at Ambergate Junction illustrating the care with which they were detailed and built; and the cutting through Belper shows that such care was not lavished solely upon those features which were generally visible. The embellishments, however, of tunnel portals at Milford and Clay Cross are lost to the modern passenger as he thunders into the darkness at inter-city speed.

Elsewhere, less dramatic but equally significant developments were changing the appearance of the county. Settlements such as the 'model' colliery villages of New Bolsover, or Ironville, built by the Butterley company were one aspect of the expanding fortunes of well established industries. The blast furnaces and cupolas of ironmaking companies such as *Handyside*, *Stanton*, and *Butterley* made iron available for all manner of purposes, for bridges such as that which carries the railway over Derby's Friar Gate, illustrating both the decorative and functional applications of iron, and for the mileposts, window frames, street and door furniture, and the myriad iron objects which became commonplace features of everyday life. In the same way, the decorative and plain brick and tile products of the brick kilns and pottery objects from the bottle ovens changed large areas of the county, in terms of the colour and texture of buildings, and the domestic wares used within them. Only in the Swadlincote area are the distinctive industrial buildings of the pottery and brickmaking industries to be seen in any numbers, and save for the stone-built blast furnaces of Morley Park, the representative buildings of the C19 ironworks are mostly gone. In an age when distinctive industrial buildings are sadly lacking, it is perhaps ironic that those most obvious and recognizable of modern industrial buildings, the great batteries of cooling towers which rise up from the Trent Valley, should relate the need for power to the availability of abundant supplies of water, thus bringing Derbyshire's industrial revolution full circle. 98

FURTHER READING

As usual the Introduction ends with a few bibliographical references. For churches the principal book used is J. C. Cox's *Notes on the Churches of Derbyshire*, 4 vols, 1875–9. This is old now and in many ways no longer up-to-date, but it is still the only fairly complete survey. Dr Cox also wrote the *Little Guide* of 1903. This has been reissued but its architectural parts hardly improved. The *Memorials of Old Derbyshire*, a symposium of 1907, was edited by Dr Cox too. Among unpublished sources, the *Rawlins Manuscript*, the *Meynell Manuscript*, and the *Browne Sketches* are also useful for churches, because they record in more or less careful watercolours the state of the exteriors before the Victorian restorations began.* For other buildings the major sources are the *Victoria County History* (2 vols, 1905) and the unpublished but accessible Department of the Environment lists of buildings of architectural and historic interest which now cover the whole county. For background information about houses there is J. Tilley's *Old Halls, Manors, and Families of Derbyshire*, 4 vols, 1892–1902, an irritating book singularly devoid of architectural information. Papers have been published mostly in the *Journal of the Derbyshire Archeological and Natural History Society* (1879 etc.), and also in the *Reliquary* (1860–1909), the *Nottinghamshire and Derbyshire Notes and Queries* (1893–8) and *Derbyshire Life and Countryside* (1931 etc.). *Country Life* is invaluable throughout and Mr Hussey's account of Haddon can still hardly be improved. Three special papers deserve mention here: that on Screens, etc., by A. Vallance (*Mem. of Old Derbys.*), that on Crosses by F. E. Routh (*Arch. J.*, XCIV, 1937), and that on Church Plate, 1491–1850, by S. A. Jeavons (*Derbys. Arch. & N.H. Soc. Jnl*, LXXXI, 1961). Of books on special church furnishings etc., E. Tyrell Green's *Fonts* (1928) contains much on Derbyshire, and A. Gardner's *Alabaster Tombs* (1940) is of particular importance to the county in which the chief quarries lay. With regard to other general literature, valuable sources for the biographies of architects and sculptors are the dictionaries of, respectively, H. M. Colvin and R. Gunnis. Guidebooks to individual churches or houses cannot here be quoted, nor special literature on towns. The Derby Public Library in 1930 printed an extremely helpful Select Catalogue to its Derbyshire Collections. But one book on one house must not be omitted from even the briefest bibliography: Mr Francis Thompson's *Chatsworth* (1950). Dr Mark Girouard's book, *Robert Smythson and the Architecture of the Elizabethan Era* (1966), should also be mentioned for the information it gives about Hardwick, Barlborough, Bolsover and other related houses in the Midlands. Of the more popular guidebooks Christopher Hobhouse's *Shell*

* The Meynell manuscript is at Meynell Langley, the Rawlins drawings are in Derby Central Library, and the Browne sketches are in the Derbyshire Record Office.

Guide of 1935 has been superseded by the Revd H. Thorold's equally informative and well illustrated edition; Mr Innes-Smith's *Notable Derbyshire Houses* (Derbyshire Countryside, 1972) provides useful photographs of inaccessible interiors.*

Finally the student will always find it useful to go from quite recent books and papers to older topographical literature, and there the most important are Lysons' *Magna Britannia*, 1819, and Glover's *History, Gazetteer and Directory of Derbyshire*, 2 vols, 1829–30 (only parishes A–D). Other *Directories* are Bagshaw's of 1846, White's of 1857, and then the various editions of Kelly. They have all been consulted and found useful.

* Very little new information about Derbyshire buildings has been published since 1953 except in the journals mentioned. We are fortunate to have been given important material from original research. Acknowledgements to the donors will be found throughout the text.

DERBYSHIRE

★

ABNEY LOW *see* GREAT HUCKLOW

ALDERWASLEY

3050

ST MARGARET. The only interesting feature of the ruined C16 chapel is the lintel above the S doorway, with crude Perp motifs in square panels. A new church was built in 1850 in the grounds of the Hall.

ALDERWASLEY HALL. Built for the Hurts. Main façade Georgian of seven bays, the central bay pedimented with tripartite central window, and tripartite semicircular window above it, and a large stone porch of 1845, stuccoed, very plain. Large C19 stone additions at the back, and further C20 extensions for the school. At the entrance two altered LODGES, originally with Diocletian above Venetian windows.

ALFRETON

4050

ST MARTIN. The church stands at the W end of the town by the entrance to the grounds of the Hall. It is a big church as Derbyshire churches go: W tower with diagonal buttresses, battlements and pinnacles, nave with clerestory and aisles of five bays, S porch, chancel, and N vestry. The W tower has a C13 ground floor (see the tower arch towards the nave) and Perp upper parts. The S arcade has octagonal piers; it may date from *c.*1325. The N arcade and the fifth bay on both sides were added in 1868 by *T. C. Hine*. Most of the windows are Perp, the E and S windows of the chancel C19. Hine moved the Perp E window to the W end of the nave. Chancel enlarged 1899–1901. The interest of the porch is its doorway with heads as label-stops (this is a feature characteristic of the church throughout) and the ogee-headed niche above; the interest of the vestry is its stone vault with broad unmoulded transverse arches (cf. porches at Ault Hucknall, etc.). – PLATE. Chalice and Paten Cover, 1702 by *Humphrey Payne*; Paten on foot, by *John Backe*, 1704; Chalice, London, 1709; Paten, by *Arte Dicken*, 1721;

large Flagon, London, 1728. – MONUMENTS. John Ormonde and Joan Chaworth † 1507. Wall-monument, brasses missing. – George Morewood † 1792, standing wall-monument of exquisite workmanship, by the *Fishers* (father and son) of York. No effigy; urn on big pedestal against the usual dark pyramid. On the pedestal a relief of a stork. All the ornamental detail admirable. – George Bonsall † 1797, tablet by *E. F. Evans* of Derby.

48

WATCHORN METHODIST CHURCH, King Street. 1929 by *F. S. Antliff & Sons* of Draycott in a fanciful Gothic style. Brick and stone with tall thin towers.

ALFRETON HALL (Adult Education Centre). The original house, built in 1724–5 for George Morewood by *Francis Smith* of Warwick, was demolished in 1968.* What survives is the E wing of 1892, similar in style to the C18 house but with a recessed Italianate loggia on the garden (S) façade. At the entrance an early C19 LODGE, stucco, with windows in arched recesses, and nearer the house C18 brick STABLES. The park is now public. To the E a leisure centre, opened in 1975. To the SW, PARKWOOD CENTRE FOR THE MENTALLY HANDICAPPED (*George Grey & Partners*, 1965–7). All CLASP buildings: the school and residence clad in tiles and timbering, the workshops in concrete.

The town is more attractive than the other industrial communities of the neighbourhood in that it possesses a main street (KING STREET) running up a hill and broadening at the top, with the Georgian GEORGE HOTEL facing down. At the bottom of the hill the HOUSE OF CONFINEMENT, 1820. Rectangular stone lock-up with round-headed doorway and two small round windows.

Eastward from the top of King Street runs HIGH STREET. Opposite the Post Office ALFRETON HOUSE, built as the Gate Inn, 1649–60. Stone, T-shaped, with central one-bay projection with porch on the ground floor. Off High Street to the S in CHAPEL STREET ALFRETON DISTRICT LIBRARY, 1974–5 by *Peter Bulwell* (*County Architect's Department*). Two storeys, red brick, with projecting square bays of tinted glass.

ALLENTON *see* DERBY, p. 189

ALLESTREE *see* DERBY, p. 189

* It was of seven bays, stone, two and a half storeys high, with giant rusticated pilasters at the angles and flanking the three centre bays and a top balustrade: square and not at all deliberately pleasing. Also demolished, a small W addition of 1855–6 by *Benjamin Wilson*.

ALPORT

2060

Unusually rewarding houses of the C17 and C18, especially MONK'S HALL, of later C16 or early C17 date, situated where the river Lathkill comes down in little cascades to join the river Bradford. Beautifully situated on the river Lathkill, an C18 CORN MILL, with its wheel and five sets of millstones intact. To the E a drying kiln with louvred roof turret.

RAENSTOR CLOSE, on the hill up to Youlgreave overlooking Alport, is a large stone house in an Arts and Crafts version of Derbyshire vernacular built in 1909–13 by *H. G. Ibbetson* of Lincoln's Inn for the Misses Melland.*

HARTHILL HALL FARM, ½ m. E. Gabled C17 house with mullioned and mullioned and transomed windows.

NINE STONE CIRCLES, on Harthill Moor, 1 m. S of Alport. Presumably of Bronze Age date.

CASTLE RING. Small, oval hill-fort of ¾ acre. It probably dates from the Iron Age, but is unexcavated.

ALSOP-EN-LE-DALE

1050

ST MICHAEL. Norman nave with a S doorway with an unusual variety of zigzag (double zigzag) in the voussoirs. Norman also the imposts of the chancel arch. The W tower is imitation Norman of 1882–3 by *F. J. Robinson*. – PLATE. Paten on foot, 1691; Flagon, 1743, by *Joseph Allen* and *Mordecai Fox*.

ALSOP HALL. C17 pre-classical, with asymmetrical front, much renewed. The three-storey gabled central block has mullioned windows meeting at the corners.

VIATOR'S BRIDGE, Milldale, 1 m. W on the footpath to Dovedale. Packhorse bridge of very rough masonry, two low segmental arches.

(HANSON GRANGE, 1 m. SW, at the entrance to Dovedale. Handsome early C19 front, but the S wall is a patchwork of earlier work with C16 or C17 mullioned and transomed windows. In the basement apparently earlier windows with arched lights. There was a grange of Burton Abbey on the site. Could the earliest work be connected with this? RE)

CROSS LOW, N of the village. Bronze Age barrow.

NAT LOW, ½ m. NW. Bronze Age barrow, the skeleton lying on a bier.

* Information from the late Mr Brian Melland via Mr Roger Evans.

MOAT LOW, ½ m. SW. Large, flat-topped mound covering a rock-cut grave containing two inhumations.

GREEN LOW, on Alsop Moor. A beaker round barrow, the contents of which show affinities with contemporary burials in Wessex.

ALTON *see* IDRIDGEHAY

ALVASTON *see* DERBY, p. 190

3050

AMBERGATE

ST ANNE. By *A. Coke Hill* (GR), consecrated 1897.

STATION. The old Jacobean-style station building of *c.* 1840 by *Francis Thompson* was demolished in 1972.* At this important junction a fine series of stone bridges, embankments, and viaducts, especially notable the viaduct carrying the railway over the Derwent.

ANCHOR CHURCH *see* FOREMARK

ARBOR LOW *see* YOULGREAVE

ARLESTON HOUSE *see* BARROW-UPON-TRENT

1040

ASHBOURNE

ST OSWALD. Ashbourne church is one of the grandest churches of Derbyshire, although its position in a valley does not allow its tall spire the effect it would have in a more prominent place. That defect disappears as soon as one is close to the church; for it lies in a graveyard a little below the road at the W end of the town and can be seen well from all sides. The church is remarkable also in its dimensions: the spire reaches a height of 212 ft, and the length of nave and chancel is 176 ft. Moreover, Ashbourne has more than regional architectural significance. It consists of nave and S aisle, crossing with crossing tower and spire, transepts with E aisles as wide as the transept, and a long

* The design was published by Thompson in 1842 and then as a villa by Loudon in the Supplement to his *Encyclopedia of . . . Villa Architecture*, 1846. (*See also* South Wingfield.)

chancel. There was no doubt a church of some size at Ashbourne in Saxon times, for in Domesday Book the town appears already as a Royal Borough. The existence of a Norman crypt was verified during excavations in 1913. Of the church now above ground, however, the oldest part is the chancel. This must have been ready when the church was dedicated in 1241. An original inscription in brass records this event (S transept S wall). The chancel has on its N and S sides three pairs of closely spaced tall lancet windows. Inside they are enriched by filleted nook-shafts. The chancel S doorway is of six orders of colonnettes (renewed), i.e. quite exceptionally sumptuous. The complex mouldings of the arch are also partly filleted. The SEDILIA have filleted shafts too. Two important alterations were made to the chancel later on, both to add light: the fourth pairs of lancets on the S and N, closest to the crossing, were replaced by large three-light ogee-reticulated windows in the C14; and the E end, no doubt originally lit by a group of lancet windows, received some time between 1392 and 1399 its seven-light window (with rather harsh long Perp panels in the tracery).*

The transepts open in tall wide two-centred arches into their E aisles, which later became the chapels of the two leading families, the Bradbournes (S; chantry founded in 1483) and the Cockaynes, later the Boothbys (N). The N transept has to the E two groups of triple lancets. Above them, in grey stone as against the earlier pink stone, is an insignificant Perp clerestory. The addition of the clerestory here and in the other parts of the church dates from *c.* 1520. The N side of the aisle has a rather bleak large five-light window with partly intersected tracery. The way in which the intersection is broken off to receive, as its top effect, a quatrefoil not in a circle is somewhat perverse and typical of *c.* 1300. The transept itself has at its N end a five-light ogee-reticulated window, i.e. a motif datable *c.* 1320–50. The S transept, on the other hand, has no E window at all, the S end of the E aisle a big Early Perp seven-light window (at the top of each half still a reminder of the Dec style), the S end of the transept itself a seven-light intersected and partly cusped window and below it an asymmetrically placed doorway with dogtooth decoration in three orders, and on the W side two plain lancets. The N side of the nave has windows of the late C13 (three-light of stepped lancets and two-light of lancets with

* Chancel restored and given battlements in 1876–8 by *George Gilbert Scott*. Redecorated inside by *S. E. Dykes Bower* in 1963.

pierced spandrel), the S aisle windows are early C14. The W front is of 1881–2 in door and lower part of the window.*

The crossing tower is a spectacular piece. It has two two-light bell-openings on each side, long, with one transom and early C14 tracery. Instead of battlements there is a pierced trefoil parapet. On the SE side a stair-turret rises higher and ends in an octagonal spirelet. The spire itself is tall and has four tiers of dormer windows, in style not later than the tower.

Now for the interior. The nave, as one enters from the W, is disappointing. The lack of a N aisle, which was no doubt projected, is painful. It means that a big NW buttress of the crossing tower sticks into the nave and a skew arch opens to its N into the transept. The S aisle, on the other hand, is wide and tall, and the four arcade arches are of fine spacious proportions. The piers are of eight shafts, the four main ones filleted. They have 13 good leaf capitals of *c.* 1300 (also heads, etc.) and head stops for short vaulting shafts never continued. The roof is Perp, much repaired. The early C14 crossing tower rests on piers with a section incorporating S-curves. Above the arches is one tier of three separate blank windows on each side. The other storeys of the tower are not visible from inside. The arcades between N transept and aisle and S transept and aisle differ. The pier on the N side has triple shafts on each of the main sides and hollows in the diagonals and carries arches of many fine mouldings; that on the S side has four filleted main shafts and in the diagonals a group of three filleted shafts. The arches are more like those of the crossing. The capitals on the N side are of big nobbly leaves except to the N, and the S respond has dogtooth decoration. On the S side the capitals are finely moulded. The triple lancets of the N transept E aisle are enriched by fine polygonal shafts with concave sides.

What can be guessed from all these details about the building history of the transepts and W parts of the church? The E parts with their lancet windows came first, probably from the middle to the later C13. The leaves of the N transept arcade and nave cannot be earlier than *c.* 1300, nor can the N transept aisle N, and the S transept S windows. The nave and aisle windows follow immediately. The N transept N window must be an early replacement. The variety of pier sections is specially remarkable at Ashbourne. It corresponds with and may well be dependent on Repton Priory.

* *G. L. Abbot* was responsible for a thorough restoration in those years. The church had previously been repaired in 1837–40 by *L. N. Cottingham.*

FURNISHINGS. FONT. C13, with trefoil arches and small fleurs de lis standing between them. – REREDOS. 1950. Designed by *Leslie Moore*, executed by *Donald Towner*. – SCREEN. N transept, with single-light openings with ogee arches and a minimum of panel tracery above them. – STALL ENDS. Two, late C15, said to come from Norbury (S transept). – CHOIR STALLS. 1876 by *George Gilbert Scott*. – STAINED GLASS. (Five medallions of C13 glass (Nativity scenes) in the N transept NE lancet. Grisaille setting, 1879. – N transept E aisle N window, jumbled C15 fragments of glass. – The E window has nineteen shields of between 1392 and 1399 in its tracery lights; main lights by *Kempe*, 1896. – Much C19 and early C20 glass. Chancel. Four N lancets, *c.* 1861, pretty, though they infuriated Ruskin who, in a letter to the Vicar in 1875, called them 'the worst piece of base Birmingham manufacture which . . . I have ever seen'. Two S lancets, fifth and sixth from E, by *Warrington*. – N transept. N window 1877 by *Hardman & Co.*; SW lancet *c.* 1857 by *Warrington*. – S transept S window by *John Hardman Powell*, 1874. – S aisle SE window, a modish Arts and Crafts piece of 1905 by *Christopher Whall*; W window 1872 by *Burlison & Grylls*. – Nave W and NE windows 1902 by *Kempe*. R. Hubbuck) – PAINTING. One panel, perhaps from a screen, late C15, with a female saint on one side, St Michael and the Image of Pity on the other. Under strong Flemish influence. Not good. – SCULPTURE. Small fragments in the Boothby Chapel, e.g. stone with Saxon interlace, stone with Norman zigzag. – PLATE. Paten with Crucifixus, 1686; Flagon, 1685; Paten, 1683.

MONUMENTS IN THE BOOTHBY CHAPEL. The Boothby Chapel (N transept) is as full of monuments as Saint-Denis Abbey. They are, starting from the entrance: Slab with a foliated cross. – Francis Cockayne † 1538 and wife, two brasses in an architectural setting with children below; tomb-chest with stumpy standing angels with shields in panels with cusped curved head and cusped curved foot. – Sir Thomas Cockayne † 1537 and wife, incised slab on tomb-chest with foiled panels. – Sir John Cockayne † 1447 and wife, recumbent alabaster effigies on a tomb-chest with stiff standing angels with shields separated by panel-tracery fields. – John † 1372 and Edmund Cockayne † 1403, on a low tomb-chest with quatrefoil panels, a fleuron frieze, and battlements. – John Cockayne † 1504 and wife, badly defaced alabaster slab. – Sir Brooke Boothby † 1789, by *Joshua Evans*, a Greek coffer on a pedestal, with surprisingly naturalistic convolvulus trails, as if it were Victorian work. – Maria Elizabeth Boothby † 1805, of the same design but with ivy trails. – Ann Boothby, née Cavendish, † 1701, not in its original state; big urn with inscription. – Penelope Boothby, 1793, *Thomas Banks*'s most famous work. White marble; the child, in the long frock of the Napoleonic fashion, lies asleep. Queen Charlotte is supposed to have broken into tears when she saw the statue at the Royal Academy exhibition. There is an inscription from Dante (Lei ch'l ciel ne mostra terra n'asconde,* etc.), one in French, one in Latin, and one in English, which says: 'She was in form and intellect most exquisite. The unfortunate Parents ventured their all on this frail Bark. And the wreck was total.' – Lady Boothby † 1838. Monument designed by *L. N. Cottingham*, carved by *B. Barrett* of London. – John Bradbourne and wife, 1483, recumbent alabaster effigies on the tomb-chest, angels below broad ogee arches. – Sir Humphrey Bradbourne † 1581 and wife, recumbent effigies, against the tomb-chest short standing figures with shields between them; attributed to the *Royleys* of Burton-on-Trent by Jeavons.

49

OTHER MONUMENTS. Robert de Kniveton † 1471, recess with broad ogee arch in the chancel N wall. – Sir Thomas Cockayne † 1592, standing wall-monument; rusticated pillars below, the figures life-size and kneeling, facing each other across a prayer-desk; pilasters l. and r. with much strapwork; arch above the figures; the children in the predella below. – George Errington † 1796, by *Sir Richard Westmacott*. – Lieut-Col. Philip Bainbridge † 1799, tablet by *Samuel Hayward* of Lichfield.

(In the churchyard a nice GRAVESTONE by *Samuel Eglinton*, one of the brothers who worked for Pickford at the Derby Assembly Rooms. ES)

CHURCHYARD GATES. E exit; wrought iron. (No documents, but evidently a mature work of *Bakewell*, *c.* 1730. ES) The stone gatepiers are capped by obelisks resting on four skulls.

ST JOHN BAPTIST, Buxton Road. A hard rock-faced *Rundbogenstil* church of 1871 for Francis Wright of Osmaston.

ALL SAINTS (R.C.), Belle Vue Road. 1887 by *Simpson* of Leeds (GR). Brick.

THE TOWN

For Public Buildings, *see* Perambulation.

* I.e. 'Those who descend into the grave are not concealed from heaven.'

The perambulation starts from the church.* To its SE the SPALDEN ALMSHOUSES, 1723–4. Three sides round a courtyard, the architecture very conservative, still with two-light low mullioned windows. Two-storeyed. Quoins and hipped roof.

CHURCH STREET is one of the finest streets of Derbyshire. It has a large variety of excellent houses and whole stretches without anything that could jar. The beginning is the GRAMMAR SCHOOL, an ambitious gabled stone building (now one of the school's boarding houses). Founded in 1585 but building continued at least until 1603. The front is symmetrical with four small gables in the middle over the schoolroom and two larger ones on the sides over the master's and usher's houses. Two doorways. On the ground floor mullioned and transomed windows. On the upper floor and in the gables low mullioned windows with arched heads to the individual lights. 58

Opposite, the MANSION. The façade is mid C18, brick, of five bays and three storeys with projecting centre. Tuscan porch, Venetian window above, tripartite semicircular window above that. It was added to the late C17 house by the Rev. John Taylor in 1764–5.‡ At the back gabled wings of *c.* 1685, Georgianized; inside, a late C17 staircase and some panelling. Between the wings a domed octagonal music room, with Rococo plasterwork, also of 1764–5. In 1784 the entrance hall was made two-storey and given a staircase with wrought-iron balustrade leading to a gallery on two Ionic alabaster columns. Taylor was a friend of Johnson, and Boswell was enthusiastic about the gardens here. All that remains is a handsome Roman Doric temple and, on the l. of the street façade, a red brick screen wall of seven blind arches against which the Orangery formerly leaned. This wall abuts on the OWLFIELD ALMSHOUSES, founded 1640. These form one composition with PEGG'S ALMSHOUSES, founded 1669. The latter stand at r. angles to the street, the former face the street. The style is identical. Stone, four-centred doorways, low mullioned windows, plain gables.§ On the other side, next to the Grammar School, the GREY HOUSE (No. 61) is mid C18, three-storey, stone. Pedimented central bay with large Roman Doric porch and Vene-

* It was substantially amended and corrected by Mr Roger Evans.

‡ (Possibly by *Joseph Pickford* of Derby (cf. the similar façade of Pickford's own house, No. 41 Friar Gate, Derby). An entry dated 1764 in Pickford's Derby Assembly Rooms account book refers to 'comeing to Ashborn for me'. ES).

§ The attic storey and gables were added to Owlfield's Almshouses in 1848, when the latrine block facing Pegg's Almshouses was also built.

tian and Diocletian windows, similar to that of the Mansion and Nos. 42–4 St John's Street. Flanking it two full-height canted bays. The basement is older fabric. No. 59 adjoining is the former stables. Further down, THE IVIES (No. 49), a plain, three-storeyed, five-bay house, late C18, with pedimented door. Again opposite, HULLAND HOUSE (No. 40), four bays, three storeys, late C18, with segmental pediment to the door and rusticated lintels (as usual at Derby). The METHODIST CHURCH follows, a pretentious building of 1889–91. Opposite another Victorian specimen, but a commendable one, the TRUSTEE SAVINGS BANK, stone-faced *à la* Barry, 1843. Again opposite: No. 34, three-storeyed of three bays with doorway with attached Tuscan columns and triangular pediment; rusticated lintels. Back to the N side: No. 27, unfortunately roughcast. The ground-floor windows with segmental, the first-floor windows with triangular pediments, *c.* 1820. After that on the S side No. 28, a big early C18 house, plain, with shell-hood over the door and modern shop fronts, then Nos. 24–6 with giant Ionic pilasters, also, alas, roughcast, and also early C18; and Nos. 16–22, the CLERGYMEN'S WIDOWS ALMSHOUSES, a Mid Georgian three-storeyed composition around three sides of a courtyard. Rainwater-head dated 1768, but building is said to have been begun in 1753. (Interior remodelled in 1969–70.) On the N side, slightly set back, VINE HOUSE (No. 15), late C18, three-storey, five-bay brick front on a stone basement with one old mullioned window; and Nos. 13–7, a nice brick group of which only No. 7 deserves special notice (stuccoed doorcase).

At the end of Church Street is VICTORIA SQUARE (the former Shambles), divided from the Market Place by an island building. No. 4, late C16 or early C17, of five bays with a timber-framed side elevation to Tigers Yard and a roughcast jettied gable to the Square, is the former Tiger Inn. BELLEVUE ROAD to the NW is reached through Tigers Yard. Here is the plain two-window-wide LOCKUP of 1844 (an inscription used to read: House of Confinement). At the E end on DOVEHOUSE GREEN DOVE HOUSE, early C18, five bays, chequered brick, with quoins, and stone window frames. Inside a good staircase and in the garden an C18 brick GAZEBO. Facing the triangular sloping MARKET PLACE the TOWN HALL, 1861 by *Benjamin Wilson* of Derby. Ashlar, with a big porch, balcony above, and a curved pediment. Otherwise several brick and stucco C18 and early C19 buildings, e.g. Nos. 12–14, brick with moulded panels; No. 16 with timber-framing and brick-nogging visible in a side passage; and the Market Fish Restaurant with fake timbering externally and the real thing within. Behind the Market Place to the NE, LOVATT'S YARD, a charming backwater with C19 brick cottages with pointed arched windows. In ST JOHN'S STREET, the continuation of Church Street, houses of the Church Street type but more modest.* Note the GREEN MAN AND BLACK'S HEAD HOTEL, Mid Georgian of seven bays, with an inn sign across the street and a picturesque little courtyard. Boswell thought that it was 'a very good inn'. On the same side further down Nos. 42–44 (Boots' store) with Venetian and Diocletian windows (cf. the Mansion and the Grey House, Church Street) and No. 50, the former Magistrates' Court, looking like a Nonconformist chapel. Again on the same side No. 54, with a broad tripartite doorway with Tuscan pilasters. On the opposite side further W No. 37 has an upstairs room painted with pastoral scenes, probably *c.* 1830 by one of the local *Bassano* family.

Back at the junction of St John's Street and Church Street, Dig Street leads S to COMPTON STREET. Here LLOYDS BANK, late C18, ashlar, with first-floor windows in shallow arched recesses and Venetian windows flanking a doorcase with an open pediment on vermiculated pilasters. It is identical to No. 44 Friar Gate, Derby, attributed to *Pickford*, but in stone, not brick. Opposite, the CLINIC, 1971–3 by *R. Kenning* (County Architect).

Further SE, in DERBY ROAD, COOPERS' ALMSHOUSES, 1800, associated with the adjoining chapel (now United Reformed). SW from Compton Street leads to CLIFTON ROAD with, on the NW side, the former RAILWAY ENGINE AND GOODS SHED, 1852. White stone with blank arches to the road and cast-iron windows on the other side.

Outside Ashbourne, 1 m. NE at Offcote, GREEN HALL, brick, two gables with balls and balustrade between, then five bays with quoins, doorway with segmental pediment, the centre bay distinguished by rusticated giant pilasters. Timber-framing internally.

SANDYBROOK HALL, ¾ m. N, E of the A515. Late Georgian. Rendered garden elevation with pediment, full-height canted bays and stone columned porch on the W.

* Several of these buildings, and others in Ashbourne, are timber-framed structures concealed by brick façades (e.g. No. 33) or by fake timbering (e.g. Nos. 26–30, Ashbourne Gingerbread Shop).

1060

ASHFORD-IN-THE-WATER

So called after the river Wye, crossed here by three BRIDGES. The one nearest the church, called Sheepwash Bridge, is still as narrow as it originally was. One of the two others is dated 1664.

HOLY TRINITY. Almost completely rebuilt in 1868–70 by *J. M. & H. Taylor*. But from the medieval church remains the Norman S tympanum with a tree of life and facing it a lion on the r. and a hog on the l. The unbuttressed W tower is in its lower part C13. The battlements and pinnacles Perp, renewed. Inside, a C14 N arcade. – FONT. Octagonal, Perp, the bowl similar to Monyash. – PULPIT. Jacobean. – ROYAL ARMS. 1724. – STAINED GLASS. N aisle W window 1880 by *Morris & Co.*, the Annunciation by *William Morris*, St John and St Gregory by *Burne-Jones*. – PLATE. Chalice, *c.* 1630–50.

In the village, many good late C18 and early C19 stone houses, a C17 TITHE BARN, and an C18 WATER MILL.

ASHFORD HALL. A small but grand house in the best Palladian manner, built about 1785, and overlooking a picturesque lake formed out of the River Wye.* It is tall and four-square, of three by five bays and two-and-a-half storeys, topped by a balustraded parapet. On the main façade, a rusticated ground floor with square-headed windows set uneasily in blind round-headed arches. The original windows were probably round-headed like those on the r. end façade. The first-floor windows have alternating triangular and segmental pediments. Central doorcase with Ionic columns supporting a pediment with Adamish decoration in the frieze. At the back, two lower wings, one the service wing, the other a later billiard room. To the l. of the façade, a pretty early C19 conservatory. Simple interior.

Behind the house, a small STABLE BLOCK and a delightful GARDENER'S HOUSE with a tetrastyle portico *in antis* and side bays with Diocletian above Venetian windows.

CHURCHDALE HALL, ½ m. NE. A low, spreading Tudor-Gothic house, mostly early C19. *John Robertson* did some work here in 1840 for the Duke of Devonshire's agent, Sidney Smithers, who lived here.

To the W, off the Buxton Road, are two ducal ESTATE COTTAGES by *Paxton* of *c.* 1849.

Ashford was the centre of the Black Marble industry, using locally

* Probably leased by the Barker family from the Dukes of Devonshire, with whom they had close connections, according to Lynn Willies.

quarried materials to produce finely inlaid ornamental work. The works of Henry Watson, founded in 1748, were in use until 1905. Most of the site lies under the A6.

FIN COP, 1 m. NW. Iron Age promontory fort of about 10 acres. Well preserved bivallate defences with a gate cut off the promontory from the SE. On Fin Cop, a BARROW containing a burial with a Food Vessel. Another barrow lies to the W side.

THORNBRIDGE HALL. *See* p. 339.

ASHOVER

3060

ALL SAINTS. Finely placed in a churchyard flanked on the S and N by old trees. The general appearance of the church typically Derbyshire, i.e. tower with spire, and the rest of the church low and embattled. The W tower was completed by the Babingtons when they had come into the parish, which was in 1419. Angle buttresses, straight-headed bell-openings, still with Dec tracery motifs. Small ogee-headed W window, battlements, and recessed spire 128 ft high. The tall tower arch to the nave has a profile with two double curves. Of other features of the church the S doorway comes first, late C13. The chancel follows, see its two low pointed trefoiled recesses in the N wall (with unexplained brackets in the middle of the back walls) and also the ogee-headed S doorway and the pretty N doorway, cusped ogee with pierced spandrels. The windows are all later Perp and all straight-headed. The N arcade of the nave is typical C14, the S arcade with very thin octagonal piers Late Perp. When it was built, four bays long, a fourth bay was added to the three-bay N arcade. Large squint from the S into the chancel. – FONT. The most important Norman font in the county. Of lead, which is interesting as there was so much lead-mining all around. England possesses altogether about thirty lead fonts. The one at Ashover is of *c.* 1200, less good in quality than early C12 examples and very small, the bowl only about 2 ft across. It has standing figures of 8 in. under arcades, only two different figures, each repeated ten times and no doubt representing the Apostles. In design the font at Dorchester, Oxon, is especially similar. – PULPIT. Plain panelled late C17. – ROOD SCREEN given by Thomas Babington, who died in 1518. Two-light openings with the centre mullion running right up into the arch. Each light with crocketed ogee arch and simple panel tracery. – PLATE. Paten on foot, 1702 by *John Backe*; Chalice and Paten, 1726, the paten made from a 1581 cup; Flagon, 1728. – MONU-

25

MENTS. Brasses to Philip Eyre, rector, † 1504, and to James Rolleston † 1507 and wife, figures of *c.* 34 in., the children kneeling below. – The alabaster tomb-chest with effigies of Thomas Babington † 1518 and his wife is the best of its date in Derbyshire. Against the chest walls small figures of saints, angels, and 'mourners' under crocketed ogee arches, one, two, or three in one panel.

Several good houses in the village, e.g. one in Church Street dated 1671 and two of the C18 in Butts Road, W of the church, WEST BANK and OLD BANK HOUSE. Just E of the church and across the road the SCHOOL, very pretty, of 1845, stone, of three bays with projecting porch bay, shaped gable, and diamond-leaded window casements.

(RAVEN HOUSE, 1¼ m. SE, at Milltown. A date stone reads 167–. Fine symmetrical gabled front, central stack, stair-tower at the back, later NW addition. The original plan was identical to Broomhill Farmhouse, Brackenfield (*see* p. 103). Staircase with splat balusters. Also at Milltown, MILLTOWN FARM, 1678, and WASH HOUSE, 1670. RE)

EASTWOOD HALL, 1 m. NE. Ruins of quite a sizeable fortified manor house, heavily garlanded with ivy. The recognizable features Elizabethan and older. It was destroyed in the Civil War.

STONE EDGE SMELT, 1½ m. NW. Remains of an C18 lead smelting site with one of the earliest surviving industrial chimneys, tall and of stone.

EDDLESTOW. *See* p. 205.

OVERTON HALL. *See* p. 296.

1030

ASTON

ASTON HALL. Very interesting to the architectural historian because of its date: 1578, in an elaborate strapwork cartouche. The house is of five bays and two storeys, with a parapet rising in the middle into a steep gable. Inside the gable a three-light window with a pediment enclosing a small figure. Small figures also in gables on the other side of the house. The front has a central doorway with sturdy Roman Doric columns on tall pedestals and a broken pediment. The door-opening itself has a four-centred arch with leaf motifs in the spandrels. The windows are of two lights and symmetrically arranged, perhaps a later adjustment.

ASTON-ON-TRENT

4020

ALL SAINTS. Some apparently Late Saxon masonry, i.e. the lower courses of the NW and NE quoins of an aisleless nave. Norman W tower strengthened by a big diagonal buttress. Norman W door, W window above, and higher up Late Norman windows with nook-shafts and zigzag decoration of the arches. The upper part Perp, and the battlements with obelisk pinnacles post-Reformation. Inside, the tower arch also Norman. Nave and aisles later C13, of three bays, separated by short circular piers with broad elementary capitals. The clerestory Perp. The S aisle windows ogee-reticulated, i.e. Dec, the N aisle windows Perp. The N door with a pretty ogee-arched surround. The N chancel chapel with an arcade similar to the aisle arcades. The S windows of the chancel are the most interesting feature of the church, tall and straight-headed with a transom band of Dec tracery (the same motif as that of ogee reticulation). Chancel and clerestory are embattled. – FONT. Plain, octagonal, C13, on five shafts. – Old PEWS preserved. – CARVING. Saxon, with interlace, built into the Saxon work on the outer E wall of the N aisle. – MONUMENT. Early C15 alabaster tomb-chest with angels holding shields. On it the recumbent effigies of a civilian and a lady holding hands.

ASTON HALL. Five-bay house with central Venetian windows on both main façades. Also on both added early C19 one-storeyed Ionic porches.* The original house is dated 1735 on a rainwater-head. Pretty staircase of that date. The house was much enlarged in 1907 for R. S. Boden. On the l. of the main front a fine ballroom with two bay-windows. Gardens by *T. H. Mawson*. Now a hospital.

Aerial photography revealed numerous PREHISTORIC MONUMENTS on the Trent gravels here. They include a Neolithic cursus, at least 5,700 ft long, several ring-ditches and barrows, a ditched earthwork which may be a henge monument, and a number of small, square ditched enclosures, possibly Iron Age burial enclosures.

ATLOW

2040

(ST PHILIP AND ST JAMES. 1874. A small stone E.E.-style church by *H. I. Stevens*.‡ Nave, chancel, and bell-turret. Interior

* Dr Gomme suspects that the house owes more of its appearance to the C19 than to 1735, e.g. the alien look of the Venetian windows.

‡ The design must have been made before Stevens's death in 1873 (RE).

enlivened with brick and coloured tiles. – PLATE. Chalice and Paten Cover on knob foot, 1668.)

AULT HUCKNALL

ST JOHN THE BAPTIST. In a lovely position just out of the industrial NE of Derbyshire with only one farm near by and the square towers of Hardwick Hall in the distance. A typical Derbyshire exterior in that it is low and all embattled, but not at all typical in that it possesses a crossing tower, as only the most ambitious churches of the county do. This crossing tower is the most interesting piece of architecture. It rests inside on a W arch towards the nave and an E arch towards the chancel. The former is obviously Norman with an outer label consisting of jumbled-up ornamental bits. The latter, however, is so narrow and low (hardly more than a doorway) that one would prefer to attribute it to a pre-Norman date, if its masonry were not un-Saxon in character; C11 anyway. Also Early Norman the nave and the N aisle. That is clearly visible in the W front, which has a blocked narrow doorway, a small N aisle W window with incised zigzag in the arch (again rather Saxon- than Norman-looking), and a highly barbaric tympanum showing a centaur (which may be St Margaret emerging from the body of the Devil) on the l. and the lamb and cross on the r. In the lintel a man (St George?) fighting a big dragon. The main W window a C14 insertion (ogee-reticulated). The upper parts of the crossing tower and the porch with pointed tunnel-vault and transverse arches Perp. Inside, the N arcade of two bays takes us back to the Early Norman period. Rectangular pier (like a chunk of wall) with the plainest capitals (like an arch impost) and unmoulded arches. The S arcade is C14, perhaps of about the same date as the nave roof, with big tie-beams and coarse trefoil tracery above (cf. North Wingfield). Restoration 1885–8 by *Butterfield*, who installed FONT, PULPIT, BENCHES, and ALTAR RAILS. His tiled floor is especially fine. – STAINED GLASS. Crucifixion, in three lights (S aisle E window), grisaille and yellow, dated 1527. – PLATE. Paten, 1778, Sheffield made; two Chalices, 1887 by *Butterfield*. – MONUMENTS. Anne Keighley, wife of the first Earl of Devonshire, dated large 1627. Big, relatively low standing wall-monument below the window of 1527. Big base with inscription and exquisite foliage decoration. Cornice and then a top like a hipped roof and, on corbels rising up from below the cornice, five free-standing allegorical figures. The whole is very Italian and not at all in the Jacobean Southwark tradition.* – In front of the monument on the floor black slab with inscription. It commemorates Thomas Hobbes, the philosopher, a protégé of the Cavendishes who died at Hardwick in 1679.

BAKEWELL

2060

ALL SAINTS. Approached from the E and below. The picture one sees is typically Derbyshire, rather low and broad, embattled, and with a tower and spire. The plan is that of the most ambitious churches of the county, with crossing tower and transepts, the S one incidentally appreciably longer than that on the N. The scale in the case of Bakewell‡ is explained by the fact that the church was collegiate. King John in 1192 gave it to the Dean and Chapter of Lichfield. Its importance, however, must go back much further, for not only are there proofs of Norman building, but in the churchyard stands an uncommonly well preserved stump of a SAXON CROSS with vine scrolls and animals and very defaced human figures, which dates from the early C9; and in addition there is exhibited in the S porch and against the W wall of the N aisle a remarkably large number of ANGLO-SAXON FRAGMENTS, of interlace work and also figures.§ They are mixed up with even more numerous NORMAN FRAGMENTS, ornamented in many ways. Moreover, the W front of the church is essentially Norman; see the W doorway of two orders of colonnettes with, in the voussoirs of the arch, two orders of beakhead and a label with small saltire crosses. Above it a fragmentary blank arcade of intersected Norman arches, now broken by the later window (of the C15, but with C19 Dec tracery). Inside the W front there are at the W ends of the aisles arches, now walled up, on the plainest imposts, and one-stepped and unchamfered. Excavations have proved them to be the former E entrances into projected but never completed W towers. So the Norman church was planned on the same ambitious scheme as Melbourne, and then during

9

* According to Dr Girouard, the source is possibly a drawing by *John Smythson*, in turn a copy of a design by Vredeman de Vries from *Pictores, Statuarii, Architecti*, 1563.

‡ The total length of the church is about 150 ft.

§ The shaft of a cross shaft with the usual interlace patterns of the C11 has been brought here from Two Dales.

building reduced. The present outer W wall is part of the revised scheme, later than the tower arches and lying 15 ft further back than the façade was originally meant to be. Of the Norman period also the first bay of the arcades between nave and aisles, with unmoulded arches on imposts as plain as those of the W wall, except for a kind of billet motif. The masonry here may indeed be Saxon and only pierced by the Norman arches. The outer wall of the S aisle is largely Norman. In the chancel walls a double plinth with roll mouldings and a few courses of masonry remain of the Norman apse.

The next stage of the church (the C13) can also be observed near the E end. The S transept, known as the Newark or 'new work', with an E aisle just as at Ashbourne, was added *c.* 1220–40. It was completely rebuilt in 1841–52 (*see* below), but the W lancets with nook-shafts inside and the piers between nave and aisle (quatrefoil section with slimmer shafts in the diagonals, the latter with shaft-rings) seem faithful to the C13 design. Then came the chancel, whose windows are of typical late C13 design (lancets of two lancet lights with pierced spandrels). Inside they have nook-shafts too. The chancel S doorway goes with the date of the chancel. So do the SEDILIA and PISCINA, the latter with a handsome twin arch with pointed trefoil cusping. The (renewed) N and S aisle windows are like those in the chancel. The widening of the N aisle must belong to this same period. So do the S and N doorways into the nave (dogtooth). The crossing tower is a reconstruction, possibly inaccurate in detail, of C13 and C14 work, made in 1841–52 by *William Flockton* of Sheffield.* It rests on piers of C13 design, with shafts filleted, moulded capitals, and double-chamfered arches. One shaft of each pier rises higher and helps to carry the vault inside the crossing tower, a vault with diagonal as well as ridge ribs. Outside only the lowest stage of the tower belongs in style to the C13. On it rises an octagonal stage with two-light bell-openings, and on that battlements and the spire. These upper parts are of *c.* 1340 in style. At the same time the S transept was rebuilt, its roof raised, and the windows above the W lancets inserted. The shape of the piers and windows, however, is said to be a faithful reproduction of the originals. The E windows on that evidence must have been enlarged and modernized in the early C14. They are big, of three lights, and have flowing

* The spire was taken down in 1825, the tower in 1830. *F. Goodwin* had made designs in 1824 for rebuilding with the tower at the W end. The present tower and spire are 16 ft shorter than the original.

tracery.* The chief Perp contributions are the S porch, the clerestory, the battlements, and the big three-light N window of the N transept, with one transom and panel tracery at the top.

In 1852 the Norman nave arcades, except the westernmost arches, were 'rebuilt in a lighter style',‡ and two Saxon windows above them destroyed. (Chancel restored in 1879–82 by *G. G. Scott Jun.*, assisted by *Temple Moore*. By *Scott* the floor, CHOIR STALLS, ALTAR, and REREDOS, and the SCREEN modelled on that in the Vernon Chapel. G. Stamp.)

FONT. Early C14, octagonal, without a separate stem. Whole figures under broad crocketed ogee arches. One of them Christ seated. – (ALTARPIECE with the Crucifixion, woodcarving by *Kuchemann* of Battersea, 1882. G. Stamp) – ALTAR and REREDOS in the N aisle by *Sir Ninian Comper*. War memorial. – CHANCEL STALLS with misericords, three, C14, very restored. – AUMBRY, S transept, with handsome frame with fleurons. – SCREEN, Vernon Chapel. Of single-light openings, the upper part of the dado also pierced; C15. – TILES. A few in the S porch, C13. – SUNDIAL, S porch. Designed by a *Mr Gauntley*, carved by *White Watson*, 1793. – STAINED GLASS. E windows 1892. Glass made for the chancel in 1881–2 by *Hardman* moved to the N transept. – Vernon Chapel, Resurrection window by *Hardman*, 1859. – (S aisle window to Louisa Blanche Foljambe † 1871. Probably one of the many windows given by *Foljambe* in memory of his wife, cf. Tideswell, E window.§ R. Hubbuck) – N aisle, window with Adoration of the Lamb, 1893 by *Henry Holiday*. – PLATE. Chalice, engraved with a lion and a lamb, and Paten, 1670; Flagon, *c.* 1706, by *Benjamin Pyne*; Paten, 1734. – MONUMENTS. A great number of headstones and coffin slabs with foliated crosses in the S porch. Many inscribed with occupational symbols.** – Sir God-

* On the other hand, it must be added that the Rawlins Manuscript does not show these windows in their present form. The whole E wall of the transept was incidentally pushed further E during the restoration, so that now it cuts into a chancel window.

‡ By *Weightman & Hadfield* of Sheffield.

§ (It is now doubted whether Foljambe designed these memorial windows himself. Some – e.g. at Buxted, Sussex – are by Heaton, Butler & Bayne. R. Hubbuck)

** These, and many others used in rebuilding or removed, were discovered in a 'parochial necropolis' during the 1841–2 restoration and form the largest and most varied group of early medieval monuments in the United Kingdom. Some fragments are still at Lomberdale Hall (*see* Middleton-by-Youlgreave); others are at Western Park Museum, Sheffield.

34 frey Foljambe and wife, an excellent and most unusual work, carved in 1385 and apparently the only surviving medieval example of a type of wall-monument popular from the C16. The figures frontal, only down to their waists, no more than one foot long, with folded hands, under a capriciously shaped arch (i.e. the attitude of recumbent effigies, but upright), the whole an internationally remarkable monument. The material is alabaster. Tablet, 1803. – The rest in the S transept E aisle (Vernon Chapel): Sir Thomas Wendesley † 1403, in armour, not well preserved. – John Vernon † 1477. Small alabaster tomb-chest. On this small figures under ogee arches and plain panels and shields between. – Sir George Vernon † 1567 and two wives, recumbent alabaster effigies on a tomb-chest with few figures, attributed to the *Royleys* of Burton-on-Trent (Jeavons). – Sir John Manners † 1584 and his wife Dorothy Vernon, standing wall-monument with the usual kneelers facing each other across a prayer-desk, the children below; not good. – Sir George Manners † 1623, big standing wall-monument of the same composition, but the kneeling children larger, in two tiers and under arches. On the arches verses from the Bible, e.g. above a baby in swaddling clothes: 'Mine age is nothing in respect of thee'; above the eldest son: 'Our generation passeth and another cometh'; and above two daughters: 'A prudent wife is from the Lord', and 'A gracious woman retaineth honour'. – Latham Woodroofe † 1648, a very late brass, S transept W wall.

PERAMBULATION

For Public Buildings *see* Perambulation.

About 1800 the Duke of Rutland tried to transform Bakewell into a spa rivalling the Duke of Devonshire's at Buxton. He realigned the streets, which had converged on a town square just below the old Town Hall (*see* p. 75), and replaced the mostly timber-framed buildings with substantial stone houses, many of which still survive.

The most important change was probably the creation in 1804 of RUTLAND SQUARE and the erection of the RUTLAND ARMS, to replace the White Horse Inn. It is stone, of five bays, with a Tuscan Doric porch and a one-bay extension to the r. To its side across the square the STABLES (Rutland Buildings), single-storey ranges round two courts. On the same side

WILLIAMS & GLYN'S BANK, a good classical composition built in 1838 as the Sheffield & Rotherham Bank.

Where the road forks opposite the hotel, BRIDGE STREET runs to the r. down to the river. First on the r., a three-storey, C18 stone house (Denman House) set back behind modern shop-fronts, then the MARKET HALL (Peak District National Park Information Centre), early C17, with low mullioned windows and originally open to the street on the NW side. Four arches have been exposed inside. NE extension and small gables added in 1858, front C20. The BRIDGE is of *c.* 1300, of five ribbed pointed arches with breakwaters. (Widened on the N side in the C19; base of a cross on the S parapet.) At its town end, BRIDGE HOUSE, a large, solid pair of early C19 houses.* Opposite, CASTLE STREET is a street of unspoilt C18 stone terrace houses in the vernacular style.

Back to the Rutland Arms, and from here KING STREET goes up towards the church. It is here that the old TOWN HALL lies, facing down the street (formerly Cornmarket). Two storeys with three-light mullioned windows in the upper storey; lower storey now glazed, but originally open to the street on square stone piers. It was built in 1602 with a Town Hall on the upper floor and St John's Hospital on the lower floor. (Evidence of sleeping cells was found against the back wall when the building was restored in 1967.) In 1709 the building was slightly altered when the row of almshouses adjoining the rear of the Town Hall was built to accommodate the almsmen. In front of the Town Hall AVENEL COURT. To the street a shop-front of 1780, but behind is a group of the earliest buildings in Bakewell including, inside, the original exterior walls of a timber-framed house. In the courtyard a partly reconstructed timber-framed building: slightly bogus, but picturesque. Opposite the side of the Town Hall CATCLIFFE HOUSE, mid-C18, ashlar, door and window surrounds with intermittent rustication, pediments to the central first-floor window, ground-floor windows, and door.

Higher up King Street becomes SOUTH CHURCH STREET skirting the S side of the churchyard. On the S side IVY HOUSE, early C17 as can be seen at the back, façade classicized in 1743 (date on rainwater-head) but still with C17 proportions. Further up the hill in MONYASH ROAD the VICARAGE, 1868–9 by

* The gardens are presumed to have been laid out by *Paxton*. (Information from records, now lost, which belonged to the Duke of Rutland's surgeon who lived in the house.)

Waterhouse, a big stone house with a Gothic porch and a triple-lancet staircase window. The garden landscaped by *Edward Milner*.

The turn r. down CHURCH LANE leads to CUNNINGHAM PLACE (Old House Museum), a parsonage house of 1543, extended *c.* 1620 and converted into tenements by Sir Richard Arkwright *c.* 1790. Inside a full-height wattle-and-daub screen, garderobe, open fireplace, etc. (Restored from 1959 by the Bakewell Historical Society.)

To the E in BAGSHAW HILL, BAGSHAW HALL (West Derbysshire Conservative Association), built in 1684, facing down the hill. Front with one-bay gabled side projections, the central bay balustraded at the top; central door with segmental pediment on brackets; attic windows pedimented. At the rear evidence of an earlier house that was incorporated, limestone rubble and mullioned windows. (Inside, original roof timbering, staircase, and some fireplaces. DOE) Bagshaw Hill leads down to BUXTON ROAD. To the r. nearest Rutland Square RUTLAND TERRACE, an early C19 stone terrace divided by pilasters and with original iron railings. Opposite RUTLAND HOUSE, early C19, stone, plain and classical, also with original railings, of a style similar to several others in the town. Off Buxton Road in BATH STREET, the BATH HOUSE, built in 1697 for the Duke of Rutland. It still contains his bath (33 ft by 16 ft), vaulted in 1705 and now forming the basement. Exterior gabled with low mullioned windows. Also in Bath Street, on the opposite side, two classical stone buildings: BANK HOUSE (NO 1), a C17 house with an C18 façade on the short side to the street (ashlar, two sash-windows, and an oval light in the gable), and DERBY SAVINGS BANK of 1848. THE BATH GARDENS, between Bath Street and Rutland Square, were laid out in 1814 as the Botanical Gardens as part of the Duke of Rutland's plans for a spa, by *White Watson*, who lived in the Bath House.

Next r. off Buxton Road is ARKWRIGHT SQUARE, industrial housing built by Arkwright in connection with Lumford Mill (*see* below). Further along Buxton Road, VICTORIA MILL (Bioquatic Laboratories), formerly Bakewell Corn Mill, built *c.* 1800. Rubble façade and cast-iron windows. At the back a huge cast-iron water wheel of *c.* 1850, preserved out of the water. Even further N LUMFORD MILL (Ferneough's), established by Arkwright in 1777. The oldest part, a stone two-storey building near the road, was built before 1824.

S from Rutland Square runs MATLOCK STREET. On the W side

THE BEECHES, an early C19 stone villa with Gothic glazing bars and deep bracketed eaves.

On the outskirts of the town on this side of the river are several buildings of interest.

Off HADDON ROAD, a continuation to the S of Matlock Street, is BURTON CLOSES.* *Paxton* and his architectural assistant *John Robertson* designed the earliest portion, in neat and picturesque Elizabethan style. It was built *c.* 1845–8 for John Allcard, a Quaker banker and stockbroker, as a summer residence in his retirement. The house was of moderate size; although it had a two-storey great hall and a spacious staircase, there were only two principal bedrooms – for Allcard and an unmarried daughter. It was gloriously sited 100 ft above the River Wye, at the intersection of two valleys, and the grounds were laid out by *Paxton*. The approach was from the E, and the drive passed below and beyond the S front, before doubling back to reach the W (entrance) front axially along a Wellingtonia avenue. Allcard partook of the current taste for rare plants, and an integral part of the design was a huge eight-bay conservatory roofed on Paxton's ridge-and-furrow system. Although Burton Closes has been credited to *Pugin*, his work was almost entirely confined to internal fitting up and decorating (1846–8). It formed one of the series of interior design commissions in his mature Houses of Parliament manner, involving *J. G. Crace* and his group of other favourite executants and craftsmen. The *ensemble* of house and landscape as first created must have been one of extreme beauty. The unclouded Mendelssohnian romanticism of Paxton and Robertson and their eclecticism, together with the whiff of ecclesiology inherent in Pugin's 'true thing', made Burton Closes a virtual epitome of Early Victorian visual taste. The transformation of this remarkable villa into a mansion began with an extension, *c.* 1856–8, for John Allcard's railway engineer son William. By *T. D. Barry* of Liverpool, it involved the dismantling of the conservatory and its re-erection on a new site. Further additions came in 1888. The whole remained largely intact until 1949, when some demolition was begun, and the interior partially stripped. The building is now flats, and much of the grounds has been given over to speculative housing.

The r. portion of the E front, with French-looking dormers, is of 1888 (architect unknown). The remainder is the asym-

* The account of Burton Closes was kindly contributed by Mr Edward Hubbard.

metrical garden front of the original *Paxton* and *Robertson* house, its main feature a gable with a ground-floor canted bay and a mullioned window with stepped lights above. A similar gable forms the S return, and at the opposite end of the S front is the conservatory, or rather its shell, reconstructed internally. Interpolated between, on the original site of the conservatory, is *Barry*'s range, in quite lively Gothic. Octagonal turret, with Perp tracery, now bereft of its spirelet. On the W a U-plan entrance court, the façade of the main block gabled and symmetrical, with stepped-light windows. On the N of the court was the service wing of the original house, and the rear of the Barry range on the S balanced this and closely matched its façade. Demolition of the N range destroyed the resulting symmetry, and a block of flats of 1972 by *Robinson Quie Associates*, taller, and in advance of the previous building line, occupies the site. The main rooms of the original house displayed characteristic elements of the style which provided so notable a vehicle for *Pugin*'s brilliance as a designer. *Crace* and the builder *George Myers* supplied between them panelled and stencilled ceilings, stone chimneypieces, panelled dadoes, and flock papers, while *Herbert Minton* made encaustic tiles and *John Hardman* metalwork and stained glass. No rooms remain complete, and subdivisions and successive conversions have confused matters, but there are substantial and worthwhile survivals, particularly ceilings, chimneypieces and glass. The great hall has lost stencilling, panelling and some screenwork, but retains a decorated ceiling, a screen, and a five-light *Hardman* window. Adjoining is Pugin's staircase, with poppyhead newels and oak-leaf and acorn dado panels. The rooms of the Barry wing were decorated in Puginistic style, presumably by *Crace*. The ENTRANCE LODGE is of the *Paxton* and *Robertson* period, as is probably a GARDENER'S COTTAGE on a cliff-edge N of the house. The STABLES, some way to the W, are likely to be *Barry*'s – a Gothic group, with an entrance arch between two cottages and a clock tower opposite it across a courtyard.

Nearer Haddon Hall is HADDON HOUSE, a low, spreading early C19 Gothic house (cf. Churchdale Hall, Ashford-in-the-Water). To the SW in SHUTTS LANE is LADY MANNERS SCHOOL. The central part of the building is neo-Georgian with lower wings (*G. H. Widdows*, County Architect, in association with *T. H. Thorpe & Partners*, 1936). Extensions in the same style (*T. H. Thorpe & Partners*, 1957–9). Further extensions in the Peak Park Authority approved style: stone, grey brick, and brown tiles, with a variety of roof shapes for interest (*J. L. Carter, County Architect's Department*, 1969–72). To the S of the school Upper Yeld Road descends to the CEMETERY. Lodge and chapels 1858 by *T. D. Barry* of Liverpool, the chapels Gothic, with polychromed roofs designed to be seen from the ridge above. Across the river to the NE in BASLOW ROAD, CASTLE HILL HOUSE (Lady Manners School Boarding House), formerly the residence of the Duke of Rutland's agent. Late C18, with a plain stuccoed five-bay front (but inside an original staircase, some original plasterwork and panelling, and two fine fireplaces: DOE). Stables, stone, to the NW.

Behind Castle Hill House ancient EARTHWORKS, popularly identified as Edward the Elder's 'burgh' of 923. A trial excavation in 1969 indicated a construction of two periods. Some time during the C12 a motte had been erected to strengthen a rubble rampart, probably square in plan, of an earlier but undetermined date.

N of Castle Hill House, also in Baslow Road, NEWHOLME HOSPITAL, the former Union Workhouse, of 1841, in Jacobean style. Attractive stone extension for geriatric patients at the back by *George Grey & Partners*, 1972–4. Off the road is BURRE HOUSE, late C18, with three-storey canted bays and lower early C19 wings, and then HOLME HALL, 1626, built by Bernard Wells. It is of three bays with a square central projection in which is the original (blocked) porch. The sides have canted bay-windows and the W windows are mullioned and transomed. The top and the tops of the bay-windows are embattled. It seems inspired by the near-by Haddon Hall. (To the N an older wing (altered) with a blocked C14 or C15 doorway. A former chapel below a terrace at the rear. DOE) In the grounds a GAZEBO, probably contemporary, and a small stone building with a pyramid roof. Near the Hall HOLME BRIDGE, a packhorse bridge of 1664 with five segmental arches, two smaller arches, cutwaters, and recesses.

(Off Baslow Road to the N in HASSOP ROAD, THE MULLIONS, by *Arnold Lowcock*, built of stone from the service wing of Burton Closes (demolished *c.* 1949; *see* above), re-using windows etc. Inside is the *Pugin* drawing-room chimneypiece from the same house, together with a little woodwork and *Hardman* glass (Edward Hubbard).)

BALL CROSS FARM, ¼ m. N of Castle Hill. Small Iron Age hill-fort of about 1¾ acres. Small-scale excavation has produced pottery of 'Brigantian' type, probably of the C1 A.D.

CATTON PASTURES, to the E of Ball Cross Farm. Five barrows out of seven visible in the C19 survive.

In fields immediately W of the town, a fine series of STRIP LYNCHETS.

GRIND LOW, 1 m. SW. Bronze Age round barrow, much mutilated.

A barrow on BURTON MOOR contained three crouched inhumations and an Anglo-Saxon secondary burial with a hanging bowl.

BOLE HILL, 2 m. SW. Chambered tomb, now largely destroyed.

BALL CROSS FARM *see* BAKEWELL

2050

BALLIDON

ALL SAINTS. A chapel in a field near the small village. Its interest was its Early Norman parts, but they are so much restored (in 1882) that they can now hardly be taken as evidence: S doorway with simple imposts and an only slightly chamfered arch, chancel arch completely unmoulded on the simplest imposts, perhaps blocked N doorway; and possibly also the W window except for its new head. – FONT. Perp, octagonal, with simple shields, tracery motifs, etc., but, most strangely, the majority of them upside down.

Earthworks and enclosures belonging to the MEDIEVAL VILLAGE are evident on the fringes of the present settlement.

The ROMAN ROAD from Little Chester to Buxton forms a stretch of the E boundary of the parish.

MINNING LOW, 1½ m. N. Chambered tomb, one of the most impressive of Derbyshire's surviving prehistoric burials. Two chambers have their capstones still in place, and another two chambers are evident. Near by, two large round barrows over stone cists.

BLACKSTONE'S LOW, ½ m. N. A bowl barrow, in which five inhumations and one cremation were found.

ROYSTONE GRANGE, 1 m. N. Bronze Age barrow, also containing an Anglo-Saxon secondary burial.

GREEN LOW, 1½ m. NE of Mining Low. Chambered tomb with a single chamber, reached through a narrow passage, now roofless, from a spacious entrance forecourt revetted by large slabs. Burials were found in the passage as well as in the chamber. Probably constructed in the Early Bronze Age.

STONEY LOW. Chambered tomb, now destroyed.

A Bronze Age barrow lies to the W of Green Low and another barrow, possibly of Roman date, NE of Minning Low.

BAMFORD

2080

ST JOHN THE BAPTIST. 1856–60 by *Butterfield*, with a typical spire similar in outline to Butterfield's All Saints, Margaret Street, London, if to no Derbyshire church. The tower is tall and slim and the spire needle-sharp and on a square, not an octagonal base. It stands at the W end of the N aisle. The aisle arcade is traditional Derbyshire. Its roof runs on with only a slight break into the steep-pitched nave roof. Fancy Dec rose window in the nave W wall. – FONT by *Butterfield*. – STAINED GLASS. E window, 1860 by *Preedy*. – PLATE. Paten by *Reily & Storer*, 1850.

The VICARAGE is also by *Butterfield*, 1862. He designed the setting round both buildings.

BAMFORD MOOR. More than twenty cairns, probably of the Bronze Age, can be seen on the moor to the N.

STANAGE EDGE. *See* Hathersage.

BANK HALL *see* CHAPEL-EN-LE-FRITH

BARLBOROUGH

4070

ST JAMES. The church belongs more to the village than to the Hall. Its earliest feature is the N arcade of four bays. The date must be *c.* 1200 or a little earlier, i.e. the arches are still round but with two slight chamfers. The capitals have waterleaf or other upright leaves, the W respond is keeled, one pier is keeled, quatrefoil in section, the other octagonal. (The S arcade, N aisle, and clerestory are of 1894–9.) The chancel arch (renewed stiff-leaf corbels, double-chamfered arch) and the W tower follow. The latter, unbuttressed, has lancet windows and a treble-chamfered arch towards the nave. The battlements and eight pinnacles are Perp. So are the chancel windows, especially the remarkably straight E window. – PAINTING. Small Crucifixion, Italian C14. – PLATE. Elizabethan Chalice; Paten, 1720; Flagon, 1732 by *William Darker*. – MONUMENT. Effigy of a Lady in sunk relief, said to be Lady Furnival who died in 1395. The effigy was apparently brought from Worksop, where she was buried.

BARLBOROUGH HALL. Built by Sir Francis Rodes, a judge in 60

the Court of Common Pleas and patronized by the Earl of Shrewsbury. Dated 1583 on the porch and 1584 on the Great Chamber overmantel. One of the not very frequent Elizabethan mansions of compact, almost square plan. It has a small inner courtyard now glazed and filled with a staircase in 1825. The S front is tall (basement with kitchen and offices and two storeys), castellated with fancy battlements, and of only five bays, the central one projecting squarely, with a doorway with coupled columns. Inside the doorway is a miniature rib-vault. The angle bays have canted bay-windows rising tower-like into third storeys. The sides of the house are asymmetrical, that on the E partly Georgianized in 1825, when a new ground-floor entrance was made; the back is like the front but with a middle projection coming forward in its centre triangularly. The house is crowned by a handsome circular cupola with mullion-and-transom-cross windows, lighting the original stone newel staircase. Otherwise the windows have two transoms and several mullions. The only exterior decoration other than the doorway is medallions with busts below the main first-floor windows. The house is plastered. Inside, the hall lies immediately to the r. of the original main entrance (S front), reached by a long flight of stone steps. It has a big wooden fireplace, a made-up piece with an overmantel of 1697 and panelling of 1825. The largest room, at r. angles to the hall, is the Great Chamber, now the chapel. It faces E and N and has a fireplace with coupled columns and a stone overmantel flanked by figures of Wisdom and Justice. The kitchens and offices are banished to the basement.

The plan has two peculiarities. Firstly, on each floor a corridor runs round the courtyard, as at Hengrave Hall, Suffolk, built in 1525–38 by another family within the Shrewsbury circle, the Kitsons, and in the 1590s at a Smythson house, Slingsby, Notts. Secondly, the internal walls are so thick that the rooms are divided by double doors with small lobbies, lighted by a single-light window, between. The architectural importance of Barlborough lies in the fact that it shares several features (chiefly the tall compact plan and projecting bays carried up into towers) with the Earl of Shrewsbury's contemporary Worksop Manor, Notts. (demolished) and his wife's later Hardwick.* Barlborough certainly belongs together with these two, and it seems likely that *Robert Smythson* supplied plans.

* It was the twin of Heath Old Hall, Yorkshire, dated 1585, which has been demolished.

A long two-storey red brick service wing stands at r. angles to the S front to the l., linked to the house by C19 corridors. Built before 1639, it has a crude classical doorway and mullion-and-transom-cross windows. Further W stone STABLES, with a small ruinous BANQUETING HOUSE attached to the S gable. Two storeys with a large semicircular bay-window and, on the upper floor, a fireplace dated 1582 or 1587 with the Rodes arms. (Near the W front good wrought-iron GATES. DOE)

(BARLBOROUGH OLD HALL. Dated 1618 over the door. Big H-plan house with ground-floor windows mullioned and transomed, upper windows only mullioned. Straight hoods. In the angles of the wings two single-storey lean-to projections, one the porch, the other formerly the bay window to the 'high' end of the hall. Stone stairs in both wings, the W one wider: several openings here with shallow arches. There are a number of elaborate plaster overmantels, one dated 1633. E wing altered by the insertion of several doors. RE)

(In the village worthy of mention are the CROSS, with sundial and orb; BARLBOROUGH HOUSE, C18, with re-used C17 panelling inside; the Regency garden front of the RECTORY, with two full-height bow windows (inside an oval dining-room); and on the other side of the street the POLE ALMSHOUSES, 1752 but still with mullioned windows. Next to the almshouses an example of ESTATE HOUSING of *c.* 1840, brick with diamond-pane casements. RE)

BARLOW

3070

ST LAURENCE. Essentially a Norman church, and because of that provided in 1867 by *S. Rollinson* with a highly demonstrative neo-Norman chancel towards the street. It is the Victorian way of putting it on thick: Mark, this is a Norman edifice! The original church consisted of nave and short chancel. Both have Norman doorways (one blocked) without decoration. One N window in the nave also has its Norman reveals. The chancel has a late C13 window; the W window is Late Tudor or C17. Transeptal S chapel with an odd posthumously Perp five-light window with five separate ogee tops. – MONUMENT. Good incised alabaster slabs to Robert Barley † 1467 and wife.

BARLOW WOODSEATS (WOODSEATS HALL). Irregular gabled C16 to C17 house with mullioned and mullioned and transomed windows. (Barn with four pairs of crucks. Mr Senior)

BARLOW WOODSEATS *see* BARLOW

4070

BARROW HILL

N of Staveley

Factory housing for the Staveley Coal and Iron Company, 'very neatly built', says Murray's *Handbook* in 1874. It dates from the 1850s and later. Some of the earliest housing has been rehabilitated by the District Council.

ST ANDREW. The earliest work of *Parker & Unwin*: 1893–5.* Red brick with short pairs of lancet windows and a friendly interior with open timber roof starting low down on corbels. No tower. *Unwin* designed the church and *Parker* all the fittings, including the mosaic REREDOS (made by *Unwin*). Chancel rails removed and re-used on the church hall steps.

3020

BARROW-UPON-TRENT

ST WILFRED. The most remarkable feature is the N arcade with (much restored) mid C13 piers, especially one circular with four shafts in the chief directions, the shafts being provided with shaft-rings. The arches are double-chamfered. The base of the W tower and the N aisle windows are early C14. The S aisle has a C14 arcade with the usual octagonal piers and the only medieval window is ogee-reticulated (in the N aisle E window). C15 the upper parts of the tower. These were altered in the C19, as was the clerestory. Squints into the chancel from N and S. – MONUMENT. Alabaster effigy of a Priest with a long series of trough-like folds down the middle of the chasuble; C14.

(WALNUT FARM. Remains of a cruck barn stand on the main street frontage. M. Todd)

(ARLESTON HOUSE, 1 m. NW across the Trent, apparently incorporates remains of the Preceptory of Yeaveley and Barrow established here by the Knights Hospitaller in the C13. On the S front seven buttresses of medieval character, the rest rebuilt in the C16 to C18. DOE)

2030

BARTON BLOUNT

BARTON HALL. The C15 gatehouse was encased in stone in the early C19. Part of the moat survives to the SW. Behind the gatehouse a 'Gothick' hall with rib-vaulting and a Perp window.

* Information from Mervyn Miller.

Some old brickwork and mullioned windows survive on the S side of the house, to the W some handsome early C18 chequered brickwork. To the NE an ashlar-faced block of 1741 (it is said) with a pedimented façade of five bays. On the terrace in front of it a balustrade said to be by *Bakewell*. The garden is now bounded by an C18 wrought-iron screen brought from Wollaton.

ST CHAD (now the private chapel of the Hall).* Medieval, but rebuilt in 1714 by *Samuel Taborer* with pilasters and pinnacles at the corners and a surprisingly big S doorway with a curly pediment. Largely rebuilt again in 1845, when lancets were inserted. A blocked N doorway is possibly medieval in origin. – ALTAR RAILS by *Horrabin* of Derby, 1926. – Squat C14 FONT. – MONUMENT. Lady wearing a wimple, *c.* 1300.

The church and the earliest parts of the Hall are all that remain of a deserted MEDIEVAL VILLAGE. Superimposed buildings dating from the Late Saxon period to the C15 have been excavated. The excavation of two crofts (1969–70) revealed C15 houses with sophisticated layouts, a four-bay barn and two superimposed houses round a cobbled courtyard, and three early structures beneath a C14 house with a hearth.

BASLOW

2070

ST ANNE. Beautifully placed with its steeple close to the river Derwent and the old bridge across the river. The tower has big angle buttresses, the spire big early broaches rising without battlements, and a tier of dormers between the broaches. Nave and aisles are embattled; so is the chancel, which was rebuilt in 1911. The church was restored in 1852–3 by the Duke of Devonshire. *Paxton* and his son-in-law, *G. H. Stokes*, were certainly involved. Aisle roofs C15. – In the porch, a fragment of a pre-Norman CROSS SHAFT with interlace. – PLATE. Cup, 1632; Paten on knob foot, 1776.

BRIDGE. Probably C17 , three arches and cutwaters. By it a tiny tollhouse with a doorway only 3½ ft high.

To the E of the church at NETHER END the PARK GATE LODGES by *Wyatville*, and PARK LODGE, built in 1840–2 by *John Robertson* for Dr Condell, the Duke's physician. The style is Italianate.

* Information from the Rev. D. H. Buckley.

BUBNELL HALL, N of the church. C17, with mullioned and mullioned and transomed windows, the W portion later than the main block. (Later alterations and additions. DOE)

(BASLOW HALL, at the N end of the village. Quite faithful to the C17 vernacular, but its date (1907) is given away by the window above the door.)

The Gritstone moors to the E contain large numbers of Bronze Age CAIRNS and other burial monuments. More than a hundred cairns lie on Big Moor, at least twenty-seven on Birchen Edge, and more than twenty on Gibbet Moor. At SWINE STY on Big Moor is a Bronze Age settlement, consisting of circular huts within a rectilinear enclosure. Above Gordom's Edge are evident traces of field-systems and enclosures outlined by stone banks. Some of the enclosures appear to contain circular huts, the date of which is likely to be Bronze Age or Iron Age. The Edge was quarried for millstones in the post-medieval period.

BATHAM GATE *see* BRADWELL

2060

BEELEY

ST ANNE. Over-restored in 1882–4 by *H. Cockbain* of Middleton. Norman S doorway. Short W tower with battlements and pinnacles. Much renewed C13 chancel. – MONUMENT. Brass to John Calvert † 1710, recumbent figure in a shroud.

OLD HALL. Early C17. Two and a half storeys with porch on the l. The first-floor windows mullioned and transomed, the others mullioned only. Straight hoods above the windows. (Inside good panelling, staircase, and other features. Outbuildings include a BARN dated 1791, and a small building with cruck trusses. RE)

Much ducal Chatsworth housing, mostly of 1838-41 by *Paxton*, with some near the Devonshire Arms of the Edensor type. Also a SCHOOL, 1841, and VICARAGE (now Dorset House), built in 1856.

BEELEY HILLTOP HOUSE, ½m. N. An important early C17 house, T-shaped, with moulded string-courses, mullioned windows and sashes. (Panelling, staircase, and overmantels including the Royal Arms of James I. DOE)

(BRIDGE, ½m. NW. One arch, ashlar-faced, by *James Paine*, 1759–60. P. Leach)

BEELEY MOOR. More than thirty barrows and cairns lie on the moor to the E.

HARLAND EDGE, 1 m. NE of Beeley. Early Bronze Age cairn, containing inhumations accompanied by Food Vessels.

HOB HURST'S HOUSE. Bronze Age barrow, surrounded by a square ditch and bank, beautifully sited on Bunker's Hill, 2 m. NE, overlooking Chatsworth.

STONE LOW, N of the A619. Bronze Age barrow.

BRAMPTON EAST MOOR, N of Hob Hurst's House. Several cairns and other burial monuments are to be seen on the moor.

BEE LOW *see* YOULGREAVE

BEIGHTON

4080

In Sheffield since 1967.

ST MARY. Perp W tower with diagonal buttresses, battlements, and eight pinnacles. The tower arch towards the nave has coarsely ornamented capitals, not a usual thing in the county. The nave arcade Perp too: octagonal piers and arches with a profile incorporating two wavy curves.

MANOR HOUSE. Five-bay Georgian with segmental pediment above the doorway and quoins. Adjoining farm buildings.

BELPER

3040

SPINNING MILL (ENGLISH SEWING LTD). The importance of Belper as an industrial town began in the C18 with the development of the textile industry here by the Strutts.* In 1771, Jedediah Strutt and Richard Arkwright built their first mill at Cromford (*see* p. 157) and in 1776 a first mill at Belper. When the partnership ended in 1781, Cromford remained Arkwright's, and Strutt and his engineer son William (born in 1756) became rulers at Belper. By 1792 Strutt owned five cotton mills at Belper, as well as one at Milford (1780), one at Derby (1786), and the Derby Silk Mill. Of the Strutts' large complex of mills only one survives, the NORTH MILL, rebuilt by William Strutt in 1804.‡ Iron-framed throughout, with arched hollow pot ceilings, it was the culmination of all his advances in metal

* In 1756 Jedediah Strutt adapted a C16 invention, the ribbed stocking frame, to commercial use (the Derby Rib). For the development of the architecture of the textile industry in Derbyshire *see* Introduction, p. 48.

‡ The South Mill of 1812, the Junction and Reeling Mills of 1807–8, and the Round Building of 1811–13 were demolished in 1959. The West Mill (1795) was demolished in 1962 and the Mule Room (1830) in 1969.

framing and fireproofing. It is a T-shaped building of five storeys, red brick, with an ashlar ground floor, windows with slightly arched tops, and large round-headed windows in the gable lighting the former top-floor schoolroom. The stone ARCHWAY over the road, of *c.* 1795, connected an earlier North Mill and the West Mill. The OFFICE BLOCK, of the early 1800s, was altered in 1912. Dominant now is the seven-storey EAST MILL, 1912, in red Accrington brick, with square corner towers and a large Italianate tower. It is similar to English Sewing Ltd's Masson Mill at Cromford of 1928.

The impressive semicircular WEIR with arcaded footwalk, upstream from the BRIDGE, rebuilt in 1796–8 by *Thomas Sykes*, County Surveyor of Bridges, was a major engineering job designed to raise the level of the Derwent to that of the mills and to form a better reservoir for their waterwheels. Begun in 1797, it was improved in the early 1800s and in 1819.

During the 1790s expansion, housing for workers was built S of the mills off Bridge Street. In LONG ROW, still with original paving stones, is NORTH ROW, gritstone, three storeys, and SOUTH ROW, also three storeys and partly of brick. To the S, in WILLIAM, GEORGE, and JOSEPH STREETS, is 'cluster' housing for Strutt's foremen, i.e. groups of four houses built back to back. (In FIELD ROW, the UNITARIAN CHAPEL, built in 1788, enlarged in the early C19; monument inside to Jedediah Strutt † 1797, 'the founder of this chapel'. CS)

Another good piece of commercial architecture, S of the Belper Mills in Chapel Street, is GEORGE BRETTLE'S WAREHOUSE, built for Brettle in 1834–5, in a dignified classical style. It is stone, of three storeys and nineteen bays with three bays at each end broken forward and pedimented, marking short N and S cross-wings.* To the S and W, and forming a courtyard with the earlier building, are wings built some time between 1850 and 1872 as a factory extension. Brick with stone dressings and also classical in style.

ST JOHN THE BAPTIST, The Butts. The old chapel of the village of Belper. Nave and chancel only, small and with smallish lancet windows (renewed, probably incorrectly). No other distinctive

* The S wing was the domestic quarters of the manager. Underneath the entrance to this wing is the date 1838. On the Tithe Award Map of 1842–4 (Derby Public Library) a separate house is shown on the site of this wing. These facts are difficult to reconcile with the appearance of the building, which looks all of the same documented date, 1834–5. We are grateful to George Brettle & Co. for allowing the use of material from an unpublished booklet about their firm.

features. The Rawlins Manuscript shows a date-stone 1634 on the porch.

ST PETER. 1824 by *Habershon*. Thin, tall W tower (big pinnacles removed). The body of the church a parallelogram with tall lancet-shaped windows with Perp tracery and angle pinnacles. The E end with a pediment-like gable, all much in the Commissioners' style, but not at all cheaply done. A well preserved pleasant interior, white and spacious, without aisles but with three galleries on cast-iron columns. – PLATE. Two-handled Cup, 1783. – MONUMENT to George Brettle † 1835 by *Sir Richard Westmacott*, a kneeling woman against a Greek stele, of the best workmanship.

CHRIST CHURCH, Bridge Foot. 1849 by *H. I. Stevens*. Ashlar, E. E. style, aisleless and towerless, but an impressive pre-Tractarian building. Inside a bold hammerbeam roof and W gallery. – STAINED GLASS. Some windows by *Kempe*, late C19.

Adjoining is the VICARAGE, 1857, also by *Stevens* and in a similar style. The façade with an oriel window closes the vista down Long Row.

TRINITY METHODIST CHURCH, Chapel Street. 1807. Stone, five bays with three-bay pediment and Tuscan porch; fine and dignified.

CEMETERY, Matlock Road. Stone chapels designed by *Edward Holmes* of Birmingham, 1857–9.

HERBERT STRUTT MIDDLE SCHOOL, Chapel Street. 1907–9 by *Hunter & Woodhouse* of Belper. Stone, Jacobethan in an Arts and Crafts manner, with copper turrets.

THE PARKS MIDDLE SCHOOL, Bargate Road. The first CLASP school in the county: 1955–6 by *F. Hamer Crossley* (County Architect) in association with the Ministry of Education (*see* Postscript to the Introduction, p. 47).

BABINGTON HOSPITAL (former Workhouse), Derby Road. An early work (1839) of *Scott & Moffatt*. Ambitious neo-Jacobean stone front with a four-storey symmetrical centre topped by a wooden lantern and three-storey ranges to the l. and r. projecting at the angles. The projections continued by one-storey wings forming a courtyard entered by a gatehouse.

PARK FOUNDRY. 1949 by *Philip Gerrard* of *C. Howitt & Partners*, worth a mention as one of the few buildings erected at the time in a contemporary style.

In BRIDGE STREET two coaching inns: the GEORGE, C18, stone, with a Doric columned porch, sashes to the street, mullioned windows to the side; and the LION, early C19, with pedimented windows* and pilasters with strange capitals based on a Greek key motif. To the E in NOTTINGHAM ROAD, near St John's church, SMITH'S ALMSHOUSES, 1713, rebuilt 1829. Stone with mullioned windows.

(Outside the town to the N up BRIDGE HILL, CROSSROADS FARM, early C19, one of several farms built by Strutt to supply his workers. Heavy version of local vernacular with mullioned windows and cast-iron casements, flanking wings, and massive stone outbuildings. (Some iron construction inside. DOE) Opposite the farm in DALLEY LANE is DALLEY HOUSE, C18, mullioned windows and a circular window above the semicircular stone hood over the door. RE)

DANNAH FARM, 2 m. NW, towards Wirksworth. Odd square mound surrounded by a slight ditch. Apparently C14.

BENTLEY HALL *see* CUBLEY

BENTY GRANGE *see* HARTINGTON

1050

BIGGIN-BY-HARTINGTON

ST THOMAS. By *E. H. Shellard*, 1844–8 (GR).

BIGGIN HALL. Dated 1642 on a stone inside. Mullioned windows still with arched tops to the lights. In the later rear wing the windows have straight-headed lights.

LIFFS LOW (or the LIFFS), 1 m. S. Beaker barrow, badly mutilated. Richly furnished with two flint axes, two flint spearheads, two flint knives, two arrow-heads, an antler hammer, and a beaker.

2040

BIGGIN-BY-HULLAND

BIGGIN HOUSE. Early Georgian stone house of five bays and two storeys. Giant Tuscan angle pilasters and a metope frieze. The doorway also has Tuscan pilasters and a metope frieze.

2060

BIRCHOVER

The Rev. Thomas Eyre († 1717) was a great admirer of the Rowtor Rocks, a cliff with many oddly shaped blocks of gritstone. They were vaguely connected with druidical practices. Mr Eyre made of three of them seats, and he also built below the cliff ROWTOR CHAPEL (CHURCH OF JESUS) (chancel added *c.* 1869). This

* The pediments added in the 1920s, according to Mrs Robson.

has been completely altered since. By the porch a number of Norman architectural fragments from an unlocated previous building on a different site. – PLATE. Chalice, 1708 by *Benjamin Pyne*; Flagon, 1759.

DRUID STONES. Behind the Druid Inn, among them two 'rocking stones'.

BIRDHOLME *see* CHESTERFIELD, p. 150

BLACKSTONE'S LOW *see* BALLIDON

BLACKWALL HOUSE *see* KIRK IRETON

BLACKWELL

4050

ST WERBURGH. 1827–8 by *Daniel Hodkin*. Rebuilt, except the tower, in 1878–9 by *J. B. Mitchell-Withers*. In the N wall inside, one circular pier of Transitional style is preserved, *c.* 1200 or a little earlier. – PLATE. Chalice and Paten Cover, 1717 by *Thomas Parr*; Flagon, 1817 by *William Gamble*. – Anglo-Saxon CROSS SHAFT in the churchyard, *c.* 5 ft preserved, in bad condition, with interlace patterns.

NEWTON OLD HALL. 1690. Small, with symmetrical three-bay front of mullioned windows. The side to the street irregular and perhaps older. Staircase with twisted balusters.

CHEE TOR. Well preserved remains of a field-system and settlement on a promontory above the River Wye. The most evident traces are enclosures containing circular huts. No dating evidence has been recovered from the site, but it probably belongs to the Iron Age or the Roman period. On the lower slopes to the E, a series of STRIP LYNCHETS overlies earlier Celtic fields.

BLADON CASTLE *see* NEWTON SOLNEY

BOLE HILL *see* BAKEWELL *and* WORMHILL

BOLSOVER

4070

ST MARY. C13 W tower of light grey stone, with broad buttresses covering the angles, W door of one order of colonnettes, double-chamfered arch (one chamfer continued into the jambs without capitals), W lancet window, two-light bell-openings, and a low, rather broad-shouldered broach-spire with one tier of dormers between the big broaches and another high up. The rest of the church was gutted by fire in 1897 and restored by *Ambler*. Damaged again by fire in 1960. New roofs, dormer windows to the nave, and octagonal vestry with conical copper-covered roof by *Taylor, Young & Partners*, 1961–2. In the nave S wall six animal-head corbels found beneath a NE buttress. The Cavendish Chapel added to the E end of the S aisle in 1624 remained intact. It is a square structure with a coved ceiling inside of wooden beams with stuccoed panels between. S chancel door Norman with odd treble-roll-moulded frame. The sculptured Crucifixion in the tympanum, badly defaced, cannot be earlier than the C13. – SCULPTURE. Nativity, large relief of the late C13; originally it must have been of very good quality. – PLATE. Chalice of *c.* 1600. – MONUMENTS. Foliated cross slabs in the N porch. – In the Cavendish Chapel two sumptuous monuments about a hundred years apart. Charles Cavendish † 1617, standing wall-monument, his recumbent effigy behind and a little above that of his wife. Kneeling children in the 'predella'. Arch between a pair of treble columns behind. The arch is coffered and in the tympanum is a rich strapwork cartouche. – Henry Cavendish, Duke of Newcastle, his wife, and one of his daughters, erected by Henrietta Cavendish Holles Harley in 1727, a very civilized marble monument of reredos type, with a big black sarcophagus between large coupled Corinthian columns supporting a pediment on which lie two allegorical figures. The design is by *Gibbs*; the sculptor was *Francis Bird*. – Buried in the churchyard are the masons John Smythson † 1634 and Huntingdon Smythson † 1648. They are probably both connected with the building of Bolsover Castle. John in addition worked for the Cavendishes at Welbeck Riding School in 1622–3.

23

BOLSOVER CASTLE. There are not many large houses in England in so impressive a position as Bolsover, stretching out along the brow of a hill which rises steeply out of a plain now all given to coalmining. Torn-open ground, long flags of smoke from chimneys, soot and mist; such is the characteristic view down from the castle, with, in the distance, the silhouettes of Sutton Scarsdale and Hardwick standing on their hills. Bolsover has a long history going back to the Conqueror, who gave the site to William Peverel. In 1155 it became a royal castle. Somewhat later, probably in 1173–9, a keep was built. The forecourt of the present Keep stands on its foundations, the massive walls

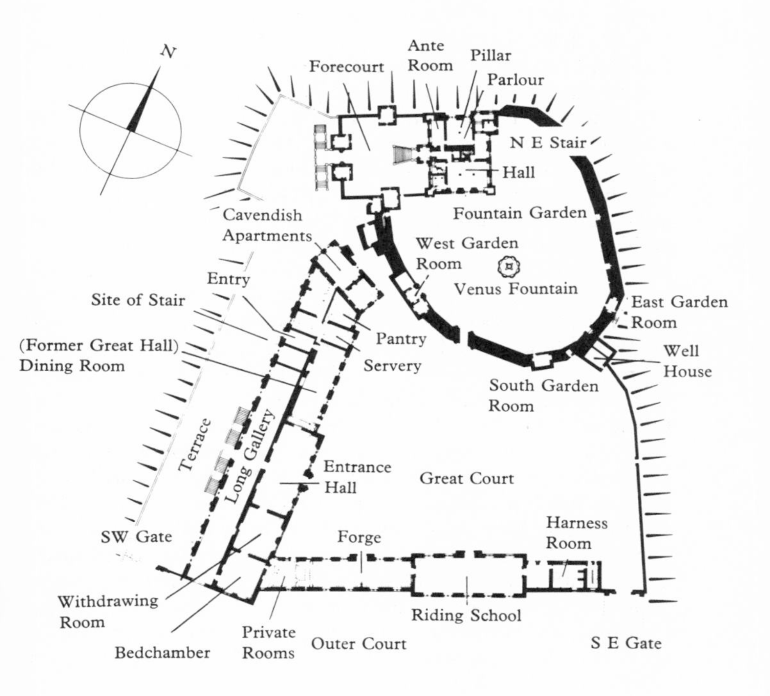

BOLSOVER CASTLE
Ground plan redrawn by permission of the HMSO

round the E garden almost coincide with the C13 inner bailey, and the main gate lies on the perimeter of the outer bailey. During the C15 and C16 the castle passed back and forth between royal and noble hands, until in 1553 it was granted to George Talbot, later Earl of Shrewsbury and the husband of Bess of Hardwick. In 1608 Bess's favourite son, Sir Charles Cavendish, leased it from his stepbrother, the seventh Earl of Shrewsbury, and in 1612 he began building a new castle here.

68 The new KEEP or Little Castle was built in 1612–21, during a period, that is, which one does not immediately connect with a structure of such an appearance. There can be no doubt that Sir Charles meant to build in a medieval style for the romantic attraction of it, a turn of taste rare but not unique in Elizabethan and Jacobean days (cf. Wollaton, Notts., and Lulworth, Dorset).* The Keep, romantic in conception, small in size, and lavish in decoration, is a country retreat, like those of C16 Italy, rather than a great mansion like Hardwick. It stands above the other buildings, raised on a basement and with a walled court in front. The block has angle turrets and at one angle a broader turret for the staircase. The turrets rise above the top battlements of the walls just as had been usual in medieval times. The tall, compact, almost square plan, which strikes one as un-Jacobean, is not really an anomaly: it corresponds to houses such as Barlborough and Hardwick, both also tall and symmetrical, and both connected with the mason-architect *Robert Smythson*. The narrow front court is also a familiar motif made special only by the use of battlements. Of the individual motifs all that deserve notice are the upright windows with one or two transoms, and the pretty cupola with its posthumously Gothic windows, like those Smythson used at Wollaton, his first great Midlands house. Robert Smythson may have been chosen to plan the Keep. He certainly had a long-standing connection with the Shrewsbury family: with Bess at Hardwick and with the sixth Earl at Worksop. However Smythson died in 1614 when the Keep had only reached ground-floor level, and we know that the balcony resting on animal corbels above the main doorway and the similar feature on the SE side were added by *John Smythson* after his visit to London in 1618. Their different, more Italianate character was in step with the latest London

* Ceremonial tournaments, which had been held at court since the Middle Ages, enjoyed a particular vogue in Elizabeth's and James I's reigns. Sir Charles's son, William, belonged to an elite group of jousters that included the Earl of Pembroke and Lord Arundel.

architecture which took its lead from Inigo Jones. In fact Smythson copied the balcony motif from Jones's recent improvements at Arundel House, but used these new forms in a decorative and linear manner. Smythson's own drawings made at Arundel House clearly show the transformation of the correctly classical into something familiar and Jacobean.* Sir Charles had died in 1617, so the completion of the Keep including the addition of these fashionable motifs was due to his son, Sir William.

As surprising as the exterior is the interior, and here even more the guest of the C17 must have felt transported back into an Arthurian world, as he desired to be. The principal rooms on the ground floor above the basement kitchens and cellars are vaulted, indeed rib-vaulted. The piers, it is true, are now columns, the bosses have scrolly ornamentation, the fireplaces with their highly unusual projecting canopy heads have Jacobean decoration, and the ribs are panelled in Jacobean taste, but the effect of venerable gloom remains all the same.‡ *John Smythson* was the creator of this fantastic decoration, so different in spirit from the hard, bright, and spacious interiors his father designed for Sir Charles's mother at Hardwick. On entering the porch its rib-vault gives an immediate clue to the medievalizing character of the interior. The hall and Pillar Parlour, on the ground floor, are really the hall and withdrawing room of a Jacobean house, although here, as in other Smythson plans, they are not in their conventional positions. The hall, with two central pillars, is entered not from the front door via a screens passage (cf. Hatfield) but from a vestibule. The Pillar Parlour is on the other side of the vestibule. Between hall and parlour is a service stair which serves them both.§ The HALL was the only room near completion when Sir Charles died in 1617. The fireplace (dated 1616), like those in some of the other rooms, has for its opening an ogee arch, i.e. a form which must be regarded as a self-conscious quotation from the lan-

69

* The drawings referred to are in the Smythson collection at the Royal Institute of British Architects Drawings Collection.

‡ The gloom has been somewhat dispelled by restoration work, but the theatrical quality of the Keep is even more pronounced.

§ This plan with vestibule and staircase between hall and parlour was occasionally used in the C16 for hunting lodges and similar retreats (e.g. Old Hall Farm, Kneesall, Notts, *c.* 1536) and in small houses (e.g. Hazelbadge Hall, 1549) where few servants were employed. Although more sophisticated, the Keep fits into this category. The plan was not in widespread use until the C17 and remained unusual in the north and west until the late C17.

guage of the past. The designs for them, however, have a Renaissance source. They are all copied from Serlio's Book VII, coloured and enriched in execution. The panelling and lunettes painted with the Labours of Hercules were added by Sir William after 1617. In the PILLAR PARLOUR is panelling clearly derived from the Elizabethan panelling at Theobalds, drawn by John Smythson on his visit there in 1618. The vault bosses like horses' heads are reminders of Sir William's preoccupation with things equestrian. Only the Gothic windows are later: inserted in 1834. In the ANTEROOM, lunettes painted with figure subjects after *Martin de Vos* and an architectural scene. Here again the planning is ingenious. The Pillar Parlour and hall are of different heights. This gives extra height to the Star (or Great) Chamber which lies on the first floor, above the Pillar Parlour, but means that the suite of rooms above the hall is reached from the Star Chamber by a flight of steps. On the ceiling of the STAR CHAMBER, the stars that give it its name. The figures of the Prophets on the arcaded panelling of the N and W walls, and those of the saints on the window reveals, are painted by someone familiar with the latest Flemish painting. 'Moses' bears the date 1621. The three-tier fireplace is the most elaborate in the Keep. The MARBLE CLOSET over the porch has a black and white colour scheme much in vogue in London at the time. In the SE angle of the building Sir William's private suite is arranged round an internal lobby. Here the ELYSIUM and HEAVEN ROOMS lead off the Best Bedchamber. Their decoration recalls the mannerist decoration of the Palazzo del Té in Mantua, the most popular of the Italian pleasure palaces. In the Elysium Room a good example of the spread of this style of decoration from Italy to France and thence to England via Flemish engravings: on the ceiling an assembly of the gods after Primaticcio's ceiling in the Galerie d'Ulysse at Fontainebleau from an engraving by Cornelius Cort. In the Heaven Room an Ascension of Christ by the artist who worked in the hall. The NE stair leads up again. Under the central lantern an octagonal lobby surrounded by arched niches and doors to less important rooms. From this top floor the service (SW) stair descends directly to the pre-1617 vaulted basement, with many original kitchen fittings.

Adjoining the Keep to the S is the FOUNTAIN GARDEN, enclosed by massive walls incorporating some masonry of the medieval inner bailey walls. In the thickness of the wall three garden rooms, perhaps on the site of the medieval towers (E and S) and gateway (W). The garden room to the W of the arched entrance is a suite of three, the central one with a groin-vault and pendant boss, the inner ones with barrel-vaults. All but one of the garden rooms have fireplaces.* In the centre of the court stands the Venus Fountain, adapted from a design by *John Smythson*, heavily rusticated and surmounted by a lumpy figure of Venus, poor by international standards but acceptable by contemporary English ones. It bears the Earl's arms, so it must date from after 1628. A walkway round the top of the walls and over an archway leads to the terrace range.

The Keep was only the first Cavendish building at Bolsover. Sir William (created Earl of Mansfield in 1628 and Duke of Newcastle at the Restoration), not content with the restricted accommodation in the Keep, built himself an independent great house to the SW of it, overlooking the valley. In spite of its unusual elongated plan it has all the accommodation (great hall, state rooms, long gallery, etc.) that one would expect to find in most contemporary great houses. Adjoining at r. angles on the SE is a RIDING SCHOOL, inspired, like that at Welbeck, Notts., by Sir William's passion for horses and the *haute école.* These buildings are among the most interesting of their date in England. They are characterized on one hand by rows of curved (Dutch) gables carrying pediments, that is a motif of the up-to-date but not courtly architecture of about 1620–50 in England (e.g. Swakeleys, Middlesex, 1638); and on the other by an excessive use of fancy rustication for doorcases, gateways and even fireplaces. There are quite a number of divers banded, diamond, and other varieties, derived presumably from such publications as Serlio's, Ducerceau's, Rubens's, and Dietterlin's. The pediments are also eccentric. The style – Baroque, not classical – corresponds to that of, say, the portal of St Mary at Oxford by Nicholas Stone (1637), the (demolished) Leathersellers' Hall in the City (1623 and later), and to other examples of the style characterized as Artisan Mannerism. The style lasted well into the 1660s and 70s, having an effect on Derby County Hall (*c.* 1660), on Nottingham Castle (1674), and on the college architecture at Cambridge. Since no documents survive the building history can only be guessed at.

The TERRACE RANGE, which runs from the SW corner of the Keep forecourt along the edge of the escarpment, lies roof-

* On the outer side of the Fountain Garden the WELL HOUSE of 1612. To the S on the hillside a number of gabled stone CONDUIT HOUSES.

less and in ruins. Damaged in the Civil War, afterwards repaired, it was stripped again in 1751 to furnish Welbeck, then the principal residence. It was built in at least three distinct phases. Our description begins with the exterior of the block at the NE end, the CAVENDISH APARTMENTS. These comprise the slanting end block and the four bays towards the terrace distinguished from the rest of the W façade by two storeys of mullion-and-transom cross windows above a basement. At the NE end are a row of shaped and pedimented gables. *John Smythson*, we know, saw and drew such gables on his visit to London, but here the gables with their more complicated profiles are closer to those used by his father on the towers at Wollaton in 1580 than to the early C17 'Dutch' or Holborn type. (He also used this early type on the stables he built for Sir William at Welbeck in 1622.) The façade must have been finished about 1630, for the NW side is studded with projecting stones initialled and dated: MC 1629, MW 1630, HS 1629, EL 1630, GD 1629.* On the second storey is a doorway dated 1633 (RIBA drawing III/1(8)), inserted when the terrace range was linked with the Keep via the garden wall walk. The four bays facing W are finished, like the rest of the W façade, with a crenellated parapet and strange 'buttresses'. It seems likely that this façade was altered for conformity when the long gallery was built.‡

Most of the rest of the terrace range roughly follows John Smythson's undated plan (RIBA III/1(4)). This shows a long gallery occupying the whole W side, as in the present building, and on the courtyard side a great hall at the N end, with state rooms to its S.

70 The LONG GALLERY is the only part attributable to *Smyth-*

* The apartments might have been begun or just planned much earlier, even before Sir Charles' death, for the vaulted basement kitchens are identical in many respects to those of the Keep. In the accounts of the Keep there are entries about new foundations begun in 1614. The Keep foundations were begun in 1612, so these must have been elsewhere.

‡ This brings us to the problem of Diepenbecke's engraving of Bolsover from the W. This is part of a plate included in the Earl's equestrian treatise 'La Nouvelle Méthode', published in 1657. It is used frequently to shed light on the building's history, but since it was made while the Earl was in exile, it must have been based on drawings, and these cannot be dated. Neither do we know whether these drawings were topographical and correct in all details, or whether they were only designs. The engraving showing the W façade of the terrace range differs in one main respect, i.e. the W side of the Cavendish apartments is shown with four curved gables surmounted by chimneys. Was it originally built like that and altered later? (According to John Harris there are early drawings (*c.* 1630s) of Bolsover Castle at Renishaw.)

son, on the basis of his drawings for the gallery doorway and the window over it (RIBA III/1(5)&(7)). Certainly planned before his death in 1634, it was probably completed for the celebrated visit of Charles I and his Queen in that year. (The entertainment, at which a masque by Ben Jonson was performed, is said to have cost £15,000, an indication of the lavish expenditure expected for such a visit.*) The Long Gallery façade is most bizarre. It is eleven bays long, standing above a basement. An outer staircase leads up from the terrace to the above-ground entrance. There are no gables – the roof-line is finished with a crenellated parapet. The pediments wilfully break the rules of classical architecture. The broken triangular one over the main doorway has a segmental piece tethered above it; those over the windows are composed of three separate sections of raking cornice. But the most remarkable feature of this façade is the attached shafts all along it that run up column-wise between the windows. But they are not columns. They start by being corbelled out of the wall, carry on banded and vermiculated, and, without capitals, die into the wall. I know of no parallel either in England or abroad. The interior is completely ruined, leaving only a slight trace of the anterooms originally at either end. At the end of the terrace, the remains of a gateway, also modelled on Jones's Arundel House gate.

Behind the N side of the gallery facing the courtyard is the GREAT HALL, converted into the dining room after the state rooms were built. The façade is unlike that of the gallery. Here the studded masonry and the windows are similar to those of the Cavendish apartments, but the windows have two transoms because of their greater height. The gables are significantly different. They are of the later 'Dutch' or Holborn type, with smooth volutes and alternating triangular and segmental pediments, a type repeated on the riding school. The gables suggest it was designed some time after the Cavendish apartments, i.e. after 1630. Inside, the slots for the hammerbeam roof and the heavily rusticated fireplace survive the later alterations. The great staircase of *Smythson*'s plan was either never built or replaced later by a narrow staircase at the S end. On the W wall the springing of its landing vault.

The doorway at the S end leads into the STATE ROOMS. The

* This entertainment, 'Love's Welcome to Bolsover', included a comment on the Earl's building mania in the form of an anti-masque satirizing the architectural profession. In it, Jonson cast his barbs at Inigo Jones's ambitions to raise architecture to the status of a liberal art.

elevation of these shows yet a further variation and, most likely, an advance in style on the rest of the terrace range. This block, independent of the adjacent hall, projects slightly from it. Above the roof-line rises the great hall's N gable. Like the gallery, the state rooms have a crenellated parapet and a lot of rustication, but no features are so bizarre or so harsh and linear as those on the gallery. They are more conventional, with fuller, more detailed mouldings and fleshier forms. The leathery strapwork round the upper windows is one of the most popular features of Artisan Mannerist style. The whole block is most reminiscent of the Earl's other major building, Nottingham Castle, not built until 1674, and designed by the Lincoln mason *Samuel Marsh*.* It must belong to the last building phase which was carried out either shortly before the Civil War (Bolsover surrendered in 1644) or even after the Res-
71 toration. The grand entrance, with the post-Restoration ducal achievement over it, leads into the roofless hall, thence through axially aligned doors into the gallery, and from there to the terrace. The other doorways are simple, with cornice hoods on consoles. The fireplaces are severely classical. To the S lie the Withdrawing Room and State Bedchamber, with a small suite of private rooms off to the E, between the terrace range and the riding school.

Unlike the terrace range, the range enclosing the court on the S side is a unified design with the five-bay RIDING SCHOOL standing slightly forward in the centre, flanked by the FORGE (W) and HARNESS ROOM (E). The whole range is surmounted by a row of Holborn gables with dormer windows. The climax of the composition is the rusticated triumphal gateway to the riding school, echoed in the smaller plainer doorway to the forge. Although the gables are just like those over the hall, the sculptural rustication and window mouldings are like those of the state rooms and no doubt of the same building phase. Part of the range is still roofed. Over the riding school is an open timber roof with ten tie-beam trusses. From the E end spectators could watch demonstrations of horsemanship through a Venetian window opening to the gallery. Below it, the rusticated doorway to the harness room. At the other end a doorway leads to the forge, a building similar to the riding school, with only half its timber roof surviving. On the S wall two forge fireplaces with pyramidal hoods.

* Vertue ascribes all the Earl's buildings at Bolsover to *Marsh*.

The court is closed from the outer court (the original outer bailey) by a gateway with rusticated piers at the SE corner.

The designer of the state rooms and the riding school is unknown. They are usually attributed to John Smythson's son, *Huntingdon Smythson*, whose 'skill in architecture' is recorded on his tomb in Bolsover church. The initials HS which appear on the Cavendish apartments might also be his, indicating that he was working for his father as a mason about 1630. Unfortunately, although it seems probable that the completion of the buildings remained in the hands of the Smythson family, we know no buildings by Huntingdon to use for comparison. Whoever built this last phase, there is clearly a certain consistency of style throughout the Earl's buildings, including Nottingham Castle. Did the Earl play a part in designing them? It was probably at the Earl's expense and at his request that John Smythson visited London in 1618 to take note of the latest architectural fashions. Did the Earl himself pick the very Italianate rectangular silhouette of the Bolsover state rooms and gallery and of Nottingham Castle, from a publication such as Rubens's *Palazzi di Genova* then quite recently published (1622)?* Does the instruction in his will to finish Nottingham Castle 'according to the form and model laid down by me' imply that he did more than just employ a mason to design the building for him? A partnership between architect and patron, common in the designing of so many earlier houses, may account for the unique and consistent character of the Earl's buildings.

NEW BOLSOVER, at the bottom of the hill W of the Castle, is a model village built in 1888–93 by the Bolsover and Creswell Colliery Co. Enlightened planning, with houses arranged round three sides of a square green, and a school etc. originally on the fourth side. Managers' detached houses to the N.

BONSALL

2050

ST JAMES. In a picturesque position on a steep hill above the village and Bonsall Brook. Perp W tower, ashlar-faced, with diagonal buttresses, battlements, pinnacles, and an unusual and handsome spire with two ornamental bands around. The church is also embattled. The N side of the chancel tells of the

* Only Jones's buildings set a precedent for this rectangular silhouette and the level parapets, but they are different in all respects. These features were really popularized much later, by Talman at Thoresby (1683) and Chatsworth (1686), and by Wren at Hampton Court (1690).

C13. The three-bay S arcade has quatrefoil piers and simple moulded capitals, some with cable decoration. This also may be C13. The N arcade has later octagonal piers. The piers of both arcades are on uncommonly high bases. All the outer walls were almost totally rebuilt by *Ewan Christian* in 1862–3. – C17 funeral HELMET, N aisle. – PLATE. Cup, 1649; Paten, *c.* 1650; Flagon, 1759 by *John Swift*. – MONUMENT. Henry Ferne, wife, and daughter, † 1763. Oval wall-monument with weeping putti.

The village possesses a fine CROSS on a circular base of thirteen steps (ball-head added 1671: DOE). It stands in the little Market Place to the W and below the church. The KING'S HEAD was established in 1677. The house has the traditional low three-light mullioned windows, and two irregular gables. There is another gabled house of *c.* 1670 (Manor House) in the High Street. Higher up the Bonsall Brook, an unusually pretty view of village houses across a pond-like widening of the brook.

Bonsall was a centre in the C18 and C19 of framework knitting. A few yards E of the Cross is one of the few remaining FRAME-WORKSHOPS, with characteristic large windows on each floor and a stairway at the side. In The Dale the remains of another shop, dated 1737 over the door.

4030

BORROWASH

ST STEPHEN. 1899 by *P. H. Currey*. Inside, an excellent wrought-iron SCREEN of C18 date, presented to the church by a member of the Pares family. It is probably the work of *Bakewell* of Derby. – (Also probably by *Bakewell* the COMMUNION RAIL said to have come from Hopwell Hall (built 1720) and an exact replica of Bakewell's garden rail of 1719 at Cholmondeley, Cheshire. ES) – (STAINED GLASS. Nave S window 1917 by *A. J. Davies* of the *Bromsgrove Guild*. Much above his average. Two angels bearing globes, surely derived from Burne-Jones's series The Days (or Angels) of Creation, painted in 1876. R. Hubbuck)

BORTHER LOW *see* ELTON

BOULTON *see* DERBY, p. 190

BOWDEN HALL *see* CHAPEL-EN-LE-FRITH

1030

BOYLESTONE

ST JOHN THE BAPTIST. The SW tower with a pyramidal roof

with conical sides is, according to an inscription, of 1844 by *Henry Duesbury*.* The chancel early C14 (but Perp E window), the S aisle windows and arcade also. In the chancel a finely moulded low N recess, also early C14. – PLATE. Cup, 1639.

BRACKENFIELD

3050

HOLY TRINITY. 1856–7 by *T. C. Hine*. Dec, low tower with broach-spire. NE chapel and vestry 1872. Inside, the C15 screen from the earlier church, TRINITY CHAPEL, the ruins of which still stand about ½ m. NNW.

ROAD NOOK FARM, ½ m. S. Smithy dated 1673, tithe barn dated 1683, both of brick, which is early for this area. The house chiefly 1840, but with old beams, etc., inside. It was originally Wessington Manor House.

(BROOMHILL FARM, ½ m. SE. Dated 1668 or 1688 on the gable. Symmetrical plan similar to Raven House, Ashover, but with plain eaves. Impressive gabled staircase tower at the back. N wing 1834. RE)

OGSTON HALL. *See* p. 294.

BRADBOURNE

2050

ALL SAINTS. The N side of the nave is partly of Saxon masonry; see, for instance, the long-and-short work at the E end. W of this a C13 lancet window. A similar window in the chancel N side. Earlier is the square unbuttressed W tower. Its date is evidently Norman. The doorway on the S side has one order of colonnettes, two orders of voussoirs with animals, and the outer order with beakheads stylized into no more than abstract tongue shapes. The twin bell-openings have zigzag arches and billet in the label. The corbel-table is also original; the battlements are later. Most of the windows of the church are renewed, but the S aisle windows show (see the label-stops) that the original windows were later C14. Inside, the Norman tower arch is broad and quite wide. The S arcade of three bays is low with keeled quatrefoil piers, i.e. *c*. 1300. The chancel arch seems to be later C14. The responds are castellated. – STAINED GLASS. Old bits in the chancel N window. – PAINTING. Large Adoration of the Shepherds; North Italian, early C17. – Primitive C16–17 wall painting in the S aisle: towers surrounding a black-letter

* Information from the Rev. D. H. Buckley.

inscription from Eccles. V.I. – CROSS SHAFT. In the churchyard, *c.* 800, with ornament typical of the date, and a scene of the Crucifixion.

BRADBOURNE HALL. Elizabethan, grey stone, with three gables, the large l. one of 1929. The staircase good and simple Jacobean.

2040

BRADLEY

ALL SAINTS. Nave and chancel, no aisles, no tower. C18 wooden bell-turret. The rest C14. The only noteworthy detail the two large corbel-heads inside l. and r. of the E window. – FONT. The bowl octagonal with trefoil arches and fleurs-de-lis between (cf. Bakewell). The foot of eight filleted shafts clustered together. C13; much restored. – PLATE. Set of silver-gilt Chalice, Paten, and Flagon given in 1641 by Lady Frances Kniveton (cf. Kirk Langley, Kniveton, Mugginton, Osmaston).

(BRADLEY HALL. An undistinguished brick exterior, but with a fine C18 staircase hall and some features in the other rooms.)

(HOLE-IN-THE-WALL. An unusual type of building, i.e. two C18 brick tenements with a central archway through which the road passes. DOE)

0080

BRADSHAW HALL

2 m. W of Chapel-en-le-Frith

Dated 1620 on the handsome gateway. The date and arms of Francis Bradshaw (recent or recut) under a double-stepped hood-mould. The house is L-shaped, gabled, and has the usual many-mullioned windows with one transom, under straight hoods, not the earlier hood-moulds that come down on the sides. Windows once blocked altered in the 1960s. Inside, original panelling and ornamental plaster ceiling over the staircase.

1080

BRADWELL

ST BARNABAS. 1867–8 by *C. C. Townsend.* Aisleless, with a tower added in 1888–91. – The PULPIT and ALTAR RAILS have early C18 carved panels said to come from a college chapel.

(PRESBYTERIAN CHAPEL (former), Smithy Hill. 1754, with mullioned and transomed windows. CS)

SMALLDALE OLD HALL. Dated 1670 but much altered.

BRADWELL HILLS. Bronze Age barrow. The Roman road from Brough to Buxton, the BATHAM GATE, passes over Bradwell Moor to the W.

BRAILSFORD

2040

ALL SAINTS. Some distance away from the village, embedded in trees. In the churchyard S of the church the poorly preserved stump of a circular mid C11 SAXON CROSS with interlace decoration, but also the figure of a man (compared by Collingwood with Penrith, Gosforth, etc., in the North, and Ilam and Leek in Staffs.). The church possesses architecturally interesting remains of Norman date. The chancel arch rests on the l. side on a circular Norman pier with many-scalloped capital. The S arcade has one circular Norman pier with a similar capital and all the arches only slightly single-chamfered. The other piers are slimmer, one octagonal and one circular. The Norman pier stands one bay from the W end of the church and is connected by an arch with the W wall. This arch lies right in front of the S wall of the W tower, a proof that the tower was built into the width of the Norman nave. The tower is ashlar-faced and has diagonal buttresses, and a Perp W door and W window. The chancel also is narrower than the Norman nave; see the odd r. side of the chancel arch with its squint. The chancel arch is early C14, as is the chancel with its characteristic windows and SEDILIA and PISCINA group. The N and S windows of the church itself are Perp (S aisle windows C19). – REREDOS with built-in old linenfold panels and Flamboyant tracery panels. – BENCH ENDS with tracery panels with shields in the main fields. – PLATE. Cup and Cover, 1594.

(On the A52 through the village, OAKLANDS, a handsome C18 brick house. RE)

BRAILSFORD HALL. A leafy road just off the A52 passes close to the façade of this red brick house, built *c.* 1905 in a restrained Jacobethan style. It faces, across the road, an ornamental park.

(CULLAND HALL, 1 m. S. 1939–41 by *Arthur Eaton* of Derby for Sir Edward Thompson. Neo-Georgian on an old site. C17 brick stables. RE)

EDNASTON. *See* p. 207.

BRAMPTON

3070

For New Brampton *see* Chesterfield, pp. 150, 151.

SS. PETER AND PAUL. Broad W tower with later angle buttresses and one Norman S window. Norman also the S doorway into the church. The blocked N doorway C13. Tower arch to the nave with keeled responds and a pointed arch of three steps of which only one is chamfered. Buttresses for the support of the tower stand out into the nave. The tower received a broach-spire of the earliest type, with big broaches not behind battlements and one tier of low-placed dormer windows. Nave, S aisle, and chancel are embattled. Perp clerestory and vaulted S porch with thick transverse arches (cf. Ault Hucknall, etc.). The nave arcades of three bays have circular and quatrefoil piers, and double-chamfered arches, the last arches being gathered under one big relieving arch. Similarly the treble-chamfered chancel arch on three orders of supports is below a coarsely depressed rounded arch. The big arches were created in 1821 when the E piers were removed. *S. Rollinson* reinstated them in 1868, and replaced most of the windows. – SCULPTURE. Small *ex-situ* figures of St Peter and St Paul, the Angel and the Virgin of the Annunciation, and Christ seated walled into the S aisle walls. Their date seems to be *c.* 1300. – MONUMENTS. Stone slab to Matilda le Caus † 1224, with Lombardic inscription. The figure is partly hidden by the inscription slab. Only her feet stick out at the bottom, and her head, shoulders, and hands holding her heart appear sunk in a quatrefoil at the top (cf. Kedleston). – Clarke Family, erected 1673, with two horribly badly carved 'Fames' holding curtains away from the inscription; a typical piece of folk art. – Geoffrey Clarke † 1734, standing wall-monument of reredos type with an urn against a grey pyramid in the middle (by *Samuel Huskisson:* DOE). – Base of a CROSS in the churchyard.

HALL, opposite the church. C16 or C17 with C19 porch and sashes. (Inside, a ribbed plaster ceiling of *c.* 1600 and heraldic overmantel. Low r. wing probably medieval. Three crucks. DOE)

ASHGATE HOUSE, Chesterfield Road. 1778, three storeys, with Venetian windows to the first floor, and Diocletian windows above.

(FRITH HALL FARMHOUSE, ¾m. S. 1804. Opposite probably the biggest cruck structure in Derbyshire, a barn with seven trusses. RE)

See p. 409

(PRATT HALL, 1 m. NW. A rambling group. The E part appears C17, the W has doors dated 1700, 1703, 1704. Plain stone mullions, oval recesses with hood-moulds in gables. RE)

CUTTHORPE HALLS. *See* p. 161.

BRAMPTON EAST MOOR *see* BEELEY

BRASSINGTON

2050

ST JAMES. Essentially a Norman church. The S arcade is uncommonly fine: three bays, circular piers, capitals both many-scalloped and of waterleaf type, and odd asymmetrically one-stepped arches (cf. Kirk Ireton). The W tower also is Norman, although it is ashlar-faced and has a diagonal buttress at the SW corner; see the tower arch towards the nave, the blocked W doorway, and especially the two-light bell-openings. The S porch is of the C13, as proved by its outer doorway. Some windows are Perp. The N aisle dates from 1879–81 (*F. J. Robinson*). But the most surprising feature is the S chancel aisle of two bays which, with its octagonal pier, coarse crocket capitals, and unmoulded arches, can hardly be later than about 1200. – SCULPTURE. Inside the tower W wall, the crude figure of a naked man with his hand on his heart.

In the centre of the village in Town Street, TUDOR HOUSE, dated 1615: two and a half storeys, L-shape, with two gables, the projecting part having the larger of the two. The windows mullioned and in the projection mullioned and transomed.

(Brassington is rich in good C18 vernacular-style houses with square-sectioned mullioned windows, e.g. WEST END MANOR, 1793, a very late dated example. RE)

RAIN'S CAVE, ½m. N. This cave contained seven Neolithic burials.

HARBOROUGH ROCKS, ½m. N. Chambered tomb, now destroyed. It contained at least sixteen individual inhumations.

RAINSTER ROCKS, ½m. NW. Iron Age and Roman settlement site.

GALLY LOW, 1½m. NW. Bronze Age barrow, also containing an Anglo-Saxon secondary burial.

SLIPER LOW, 2m. NW. Beaker barrow.

The ROMAN ROAD from Little Chester to Buxton is followed by the W boundary of the parish.

BREADSALL

3030

ALL SAINTS. The finest steeple near Derby, C13 tower and slim, elegant, recessed, early C14 spire. The tower is of four stages. On the ground floor a W doorway of two orders and a treble-chamfered tower arch to the nave, first floor double-chamfered lancets, second floor two-light windows under hood-moulds

11

with dogtooth ornament, third floor two two-light double-chamfered lancets as bell-openings. The battlements belong in date to the spire (grey stone, the older parts pink). Older than the tower is the Norman S doorway of two orders of colonnettes, a zigzag arch, and a simply decorated label. Again to the C13 belong the chancel (one N lancet window replaced Perp) and the N arcade (circular piers with octagonal capitals with nail-head decoration), or rather belonged; for the church was set on fire by suffragettes in 1914 and had to be very extensively restored. This was done well and carefully by *Caröe* in 1915. The nave S windows were of a handsome Late Dec variety, ogee-reticulated but straight-headed, with hood-moulds, the N aisle windows partly also Dec (intersected cusped tracery) and partly Perp. Squint from the N aisle into the chancel. SEDILIA late C14 or C15 with ogee heads and shields in the spandrels; rather bare (cf. Horsley). – SCULPTURE. A wooden, partly gessoed, Pietà, late C14, was found below the floor during the restoration of 1877. It is small, austere, and somewhat strident in expression; most probably of German origin. – PLATE. Chalice and Paten Cover, *c.* 1635; Flagon, 1774 by *Charles Woodward.*

OLD HALL. Opposite the W end of the church. Medieval stonework and half-timbering, but very badly tampered with and added to. (Inside exposed timber-framed walls. The hall has a medieval fitted bench round two sides. DOE)

BREADSALL PRIORY. On the site of an Augustinian priory founded in the C13. Of this only an arch and a drain survive in the basement of the Jacobean house built by Sir John Bentley, a London lawyer. The three-storey, E-plan house survives intact on the top floor and is visible on the outside in a few gables. The extensive Gothic enlargements are of *c.* 1861 by *Robert Scrivener* of Hanley for Francis Morley of the hosiery firm. Elizabethan W wing added after 1899 by Sir Alfred Haslam. Inside, in the entrance hall, a large neo-Gothic door made by Mr *Haslam* for the 1851 exhibition. (Also a fine billiard room with a gallery in Moorish style. RE) Rose garden 1909 by *T. H. Mawson.* The house was the home of Erasmus Darwin, who died here in 1802. It is now an hotel.

4030

BREASTON

ST MICHAEL. Unbuttressed C13 W tower, crowned by a short broached spire. S aisle also C13; see the blocked doorway with dogtooth ornament and the windows of three lancet lights, the middle one higher than the others. The arcade of three bays to the nave has octagonal piers and double-chamfered arches. The date also late C13 or a little later; i.e. perhaps of the same time as the chancel E window, which has Dec tracery. Restoration and vestry 1895 by *Evans & Jolly*. – FONT, 1720, and PLATE, 1721 (Chalice, Paten Cover on knob foot, and two Patens, all by *Thomas Morse*) given by Elizabeth Gray. – No other furnishings of interest.

BRETBY PARK

3020

95

An impressive castellated mansion overlooking extensive grounds and to the E a series of artificial lakes contrived by Philip Stanhope (created Earl of Chesterfield 1628) near the mansion he began *c.* 1610. Its gardens (*c.* 1669) and waterworks (1684–1702), laid out by the second Earl, were praised by Tallard as the finest in Europe except Versailles. The C17 house was demolished before the end of the C18, and by 1813 the fifth Earl had begun a new mansion to designs by *Sir Jeffry Wyatville*. It was left unfinished at the Earl's death in 1815. To a Jacobean range, SE of the previous house, were added three further ranges including the show E front, with circular towers at the angles and a central projection with angle turrets, and a S front (never completed) with a big gateway into the square courtyard, the W side of which is a screen wall concealing the C17 building. A chapel was intended to fill the space between the S and W wings. The building is of solid stone oddly tooled with a system of diagonal spots. The windows are mostly rectangular, but some are lancet-shaped with the characteristic early C19 revival of the C13 type with two lancet lights with a pierced spandrel in the main lancet. As far as they are original the interiors, still unfinished in 1828, are mostly classical, especially handsome the Music Room in the SE tower. In the E wing some thinly applied Gothic–Tudor plaster and woodwork. Boudoir of 1838 by *Samuel Beazley*.

Although Wyatville must have been mainly responsible for the present building, *James Wyatt* worked here before 1813 and other members of the *Wyatt* family before the Earl's death. *William Martin*, the Earl's resident architect, supervised the building of the Hall and various estate buildings (1805–15).*

* D. Linstrum (*Sir Jeffry Wyatville*, 1972, p. 231) believes that Wyatville's responsibility was limited, perhaps to the W front, for which he exhibited designs.

ST WYSTAN, of 1877, has a good set of PLATE of *c.* 1685 given to the church about the time of its rebuilding (Chalice, Paten Cover on knob foot, and Flagon). The maker's mark appears to be *Benjamin Bathurst*'s.

(By the church BRETBY GREEN, the estate hamlet. Former SCHOOL, 1806, and to the W BRETBY FARM, mostly demolished but retaining remnants of *Martin*'s model farm including a marble-lined DAIRY, now part of the house. RE) It was illustrated by Glover in 1831 as a model farm for the county.

CASTLEFIELDS, SW of the church. Prominent earthworks, the site of the castle pulled down by Philip Stanhope.

4070

BRIMINGTON

ST MICHAEL. 1847 by *Mitchell* of Sheffield, except the tower of 1796, and the chancel of 1891 by *Naylor & Sale*.

RINGWOOD HOUSE (CLUB), Chesterfield Road. Early C19, with veranda of coupled Ionic columns and entrance porch also of coupled Ionic columns.

(TAPTON GROVE, Grove Road, 1 m. SW. Late C18. It may be the 'House at Tapton Grove Sheffield' in R. E. Leader's *Surveyors and Architects of Sheffield* (Colvin) and thus by *Joseph Badger*, who worked at Renishaw Hall. RE)

2020

BRIZLINCOTE HALL

Built in 1707 by the second Earl of Chesterfield. The inscribed date 1714 is a later addition. Brick, five bays and two storeys, with quoins, pedimented doorway, and alternating pediments to the upper windows. Hipped roof. So far nothing remarkable. But across the whole front extends a monstrous segmental pediment (cf. Hopton Hall), big enough to contain five windows, the outer ones small and circular. Garden and entrance fronts are almost identical; the shorter side elevations also have segmental pediments only slightly less gargantuan. (On both main fronts the doorcases have handsome swan's-neck pediments on particularly scrumptious consoles, oddly repeated at right angles along the face of the wall, an apparently unique feature. A. Gomme)

See p. 409

BROCKSFORD HALL *see* DOVERIDGE

BROOKFIELD MANOR

2080

1 m. N of Hathersage

In a picturesque position by a brook, a romantic castellated house incorporating a C16 and C17 stone house, which forms one side of the building, with 1656 over a blocked doorway. Transformed in 1825, and again in 1870, when the semicircular drawing room now dominating the front, an arched gateway, coats of arms, and probably a lot of crenellation were added. Incorporated in the gateway an interesting arch on slightly elaborate springers, possibly a vestige of a medieval house.*

BROOKHILL HALL

4050

½ m. E of Pinxton

The building is essentially Jacobean and L-shaped; see the surviving mullioned or mullioned and transomed windows and gables. But the S front has been Georgianized (five bays, two storeys) and a fine drawing room added to the W range *c.* 1770.‡ Panelling and a fireplace in the dining room from Kirkby Old Hall, Notts. At the back, forming a courtyard, additions of 1896–1902. C18 STABLES, red brick with Gothick arches and a clock tower.

BROOMHILL FARM *see* BRACKENFIELD

BROUGH-ON-NOE

1080

1¾ m. E of Castleton

The plan of the Roman auxiliary fort of NAVIO has recently been recovered by excavations. The fort is small, and may have been designed for only part of an auxiliary regiment. It was an important control centre for the Peak District and possibly a collecting point for the lead and silver products of the region. Several periods of occupation are evident. Originating in a timber fort of *c.* A.D. 75/80, which was held until *c.* 120, the site was reoccupied *c.* 154–8 under the governor Julius Verus. The orientation of the fort was then changed, perhaps through 90 degrees, and the barracks, granaries, headquarters, and commandant's house were thoroughly reconstructed. At the beginning of the C3 the headquarters and granaries were rebuilt in stone, and

* Information about Brookfield Manor kindly given by Miss Meredith.
‡ And some medieval masonry is probably incorporated.

there were further changes to the barracks. The final phase of military occupation was the early C4, when many of the principal buildings were again remodelled. The end came shortly after the middle of the C4. Outside the fort lay a sizable extramural village.

BUBNELL HALL *see* BASLOW

BULL RING *see* CHAPEL-EN-LE-FRITH

0070

BURBAGE

Now a suburb of Buxton.

CHRIST CHURCH. 1860 by *H. Currey*, one of the buildings erected in connexion with the seventh Duke of Devonshire's plan for the development of Buxton. The church is atrociously ugly, with its tower which has twin circular bell-openings, a parapet which rises into a triangle in the middle of each side, and a pyramid roof. The aisles are separated from the nave by wooden piers and wooden arches of a fancy shape and with pierced spandrels. – STAINED GLASS. S aisle middle window 1915 by *Morris & Co.*, the design of Christ and Mary Magdalene in the Garden of Gethsemane by *Burne-Jones*.

GRIN LOW, ¾ m. SW. Bronze Age barrow, now surrounded by the look-out tower called Solomon's Temple, built by Solomon Mycock in 1896. The mound contained four primary inhumations and at least two later cremations.

FOX LOW, 1 m. SW. Bronze Age barrow.

BURR TOR *see* GREAT HUCKLOW

BURTON MOOR *see* BAKEWELL

0070

BUXTON

The waters of Buxton were known to the Romans. A Roman fort of the later C1 probably lay at Silverlands on the hill above the town. Later, a Roman spa and settlement (Aquae Arnemetiae) grew up on the valley floor close to the mineral springs. Remains of Roman baths have been revealed beneath the Crescent buildings and close to St Ann's Well, and still lie beneath the present spa buildings. The waters were used in the Middle Ages and were much in favour in the Elizabethan age. Mary Queen of Scots was brought here by the Earl of Shrewsbury, and the Earls of Leicester and Warwick made use of the springs. But the conversion into a fashionable C18 and C19 spa is due chiefly to three later Dukes of Devonshire, the fifth, sixth, and seventh.* Their spa developed in the valley below the old town, and a division between the old market town (the highest in England) and the spa is still noticeable now. The old town strangely enough possessed no church of any size.

ST ANNE, tucked away behind the W end of the High Street. A church of chapel size, with no tower, no aisles, and no division between nave and chancel. Very low big tie-beams about 9 ft from the ground, low three-light mullioned windows. Rendered. The date over the N porch is 1625. Late C19 furnishings. – STAINED GLASS. N side, two windows by *J. E. Nuttgens*, 1947.

The only buildings in the high town which need recording belong to the C18 and C19.‡ In the MARKET PLACE the EAGLE HOTEL, C18, of nine bays and three and a half storeys, erected by the fifth Duke to replace an earlier inn, and the TOWN HALL, 1887–9 by *W. Pollard* of Manchester, rather poor, with a thin tower in the middle of the façade.

The spa development began about 1779, when the fifth Duke of Devonshire, as lord of the manor, conceived the idea of making Buxton into a second Bath. So he obtained the services of *John Carr* of York and had the CRESCENT built close to the original St Ann's Well at the foot of St Ann's Cliff, then a bleak hillside, in a rather cramped position, since the owner of part of the proposed site refused to sell except at an exorbitant figure.§ The first payments for work are dated April 1780, the last June 1790; total cost £38,601 18*s*. 4*d*. The Crescent, partly occupied in 1786, is small compared with the Royal Crescent at Bath, completed only in 1775. Even so, it has a breadth of 57 ft, a total length of 360 ft, 42 pilasters and 378 windows! In plan, the Royal Crescent is semi-elliptical, Buxton Crescent is semicircular, but whereas the former comprised a number of similar house units, the latter contained a variety of accommodation, shops, lodgings, and two hotels – St Ann's (W) and the Great (or Grand). Shortly after completion the central position was

91

* Although *John Barker* built a new bath house (demolished by Carr) for the first Duke *c*. 1710 (ES).

‡ Except, in the Market Place, the three-step base and shaft of a medieval CROSS.

§ The revised description of the Crescent and information about Carr's work at Buxton were kindly given by Mr R. B. Wragg.

used as a hotel, the Centre. The elevation detail possibly owes something to Inigo Jones's Covent Garden piazza or even to No. 20 St James's Square by Robert Adam: giant pilasters of the Roman Doric order above rusticated arcades with triglyphs, metopes, frieze, cornice, and top balustrade. The rear elevation, visible on the NE, is simple. The massive chimneystacks, cruciform in plan, are distinctive. Central and surmounting the lodging once occupied by the Duke is the Cavendish coat of arms carved by *Thomas Waterworth* of Doncaster at a cost of £65. Inside the former Great Hotel, completely restored by Derbyshire County Council in 1970–3 for use as an Area Library, a fine semicircular staircase and the ASSEMBLY ROOM, a large, elegant room in Adam style with giant Corinthian pilasters, elaborate plasterwork by *James Henderson Jun.* of York, at the ends shallow niches screened off by pairs of Corinthian columns, and original chandeliers.

In 1785–90 the Duke and *Carr* followed the Crescent by a large STABLES establishment to the N. This survives, with additions, as the DEVONSHIRE ROYAL HOSPITAL, converted in 1859 'for the use of the sick poor' by the sixth Duke's architect at Buxton, the Londoner *Henry Currey* († 1900). The original buildings, erected to *Carr*'s designs by the masons *Robert Smith* and *William Booth* of Stony Middleton,* was a square with chamfered corners and central pediments, of very restrained architecture. The centre was a large circular court with a colonnade of big Tuscan columns for riding exercises. In 1881–2 *R. R. Duke* covered the courtyard with a huge dome, 156 ft in diameter and at the time the largest in the world. He also added angle turrets and a clock tower asymmetrically on the SE side. The urn on the SE pediment by *Thomas Waterworth* of Doncaster formerly crowned the (demolished) Well House of 1782 by *Carr*. Further additions to the hospital in 1914 and 1921.

Completed by 1811 were Nos. 29, 30, and 31 HALL BANK, the remaining (altered?) houses of a rising terrace on the W side of The Slopes, and the SQUARE, with three outward-facing façades of ten by sixteen bays on arcades.‡ The Square lies to the W of the Crescent and opposite the later Pavilion Gardens. Between it and the Crescent at the corner, OLD HALL, the

* They also built the Crescent.

‡ A. Jewitt in his *History of Buxton* (1811) tells us that Hall Bank and the Square have been 'lately finished'. Although they are traditionally attributed to Carr their plainness suggests that they are by a local mason or architect, possibly working to Carr's directions.

oldest of the buildings of lower Buxton. It was here that the Queen of Scots stayed in 1573, but from the time of her sojourn nothing survives.* The present building is of 1670 with late C18 additions behind. It has a five-bay front with slightly projecting angle bays, thick quoins, a semicircular porch on Tuscan columns and a window above it with a characteristic semicircular pediment (cf. the Peacock at Rowsley, 1652).

The first work at Buxton connected with the sixth Duke was the provision of a church for the spa.

ST JOHN THE BAPTIST, W of the riding stables and at first quite isolated, was built in 1811, probably by *John White* (Colvin). The exterior had an E entrance portico of heavy Tuscan columns, closed in to form a chancel in 1896–7 by *Blomfield & Son*, and a W elevation with Tuscan pilasters and above the pediment a tower rising to a domed top. The detail of the tower is remarkably free, and the domed top has no parallel in the normal neo-classical church types of 1810–20. The forms are rather Italian than classical. Interior without aisles, but with shallow transepts, the walls ashlar-faced, with pilasters. W gallery 1911. Chancel decorated with mosaics in 1902. Opulent Victorian furnishings: PULPIT, 1867; FONT, 1875; REREDOS, 1896–7. – STAINED GLASS. Two N windows with classical motifs by *Kempe*, c. 1897–1903. S window put in in 1920. Similar but more colourful E window. Both by *Kempe & Co.*? – PLATE. Unusual set decorated with thorn branches (two Chalices, two Patens, and Flagon), 1839 by *Edward Barnard & Sons*. 32

The sixth Duke's architect at Chatsworth, *Wyatville*, probably laid out the gardens (THE SLOPES) up St Ann's Cliff facing the Crescent, *c.* 1818. (The Palladian vases are part of the original layout and are said to have come from Londesborough, Yorks, Lord Burlington's seat. T. Cocke) This layout was modified by *Joseph Paxton*, the sixth Duke's confidant and gardener, about 1840. In 1852, Paxton also made an initial design for THE PARK, a residential area to the W of the stables and St John, with a circular open space inside and houses around, like his Birkenhead Park of 1843–7 somewhat on the pattern of Nash's original idea for Regent's Park. Its final form differs considerably from Paxton's plan (only Athelstone Ter-

* The Hall, erected by Lord Shrewsbury 'for the convenience of bathers', is described by Dr Jones in 1572 as 'four square, four stories hye, so well compacte with houses of offices, beneath and above', and seems to be related to other 'high houses' in the Midlands (cf. Elizabethan Chatsworth, Barlborough Hall, Hardwick, and North Lees). It is shown on Speed's map of Derbyshire (1610).

race appears on his map), and the houses, mostly of the 1870s, are not to his design. (In The Park is early work by *Barry Parker*: STRACHUR and LONGFORD (1904) in Park Road, both typical late C19 Buxton houses. Between them was MOORLANDS, the Parker home, now demolished. GREENMOOR, Carlisle Road, with a continuous oak-framed window curving round the corner on the first floor, is a rather eclectic early house by *Parker & Unwin*, 1897–1900. Mervyn Miller)*

The THERMAL and NATURAL BATHS were begun soon after in 1853. The Natural Baths, between the Old Hall and the Crescent, were built by *H. Currey* and rebuilt in 1924 by *F. Langley* (Borough Architect), who retained the original arcaded façade. At the other end of the Crescent are the Thermal Baths, also with an arcaded front and probably also by *Currey* but with *Paxton*'s co-operation. The glazed roof, removed early this century, was of the ridge and furrow type (cf. Chatsworth Lily House, 1849–50). The PUMP ROOM, opposite the Crescent, was built in 1894 by *Currey*; the arcades were glazed and the domes removed from the end pavilions in 1912. Round the corner the COLONNADE, a row of shops with an elegant iron veranda. A similar feature was removed from the Thermal Baths in 1967. Opposite (SE) the GROVE HOTEL has more extravagant ironwork.

A larger scale of development started after the sixth Duke's death, when the railway finally reached Buxton in 1863. At the STATION only one end wall, with giant fan window, and a waiting-room building survive from the two identical and adjacent stations designed by *J. Smith*, with *Paxton*'s advice, for the Midland and the London & North Western Railway Companies. The major part was demolished in 1969–70. In 1868 the seventh Duke's architect, *Henry Currey*, built the château-style PALACE HOTEL to the NW of the station. More churches were also provided.‡

ST ANNE (R.C.), Terrace Road. 1861 by *Scoles*. Lancet style, no tower.

HOLY TRINITY, Hardwick Mount. Nave 1873 by *R. R. Duke*.

* In the S of the town SOMERSBY and FARRINGFORD, College Road, are an interesting pair of houses of 1895 by *Parker*. Stone with timber framing in the gables and restless detail, strongly influenced by the 'Cheshire Revival' style of Faulkner Armitage, to whom Parker was articled. By *Parker & Unwin* the Spencer Road extension (1902) to THE TOWERS, College Road, and two pairs of houses in Lightwood Road (Nos. 195–201), 1903–4 (Mervyn Miller).

‡ ST JAMES, Bath Road, of 1869–70 by *J. M. & H. Taylor*, was demolished in 1975.

E transept added 1883 and spindly Perp tower completed 1906 by *Wills & Son* of London. Light and dark grey limestone. (Well preserved Evangelical interior: it was built as a proprietary chapel. T. Cocke)

UNITED REFORMED CHURCH (formerly Congregational), Hardwick Street. 1859 by *H. Currey*. Coarse Dec details and a spire.

(METHODIST CHURCH, Eagle Parade. Stone, 1849, in C14 Gothic style, with later chancel and transepts. CS)

Finally, in 1871, Buxton established itself as a proper Victorian spa by the erection of the PAVILION and the pretty PAVILION GARDENS in front of it. The Pavilion is a utilitarian, quite graceful iron and glass structure by *Edward Milner* of Sydenham, Paxton's assistant during the erection of the Crystal Palace. It was enlarged in 1875 by a CONCERT HALL on the W, an octagonal structure, heavier in the details, by *R. R. Duke*. Joined to the W of this SWIMMING BATHS, 1969–72, begun by *J. Poulson* and completed by *Booth, Hancock & Johnson* of Pontefract. The slate mansard roof echoes the massive slate dome of the Concert Hall. *Milner* also created the Pavilion Gardens on the site of THE SERPENTINE WALKS, which were almost certainly laid out by *Paxton* and which partly survive to the W. The character of the spa derives a great deal from the solid Victorian houses, many built as guest and lodging houses: e.g. Italianate villas in the BROAD WALK, with original iron lamp standards and bollards, and the larger and later mansions in BURLINGTON ROAD.

Dating from early this century were the EMPIRE HOTEL (demolished 1964) by *Thomas Garner*, *c.* 1906, to the NW of the Park; the OPERA HOUSE, 1903 by *Frank Matcham*, with a sumptuous interior by the *Dejong Company* of London, at the E end of the Pavilion; and another church in the S of the town.

ST MARY THE VIRGIN, West Road. 1914–15 by *P. Currey & C. C. Thompson*. Very attractive stone Arts-and-Crafts-style church. Steep undulating roof spanning the nave and very low aisles. Eyebrow dormers instead of clerestory windows; lancets at the E and W ends and in the transepts. Small central belfry, the chancel under the crossing. Inside, good contemporary fittings, close to work of *c.* 1900 by the Northern Art Workers Guild. 20

There is little new building, and most is inconspicuous; e.g. High Peak Borough Council SHELTERED HOUSING, HARTINGTON ROAD, by the *Francis Jones Partnership*, 1973–6, in imitation of nearby C19 stone terraces, with full-height wooden bay-windows.

STADEN LOW, 1 m. SE. Earthworks near the railway line have been claimed as a possible henge monument, but this is unlikely.

COW LOW, 1½ m. E. Bronze Age barrow, containing also an Anglo-Saxon secondary burial.

HASLING HOUSE, 1½ m. S. Bronze Age barrow.

BURBAGE. *See* p. 112.

FAIRFIELD. *See* p. 214.

0080

BUXWORTH

ST JAMES. 1874 by *J. Lowe* (GR). Stone, lancet style, with a polygonal spire and bellcote. – (STAINED GLASS. S window, sensitively coloured abstract design, 1962. T. Cocke)

(BUGSWORTH HALL, dated 1627, is many-gabled and partly plastered, with stone mullioned windows of narrow lights. RE)

In the village, the terminal CANAL BASIN of the Peak Forest Canal, designed to join the Manchester, Ashton & Oldham Canal with Chapel Milton and Whaley Bridge and completed in 1800 by *Benjamin Outram*. Notable are the highly finished stonework of the upper, middle, and lower basins, together with numerous bridges to carry tramways to the wharves and the lime kilns associated with them; the gauging lock at the approach to the basin; the wharfinger's cottage by the basin; and well preserved remains of the TRAMWAY, including bridges, embankments, and a series of tramway blocks *in situ*. The tramway, constructed by *Outram* in 1800, linked the basin with nearby gritstone workings and with limestone quarries at Doveholes.

2010

CALDWELL

ST GILES. Chapel consisting of nave with bellcote and lower chancel in the grounds of the house. The chapel is Norman though much renewed; see the small round-headed windows on the N side of nave and chancel and the S side of the nave. On the N side also a blocked round-headed doorway. In the W window two roundels of STAINED GLASS, probably *c.* 1400. – PLATE. Elizabethan Chalice and Paten Cover.

CALDWELL HALL. Eleven-bay brick mansion of two and a half storeys, plain, with parapet. To the r. of the entrance a lower, pedimented range of seven bays with windows with one mullion and one transom. Date on a rainwater-head 1678. NW wing c. 1875.

(MANOR FARM, opposite the Hall, and PRIORY FARM, at the other end of the village, are both C18 brick houses, the former with a Doric columned and pedimented porch. RE)

CALKE

3020

CALKE ABBEY lies in a dip, in extensive grounds, a large stone mansion dated 1703, all but unknown to architectural literature. It lies on the site of the Augustinian priory of St Giles, founded from Repton c. 1131. The house, built by Sir John Harpur to replace his huge mansion at Swarkestone, is very ambitious in scale if somewhat coarse in detail. Low ground floor plus two large upper floors. The entrance (S) front is thirteen bays wide, the middle seven recessed: at the corners of the three-bay angle projections are fluted Ionic pilasters on high pedestals, their capitals well below the top of the upper windows so that no continuous entablature is possible. Other pilasters used to flank the three central bays. A staircase, apparently of 1727, designed by *Gibbs* and built by *Francis Smith* of Warwick and now removed, led up to the main entrance on the first floor: the door has an exceptionally sumptuous moulded surround with square ears, a keystone carrying an elaborately carved monogram (probably later), a sculptured frieze, and a broken segmental pediment on lavish consoles. The W front is equally large and similar, but the recession is three bays deep with further recessions in the re-entrant angles, though the cornice is continuous – a provincial gaucherie like the handling of the corner pilasters, which stand side to back without forming a pillar. Here also a barbaric version of a Gibbs doorcase without pediment but carrying debased volutes on either side of the central window. On the E front the projections are of only two bays and the recession shallow. The plan is related to houses by *Smith*, i.e. the lost Sandwell Hall, Staffs., and the previous Kedleston; but the general style is not distinctive. The original entrance door now opens on to a large pedimented portico or loggia, with four unfluted Ionic columns, which replaced the Gibbs staircase in c. 1804. It stands on a row of pilastered piers whose triglyph frieze indicates that oddly no new staircase was provided.

So one now enters through the undercroft of the portico into a low vestibule giving on to the rather narrow staircase hall which climbs through the full height of the house. The staircase has two balusters per tread, each standing on a handsomely carved miniature urn; carved treads and richly panelled dado. On the landings arched doors and wooden Corinthian pilasters, much more finely executed than the exterior. In the middle of the S range is the original hall, later converted to the saloon: two storeys high with, at each end, a fireplace flanked by coupled Corinthian pilasters carrying an enormous broken segmental pediment without bedmould; the upper stages of the walls have rather arbitrary patterns of panelling. The ceiling is heavily coffered and was evidently given its present form in 1804 when much of the interior was recast: the dining room received two hefty Ionic columns and also two fine, specially designed, Sheraton sideboards. The architectural work of this date is unfortunately very coarse.

Stately brick STABLES of 1712–16 by *William Gilkes* of Burton (was he capable of the house?): two storeys, thirteen bays wide, the centre three bays projecting under a pediment with a big segmental carriage arch; symmetrical five-bay wings with bolection moulding round the central doorways; quoins at all angles. Above the pediment a quite large octagonal cupola with an onion dome. LODGES at the Ticknall entrance by *Wilkins*, who presumably made the early C19 alterations to the house.* Outside the main gates a TUNNEL, constructed to hide the traffic from the Ticknall lime quarries along the Ticknall Tramway, built in 1795–1805 by *Benjamin Outram.*

ST GILES, in the grounds of the house, but not near to it. Rebuilt in 1826, with a narrow W tower and a castellated nave. – PLATE. Chalice, 1683, possibly brought from Swarkeston; Paten Cover on knob foot, Paten on foot, and Flagon, all by *Edward Pearce* and all given by the Harpurs in 1709; Sweetmeat Dish, *c.* 1717 by *Paul Lamerie.* – MONUMENT to Sir John Harpur † 1741 and his wife, of excellent workmanship, by *Cheere* (Gunnis). Inscription plate with lovely cherubs' heads below. Above the usual pyramid, and to the l. and r. portrait busts.

2050

CALLOW

1 m. SW of Wirksworth

(CALLOW HALL. Farmhouse of 1865. Built into the double-pile house odd bits of Gothic masonry: a head and carved stone

* This description of the Abbey was kindly revised by Dr Andor Gomme.

above the date-stone, the head of an E.E. double window in the N gable. Older masonry in the rear block, and inside it remains of real interest, namely, a four-bay vaulted undercroft with chamfered rib-vaults springing from moulded corbels of C13 character, also carrying transverse arches. In the third bay of the E wall a stone chimneypiece, also medieval, the mantel a flat arch composed of joggled stones (cf. Conisbrough Castle keep, Yorks.) supported on columns with two tiers of cushion capitals with crude faces. No visible bases to the columns and no direct connection to a flue. Has the fireplace been moved? To the W remains of a moat. Barns 1825 and 1826. RE)

CALOW

4070

(ST PETER. 1869 by *S. Rollinson*. Unusual steeple and spire of 1887. RE)

CALVER

2070

CALVER MILL. The main six-storeyed stone block was built by Arkwright in 1803–4, to replace a mill of the 1780s. Pediment to the front and small E and W projections; central wing on the other side. It has circular cast-iron pillars, but originally the floor supports were of wood. Wheelhouse of 1834, with segmental arches. Early C19 two-storey manager's house and a one-storey office building in a landscaped setting, 1972–3 by *Hadfield, Cawkwell, Davidson & Partners*. 99

(BRIDGE. C18, three segmental arches. RE)

STOKE HALL. *See* p. 329.

CARDER LOW *see* HARTINGTON

CARLWARK*

2080

1¾ m. E of Hathersage

Superb hill-fort of about two acres in area. The great fortress is built at an altitude of over 1,200 ft on a wild moorland summit littered with boulders and outcrops of millstone grit. Subrectangular in outline, certain sectors of the defences still stand to a height of 10 ft. Gates can be observed in the E side and close to the S W angle. The interior is unexcavated. The site may well belong to the Iron Age, but the fact that its defences in-

* Now in Yorkshire.

corporate a rampart of turf fronted by large stone blocks has led some to argue that the fort may date from immediately after the Roman period. On the Longshaw Estate to the S lie two enclosed settlements, one of them with two oval huts within the walls. Their date is unknown, but the Iron Age or the Roman period seems the most likely context.

4050

CARNFIELD HALL

1 m. E of Alfreton

An early C17 stone mansion built by the Revells, with classicized E front. The latter is of nine bays and two storeys, the three side bays on each side projecting somewhat. Central doorway with broken segmental pediment. But early C17 twin gables appear above the projections to remind one of the real date of the house, which is impressively obvious at the back. Here the side parts project more, and one of them is continued as a lower range. The windows are mullioned and mullioned and transomed. Opposite the back a stable range apparently of the early C18. Inside, the staircases are original, and one upper room with panelling. More C16–17 woodwork was evidently brought from outside.

See p. 409

2050

CARSINGTON

ST MARGARET. Nave and chancel in one, embattled, with straight-headed three-light Perp windows. Yet the sundial in the E wall says 'Re-edified 1648'. It is an interesting, because specially complete case of Gothic Survival. Only the W end was altered in the C19 (pediment, bellcote), and possibly the E window (intersecting Y-tracery).

(SCHOOL. 1726, erected by Temperance Gell in a C17 manner, with mullioned and transomed cross windows. DOE)

OWSLOW FARM. Romano-British settlement.

HOPTON HALL. *See* p. 248.

CARTLEDGE HALL *see* HOLMESFIELD

CASTLE NAZE *see* CHAPEL-EN-LE-FRITH

CASTLETON

1080

Splendidly situated immediately below the towering Peveril Castle and with a view of the summits of the High Peak closing in to the W.

ST EDMUND. Broad Norman chancel arch of one order of colonnettes with block capitals. Big coarse zigzag in the arch. The rest essentially of the restoration of *c.* 1837. The aisles were then removed, so that the nave now has the proportions of Commissioners' churches, and the windows given their lancet shapes and typical neo-late-C13 tracery. Perp W tower, ashlar-faced, with diagonal buttresses, battlements, and eight pinnacles. – BOX PEWS. Excellently preserved throughout; C17, with various dates on (1661, 1662, 1663, 1676). – PLATE. Paten Cover, 1664.

CASTLETON HALL (Y.H.A.). C17 and later. A rustic Baroque façade of seven bays divided by pilasters of a sort. All the attempts at classical detail comically ignorant.

(CAUSEY HOUSE. Cruck-trussed house of two bays, originally timber-framed, now encased in stone and heightened. Substantial evidence of three pairs of large crucks. Taken with another cruck building in Low Lane, two early alignments of the medieval street are confirmed. Stanley Jones)

PEVERIL CASTLE. *See* p. 298.

MAM TOR, 1½ m. W. This Late Bronze Age and Iron Age hillfort encloses 16 acres and lies at an altitude of 1,700 feet. The defences consist of a single rampart and ditch on three sides, doubled on the S. Recent occupation has suggested that Mam Tor's origins may lie in the Bronze Age, a radiocarbon date of 1180 B.C. having been obtained for occupation in the interior.

GREY DITCH. This linear earthwork blocks the entry into Bradwell Dale from the Hope valley. Three sectors of the bank and ditch survive, the best preserved lengths being 21 ft wide and 8 ft high. Its date is not certain, but the period immediately following the end of Roman rule is the most probable.

LORD'S SEAT, 2½ m. W. Bronze Age round barrow on Rushup Edge.

CASTLE WOOD *see* PINXTON

CATTON HALL

2010

A large, plain, but stately brick house, begun in 1741–2 for Christopher Horton. *James Gibbs* prepared designs but one by

William Smith of Warwick for a much larger house was accepted in 1741.* (Smith was contractor for Gibbs's Radcliffe Camera in Oxford at the time.) The contractor here was *Mr Pickford*, probably *William Pickford*, who had worked for the Smiths at Trentham Park, Staffs.‡ Three storeys high plus a stone-faced basement. The main (SW) front is nine bays wide with the three central bays slightly projecting. The only decoration is the Doric doorcase. The NW side is similar but of seven bays. The NE front has a recessed centre of five bays. A new (SE) entrance was contrived in the early C19, and to the l. a Queen Anne style wing of 1907 by *T. G. Jackson*. (Very rich interiors. The best room is the so-called great hall, with pedimented overmantels (cf. Radburne) and strange, rather nervous Rococo drops originally ending in mirrors: also panels of musical instruments. The carving is wiry and linear. On the ceiling richly decorated exposed beams. The drawing room is similar but plainer, with long volutes above the chimneypiece. Staircase with balusters on a continuous string (cf. Radburne) and an arcaded landing. Modillion cornices everywhere and some fine original furniture. It seems a classic case of the very plain exterior with all the money lavished on the interior. A. Gomme) Behind the hall a brick CHAPEL, built in 1892, with a Norman FONT.

CATTON PASTURES *see* BAKEWELL

CHADDESDEN *see* DERBY, p. 291

0080

CHAPEL-EN-LE-FRITH

ST THOMAS BECKET. The first church was a chapel built by the foresters of the Peak Forest about 1225. Hence the name of the town (in-the-Forest). The present church is chiefly of the early C14, and quite large and wide. Nave and aisles of four bays, the piers octagonal, of red stone, with moulded capitals showing discreet nailhead decoration in the S arcade, and double-chamfered arches. The chancel arch appears of the same date. The chancel was much altered in 1890–3 by *Darbyshire & Smith* and is over-restored. The W tower and the S front of the church altogether received new clothes in 1731–3. The architect of the modernization was *G. Platt* of Rotherham. The

* For Gibbs's designs see A. Gomme's article in *The Country Seat*, ed. J. Harris and H. M. Colvin, 1970, p. 157.

‡ William Pickford was the father of Joseph Pickford of Derby (ES).

arched windows, the central one with alternating rustication, the S porch, and the tower with its parapet and obelisk pinnacles are all essentially in the medieval tradition. It is only the motifs which have been changed. – BOX PEWS, early C19. – FONT. C15. – ALTAR RAILS (W end). 1681. – CHANDELIER. 1731. – STAINED GLASS. E window 1890–3 by *Heaton, Butler & Bayne*. – PLATE. Paten on foot, 1710, inscribed 1747; Flagon, 1736 by *Francis Spilsbury*. – In the churchyard a pre-Conquest CROSS SHAFT.

CHRIST CHURCH dates from 1903 and has a small S tower with thick buttresses. It goes octagonal on top and ends in a spire.

In the Market Place, a medieval MARKET CROSS. Below, in Market Street, a few houses worth passing notice, chiefly WILLIAMS AND GLYN'S BANK, with a fine Art Nouveau ground storey, and further E the HEARSE HOUSE, dated 1818. On the Manchester Road THE ELMS, the former Workhouse, of 1840, well preserved in its various parts. Opposite, the road to the STATION, 1867 by *Edward Walters*, altered.

See p. 409

(BOWDEN HALL, 1 m. NE. Mostly of 1844 by *Richard Lane*. Tudor Gothic. Partly demolished. H. M. Colvin)

BANK HALL, 1–2 m. SSW. Plain Early Victorian house of no great merit but with a single room by *Eden Nesfield*, 1872–4, for Henry Renshaw of Manchester. Bay-window to the drive. It is Nesfield's most complete surviving interior, most of it exhibited in London in 1875. Oak sideboard dated 1873, like Shaw's at Cragside; panelling; canvases in a frieze painted by *Armstrong & Caldecott*; fine fireplace, tiles, and plaster ceiling; and amusing botanical painted glass. Lodge to the S by *Nesfield*.*

See p. 409

BULL RING henge monument, Dove Holes, 2 m. SE. A roughly circular earthwork, 250 ft in diameter, with opposed entrances. Large stones originally lay within, but none now survive. Like Arbor Low (*see* Youlgreave), this henge presumably dates from the Early Bronze Age.

CASTLE NAZE, Combs Moss, 1½ m. W of the Bull Ring. Iron Age promontory fort, 2¼ acres in area. The double ramparts are still well preserved on the SE side, standing to a height of 7–9 ft. They appear to embody two phases of construction.

FORD HALL. *See* p. 216.

COW LOW, 2 m. NE. Large cairn, now badly damaged.

LADY LOW, 2 m. S. Large cairn.

GANTRY'S HILL, 3 m. E. Bronze Age round barrow.

* Information from Mr Andrew Saint and Mr Thomas Cocke.

SPARROW PIT, 3 m. E. Bronze Age round barrow.
WHITEHOUGH. *See* p. 352.

0090

CHARLESWORTH

ST JOHN THE BAPTIST. 1848–9 by *J. Mitchell*, still in the pre-archaeological lancet style. Big S tower.

CONGREGATIONAL (United Reformed) CHAPEL. On the site of the original chapel of Charlesworth. Rebuilt for the Congregationalists in 1797. Big, with gable and central Venetian window on ground floor and upper floor.

(PARTICULAR BAPTIST CHAPEL. Stone, 1835, with two heights of round-arched windows. C. Stell)

(BROADBOTTOM BRIDGE. 1683, with one segmental arch of 70 ft, ribbed underneath. The other end is in Cheshire. RE)

COOMBS EDGE, 1 m. SE. Bronze Age cairn.

2070

CHATSWORTH*

INTRODUCTION

Visitors to Derbyshire may argue whether Haddon or Hardwick or Chatsworth is the most impressive mansion in the county. Haddon is no doubt more romantic than either of the others, and Hardwick is, also undoubtedly, of an architectural unity which Chatsworth fails to achieve. The grounds of Chatsworth, on the other hand, are not matched by Haddon or Hardwick or indeed more than perhaps half-a-dozen of the country houses of Britain. The lack of unity of Chatsworth is not at once noticed as one sees the house from a distance and even as one approaches it quite closely. This is due to a relatively short main building period, that of the first Duke of Devonshire (1687–1707), and to the great tact and understanding with which the second main building period, that of the sixth Duke (1820–42) and his architect *Sir Jeffry Wyatville*, treated the first, at least as far as alterations to the first Duke's palace went; for the sixth Duke added a highly palatial new wing which certainly lacks tact, even if it makes up for that by the rare combination of self-assurance and sobriety of detail.

Today Chatsworth is richer in its contents than previously, with the addition of the best of the furniture, pictures, and

* We owe the revision of this account of Chatsworth to Mr T. Wragg, Librarian and Keeper of the Devonshire Collections.

objects from Devonshire House and Chiswick to its already important collections.

William Cavendish, fourth Earl of Devonshire (1640–1707), was made first Duke in 1694 in recognition of his share in the events of 1688 and the safe establishment of William of Orange. When he took possession of Chatsworth after his father's death in 1684, he found an ELIZABETHAN HOUSE no smaller than the one he was to build. It had been begun in 1552 (to a plan made by *Roger Worthe* in 1551) by Sir William Cavendish and his wife Bess of Hardwick. The first of her many houses, it was a square built around an inner courtyard, just like its successor, and had four storeys, square angle turrets, and a tall gatehouse on the W with triangularly projecting turrets. Nothing externally visible survives of this house. However, of the smaller structures of its garden and further away, two still exist: the HUNTING TOWER or STAND, a look-out tower capping the wooded hill to the NE with four circular angle turrets with domed caps and windows with mullion-and-transom cross, and QUEEN MARY'S BOWER, NW of the N entrance of the house. The Hunting Tower was a gazebo of Bess of Hardwick at the NE corner of her park wall. Inside are three small rooms. The turrets on the uppermost floor have ceilings of decorative plasterwork of *c.* 1580. Queen Mary's Bower, restored by *Wyatville* for the sixth Duke, was possibly used by Mary Queen of Scots to take the air during her periods of captivity at Chatsworth in 1570, 1573, 1577, 1578, and 1581. Enclosing an ancient earthwork, it is a low square tower reached by steps which form a bridge over the moat, the only remnant of the several large ponds which filled the area NW of the house until the mid C17.

EXTERIOR

When the first Duke started building, he did not at first intend a complete replacement of Bess of Hardwick's house. That idea came only gradually. He began by putting up a new SOUTH WING (1687–9). This was designed by *William Talman*, who had designed Thoresby for the Duke of Kingston shortly before, but was a relatively unknown architect to be entrusted with so big an enterprise. The artists engaged for interior work, on the other hand, were mostly men close to the court: *Laguerre* and *Verrio* for the painting, *Cibber* for sculpture, and *Tijou* for ironwork. All four also appear at Hampton Court, where the new King, for whom the Duke had done so much, was to start

77

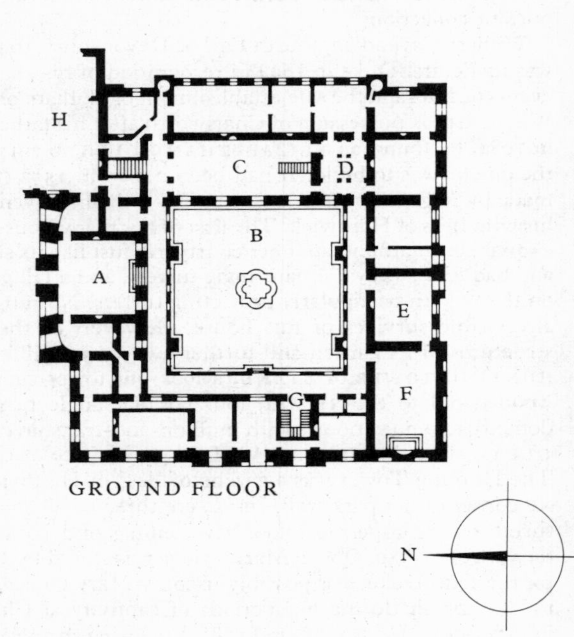

CHATSWORTH

GROUND FLOOR

A. Entrance Hall
B. Inner Court
C. Painted Hall
D. Grotto
E. Oak Room
F. Chapel
G. West Stairs
H. North Wing

FIRST FLOOR

C. Painted Hall
F. Chapel
H. North Wing
I. Great Stairs
J. Library
K. Ante-library

SECOND FLOOR

H. North Wing
L. Leicester Rooms
M. Queen of Scots Ro
N. State Dining Room
O. State Drawing Roo
P. State Music Room
Q. State Bedroom
R. State Dressing Roo
S. Sabine Room

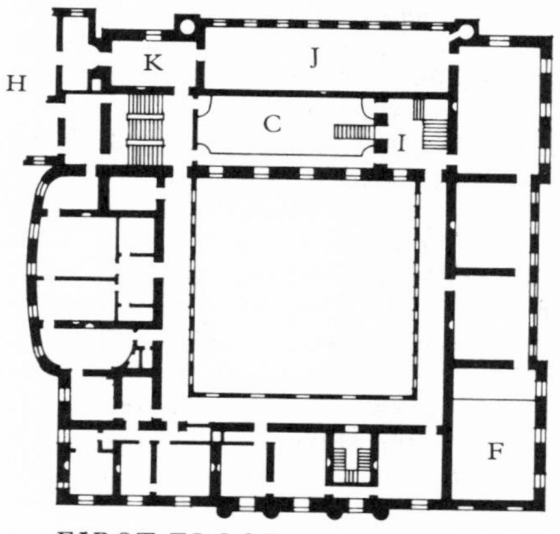

FIRST FLOOR

SECOND FLOOR

and carry on almost exactly contemporaneously with Chatsworth. But the woodwork at Chatsworth, which is every bit as good as that at Hampton Court, and Kensington Palace, is not by Grinling Gibbons, as tradition had it, but by the London team, *Young*, *Davis*, and *Lobb*, and their local associate *Samuel Watson* (*see* Heanor) who after 1694 became the principal sculptor both in wood and stone.*

Talman's SOUTH FRONT, possibly derived from an unexecuted design by Bernini for the Louvre, is eleven bays wide and consists of a rusticated basement and two upper floors of equal height. The centre is emphasized only by the outer staircase by *Wyatville* (1837) replacing Talman's original horseshoe, which had a balustrade by *Tijou*. The main emphases lie on the slightly projecting angle pavilions of three bays which have giant pilasters and some decoration in the frieze. The whole is crowned by a balustrade surmounted by urns.

Early in 1688 the Duke decided to replace the Elizabethan Great Staircase. It lay in the S corner of the old E wing, adjoining the rising new range. On the other side it adjoined the Elizabethan Hall, placed as usual (*see* Haddon and South Wingfield) across the courtyard opposite the gatehouse. At first the old Hall was meant to remain, but then, in 1689–91, this was also replaced. Once so much of the Elizabethan E range had been destroyed, the rest was taken down too, and *Talman* designed a new EAST FRONT. Its most striking features were the two narrow projections one bay from the angles, now decorated with coupled giant pilasters added by *Wyatville*, who at the same time removed the top attic windows to the back and changed the balustrade to match that on the S. Otherwise the front was plainly utilitarian, eleven bays wide. The projections hide spiral staircases, and most probably Elizabethan masonry. Owing to the rise of the ground the basement is hardly visible on this side. In 1696 this front was complete. In the same year Talman was dismissed by the Duke, who had quarrelled with his London craftsmen and regarded Talman as partly responsible for their overcharging.

Between 1696 and 1700 only minor additions were made, mostly external, to the house and especially the TERRACE and STAIRS in front of the future new WEST FRONT. But in 1700 a new phase began, when Bess's W front itself with its gatehouse was demolished to make way for the grandest of the Chatsworth façades. This was built in 1700–3, and, strangely enough, it is

78

* Watson however had been apprenticed in London, to Charles Oakley (ES).

not known for certain who designed it. After Talman's dismissal no architect appears to have been directly employed on the building. The final approved elevation is signed by *John Fitch*, the master mason, but is probably based on a design by *Archer* derived from Marly.*

The W wing is nine bays wide. It is the only one distinguished by a pediment and four all-round attached columns to carry it. The remaining six bays to the l. and r. have giant pilasters. The rusticated basement here has the height of a proper ground floor, and its centre was indeed the first Duke's main entrance into the house, a curiously insignificant entrance. This ground floor forms the base on which the giant pilasters and columns stand, a more crowded and more Baroque effect than that of the previous façades. There is a remarkably Baroque restlessness in the details of the design, the projections and recessions within the ground-floor centre, the garlands round the central windows, the ornamentation of the frieze (taken over from the S range), and the carvings inside the pediment. The garlands are by *Nadauld*; the decoration of the pediment is *Watson*'s work.

In 1703–4 a colonnade was added to the S wing on the courtyard side to make communication easier; to this was added a first-floor gallery, matching the Elizabethan one on the opposite side of the court. The colonnade was abolished by *Wyatville* when he completed the present enclosed corridors on three sides of the courtyard. Finally in 1705–7 came the last stage in the reconstruction of the house, the new NORTH FRONT. It is chiefly in the form of a shallow curve to connect the E and W wings, which differed in their extent to the N by as much as 9 ft. The bow has five windows and giant pilasters above the ground floor where *Wyatville* added the present squared projection, at the same time replacing the original oval attic windows and changing the windows on the first and second floors from round-headed to square. He also altered the frieze and substituted fluted pillars for the original rusticated ones. The wide centre part is raised, the only break in the continuity of the balustrade. The motif goes well with the style of its

* The attribution to *Archer* is made by K. Downes (*English Baroque Architecture*, 1966, pp. 62–3). It was previously attributed by M. Whiffen to *Thornhill* on the basis of an inscription in *Vitruvius Britannicus*. Thornhill was painting here in 1700 but is not known to have made any architectural designs before 1716. Sir John Summerson considers that the proportions of the façade and emphatic keystones are closer to Le Vau's Vaux-le-Vicomte.

designer, who was almost certainly *Thomas Archer*. Archer spent some time at Chatsworth in 1704 or 1705 and was left £200 by the Duke in his will for 'his favour and his care and trouble touching the building of the house'.

In spite of this complex building history, Chatsworth as it appeared in Early Georgian days possessed a convincing unity of style. This was partly due to the square, compact shape of the block and partly, as has been said before, to the short intervals between the various phases. The next substantial addition was due to the fourth Duke, who succeeded to the title in 1755. He employed *James Paine* to complete a comprehensive plan for clearing the surroundings and improving the approach to the house, in conjunction with the building of the new main road running N–S through the park. A new bridge was built and extensive stables to the NE provided. A new entrance hall (cf. below) was contrived in place of the previous kitchen in the middle of the N bow, an additional low wing from the NE angle, forming one side of an entrance court housing the kitchen and offices (1756–60). The stables remain, but for the office wing a more substantial and infinitely more ambitious wing was substituted by the sixth Duke.

The sixth Duke (1790–1858) had succeeded in 1811. His first job was an internal adjustment, the conversion of the long gallery into a library (1815; cf. below).* He did not taste of the sweet taste of building until 1820, when work began on the new

77 NORTH WING and many more changes inside the house. His architect was *Jeffry Wyatt*, later *Sir Jeffry Wyatville*, who had made a name by his previous work for Longleat (1801 etc.) and Wollaton (1804) in the Elizabethan style, and Ashridge (1814 etc.) in the Gothic style. The main function of the N wing, which is 357 ft long, was to provide a suite of rooms, including a dining or ballroom and a gallery for sculpture, longer, more easily accessible, and grander than the first Duke's state rooms on the second floor of the S range had been. The wing also provided new kitchens and offices and accommodation for less important guests and servants. The C17 state rooms were to become 'a museum of old furniture and a walk in wet weather'.

The architects of the Romantic period (and Wyatville was emphatically one of them, even where he used the chastest classical forms) disliked the symmetry of the Age of Reason. The Picturesque was their watchword, and so neither the Duke nor his architect was worried by the fact that the new wing de-

* According to the Duke's own Handbook of Chatsworth (1845).

stroyed the compactness of the old house. The length of the jutting-out new range seemed to add just what was needed, especially when, in 1827, an orangery was added at the N end as an afterthought and after that a swimming bath with a theatre above. Finally, to top this achievement, the Duke out of his own mind finished the wing by the Temple Attic, the big belvedere storey at the N end.* Its self-assertiveness hurts people, but as a symbol of the man who built it and of his time it could not be better. And it is besides in its somewhat Genoese Cinquecento character by no means offensive. Due to *Wyatville* also are the ENTRANCE LODGES and GATEWAYS, on the N, which replaced the screen wall with an archway provided by *Paine* in 1764, a monumental overture in the Tuscan style to the N forecourt (with its fine weeping ash) and to the house.

INTERIOR

The interior of the house will be discussed in the order in which visitors (at the time of writing) see it. Parts not shown but architecturally of significance will follow after that, and then the outbuildings, gardens, and grounds. In accordance with the principles of *The Buildings of England*, neither furniture nor paintings will be mentioned, unless they can be considered fixtures and fitments.

The ENTRANCE HALL was contrived out of the first Duke's kitchen by *James Paine* for the fourth Duke *c.* 1756–60. The columns are copies of one by *Kent* in the grounds of Lord Burlington's Palladian villa at Chiswick, which had come into the possession of the Duke in 1753. The staircase was widened by *Wyatville*, who also replaced the chimneypieces by new ones and opened out the windows on the l. and r. of the stairs. The CORRIDORS in their present form are all *Wyatville*'s work. To reach the Painted Hall and the main stairs the C18 visitor had to pass through the first Duke's open colonnade, an eminently inconvenient approach, even if one slightly more convenient than the original one, which from the low entrance hall in the middle of the W front had to be reached across the open courtyard, as if the house had been one of the dark Middle Ages.

The PAINTED HALL is 64 by 26 ft in size. Originally two flights of stairs curved up to the first-floor landing at the S end. This arrangement has been altered twice, first under the sixth Duke (1833), who also added as an easier access to the first floor

* In fact the idea of a belvedere in the new wing had been conceived in 1818, when the Duke first met Wyatville, and drawings were made in 1824.

the Oak Stairs N of the hall with their domed skylight (1823–9), and again in 1911–12, when the present hall staircase and galleries were built (by *W. H. Romaine-Walker*). The hall has a ceiling and walls painted by *Laguerre*, assisted by *Ricard*, in 1694. They represent the Life of Julius Caesar. They are intended to be grand in the Baroque manner but do not succeed in this. Their colouring lacks fire and their compositions brio. It is particularly unfortunate that there is no framing with gilt and stucco round the ceiling painting. It makes the paintwork appear flat and just stuck on. The painted architecture on the walls has the same quality of flatness. *Samuel Watson*'s stone-carvings, on the other hand, are superb.

The Great Stairs are approached by means of the staircase in the hall. Originally they were meant to start from the ground floor. The change of plan left no function for the dark square space on the ground floor beneath the Great Stairs. So the first Duke decided to make it into a GROTTO, not really one with shell-studded walls and rockery, but at least a room the *point de vue* of which was a fountain. This, or rather the relief of Diana, was bought in London in 1692. It must be French work of *c.* 1600 and is of higher quality than contemporary figure work in England. *Watson*'s stone-carving here is the most sumptuous he did inside the house. The ceiling of the grotto is supported by four heavy Tuscan columns. If the room is less gloomy now than one might expect, this is due to the piercing of four openings by the sixth Duke.

From the grotto visitors go by way of the chapel corridor through the OAK ROOM, fitted out with carvings of *c.* 1700 acquired by the sixth Duke from a German monastery, to the CHAPEL, the finest room at Chatsworth. It runs through two storeys with an E gallery on the first floor. The walls are cedar-panelled with limewood carvings of garlands of fruit and foliage in the manner of Gibbons. Against the W wall is a magnificent reredos of alabaster, with columns of black Derbyshire marble, carved by *Samuel Watson* after a design by *Cibber*. The apse behind the altar is surmounted by a broken pediment and an upper storey with a large painting of Doubting Thomas by *Verrio* flanked by allegorical statues of Faith and Justice by *Cibber*. The top is a broken segmental pediment. The figures are matched by feigned sculpture by *Ricard* on the adjoining walls. In this work, completed in 1694, England is certainly as Baroque in the Continental sense, that is as magnificent and swaggering, as she ever was. *Laguerre*'s walls and ceiling again

79

fail to keep up this high pitch. They appear dull and slaty next to Verrio's painting and Cibber's sculpture. But even Verrio seems staid and somewhat phlegmatic if compared with *Sir James Thornhill*'s early ceiling painting (1706) on the WEST STAIRS. It represents the Fall of Phaeton and shows that he owed as much to Rubens as to Italy.

The ironwork of the balustrade (1702) is the work of *John Gardom*, the local smith who earlier worked with Tijou. It should be remembered that in the first Duke's day the staircase was lit by windows looking into the courtyard on every floor.

Visitors go up the West Stairs straight to the second floor and enter the STATE ROOMS through the W Sketch Gallery, now hung with family portraits, and the China Closet. To the N of the staircase is the SABINE ROOM, painted by *Thornhill* (1708), one of the greatest English Baroque interiors, which is at times included in the public route.

To have the best suite on the second floor is an anomaly, explained by the fact that the ground floor was regarded as a basement, and owing to the fall of the site was indeed on the E side (where hall and Great Stairs are placed) no more than a basement. It follows the precedent of Bess of Hardwick's Chatsworth, and her last great house at Hardwick. The state rooms (five in number) are of a type familiar from Hampton Court and Kensington Palace, with the doors in *enfilade*, made more impressive by continuing them at the E end with a mirror (costing the fabulous sum of £105, but replaced with plate glass by the sixth Duke) to double their length in appearance. The suite has ceilings painted by *Verrio*, *Laguerre*, and *Ricard*,* and a profusion of exquisite ornamental wood-carving by the London carvers *Lobb*, *Davis*, and *Young*, assisted by *Watson*. The rooms were decorated in 1689–99, but only the DINING ROOM survives in its original state. The sixth Duke placed the embossed and gilt leather on the walls of the BEDROOM and MUSIC ROOM; the Mortlake tapestries were framed on the walls of the drawing room at an earlier date. The so-called STATE DINING ROOM was of course never a dining room. Its original name was the Great Chamber. The gilt side tables in this room were designed by *Kent* for Lord Burlington's Chis-

* By *Verrio* the Virtues and Vices (1691), State Dining Room; all the others by *Laguerre* assisted by *Ricard*, 1689–94. The finest, that in the State Bedroom, the Triumph of Diana. State Music Room, Phaeton and Apollo; State Drawing Room, an Assembly of the Gods; State Dressing Room, Dispatch of the Apple of Discord.

wick villa. The large centre table, also by *Kent*, was brought from Wanstead.

Beyond are the GREAT STAIRS (1689–90) designed by *Talman*. The ceiling here is by *Verrio* (Triumph of Semele, 1691), the grisaille panels on the walls by unrecorded painters. Originally the first Duke intended Verrio to paint the walls, and the beginnings of his scheme remain. The statues and doorcases are by *Cibber*. *Tijou*, the most famous artist in wrought iron ever working in England, did the stair balustrade and received £250 for it. The pattern is one (none too felicitous) of square balusters represented flat and in outline. From the landing one either returns to the Painted Hall or enters the QUEEN OF SCOTS APARTMENTS. The rooms on the courtyard side were rebuilt by *Talman* (1689–91) on the site of the rooms used by Mary Stuart in the old house. Planned as an addition to the state rooms, they had carvings by *Watson* and a ceiling by *Verrio*, and were completely separated from the rooms on the E side. The whole floor was altered by *Wyatville* and redecorated for the sixth Duke around 1830. The ceilings were lowered and the two large rooms reduced by the provision of a lobby and passage.*

The next room shown to the public is the ANTE-LIBRARY, formerly the Little Dining Room, with a ceiling painting by *Hayter* c. 1820. The LIBRARY is seen, but not entered, from this room. This is on the first floor and fills most of the E front. 90 ft long, it was originally the GALLERY, fitted out by the first Duke in 1694–1700 with plasterwork by *Goudge* of London and painted panels by *Chéron* and *Thornhill* (now in the theatre). Twice refitted as a library for the sixth Duke, the present scheme by *Wyatville* with woodwork and fittings by *Armstrong & Siddons* dates from 1832. Of the original work only the plasterwork of the ceiling and its painted medallions by *Verrio* remain.

The redecoration of the Gallery started the sixth Duke on his much more ambitious scheme of creating a whole new suite of rooms, larger and grander than the old building could provide anywhere. So the new N wing (i.e. the wing projecting from the NE corner to the N) was designed by *Wyatville*, begun in 1818, and completed in the 1830s. Nearly 600 ft in length and terminating in the Theatre Tower with the Duke's own belve-

* These rooms are an optional addition to the route, first opened to the public in 1966. The Green Satin Room (now plainly papered) was originally the Leicester Drawing Room.

dere which originally had a swimming bath on the ground floor, it contains kitchens and offices on the ground floor, and the new State Suite on the first, with bachelors' bedrooms behind. *Wyatville* in his interiors kept to a grand classical manner and forgot about the fancies he was able to put into his Gothic work. The suite consists of the DOME ROOM, an ante-room with bust columns of *pavonazza* and *gialastro* and two slender vases of the rare *occhio di paone*; the DINING ROOM with its curved and coffered ceiling, and its chimneypieces flanked with figures by *Westmacott* the younger and *Sievier*; the SCULPTURE GALLERY with three square lantern skylights; and the ORANGERY, added in 1827 as an afterthought. In the sculpture gallery the very expensive ormolu capitals of the large columns at the N end are by *Delafontaine* of Paris. The bas reliefs on the E wall are by *Thorwaldsen* (1827–32) and the room contains the best of the neo-classical sculpture acquired by the sixth Duke, which overflows into the orangery. It was a regally expensive job throughout.

The THEATRE is now a gallery for special exhibitions. Originally designed by *Wyatville* in 1833 as a banqueting chamber, it was later fitted out as a theatre by *Crace*, the painted panels which originally decorated what are now the library and ante-library being placed on its ceiling.

Most of *Wyatville*'s work inside the first Duke's block is not seen by the normal visitor. It comprised alterations to the suite below the state rooms, the principal living rooms for the family and occasionally used for larger-scale entertaining (1827–33), and the LOWER LIBRARY, decorated by *Crace*, 1844. It also comprised the introduction of more commodious corridors at the back of the S and W ranges facing the courtyard (1830s).

STABLES

Close to Wyatville's N wing is the big quadrangle of *Paine*'s stables, built for the fourth Duke in 1758–63. The design is characterized by a free use of cyclopic rustication (on the pattern of Giulio Romano and Serlio). The front has a central triumphal-arch motif with four attached columns and the usual clock-turret with open cupola above (cf. C18 Burlington House, according to Walpole). The columns are given big blocks of heavy rustication at intervals. Over the entrance is a coat of arms carved by *Henry Watson*, and inside the courtyard four rusticated giant gateways and an open ground-floor arcade rusticated throughout. The walls above it are ashlar-faced.

GARDENS AND GROUNDS

The gardens and grounds are basically due to the first Duke, in spite of many later alterations. He did as much outdoors as he did to the house. In 1699 the house was reached from the W, not the N (cf. above). An unornamental bridge crossed the river to the S of the house and led to a forecourt on the W front, with iron palisade by *Tijou*, and the stables and outbuildings in line on the N. To the SW, S, SE, and E were formal parterres with fountains and statuary and the bowling green. The parterres were laid out by the King's Gardeners *George London* and *Henry Wise*, each in the taste of the time a separate rectangle. On the S side of the Bowling Green stood the TEMPLE OF FLORA (1693–5), moved to the N end of the E front *c.* 1765, with its four slim Roman Doric columns and top balustrade.

To the S was the CANAL (dug 1702), an indispensable piece of French garden design, and to the E the most dramatic piece, the CASCADE, begun in 1694. The canal now contains *Paxton*'s EMPEROR FOUNTAIN which, fed by the Emperor Lake dug for the purpose on top of the hill to the E, first played in 1843. The CASCADE and other waterworks of the first Duke's formal garden were designed by *Grillet*, a pupil of Le Nôtre, but the 80 CASCADE HOUSE, designed by *Thomas Archer*, was added later (1702). It has a stepped little dome, corners with intermittently rusticated pilasters coming forward in a curve, two twisting dolphins flanking the entrance arch, and rockery and figures on the parapet. Behind the Cascade House, the Cascade Pond is fed by water from ponds on the hill top led to an AQUEDUCT, a piece of Baroque romanticism inspired by Wilhelmshöhe near Kassel, built for the sixth Duke: four rudely rusticated arches in the woods, ending abruptly, which no visitor should miss.

The gardens remained in their state of 1707 until the fourth Duke, probably influenced by his father-in-law Lord Burlington, began his improvements. They all belong to his last ten years, their purpose to convert the first Duke's formal gardens and the park to the W into a landscape in the sense of *Capability Brown*, who was indeed called in in 1761. New lawns coming close to the house and merging into the park with a handsome new BRIDGE (with re-used *Cibber* sculpture) and a new gracefully winding approach road (by *Paine*, 1760–4) were made, and thereby the surroundings of the house created which we admire today. *Paine* also built the one-arch bridge at the S of the park to carry the new road from Edensor to Beeley and the MILL (now a ruin) near by (1759–60). This has one of Paine's favourite devices, an interlocking pediment derived from Palladio's Venetian churches, which also occurred in the office wing (P. Leach).

Yet the sixth Duke's taste also appears in the garden, as it does everywhere. As can be seen in the case of so many properties landscaped in the C18, the Victorian taste insisted on the restoration of a more formal layout near the house. So statues and clipped trees arranged symmetrically came back, and even embroidery parterres. In addition large structures went up for horticultural purposes, due at first more to the Duke's gardener, the great *Paxton*, who was employed to lay out the gardens in 1826–44, than to the Duke himself. The most impressive of these, the GREAT CONSERVATORY (1836–40), 277 ft long, 67 ft high, 'the glory of Chatsworth and the most extensive in the world' (Murray's *Handbook*, 1874), was unfortunately demolished in 1920.* In more than one way it was the immediate predecessor of Paxton's Crystal Palace. But Paxton's forcing wall, glazed in 1848, survives, running E from the Temple of Flora and the N end of Wyatville's new wing, and the ARBORETUM and PINETUM planted under his direction remain a feature of the garden.

GREENHOUSE (1970) designed by *G. A. H. Pearce* to the rear of the sixth Duke's greenhouse. Appropriately novel construction, the roof being supported by external bracing. Inside the largest and hottest of three compartments contains a pool for the Victoria Lily.

Finally, some buildings which the sixth Duke built further out in the park must be mentioned – the Baslow GATE LODGES, designed by *Wyatville* in 1837 and finished by *Paxton*, 1842; the SWISS COTTAGE, 1839, with rather fanciful bargeboarding, by the Swiss Lake (and altogether the surprising lake and hill scenery to the E of the house, landscaped by *Paxton*); and the RUSSIAN COTTAGE, 1855, overlooking Calton Pasture to the W of the Beeley Bridge, based on a model of a Russian farm sent to the Duke by the Tsar.

For estate buildings *see* Baslow, Beeley, Edensor, and Pilsley.

* Paxton may have been assisted by *Decimus Burton* in designing it.

CHEE TOR *see* BLACKWELL

CHELLASTON *see* DERBY, p. 192

1070

CHELMORTON

ST JOHN THE BAPTIST. Low broad W tower with battlements and recessed spire. The spire has one tier of dormers low down and a girdle high up. The rest of the church of a lighter stone. It has a three-bay arcade between nave and S aisle with plain octagonal piers and double-chamfered round arches, and a four-bay N arcade with fine capitals and pointed arches. At the time when the N arcade was built, the S arcade was lengthened by one bay to match it. This fourth bay opens into the S transept. The E wall of this is not in line with the chancel arch. So the building history is complex. As to dating, the S arcade can hardly be later than *c.* 1200. The S transept has a genuine S window of three stepped lancet lights and an E window of two lancet lights with pierced spandrel, i.e. a date *c.* 1300. The N aisle doorway (blocked) has a plain steeply pointed trefoil head, i.e. again *c.* 1300. Regarding the date of the chancel, its SEDILIA and PISCINA look mid C14. Perp clerestory on the S side only (altered C19) and porch. – FONT. Octagonal, Perp. – ROOD SCREEN. Stone, Perp, low, embattled, with blank ogee arcade, and below the battlements openwork quatrefoils. – STAINED GLASS. E window 1880 by *Jones & Willis* (TK). – PLATE. Paten, 1614; Cup, 1625. – (MONUMENT. George Dale † 1683, a surprisingly up-to-date Baroque tablet. T. Cocke)

At the entrance to this typically one-street village, TOWNEND FARMHOUSE, C18, plastered front with stone parapet, four Venetian windows, and a doorway with fluted pilasters and a pediment. Good C18 stone barn behind.

CHELMORTON LOWS. Two round barrows.

NETHER LOW. Barrow with four inhumations, ¼ m. S. Near by, an Anglo-Saxon barrow.

FIVE WELLS *see* Taddington.

3070

CHESTERFIELD

CHURCHES

ST MARY AND ALL SAINTS.* A big, long church (173 by 110 ft)

* A ROMAN FORT, which passed through several phases of occupation, lay at the centre of the town near to the church. Originating in the late C1, it appears to have been held until the middle of the C2.

of cleaned grey ashlar stone with a crossing tower, lying in the centre of the old part of the town. It is nationally famous owing to the freak that its timber and lead spire has warped into a comically twisted shape. It is 228 ft high and leans 7½ ft to the S, 10½ ft to the SW, and 3 ft to the W. The warping is due to each stage of the wooden framework having turned round a few degrees upon the one beneath. It is made more peculiar to the eye by the lead plates being laid herringbone fashion, so that the whole spire looks channelled, although the eight sides are in fact perfectly flat. The church consists of nave and aisles of six bays, S and N transepts (the latter rebuilt and provided with a pediment in 1769, vestry added 1963), and an E end of unusual complexity. The chancel is flanked by two-bay chancel chapels as long as the chancel (St Katherine's N, Lady Chapel S), and to the S of the southern one follows a much shorter chapel with polygonal E end (Lesser Lady Chapel), an unusual feature in England though common on the Continent, and to the N of the northern a short rectangular chapel (Holy Cross) with the vestry E of it. This multiplicity of chapels is due to the wealth of guilds in the town. The earliest, the Guild of Our Lady and the Holy Cross, was founded in 1218.

The oldest architectural piece in the church is the PISCINA in the Holy Cross Chapel, trefoiled, E.E. The oldest major parts are the supports of the crossing tower, dedicated in 1234, and the transepts with the piers separating them from an E aisle later converted into the chapels mentioned above. The latter date from the late C13 or a little later; see the S transept S respond (many slim shafts with shaft-rings) and N respond (three sturdier shafts with fillets) – the pier between was later converted into a semi-Perp shape – the W respond of the S chancel chapel, the beautifully stiff-leaf-decorated N respond and pier of the N transept (the latter octagonal and with ornamentation, including human heads), and the crossing piers, each facing the crossing with six big shafts, the two main axial ones filleted. The crossing arches are treble-chamfered.

Most of the rest of the church is Dec, or *c.* 1325–50. Outside, the central W window is of seven lights with one transom and flowing tracery, the side parts chiefly ogee-reticulated, the centre branching out in divers leaf shapes. The W door (and the great E window) date from *Gilbert Scott*'s restoration of 1843. The N transept N window is original Dec, the S transept S window of 1875. All the aisle windows are simple three-light Dec, the tall slim windows of the Lesser Lady Chapel two-light

Dec (inside a PISCINA with ogee-trefoil head), the Lady Chapel S windows ogee-reticulated. Perp replacement windows appear chiefly at the W ends of the aisles and at the E ends of the chancel aisles, and also in the clerestory. The main S doorway is typical C14 in its fine filleted shafts and arch mouldings. The S transept doorway and N doorway are C19; the N transept doorway dates from 1769 (with pediment). The upper parts of the crossing tower have two two-light bell-openings on each side and a parapet instead of battlements.

As to the interior architecture, nothing has yet been said of the nave, which is very different in feeling from the accepted Derbyshire types. The piers are quatrefoil with hollows in the diagonals and fillets on the main shafts, very tall and thin, the capitals moulded and the arches provided with two wavy mouldings. The date is apparently later than the rest, *c.* 1350–75 perhaps. Crocketed ogee-headed recess in the S aisle. The only old roof is in the S transept; Late Perp. The W gallery is a reminder of the restoration of 1842–3, carried out by *Gilbert Scott*, an early work of his, not yet as archaeologically competent as his later jobs.

17

FURNISHINGS. REREDOSES. High altar by *Temple Moore*, 1898; Holy Cross altar with a centre panel from Oberammergau, side panels by *Leslie Moore*, 1934. – FONT. Norman, tub-shaped, with leaf decoration; also a foliated cross; badly preserved. – PULPIT. Uncommonly courtly work of Jacobean style; note the openwork plaited balusters of the stair. Perhaps by the carvers of the long gallery at Haddon. – SCREENS. S transept with original ribbed coving. Each section is of four lights with a depressed arched top; each light ends in a steep crocketed arch; no panel tracery. The date is *c.* 1500. – N transept, St Katherine's Chapel (not in its original position), with three-light sections and simple Perp tracery. This was originally the rood screen of *c.* 1475. – N transept, Holy Cross Chapel (towards the choir vestry), Perp, originally belonging to the Foljambe Chapel (1503–4). The present rood screen is of 1915 by *Temple Moore*. – CANDELABRUM. S chancel chapel, presented in 1760, originally in the nave. It is in two tiers and has, above the upper tier, lovely wrought-iron decoration nearly up to the very top. – SCULPTURE. Head-corbels in the N transept E and W walls; also in the Lesser Lady Chapel. – STAINED GLASS. Lady Chapel (1844) and St Katherine's Chapel E (1868) by *Warrington*. – S transept by *Hardman*, 1875. – Nave W by *Heaton, Butler & Bayne*, 1890. – Holy Cross Chapel E by

Comper, 1941. – St Peter's Chapel by the same and Miss *Aldrich Rope*, 1943. – Lady Chapel E (1947) and chancel E (1953) by *Christopher Webb*. – PROCESSIONAL CROSS (at the back of the bishop's chair), said to be Italian, early C16. From Wingerworth. – PLATE. Two large Flagons, given 1733; two Chalices, Paten on foot, and large Almsdish of 1808, by *William & Peter Bateman*.

MONUMENTS. Effigy of a Priest, two angels by his pillow, early C14(?), in the S aisle recess. – Members of the Foljambe family at the E end of the Lady Chapel: Henry Foljambe † 1510 and wife. Alabaster tomb-chest (with brasses), made at Burton-on-Trent by *Harper* and *Moorecock*, who were paid £10. Against the chest walls standing figures of mourners under crocketed ogee arches, mostly two in one panel, under a twin arch. – On the top of this monument kneeling figure of a boy, probably Sir Thomas † 1604 (the head does not belong to the body). – Sir Godfrey † 1529 and wife, brasses (remade), kneeling children below. – Sir Godfrey † 1585 and wife, big Renaissance tomb-chest with recumbent effigies, of the best quality available, both in the portraits and the strap decoration of the chest. – George † 1588, damaged incised alabaster slab. – Godfrey and wife † 1594 (S wall). Very cosmopolitan big standing wall- 42 monument. A framed panel is dated 1592. It was ordered before his death. Two recumbent effigies on a straw mat. They lie not on a tomb-chest but on a bulgy sarcophagus with sirens and thick garlands. Back wall with two Sansovinesque standing allegorical figures between columns to the l. and r. of the inscribed tablet, and above in the scrolly pediment two reclining allegories and more ornament and fruit bunches. – The same Godfrey was responsible for the erection of the large tablet with kneeling figure to Sir James Foljambe who had died in 1558. It is unusually flat and as delicate as Godfrey's own tomb. Note especially the fine representation of the children below. To the l. and r. of the kneeler are panels with fruit, etc., and to the l. and r. of these thin caryatids. – Finally there is, arranged symmetrically with the previous monument, that of another ancestor left without any inscription. This was also commissioned by Godfrey. It has the figure all bundled up in a shroud (as 41 at Fenny Bentley). Above, a tripartite 'reredos' with fine fluted pilasters and Death in the middle and Old Age and Childhood l. and r. Bones, shovels, and hoes and the 'predella' below – a mysterious and extremely fascinating monument. – Among the wall-tablets the following are signed: Godfrey Heathcote

† 1773, by *John Fisher, elder and younger*, of York. – Mary Boucher † 1791, by *William Stead* of York. – Elizabeth Bapshaw † 1792, by *John Blagden* of Sheffield.

HOLY TRINITY, Newbold Road. Of elephant grey ashlar. Lancet windows, W tower with pinnacles. 1838 by *Thomas Johnson*, altered in 1888–9 by *S. Rollinson*. – The STAINED GLASS in the E window is a memorial (1848) to George Stephenson the engineer, who is buried in the church.

ANNUNCIATION (R.C.), Spencer Street. 1854 by *Joseph Hansom*. Quite big, the most impressive part the *Westwerk*, as the Germans call it, i.e. the big broad tower-like erection at the W end. This was added in 1874. Attached is a presbytery in the same style.

METHODIST CHURCH, Saltergate. 1870. Big, of stone, seven bays long, with a spectacular Renaissance front with attached portico of giant Ionic columns and pediment.

UNITED REFORMED (Congregational) CHURCH, Rosehill. Formerly an Independent Chapel. 1822, much re-done. The Tuscan doorway is original.

ELDER YARD CHAPEL (Unitarian), Elder Way. 1694, but altered. (Rendered S front of five bays, enlarged to six, three-bay pediment, central doorway, and mullion-and-transom cross windows. CS) The side elevation to Elder Way has quoins, plain horizontal string courses, a central door, and two low mullioned windows.

FRIENDS MEETING HOUSE, Goldwell Hill. 1971–2 by *Bartlett & Gray*, skilfully fitted on to a steeply sloping site with much mature vegetation. It replaces the C18 Meeting House in Saltergate, demolished 1974.*

PUBLIC BUILDINGS

TOWN HALL, Rosehill. By *Bradshaw, Gass & Hope*, 1937–8. In a fine position overlooking the valley. It is of a scale quite different from the Chesterfield of before, and it has the ostentation-cum-gentility so favoured for such buildings. Brick and stone, with a central portico of six giant columns.‡ – PLATE. Silver-gilt Mace, 1671–2; Tankard by *Richard Bayley*, 1730–1; Seal, apparently C14.

* This was late C18 with a C19 E wall and staircase. N and W walls of stone, S, E, and staircase of brick. Inside a gallery and some C18 and C19 panelling.

‡ The earlier Town Hall stood at the corner of the Market Place, the corner of Glumangate and High Street, and was built in 1787–8 by *Carr* of York for the Duke of Portland.

COURT HOUSE, Shentall Gardens. 1963–5, sited in the gardens sloping down to West Bars below the Town Hall, and visible from all sides and from above. The architects (*J. S. Allen* in association with *R. Keenleyside*) have taken this into consideration. The building is composed of two sections, fanning outwards from a central core. Both the curved outer concrete-framed walls of the jettied-out upper floor and the roofs have restless zigzag profiles, the roofs constructed with box-beams at 30 degrees to the horizontal, the outer walls with angled blue granite infill panels. The side walls of each fan have long windows divided by quartz aggregate louvres lighting the courtrooms. Beneath, lower offices also with louvred panels. Small-scale and fussy when compared with the Town Hall on one side of it and the almost contemporary Chetwynd House on the other.

POSTAL FINANCE DEPARTMENT (CHETWYND HOUSE), West Bars. 1960–3. The first of the large decentralized government offices built under the Fleming Plan (architect: *J. W. Parr*, Ministry of Public Building and Works). It occupies an attractive site between Shentall Gardens and Queens Park. At r. angles to West Bars is a ten-storey glass and concrete tower divided on the W by a piazza (with a sculpture by *Barbara Hepworth*) from three-storey blocks ranged round a courtyard. Housing for workers has been provided at Loundsley Green (*see* p. 148) and other areas to the N of the town.

MARKET HALL, Market Place. 1857 by *Davies & Sons*. The crudest show of High Victorian provincial prosperity. Brick, symmetrical, with a tall tower.

CHESTERFIELD COLLEGE OF ART AND DESIGN (Annexe), Sheffield Road, is the former Grammar School for Boys (1846 by *Patterson & Hine* plus 1860 and 1862), in a gloomy rock-faced Tudor. Behind it purpose-built College of Art buildings by *R. Kenning* (County Architect), 1968–76.

ST HELENA SCHOOL FOR GIRLS, Sheffield Road, forms a contrast with the boys' school characteristic of many boys' and girls' schools. It is of 1911 by *G. H. Widdows* (County Architect) in brick with a cupola and a cheerful mixture of Baroque and Tudor motifs.

PERAMBULATION

The centre of the town is the MARKET PLACE. In the late C18 an attempt was made to impose axial formality on this big, sloping, wedge-shaped space by emphasizing the centre of each side. At the W end was an ancient arcaded Market Hall, demolished before 1839, probably *c.* 1802. Facing it was the CATHEDRAL VAULTS, now demolished but with its five-bay arcade partly retained. At the centre of the N side (High Street) was the KING AND MILLER INN, which also had an arcade. It was demolished in 1968 and replaced by the out-of-scale LITTLEWOOD'S STORE. On the S is LOW PAVEMENT, a picturesque range of different periods, now decrepit after years of 'planning blight'.* In the centre still, the former CASTLE INN (No. 41), also with an arcade on the street façade. Adjoining on the W, Nos. 43 and 45, also C18, No. 45 with a Baroque stone surround and pediment to the central window.‡ A little further W, the PEACOCK INN, found on stripping later casing (1974) to be a three-bay timber-framed building of *c.* 1500, of which two bays survive. It had a first floor of impressive dimensions and may have been the hall of the town's most important guild, that of the Blessed Mary. Evidence of occupation from the late C13 was found, and a C15 stone house immediately preceded the present structure. Ending Low Pavement to the E the former FALCON INN (No. 1, now Boden's Restaurant), timber-framed, with each storey jettied out and supported over the pavement by two large stone Tuscan columns. (Late Elizabethan and more characteristic of Devon, e.g. Totnes, than of Derbyshire. DOE)

Opposite Boden's Restaurant, between Packer's Row and the Market Place, is the area popularly known as the SHAMBLES. In layout it retains its medieval character, but the only really old building is the ROYAL OAK, tidied up and a little embellished but essentially a sound C16 timber-framed building. Packer's Row leads into HIGH STREET, where the upper part of the GENERAL POST OFFICE is a pedimented brick C18 building. At the W end of the High Street in NEW SQUARE, No. 87 (ARCHBISHOP SECKER'S HOUSE), a late

* Since the war development plans have been under consideration. In 1973 planning permission was granted for a commercial development (architects *Bernard Engle & Partners*) which would have involved the destruction of almost the whole of Low Pavement and which would have occupied most of the Market Place. Fortunately these plans were rejected in 1975 and new plans, conserving this area, are being implemented (1977; architects *Feilden & Mawson*). A large part of the town centre is now a conservation area.

‡ We are indebted to Mr Roger Evans for the information in the preceding lines of the Perambulation.

C18 three-storey brick house with a pedimented doorway and two two-storey canted bays flanking it.

Round the corner from New Square in WEST BARS, No. 23 is of c. 1830 but completely in the Georgian tradition, which lasted until late here. Red brick, of two storeys and three bays, with a doorway with fluted Doric half-columns. From the N side of New Square, Soresby Street leads to SALTERGATE. Almost opposite the end of Soresby Street, MARSDEN STREET turns off Saltergate. There, the BRAYSHAW BUILDING is the former United Methodist Free Church, built in 1869–70 by a Mr *Simpson*. Florentine C15 palazzo style with biforated windows which have cast-iron tracery. Behind it, the former Sunday School, 1874.* At the E end of Saltergate, SALTERGATE TERRACE (Nos. 69–79) is like No. 23 West Bars, of c. 1830 but still Georgian. Brick with doorways with recessed Roman Doric columns and a four-bay pediment. On the island site at the corner of HOLYWELL STREET a new development was at planning stage in 1975. Facing this the mid-C19 classical ROYAL HOSPITAL. In the grounds, HOLYWELL HOUSE of c. 1800 is of two storeys and three bays with a semicircular columned porch (cf. Hasland Hall, p. 151). Next along Holywell Street, HOLYWELL CROSS POST OFFICE, a C17 house with the upper storey jettied out. At the end of Holywell Street a turn right leads into ST MARY'S GATE. Notable are No. 2 (with a late C19 exterior concealing some early C17 panelled rooms and an ornamental plastered ceiling: DOE) and No. 42, a Late Georgian five-bay three-storeyed brick house with stone dressings and quoins. St Mary's Gate ends at the main E–W road through the town (Vicars Lane/Low Pavement/West Bars). S of this there is testimony of early industry. In MARKHAM ROAD was the former SILK MILL of c. 1757, demolished in 1967. The following buildings are incorporated into the large factory of ROBINSON & SON (entrance in Wheatbridge Road). To the S in DOCK WALK is the CANNON MILL, originally part of the Griffin Foundry of John and Ebenezer Smith & Co., 1775–1838. Square, two-storey, red brick, coped gable end with ornamental cresting. Large iron water wheel. On the side are three sham Gothic arches with an oval iron plaque dated 1816 displaying a cannon. (Restored 1957.) In the main complex are some early buildings with cast-iron stanchions (Nixon). Major modern extensions to Robinson & Son Ltd have been designed by *Hadfield, Cawkwell, Davidson*

* There is a similar former chapel by the hospital in BREWERY STREET.

& Partners. Large landscaped offices on the German *Büro-landschaft* principle, 1972–5.

OUTER CHESTERFIELD

Chesterfield also includes outlying suburbs and villages and several interesting houses. It is most convenient to divide the area topographically into two sections. (1) To the N of the main E–W axis (i.e. the A619 to Bakewell and the A632 to Bolsover) lie Littlemoor, Newbold Moor, New Whittington, Sheepbridge, Stonegravels, Tapton, Whittington, and Whittington Moor.
(2) To the S of it lie Birdholme, Boythorpe, Hasland, and Hadyhill. On the W, the A619 (Chatsworth Road) runs through New Brampton.

NORTH

CHRIST CHURCH, Sheffield Road, Stonegravels. 1869 by *S. Rollinson*, aisles 1913–14 by *Rollinson & Sons*. Red brick, lancet style.

ST BARTHOLOMEW, Church Street North, Whittington. 1896 by *E. R. Rollinson*. Stone with a spire. – STAINED GLASS. N aisle window 1915 by *Morris & Co*. – PLATE. Elizabethan Chalice; Paten Cover, 1620; Paten and Flagon, 1753, inscribed IS, possibly by *John Swift*.

ST JOHN EVANGELIST, St John's Road, Littlemoor. Small stone church of 1887, with wide aisles added in 1957. – PLATE. Two Chalices, 1803. – Next to the church a large, attractive stone VICARAGE, Gothic.

ROMAN CATHOLIC CHAPEL, Newbold Moor. Disused. Doorway with almost completely defaced Norman tympanum. Windows Perp, no windows on the N side. Roof with bosses on the tiebeams. The chapel is only 36 by 18 ft. It was granted by James II for Roman Catholic worship and sacked by a Protestant mob in 1688. The pediment-like gable with its pinnacles may be part of the restoration after that event.

ST ANDREW UNITED REFORMED CHURCH, Newbold Road. Opened 1955; designed by *S. Welsh*.

METHODIST CHURCH, Cuttholme Road, Loundsley Green. 1962–4 by *E. D. Mills & Partners*. In appearance a rectangular slate-hung central block, supported on a larger brick block. In fact the church, steel-framed and clerestory-lit, is in the centre of the building and rises above the brick-built ancillary rooms that surround it. Inside TAPESTRIES by *Anne Butler*. This

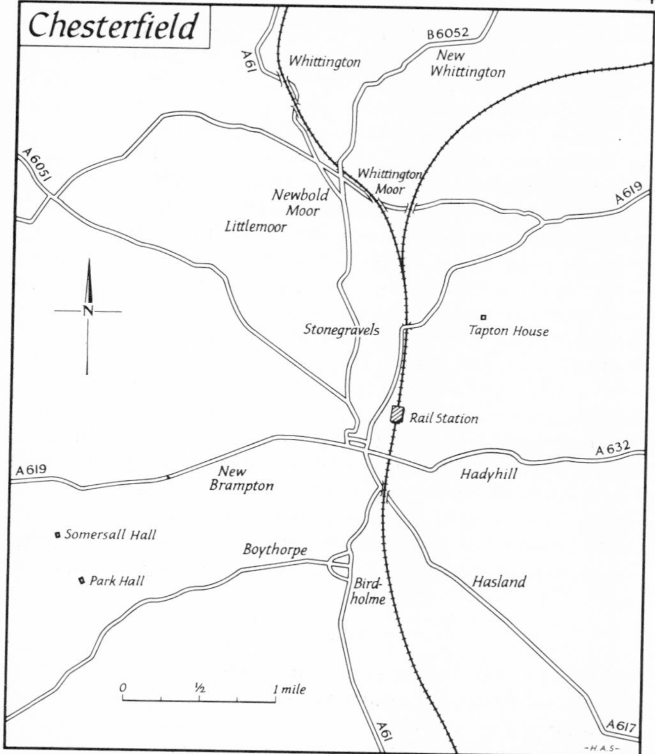

church is opposite a very basic C of E church, and both serve an estate built during the 1960s.

SCHOOL FOR THE HANDICAPPED, Ashgate Road. 1957–9 by *Bartlett & Gray*, in collaboration with *F. Hamer Crossley* (County Architect). A small brick-faced, steel-framed school, pleasing on both main façades. Three wings of varying heights; almost completely glazed S wall.

Starting in the N of the area, WHITTINGTON retains an attractive village centre (especially CHURCH STREET NORTH), although one of the best buildings, MANOR FARM, was demolished in 1970. Its fine barns survive to the W of the church. Further W is HOLLY HOUSE (D.C.C. Residential Home), *c.* 1800, ashlar, with a three-bay façade and shallow-hipped roof. The windows have channelled lintels, the doorcase

Doric columns and an open pediment. S of the church, the GREEN with a few old stone houses, including REVOLUTION HOUSE (the remains of an inn where the 1688 conspirators met), allegedly C16 but much restored, and further E, No. 87 HIGH STREET, a dignified Georgian brick house.

S of Whittington at NEWBOLD MOOR is OLD HOUSE HOTEL (formerly Green Farm), dated 1678 yet still gabled with mullioned windows. Extended in 1973–5. Predominant in this area are post-war housing estates of altogether 1,450 dwellings, built in 1945–58. SE of Newbold Moor is TAPTON HOUSE (school), a large brick house standing on a hill. Seven by five bays with three-bay pediment. Built *c.* 1800 and once the residence of George Stephenson, the engineer. (For TAPTON GROVE *see* Brimington.) (At SHEEPBRIDGE, SW of Newbold Moor, is DUNSTAN HALL, C17, extended in the C18 and again in 1826 (date on the porch). Four-gabled front, part two storeys and part three, with Gothic revival details including the porch on the l. Good parkland setting and Gothic-style park railings. On the road to Brampton (Ashgate Road) on the W side of the town, THE HOMESTEAD by *Parker & Unwin*, *c.* 1903–5. Gritstone, mullioned windows, two bow-windows to the garden, buttressed ends with batter à la Voysey, big hipped roof.* RE)

SOUTH

ST AUGUSTINE, Derby Road, Birdholme. 1931 by *Hicks & Charlwood*. Brick, in Lombard Romanesque style, with a three-sided apse, the side chapel and vestry almost detached from the church under separate gables. – (STAINED GLASS in the S chapel by *Nuttgens*, 1959. R. Hubbuck)

ST PAUL, Churchside, Hasland (just over the borough boundary). 1850–1 by *T. C. Hine*. Stone, simple Dec Gothic, with bell-turret.

ST THOMAS, Chatsworth Road, New Brampton. 1830–2 by *Woodhead & Hurst* (GR). The Commissioners' type, with a rather narrow W tower crowned by clumsily big pinnacles. The tower is flanked by entrance bays. Nave without aisles, and tall lancet-like three-light windows. Chancel 1891 by *Naylor & Sale* (GR).

Starting in the S of the area at BIRDHOLME, BIRDHOLME HOUSE, half way to Wingerworth, was the dower house of the

* It originally had a superb Arts and Crafts interior, now gutted (Mervyn Miller).

demolished Wingerworth Hall (*see* p. 356). It is partly early and partly late C17 (the late part with mullioned windows tied to a string-course above to systematize them). To the SE at HASLAND, now a large suburb, HASLAND HALL (school), Mansfield Road, is of *c.* 1800, ashlar, with sash-windows and a semicircular Doric porch, very similar to Holywell House in the hospital grounds (*see* Chesterfield, p. 147). (By HASLAND GREEN, the MANOR HOUSE, rendered and unremarkable externally, but medieval and C16–17 with internal features of interest. DOE) To the SW of the area PARK HALL, Walton Back Lane, looks late C17 (reset date-stone 1661 : DOE). SOMERSALL HALL, a three-bay house of 1763 with pedimented doorway, has unusually attractive outbuildings, partly C17 and partly Gothick. Close to the back of the Hall is a GAZEBO, C17, gabled, probably built for the purpose and not converted from the remains of an earlier Hall, as previously suggested. (In Chatsworth Road, the former LODGES of Somersall Hall are tiny octagonal boxes with Gothic openings, with modern extensions behind both. RE) On the N side of Chatsworth Road the MANOR HOUSE, Manor Road, NEW BRAMPTON. Just a few C17 mullioned windows remain (it was refaced in the early C19), and an early C18 summer house with an ogee top with fishscale stone slates.* (Also surviving is a BARN with two good sets of crucks. RE) (Also in Chatsworth Road, No. 134 is by *Parker*, typical of his late work, i.e. not much different from the speculative housing of the period. Mervyn Miller) (In OLD ROAD, No. 216 is an example of the survival of good C18 building traditions into the C19. RE) In WALTON ROAD S of the main road a coach house and outbuildings are all that remain of the C18 WALTON CORN MILL. In the N and S of the borough are several large Late Georgian houses, e.g. WHITTINGTON HALL (Hospital) and DRYHURST at HADYHILL.

See p. 40

BELMONT. *See* Walton.
WALTON. *See* p. 348.

CHINLEY

0080

ST MARY THE VIRGIN. 1907. (Ingenious E extension by *J. B. Blagney*, 1957–72, to a simple nave. E wall of glass with an enclosed courtyard over ancillary rooms beyond it. T. Cocke)
(INDEPENDENT CHAPEL, Chapel Milton. Stone, 1711, long and narrow, with two heights of mullioned windows. Galleried

* (Associated with the gazebo an alcove seat with a coved cornice above.)

interior with box pews. The pulpit is in the centre of the N wall. CS) S windows more classical and up-to-date.

Towering over the chapel two massive stone RAILWAY VIADUCTS of *c.* 1867 by *Barlow* and *Campion.*

9090

CHISWORTH

(FOLD FARM, Higher Chisworth. Dated 1697 on the porch. T-shape, with mullioned windows. The porch is two-storeyed, with lintel stones formed into arches. Unspoiled hamlet near the farm. RE)

INTAKES FARM, Higher Chisworth. Bronze Age CAIRN.

2030

CHURCH BROUGHTON

ST MICHAEL. Mostly early C14, but the NE arcade respond semicircular with scalloped capital, i.e. Norman. Of external early C14 features note that the windows of the lower parts of the tower (with angle buttresses; the upper part with C19 pinnacles and big gargoyles beneath the battlements), the S aisle S doorway and windows, and the chancel windows. The N aisle E and W windows look a little earlier. Inside, the arcade on circular piers and the tower arch on semicircular imposts are clearly early C14. The first pier of the arcade from the W is wider than the others, consisting, as it were, of two imposts and a piece of wall between. At capital height the wall-piece has a head and a demi-caryatid instead of a capital. The arches two-stepped and only slightly chamfered. Good SEDILIA and PISCINA group in the chancel, ogee-headed, i.e. also early C14. Perp clerestory and roof, modified in the early C18. – FONT. Norman, of tapering tub shape, with a large zigzag motif and, superimposed on it, large intersected circles. – PLATE. Paten, 1707 by *Joseph Ward*; Chalice, *c.* 1720.

(OLD HALL, Hall Lane. A complete C16 timber-framed building with hall and cross-wing and big central stone stack concealed by brick and rendered casing dated 1702. Small porch turret in the W angle. RE)

CHURCHDALE HALL *see* ASHFORD-IN-THE-WATER

2010

CHURCH GRESLEY

ST GEORGE AND ST MARY. A priory of Austin Canons was founded here in the early C12. The present parish church incorporates the tower of the conventual church. In its E wall inside is a blocked treble-chamfered arch. The rest of the church and the top parts of the tower date from *c.* 1820 (chancel 1872 by *A. W. Blomfield*). Nave and N aisle with the typical lancet windows of two lancet lights. The arcade looks as if it might be old and only heavily restored (octagonal piers, treble-chamfered arches). – STALLS with misericords from Drakelowe Hall, three in the chancel, seven at the W end. The stalls are mid C17, beautifully carved in continental style and identical to those of 1660 by *Quellin* in St Jacobus, Antwerp. The MISERICORDS are also mid C17 but probably matched up with the stalls at some time. – PLATE. Chalice, 1724 by *Gabriel Sleath*. – MONUMENT. Thomas Gresley † 1699, life-size kneeling figure with two standing putti to the l. and r. (By *Sir William Wilson*. ES)

GREENS POTTERY. Late C19, with four traditional bottle kilns in excellent condition, some with kiln furniture. They are of differing designs and form the core of the building, the roof trusses for the surrounding pottery sprung from kneelers in the outer kiln walls. (Part seems to be early C19. ES)

CHURCH WILNE *see* WILNE

CLAY CROSS

3060

ST BARTHOLOMEW. 1851 by *Stevens*, with broach-spire built slightly later to his design. Vestry added on the N side of the chancel in 1858–9 by *G. E. Street*. S aisle refenestrated in 1879 by *F. J. Robinson*. – STAINED GLASS. S aisle window 1879 by *Morris & Co.*, Sts John, Peter, and James to a *Burne-Jones* design.

WOODTHORPE HALL. Small C17 manor house.

PITHEAD BATHS. By *J. W. M. Dudding*, one of the many exemplary structures put up by the Miners' Welfare Commission in the 1940s.

CLIFTON

1040

HOLY TRINITY. 1845 by *H. I. Stevens*. Apse and bell-tower 1868 by *Slater & Carpenter*. – (STAINED GLASS. Apse windows by *Clayton & Bell* to a person † 1882. R. Hubbuck). – PLATE. Paten on foot, Dublin-made, 1726.

HANGING BRIDGE, ¾m. NW, across the river Dove. Of five

pointed arches with chamfered ribs. The roadway has been much widened.

4070

CLOWNE

ST JOHN THE BAPTIST. Outside the industrialized village. Perp W tower with diagonal buttresses, battlements, and pinnacles. Nave and chancel essentially Norman. (Chancel rebuilt 1955. DOE) S doorway with an order of colonnettes; the capitals have spiral decoration and the arch one roll-moulding. Norman chancel arch on imposts with three shafts; capitals with several volute and similar varieties. To the S of the chancel arch a Norman recess, perhaps in connexion with the altar at the E end of a former S aisle. Norman chancel doorway plain and narrow. In the S wall also one big lancet window. The E window Perp. – ALTARPIECE signed by *Bouttats* of Antwerp and dated 1724. Panels with Commandments, Creed, Lord's Prayer, and the Ascension. – (STAINED GLASS, S wall. Three two-light windows by *Clare Dawson*, 1950. R. Hubbuck) – PLATE. Chalice, 1698 by *John Shepherd*.

4040

CODNOR

ST JAMES. 1843 by *Robert Barker* (GR), quite pretty. Stone, with narrow W tower, the body of the church an aisleless parallelogram with lancet windows, white inside, and with a W gallery on cast-iron columns. Chancel 1888–90 by *J. Holden* (GR). – FONT found in the precincts of the castle.

CODNOR CASTLE, 1 m. E. Visually impressive, with its cliff-like fragments of masonry rising to a height of 18 ft, but archaeologically not very telling, unless one is provided with a plan of the results of excavations. Codnor Castle was built by the Lords Grey of Codnor and passed to the Zouche family in 1496. It was surrounded by a park of 1,500 acres. It consisted of a lower and an upper court. The former lies W and NW of the present farmhouse of *c.* 1640 which occupies the E side of the court. It was separated from the upper court by a wall with two circular towers at the end and two circular turrets flanking the gateway. In the middle of its W side were two slightly projecting rectangular turrets. The upper court contained the most important living quarters, a three-storeyed structure. Masonry dates from two periods, the early C13 and the early C14. The lower court was an addition to the earlier upper court.

COMBS MOSS *see* CHAPEL-EN-LE-FRITH

COOMBS EDGE *see* CHARLESWORTH

COTMANHAY

4040

Part of Ilkeston

CHRIST CHURCH. 1847–8 by *Stevens* (GR). Small, of stone, with lancet windows and a polygonal bell-turret of the restraint typical of Stevens. – PLATE. Flagon, 1836 by *John Keith*, the first in Gothic Revival style in Derbyshire.

COTON-IN-THE-ELMS

2010

ST MARY. 1844–6 by *Stevens*. Narrow W tower with recessed spire. The nave (unaisled) is wider than the tower. Two-light lancet windows with Dec tracery. The stone diagonally tooled; Stevens liked all kinds of tooling of his walls.

COW LOW *see* BUXTON, CHAPEL-EN-LE-FRITH, *and* FAIRFIELD

COXBENCH HALL *see* HORSLEY

CRAKE LOW *see* TISSINGTON

CRESSBROOK

1070

CRESSBROOK MILL, 1½ m. from Litton. The main building of twelve-bay width with a four-bay pediment and a lantern on the hipped roof is still entirely Georgian in appearance. Inside it has the typical early slender cross-shaped cast-iron columns but timber beams. The date is 1815. It was built by William Newton to replace Arkwright's mill of 1779. There are some remains of this at the W end. Behind it an older building with a narrow Gothic front towards the mill-stream: turrets, lancet windows, etc., similar in style to Castle Mill, Papplewick, Notts. It was Arkwright's Apprentice House. Associated with the mill, some three-storey stone terrace houses, probably of the same date as the earlier mill.

CRESWELL

5070

ST MARY MAGDALENE. Built in 1899 by *L. Ambler* for the Duke of Portland. Aisles 1914, tower 1927 also by *Ambler*. –

(STAINED GLASS. Two windows (E and Miners' Memorial) by *Clare Dawson*, 1951. R. Hubbuck)

MODEL VILLAGE. 1896–1900 by *Percy B. Houfton* for the Bolsover & Creswell Colliery Co. (cf. New Bolsover). Houses face a big oval green.

5070

CRESWELL CRAGS

The caves in this impressive limestone gorge on the border with Nottinghamshire have produced major evidence for the Palaeolithic culture named Creswellian after the finds of flint implements made here. The most important caves are Pinhole Cave, Robin Hood's Cave, and Mother Grundy's Parlour. A radiocarbon date of 8000 B.C. or earlier has been obtained for the later Palaeolithic occupation in Robin Hood's Cave, but still earlier occupation is virtually certain. In addition to the caves, there are numbers of rock shelters along the gorge, and both caves and shelters have produced considerable quantities of early prehistoric, Iron Age, and Roman artifacts.

3050

CRICH

ST MICHAEL. Quite an important church. The N arcade of three bays Norman with circular piers, round unchamfered arches of two steps, scalloped capitals to the E and W responds, and extremely elementary moulded capitals to the piers. S arcade with slightly more detailed capitals and single-chamfered arches, Late Norman. At each end a narrower pointed arch was inserted to connect the earlier work with the C14 chancel. This has ogee-reticulated (renewed) windows, i.e. *c.* 1320–50, and plain ogee-headed SEDILIA. The N and S aisle windows are partly Dec and partly Perp. The Perp W tower has angle buttresses, a handsome parapet (with a wavy band with trefoils) instead of battlements, and a recessed spire with two tiers of dormer windows. In the outer wall of the N aisle as well as the inner wall are low ogee-headed tomb recesses. In the chancel N wall one of the rare built-in stone bible rests (cf. Spondon (Derby), Chaddesden (Derby), Etwall, etc.). – FONT. Plain Norman. – TWO BENCH ENDS with poppy-heads (one in the vestry). – PLATE. Two Chalices presented 1712. – MONUMENTS. In the N aisle recess good late C14 effigy of a bearded man in a long frock, presumed to be Sir William de Wakebridge † 1369. – Godfrey Beresford † 1513, carved figure of a knight, chancel S side. – Incised slab to German Pole † 1588 and wife, the inscription below, and the slab upright in the chancel wall.

– Below it incised slab on tomb-chest to John Claye † 1632 and his two wives, kneeling children against the tomb-chest. – Ephraim Shelmardine † 1637, brass memorial to a baby, with portrait, the plate 5 by 8 in. in size. – Wall-monument to Captain German Wheatcroft † 1857 by *S. Manning* of London still completely in the classical tradition.

(WESLEYAN CHAPEL. Stone, *c.* 1770, two doorways, round-arched upper windows, galleries. C. Stell)

In the main street an C18 FRAME SHOP, of three storeys with a long upper window.

THE TRAMWAY MUSEUM, in an old quarry N of the village. Stone workshops for building quarry wagons by *Stephenson*, 1841. The façade of the DERBY ASSEMBLY ROOMS (*see* p. 175n) has been re-erected here and it is proposed to build a museum, lecture hall, etc. behind it. Other buildings (e.g. pub, bandstand) are being re-erected (1976) to form an Edwardian street through which the trams will run (architect, *Roderick Gradidge**). 89

CHASE CLIFFE, on the road to Whatstandwell, is by *Ferrey*, 1859–61. According to Eastlake, 'Tudor, for Messrs. Hurt, in character with the ancient domestic architecture of the county.'‡

CROCKENDALE PASTURES *see* HASSOP

CROMFORD

2050

It was at Cromford that Richard Arkwright started the first successful cotton-spinning mill worked by water power. The foundation date is 1771, and the original MILL still stands S of the bridge at r. angles to Mill Road W of the entrance (now a colour works). It is three storeys high but was originally five, two storeys having been removed after a fire in 1930. The stone block at the W end of the group is also early (before 1777): three storeys, mullioned windows, and lintels and sills forming continuous bands. Of the big seven-storey block at the E end, under construction according to Bray in 1777, only fragments remain after a fire in the C19. The buildings of *c.* 1790 along the road have no windows on the lower floors and suggest a defence against industrial spies and rioters. The buildings, all constructed with timber and not fireproof like those at Belper, are grouped round an irregular courtyard. It looks rather grim now and must always have looked forbidding. Bray tells us that 200

* Who supplied the information.

‡ *History of the Gothic Revival*, 1872, appendix 172.

were employed, 'chiefly children. They work by turns night and day'. Least grim is a small brick building with sash-windows, a dentil cornice, and hipped roof at the W end. Was it the original offices? The water was supplied partly by the Bonsall Stream and partly by an adit for draining mines called the Cromford Mear Slough and was carried across the road by a wooden launder, replaced in 1821 by the present cast-iron aqueduct. The same stream is the chief source of the CROMFORD CANAL, which accompanies the view from Cromford downwards. It was built by *William Jessop* and *Benjamin Outram* for a consortium including Arkwright and opened in 1793. It runs parallel with the Derwent for twelve and a half miles to Langley Mill, where it joins the Erewash Canal, from whence the major canal routes could be reached. Just past the mill is its Derbyshire terminus at Cromford Wharf. One of the two warehouses still has its overhead canopy. Opposite the mill is the manager's house (THE SHRUBBERY) and set back in grounds ROCK HOUSE, Arkwright's early residence, and its coach house.

97 In 1783 Arkwright built the MASSON MILLS a little higher up and round a big bend in the river. These were developed into a big modern building in the early C20, but the middle is still the original six-storey building with the staircase in a projection and a top cupola. The projection has an odd rhythm of small semicircular between Venetian (one altered) windows. The second mill is of brick and also still with timber beams. To the S a large red brick building, its Italianate tower with Art Nouveau lettering and the date 1928 (cf. Belper East Mill, 1912, also for English Sewing Ltd).

Between the two mills the dramatic break through the limestone rocks which is called Scarthin Nick. Behind this, away from the river to the S, Cromford village, the settlement created by Arkwright round his mill. In the Market Place the GREYHOUND INN of 1778, a fine house like a minor town hall, five bays with a three-bay quoined and pedimented centre and a Roman Doric doorcase. SE of the Market Place is NORTH STREET, a complete street of housing built in 1771–6 by Arkwright for his employees. Two three-storey stone terraces with mullioned windows, originally larger in the attics, which were intended as framework knitting rooms.* At the end of the street

* A number of houses on the E side have had their original attic windows reopened as part of a programme of repair for the Landmark Trust (architect: *G. Robb*).

the SCHOOL (C of E), built in 1832, enlarged later. Stone with round-headed windows. On Cromford Hill later industrial housing, and in WATER LANE to the W of the Market Place more by Arkwright and the ARKWRIGHT CENTRE, an C18 watermill, plain but with a Venetian window in the rear wing. Believed to have been built *c.* 1780 as the corn mill of the factory village.

N of the Market Place across the A6 (Derby Road) is Mill Road. Past the Old Mill the church of Cromford, ST MARY, is reached. This was begun by Arkwright before his death in 1792,* completed in 1797, and gothicized in 1858. It now has the old narrow W turret, but in front of it a three-bay open Perp porch. The windows are Perp lancets. An apsidal chancel was added. – The WALL PAINTINGS and the STAINED GLASS inside by *A. O. Hemming*, 1897. – PLATE. Paten on knob foot, 1732 by *Thomas Mason*; Flagon and Paten, 1776; Chalice, 1780; Chalice and Paten Cover, 1796. – MONUMENTS to Mrs Arkwright † 1820 by *Chantrey* and to Charles Arkwright † 1850 by *H. Weekes*.

By St Mary CROMFORD BRIDGE. This is C15, like Matlock Bridge (three pointed arches). At the Cromford end an early C18 FISHING PAVILION, square with pyramidal roof, and the inscription 'Piscatoribus sacrum'. (It appears to be a near-replica of Walton and Cotton's more celebrated pavilion in Beresford Dale. DOE) Then, attached to the bridge, ruins of a C15 CHAPEL (W doorway and one two-light mullioned window to its l. remain). Across the bridge the turn r. leads to the STATION. The ornate French château-style up-platform waiting room and station-master's house are of *c.* 1860, attributed to Paxton's son-in-law, *G. H. Stokes*. (The larger, plainer building is later. RE) Back to the bridge and in Lea Road BRIDGE HOUSE, partly Jacobean and partly Georgian, and nearer the bridge the LODGE (square and classical, but with two blank quatrefoils and an irregular roof-line) to Willersley Castle. It was designed by *Thomas Gardner*.

WILLERSLEY CASTLE was built as Sir Richard Arkwright's residence in 1789–90 by *William Thomas* of London. Arkwright died before he could move in. It is an ambitious seven-bay stone structure of two and a half storeys with lower side wings front- 93

* And was probably designed by *Thomas Gardner* of Uttoxeter. His account for Willersley Castle refers to 'its chapel' and the original design was similar to his church at Wiggington, Staffs. (ES).

ing the sheer face of the cliff across the sloping lawn and across the river. The house is entirely classical in conception, but romanticized by battlements and by semicircular turrets flanking the broad centre and smaller circular turrets at the angles of the wing. Torrington in 1790 called it 'an effort of inconvenient ill taste'. The interior was burnt out in 1791 and redone by *Thomas Gardner* of Uttoxeter.* The finest room is an oval hall with galleries on both upper storeys, a domed skylight, and plasterwork. In the grounds near the gate HOME FARMHOUSE, which must be contemporary.

At HIGH PEAK JUNCTION, 1 m. S along the A6 and canal, is a group of buildings belonging to the transhipment point between the High Peak railway and the canal. There are two major architectural monuments: the CANAL AQUEDUCT over the Derwent, 1792 by *Jessop*, ashlar, a beautiful single-span bridge with wide elliptical arch, rebuilt at the engineer's own expense after the first one collapsed; and the PUMP HOUSE to pump water from the river to the canal, a tall, narrow, rock-faced stone structure with pediments and voussoired arched windows, and a tall elegant chimney with cast-iron capping. (It contains a notable pumping engine of 1849 by *Graham & Co.*, Milton Iron Works. DOE) Associated with the railway at the bottom of Sheep Pasture incline are railway repair workshops, the bottom pulley wheel pit of the incline, and the water tank used by locomotives. Further up, a catchpit to catch runaway trucks, and on the main road the LOCO AND AGENT'S HOUSES, an early C19 pair.

CROSS LOW *see* ALSOP-EN-LE-DALE

CUBLEY

1030

ST ANDREW. Late Perp W tower with angle buttresses, large W door and large W window, and tall tower arch towards the nave, restored in 1874 by *J. P. St Aubyn*. Nave and S aisle have C17 windows with one mullion and one transom; they are much larger on the S side. The chancel is C13 with a broad five-light E window (restored in 1872 by *St Aubyn*). The chancel arch has semicircular responds with rude faces. The arch is double-chamfered. The interior shows, however, that the earliest part of the church is the nave arcade, with circular piers, un-

* According to Mr Saunders.

chamfered arches, and one capital with a rudimentary leaf motif. The W respond rests on a head bracket. – FONT. Plain Norman. – PAINTING. Yellow and black ornamental painting on the chancel arch and the last arcade arch to the E. – STAINED GLASS. Fragments of C14 figures in the chancel windows. – MONUMENTS. Alabaster tomb-chest to Sir Nicholas Montgomery † 1494, the effigy defaced; the four angels holding shields who stand against the tomb-chest are in better preservation. – One side of an alabaster tomb-chest without effigy but with good figures against the chest, e.g. one saint in an amply draped mantle. The weepers hold shields. The monument is ascribed by Mr Gardner to *Harper* and *Moorecock* of Burton (cf. Chesterfield), i.e. 1500.

BENTLEY HALL, 1 m. E. Elizabethan or Jacobean brick and stone building with flat quoins. The front has a central canted bay-window (the conversion of the ground floor into a porch in the C19). Added on the W side is a late C17 wing with rusticated quoins and a centre that has a doorway with a scrolly pediment, two giant pilasters, and a segmental top pediment. The style is so similar to that of Sudbury Hall that it may well be by *Sir William Wilson.*

The Hall is all that is left of the village of HUNGRY BENTLEY, except a clearly defined street pattern in the surrounding fields. It is the best deserted medieval village site in the county. Further E more earthworks of the deserted village of ALKMONTON.

CULLAND HALL *see* BRAILSFORD

CURBAR

2070

ALL SAINTS. 1868 by *Salvin Jun.* (GR). Nave, chancel, N aisle, and bellcote; rock-faced.

LOCKUP. Circular with conical roof. At the top end of the village, S of the village street.

FROGGATT EDGE, 1 m. N. Ring cairn consisting of nine upright stones.

CUTTHORPE HALLS

NW of Chesterfield

3070

(OLD HALL consists of the Old Manor House, with the main rooms in three storeys above each other and the staircase in an attached wing, and Old Hall Cottages, the two-storey, two-bay wing to the l. It was built by Ralph Clarke, first Mayor of Chesterfield, † 1660. CUTTHORPE HALL, ½ m. away, is the product of growth, C16 to C18 parts, it seems. Near it, the C16 or C17 gabled DOWER HOUSE.)

2030

DALBURY

ALL SAINTS. Small with embattled bellcote. The only noteworthy old feature the small lancet on the S side. In it a blackened STAINED GLASS figure of St Michael. The other lancets, however, also occur already in drawings of the 1820s. These show the bellcote in its present state too. (N aisle 1849. Complete set of BOX PEWS, C17 or early C18 FONT COVER, early C19 ORGAN CASE. DOE) – PLATE. Elizabethan Chalice; Cup of *lignum vitae* and Cover, *c.* 1680; Chalice, Paten Cover on knob foot, and Flagon, 1749 by *John Swift*, replicas of those at Sutton-on-the-Hill also given by Humphrey Chetham.

4030

DALE ABBEY

DALE ABBEY was a house of Premonstratensian Canons founded about the year 1200. Little of it remains now on its delightful site below the sandstone cliffs, where a Derby baker whom a vision had compelled to abandon his worldly goods and live as a recluse had made his hermitage. His cave was enlarged in the C18 by Sir Robert Burdett, who entertained in it. The chief surviving architectural fragment of the abbey is the great arch of the chancel E window (over 17 ft) with indications of ripe geometrical tracery, similar probably to Newstead Abbey and the Angel Choir at Lincoln, i.e. late C13. Excavations have shown the church to have possessed transepts 100 ft in length, a crossing tower, S chancel chapel, a cloister 85 ft square, and a nave of unknown length. The CHAPTER HOUSE on the E side of the cloister is still recognizable. It has a doorway of four orders of colonnettes and two piers along its centre. It is now the museum of the scanty finds made on the site (many foliated cross slabs, floor tiles, the effigy of a canon). To the S of the cloister the N wall of a cow-house indicates some vaulting of the former REFECTORY, and further SW an end of a cottage is locally connected with the monastic KITCHEN. Still further away, to the NW of the site of the abbey, are the remains of the GATEHOUSE.

12

ALL SAINTS, the present church of the village of Dale Abbey, is in no provable way connected with the abbey, although it has been suggested that the whole structure was the infirmary and infirmary chapel. It is one of the smallest and oddest of English churches. Its size is 26 by 25 ft and it is under the same roof with a dwelling house.* The interior is cram-full of box pews, has a gallery, a pulpit of 1634 to the l. of the altar high up, an altar fitted with doors and drawers for communion plate, and some interesting wall paintings (Annunciation, Visitation, Nativity, N wall, all late C13). There is also a badly preserved incised slab. The masonry of the nave is Norman (perhaps the Chapel of Depedale, mentioned in the late C12), the aisle was added soon after. Most of the details are Perp, especially the addition of the upper storey with its open timber roof. – PLATE. Chalice, 1701 by *Willoughby Masham.*

(POPLAR FARM OR FRIARS HOUSE. Mostly C18, but with an impressive C16 timber-framed front, jettied upper storey, close-studding.‡ Original staircase. RE)

CAT AND FIDDLE MILL. The only Derbyshire windmill in working order, the only post mill, and one of only two surviving windmills in the county. The other is the tower mill at Heage.

DANNAH FARM *see* BELPER

DARLEY ABBEY *see* DERBY, p. 193

DARLEY DALE

2060

Part of Matlock

ST HELEN. A cruciform church (cf. Ashbourne, Wirksworth, Hartington). The S transept has lancets on its E side, and the chancel has a S lancet. The N arcade inside (three bays) goes with that: circular piers, moulded capitals, double-chamfered arches. The chancel arch of the same design.§ The S arcade is a little later: octagonal piers. Its date may be that of the tall steep three-light Dec S window of the S transept and the identical N window of the N transept. The S aisle windows are C19. Perp E window of five lights, Perp N aisle windows, Perp battlements on nave and transepts, Perp nave roof with bosses, Perp W tower with angle buttresses and W door and W window

* Once the village inn! (A. Gomme).

‡ Much altered in 1975. Part of the close-studded wall remains, but most of the house is brick-clad or brick-built.

§ The S doorway into the nave is completely renewed, if not new. Its design is of C13 style. The N aisle and most of the S aisle were rebuilt in 1854 by *Stevens.*

decorated with head label-stops, etc. – FONTS. One circular, Norman, small, with ribbed edges, the other octagonal, Perp, with tracery motifs similar to Hartington. – SAXON CROSS. Fragment of a shaft, discovered *c.* 1950 and of great interest because of its remarkably antique geometrical ornament. – PARCLOSE SCREEN, S aisle. Stone, single-light openings, plain Perp design. – STAINED GLASS. Raphael Gillum memorial window, S transept, 1862–3, four tiers of three small storeys, with the Song of Solomon, in the most excellent early style of *Burne-Jones* for *Morris & Co.* – E window also a *Burne-Jones* design, 1892. – PLATE. Almsdish, 1785, Chalice and Flagon, 1791, all by *T. Daniel.* – MONUMENTS. Several coffin lids with foliated crosses. – Sir John de Darley, *c.* 1330(?), a cross-legged, bearded, and moustached knight, holding his heart in his hand (N transept). – Incised slab, ruinous, S aisle. – Incised slab to John Rollesley † 1513 and wife, incised slab to John Rollesley † 1535 and wife (N transept).

31

In the churchyard the battered remains of a huge yew tree, one of the largest in girth in England (4 ft from the ground it is 33 ft in circumference).

DARLEY BRIDGE. C15, two pointed arches with ribs.

STATION (disused). Built *c.* 1860, stone, Gothic. (Possibly by *Edward Walters*, cf. Great Longstone. D. Lloyd) Near by a pair of COTTAGES by *Paxton*, *c.* 1850.

(WHITWORTH INSTITUTE, Dale Road. Late C19. Impressive stone building in a 'free Tudor' style. The main block has an arcaded ground floor, three tall windows above with dormer gables, and a steep roof with cupola. Attached at the S end the WHITWORTH HOTEL of similar design. RE)

ST ELPHINS SCHOOL, built as Darley Dale Hydro in the late C19. Tudor style. Extensions 1967–75 by *Hadfield, Cawkwell, Davidson & Partners.*

STANCLIFFE HALL (School), Whitworth Road. C17 S range with considerable enlargements of 1872 by *T. Roger Smith* and of 1879 by *E. M. Barry* for Sir Joseph Whitworth. Winter garden added 1885. (Minor and disappointing work inside by *Crace.* RE) LODGE on the A6 in François I style, probably by *T. R. Smith.*

To the SE, at Two Dales, HOLT HOUSE, Ladygrove Road. Very handsome, three-bay, one-and-a-half storey stone house with extremely elongated main-floor windows and extremely elongated thin giant Ionic pilasters at the sides and centre. It was built by D. Dakeyne Jun. in 1800–1 and was the headquarters of a small local bank. In the grounds a Gothic building with lancet windows and a bogus 1416 datestone.

(SYDNOPE HALL, 1½ m. E. Long irregular battlemented house bearing all the characteristics of the enlargement in 1826 by Sir Francis Darwin. J. Barron Wright)* Gothick eyecatcher, now a cottage.

DENBY

3040

ST MARY. Small, the earlier parts of brown stone, the later pink and grey. C14 W tower with angle buttresses connected at the top by a horizontal band, and broach-spire rising behind a parapet with a handsome frieze of pierced pointed trefoils. No W door, but an ogee-headed niche higher up on the W side. The chancel Dec with a characteristic three-light E window and equally characteristic two-light N and S windows. Nave with C15 clerestory and S aisle. The arcade is the oldest surviving part of the church: two bays, Transitional or earliest C13: circular pier with very plain moulded capital and double-chamfered arches. One of the responds with a little nailhead decoration. The Perp N arcade was removed in 1838 and a gallery put in. But the FONT may well be part of the pier. A special showpiece the S porch, not axial with the S door, stone-vaulted, with the side walls divided into two panels by a vertical shaft. The church was restored in 1901–3 by *J. Oldrid Scott*.

(PARK HALL. 1702 but Jacobean in style with gables, mullioned windows, and an C18 brick porch. Good early C18 stairwell. DOE)

* According to the Secretary of the Darley Dale Historical Society the work was carried out by *Samuel Wood* or *James Oldershaw*.

3030

DERBY

INTRODUCTION

Little Chester, just N of the city centre, was a Roman site succeeding a camp situated on the high ground on the opposite side of the Derwent. The remains of a Saxon church belonging to the Saxon settlement of Northworthy have been excavated on the site of the demolished St Alkmund, and Saxon sculptural fragments are now in the museum. Under the Danish occupation Derby was one of the five burghs of the Midlands. All Saints and St Alkmund had pre-Conquest collegiate foundations, and St Peter has structural remains of interest proving the church to be the successor to a Norman one. The town had several religious houses, including St Helen, on the site of St Helen's Street (founded as a cell of the Austin Canons in 1137 and made a hospital dependent on Darley Abbey *c.* 1160); St James (a Cluniac cell dependent on Bermondsey, founded in 1140) and its hospital of St James and St Anthony; the Benedictine Nunnery of King's Mead sited SW of the centre (founded 1149–59); and Blackfriars, on the site of Friary Street (founded 1239). The tower of All Saints is one of the biggest Perp towers in England, testifying to the trading prosperity of the town. The main trades were wool fulling and malting. A Guild Merchant had been formed by permission of King John's charter of 1204. The old town went roughly from Bridge Gate on the N by St Helen's Street and Ford Street on the W, and on by Friary Street to St Peter's Street, the castle,* and Morledge to the S. Surviving architectural evidence of before the C18 is deplorably scarce. The Jacobean House of 1677 in Wardwick is the chief domestic building, the County Hall of 1660 the chief – and indeed a very interesting – public building. The industrialization of Derby began with the erection in 1717 or 1718 of John and Thomas Lombe's Silk Mill, the earliest built in England. The wealth of the town in the C18 is obvious from the few remaining sturdy, massive, and matter-of-fact red brick houses in the centre, replacing the half-timbered Derby of the past, and the only slightly more elegant dwelling houses *ante portas*, chiefly in Friar Gate. Throughout the C19 there was a gradual increase in area and population (1801 *c.* 11,000, 1821 *c.* 17,500, 1841 *c.* 33,000, 1861 *c.* 43,000, 1881 *c.* 58,000, 1901 *c.* 69,000). The railway arrived in 1839, and until 1846 almost all the traffic to the North of England

* The exact location of this is unknown, although the street nomenclature (Castlefields, Castle Street, etc.) supports the probability of its existence.

passed through Derby. After 1867 it became a major station on the route from London to Manchester,* and in 1878, the Crown Derby Porcelain Co. Ltd expanded. The growth of the town did not bring it much additional architectural character. The chief Victorian improvement in the centre was the culverting of the stream, the Markeaton Brook, which ran through Victoria Street (then Brookside) and the making of Albert Street, Victoria Street, and the Strand between 1875 and 1878. Neither the C19 public buildings nor the Victorian churches are in any way remarkable. Commercial architecture was on the whole sober and dignified all through the C19. Abominations are absent, but also the pleasures of fantasy and folly. In the first third of the C20 Derby suddenly grew from a provincial town into a thriving industrial centre (population in 1931 *c.* 142,000). Rolls Royce opened their first factory here in 1907, and during World War I British Celanese opened a huge plant then just outside the borough at Spondon.

The twenty-four years since 1953 have brought extensive clearance of buildings of all types. Much of C18 Derby has now gone. Bridge Gate and St Alkmund's Churchyard and most of Full Street were victims of the inner ring road constructed in 1967. The Assembly Rooms were gutted by fire and the façade removed (to Crich), and all but one of the pre-1850 Nonconformist chapels have been demolished. The C19 St Alkmund's was also sacrificed to the traffic scheme.‡ Other areas have been replaced by office blocks, stores, and shopping precincts, none of great merit. In 1966 the boundary was changed to form the County Borough (from 1977 the City) of Derby, which now includes many surrounding villages and their housing estates. The population therefore has risen dramatically from 141,267 (1965) to 217,930 (1974). New facilities have been provided for the enlarged town, i.e. a civic centre, theatre, and large shopping complex.

CHURCHES

CATHEDRAL CHURCH OF ALL SAINTS.§ Raised to the rank

* Despite the closure of the Derby to Manchester line in 1967 Derby has remained important as a centre for the development of railway technology etc.

‡ But fortunately some buildings worthy of preservation survive, not only in Wardwick and its continuation, Friar Gate and Ashbourne Road, where the houses have been admirably restored, but scattered throughout the town centre (*see* Perambulation).

§ Details amended and corrected by Mrs M. Mallender, Honorary Cathedral Archivist.

of a cathedral in 1927. Until then the chief parish church of
See p. 409 the town, with a pre-Conquest collegiate foundation. Its W tower dates from the early C16; the rest was rebuilt by *James Gibbs* in 1723–5 (builders: *William* (d. 1724) and *Francis Smith* of Warwick).* Both parts are of high architectural quality. The 18 tower is tall, square, broad, and stately, the one powerful accent in the skyline of Derby. It has three tall storeys, all highly decorated with friezes, canopies, etc. The buttresses nearly meet at the angles. The ground floor has a big W door, the second stage large blank three-light windows with four-centred tops and blank decorative niches. The bell-openings on the third stage are equally large, of four lights with panelled tracery. The top of the tower has ornamented battlements, and very big pinnacles. The body of the church appears low compared with the C16 work.‡ It spreads out broadly, has only one storey of large round-headed windows, and is crowned by a balustrade. Door and window surrounds show a surfeit of Gibbs's favourite motif of intermittent rustication. As the windows are all separated from each other by coupled pilasters, the rhythm of the sides is comfortably unhurried. Gibbs's church had a rectangular E end with a big pediment across nave and aisles and a Venetian window. The window was removed when the E extension was built in 1967–72, to designs by *Sebastian Comper*.§ The two-bay-long retrochoir follows the C18 elevation, without Gibbs's rustication, and ends in a shallow V-shaped apse. Underneath the Chapter Room, Song School, etc., present a plain façade to Full Street.

* Dr Hutchinson, appointed to the living in 1719, led the rebuilding campaign. In November 1719 the Vestry asked 'Mr Smith of Warwick having made a Draught about the building of this church' for an estimate. In 1722 they resolved to demolish and early in 1723 a new plan was presented 'by Mr Gibbs and Mr Smiths'. The Corporation delayed, so Dr Hutchinson ordered the demolition himself on 18 February 1723.

‡ It was intentionally so. *Gibbs*, who published the design in *A Book of Architecture* (1728), stated that 'the plainness of the Building makes it less expensive and renders it more suitable to the old steeple'. The exterior is a combination of the first design for St Mary-le-Strand and an early, rejected design for St Martin-in-the-Fields.

§ Soon after the Diocese was formed in 1927, extensions were envisaged to adapt the church to cathedral status and functions. In 1939 *Sir Ninian Comper* made plans (revised in the early 1950s) for a large, overpowering extension of choir and sanctuary raised above ancillary rooms. Sebastian Comper made completely new and more sympathetic plans in 1954 and 1958. Final plans were accepted in 1967 and work begun. It was completed after Comper's retirement in 1969 by *Anthony New* for the *Seely & Paget Partnership*.

The INTERIOR also appears broad and relatively low. It is designed on the same principle as Gibbs's St Martin-in-the-Fields. Nave and aisles are separated by Tuscan columns on tall pedestals (to allow for box pews). The aisles are groin-vaulted, the nave tunnel-vaulted. The arcade arches cut into the tunnel-vault. The vaults are rather poorly decorated with panels. The retrochoir has a plain groin-vault and a minimum of ornamentation. It is tactful but dull. The whole interior was given a new colour scheme of mauvish-grey, white, and gold by *Anthony New*, 1972.*

19

FURNISHINGS. PULPIT, 1873 by *Temple Moore*, with tester on two columns, 1945 by *Sir Ninian Comper*. – BALUSTER FONT in Pentelicon marble, made in 1974 to a design in Gibbs's *A Book of Architecture* (1728). – BALDACCHINO by *Sebastian Comper*, of Early Christian type but strictly classical: canopy on Corinthian columns. – In the chancel, SEDILIA, 1941 by *Sir Ninian Comper*; CANONS' STALLS, reconstructed 1972 from choir stalls of 1894 by *Temple Moore*. – COUNTY COUNCIL PEW of wrought iron with symbols of local government by *Anthony New*, 1972. – PANELLING and raised seat in the N chancel chapel (Consistory Court), C17. – WEST GALLERY. 1732–3, on fluted Ionic columns, extended through the aisles in 1841. The old centre part curves back gracefully and carries the organ, by *Compton*, 1939; case by *J. S. Comper*, 1963. – BISHOP'S THRONE. C18; from Constantinople. – CUPBOARD at the W end of the N aisle. Early C18, richly carved, Flemish. – CHANCEL SCREEN. The most important possession of the cathedral. Wrought ironwork by *Robert Bakewell*, the brilliant local smith who died in 1752. The screens to the chancel chapels were assembled *c*. 1900. Also by *Bakewell* the COMMUNION RAILS, the STANDS for mace and sword belonging to the Corporation Pew, the SUPPORT of the altar table in the S chapel, and the RAILS to Thomas Chambers's monument (*see* below) at the E end of the N aisle. – STAINED GLASS.‡ E windows of both aisles 1967, designed by *Ceri Richards* and made by *Patrick Reyntiens*, representing All Souls (N) and All Saints (S). Vivid blues and yellows in conflict with the later colour scheme. – PLATE. Chalice and Paten, 1693; set of two Chalices and Patens and two Flagons, all by *George Wickes*, and one Almsdish, Lon-

28

* Restorations were made in 1873–4 by *J. Young*, who discarded Gibbs's furnishings; in 1904–5 by *Temple Moore*; and in 1928 by *Sir Ninian Comper*.

‡ Glass from the E window with Crucifixion by *Clayton & Bell*, 1863, is now in store. It is surprisingly vigorous for its date; strong colours, good faces.

don-made, given by the Earl of Exeter in 1727; Chalice, Paten Cover, and Almsdish, 1764; two tall Vases, given in 1828, their shape and decoration already very close to the Victorian taste; two Chalices, two Patens, and one Ciborium, 1962 by *W. Hall* of Derby; Chalice, Paten, and Almsdish, 1974 by *Brian Asquith.*

MONUMENTS. Alabaster slab to Sub-Dean Lawe, *c.* 1480; incised figure surrounded by architecture with smaller decorative figures; the workmanship mediocre (N chancel chapel). – Timber monument with decayed timber effigy, small figures of mourners, and fragment of a gisant or cadaver below (perhaps Sub-Dean Johnson, *c.* 1527; S aisle). – Elizabeth, Countess of Shrewsbury, † 1607, better known as Bess of Hardwick (*see* Hardwick for her life). Standing wall-monument, designed by *John Smythson.* In 1601 it was finished 'and wanteth nothing but setting up'. Recumbent effigy of alabaster, not especially good. Black columns to the l. and r., and between them a shallow coffered arch. Back wall with inscription and strapwork cartouche. Above the entablature two obelisks and a tall central achievement. The monument stands in the S chancel chapel, which was the Cavendish Chapel. In the middle stood until 1876 the monument to the second Earl of Devonshire († 1628) by *Edward Marshall.* In the vault beneath the chapel over forty members of the family were buried between 1607 and 1848 (see the mounted coffin plates). – Richard Crowshawe † 1631, wall-monument with kneeling figures (N aisle). – William Allestry † 1655 and his wife † 1638, wall-monument with sarcophagus and four columns; no effigies (N aisle). – Sir William Wheler † 1666, large wall-monument with two busts high up (N aisle). – Thomas Chambers † 1726 and his wife † 1735, by *Roubiliac*, a tripartite composition with the centre filled by the inscription below a pediment; in the sides two fine busts in circular niches. – Sarah Ballidon † 1736, wall-monument to a design in *Gibbs*'s *Book of Architecture* (1728). – Caroline Countess of Bessborough † 1760, daughter of the third Duke of Devonshire, by *Rysbrack.* Standing wall-monument; seated allegorical figure with bust behind to her l. on a bracket, the whole against a black pyramid. – Will. Ponsonby Earl of Bessborough † 1793, by *Nollekens*, wall-monument with bust above a sarcophagus. – Richard Bateman † 1821, signed by *Chantrey* (who was born on the Derbyshire border), 1822, wall-monument with weeping seated female by an urn. – Mary Elizabeth Chichester † 1830, by *Sir R. Westmacott*, small wall-monument with reclining figure on a couch in a gently recessed oval panel. – Innumerable minor wall-tablets. The following two are signed: Thomas Swanwick † 1814, by *James Sherwood* of Derby. – John Hope † 1819, by *Joseph Hall the Younger* of Derby.

ST ALKMUND, Bridge Gate, 1846 by *H. I. Stevens*, was demolished in 1967 to make way for the inner ring road.*

ST JOHN THE EVANGELIST, Bridge Street. 1826–7 by *Francis Goodwin*; apsidal chancel 1871 by *Giles*. Ashlar-faced parallelogram with aisles and galleries. Tall coupled side windows with a little geometrical cast-iron tracery; tall entrance niche. No tower, but four angle-turrets and odd pinnacles with far-projecting castellated tops. – PLATE. Two Cover Patens on knob feet, 1751; Flagon, 1773 by *John Kenteber*.

ST MARY (R.C.), Bridge Gate. *A. W. Pugin*'s first large parish church.‡ Ashlar-faced. Tall, rather narrow W tower (ritual W; in fact S) of four stages. The projected spire was never built. The lean-to roofs of the aisles appear behind it, also rather tight. Tall narrow nave separated from the aisles by slender piers without capitals. Clerestory with twice as many windows as bays in the arcade. All the detail still Perp. Later Pugin preferred the late C13 and early C14. The finest motif is the slightly lower, vaulted choir with an apse, all glazed above the base. – ROOD, supported by a fragile arch, possibly inspired by that in St Elizabeth, Marburg. – PIETÀ in the NE chapel by *Earp*. – STAINED GLASS. Apse window in an *altdeutscher* style by *Warrington*. – Other windows by *Hardman*, 1919–31. – In 1854 *E. W. Pugin* added a large NW Lady Chapel in place of the elaborate N chapels originally planned. It is in his father's late manner, Dec, with stencilled wall decoration. – GATES to the NW chapel and chancel SCREEN, 1854 by *Hardman*. – (The small

* It was an ambitious building marking the beginning of Victorian prosperity. Ashlar stone slightly rock-tooled, tall nave with openwork balustrade, aisles, tall C14-looking piers inside, tall tower with spire supported by flying buttresses. It stood on a Saxon site. The oldest building found beneath in 1968 consisted of a nave (44 by 19 ft) with a smaller E annexe (16 ft square) and similar annexes to N and S and suggested a date not later than the C9. This church was extended to the E in the C12. S aisle widened and N aisle remodelled in the late C13 or early C14 and extended to the W in the C15. A C9 SARCOPHAGUS, believed to be the tomb of St Alkmund, was found (now in the Derby Museum and Art Gallery, together with other Saxon fragments found earlier). For the new St Alkmund *see* Outer Derby, p. 184.

‡ And one of the many paid for by Lord Shrewsbury – cf. St Alban Macclesfield, Cheshire, Pugin's other large Perp church, similar in plan though without the apse and with a sturdier tower (A. Gomme).

RECTORY to the E, brick with Gothic details, was also by *A. W. Pugin*. It has alas been demolished.)

ST MARY'S CHAPEL, Bridge Gate. One of the few surviving chapels built on bridges. The original C14 chapel was of stone, and the springing of the first arch of the old bridge can still be seen below the E end. It is a picturesque sight with the straight-headed Perp E window and half-timbered gable above. Much repair work in brick. Small aisleless interior. – STAINED GLASS. E window 1973 by *Mary Robson*. – Adjoining the chapel is ST MARY'S BRIDGE HOUSE, C17, gabled, with C18 fenestration.

ST MICHAEL, Queen Street. 1858 by *H. I. Stevens*. Stone-faced, with a curious horizontal ribbed rock-facing. Imitation C13 detail, the interior inspired by St Peter's.*

ST PETER, St Peter Street. The only medieval church of Derby, but very heavily restored and partly rebuilt. The chancel was restored in 1851–3 by *G. G. Place* of Nottingham, the rest of the church in 1859 by *G. E. Street*. (Street removed C18 pews, galleries, etc., and renewed the roofs, arcades, and window tracery.) In 1898 the W tower was rebuilt and the nave extended by one bay. The W end is now masked by a two-storey extension for parish rooms, *c.* 1972. The S aisle windows are of five lights with strongly elongated, uncusped ogee-reticulation. The N aisle and the W parts of the chancel have normal ogee-reticulated tracery. The E end has a five-light Perp window. The picturesque two-storeyed NE vestry was added after the completion of the aisle and the W parts of the chancel (blocked windows), and rebuilt in 1865. The interior reveals the E wall of the nave to be Norman. The responds of the nave arcades have scalloped capitals. The rest of the N arcade has slim circular piers with simple moulded capitals, of the S arcade octagonal piers. The arches are double-chamfered. The aisles are comfortably wide and have lean-to roofs of flat pitch. The bulk of the church is evidently an early C14 rebuilding. – PULPIT. 1859 by *Street*. – CHEST with heavy tracery. Medieval. – STAINED GLASS. E window before 1858 by *Barber* of York (TK), very yellow and with much heavy canopy-work.‡

ST WERBURGH, Friar Gate.§ The C15 tower collapsed and was rebuilt in 1601 (see the Gothic bell-openings and the obelisk pinnacles). The church was rebuilt in 1699. Of that building

* Made redundant in 1977.

‡ Information about C19 restorations from P. Joyce. *Robert Bakewell* is buried here. No monument.

§ Dr Johnson was married here in 1735.

only the chancel remains. The rest was again rebuilt in 1892–4 by *Sir Arthur Blomfield*, Dec-style and rock-faced. He changed the orientation so that the altar is now on the N, and the old chancel is a long side chapel. This still possesses its fine REREDOS of 1708* with carved Royal Arms above, and some other woodwork. Above the W end of the nave has been suspended a social centre, i.e. a timber-framed box by *G. I. Larkin* for *T. H. Thorpe & Partners*, 1971, with relief panels by *Ronald Pope*. It has been designed as an independent structure, competing with Blomfield's nave. – FONT COVER of wrought iron by *Bakewell*, 1716, with scrolly leaf motifs; very attractive. – PULPIT. Wrought iron, designed by *Blomfield*, 1894. – STAINED GLASS by *Kempe*, 1894–9. – PLATE. Paten on truncated foot, 1699; Chalice, *c.* 1700; two Flagons, 1717 by *Richard Green*; Chalice and two Almsdishes, 1757 by *John Swift*; Paten on foot, 1757; Silver Spoon, C18. – MONUMENTS. Sarah Winyates, by *Chantrey*, 1832, kneeling female by urn, rather hard. – Many minor wall-tablets. – By the church, particularly fine wrought-iron GATES in *Bakewell*'s style. (Probably the work of *Benjamin* or *William Yates*. ES)

NONCONFORMIST CHURCHES. Derby had five interesting, and one fine, pre-1850 Nonconformist churches. Only one of these still stands: the rest have been demolished within the last ten years (1966–76).‡

FRIENDS' MEETING HOUSE, St Helen's Street. 1808. Plain stone-faced rectangle with arched windows and hipped roof. Modern porches.

PUBLIC BUILDINGS

COUNTY HALL (now CROWN COURT), St Mary's Gate. A re- 72

* By *Henry Huss* of Derby, according to Mr Saunders.

‡ METHODIST CHURCH, King Street. 1841 by *James Simpson* of Leeds. A fine, stately Grecian front with one-storeyed Greek Doric porch, and an upper floor with Ionic pilasters, arched windows and a pediment. Lower projecting wings, which were minister's houses. Demolished 1966.

METHODIST CHAPEL, St Michael's Lane, the first in Derby: in it Wesley preached in 1765. It was a brick rectangle, very plain, with arched windows. Demolished in 1971 after being used for other purposes for many years.

UNITARIAN CHURCH, Friar Gate. The building was late C17, brick, with stone quoins. What was visible belonged largely to 1890. The church was originally Presbyterian. Demolished 1974.

BAPTIST CHAPEL, St Mary's Gate. The former mansion of the Osbornes, *c.* 1750, converted to a chapel in 1841. Gates by *Bakewell* removed to the cathedral (*see* p. 169).

markably interesting building of *c.* 1660.* It lies back from the road, with the Sub Police Station (*see* Perambulation p. 178) on one side of the *cour d'honneur* and a brick former Judges' Lodgings of 1811 on the other. The façade of the Hall is of five bays, with tall arched windows in the first, third, and fifth bays (the mullions and transoms are typical of the date) and ornate doorways in the second and fourth. These have scrolly broken pediments of a style similar to the C17 buildings at Bolsover and Nottingham Castle. The inside is a large court with sparing classical decoration and behind it two court rooms, built in 1829. – MONUMENT to F. N. Clarke Mundy, with bust, by *Chantrey*, 1817.

COUNTY OFFICES, St Mary's Gate. A group of buildings on either side of the street built as the County Council headquarters and begun in 1895 with the part now at the back on the S side. Red brick with stone dressings. Rather laboured Renaissance-style façades behind shallow forecourts. Inside, the Council Chamber has its original ceiling but no other fittings. Quite opulent hall and staircase with quantities of simulated marble and stained glass.‡

GUILD HALL, Market Place. Built in 1828 by *Habershon* with a classical façade: four Ionic columns supporting a pediment over a rusticated arcade. It was remodelled in 1842 by *Duesbury & Lee* after a fire the year before and given a central tower with a domical cap. Flanking it two reliefs by *John Bell:* 'Scientia' and 'Industria'. The detail late classical. The inscription proudly calls it the Forum Municipale. *The Builder*, in 1897, said of it that 'the detail is largely tinctured with Greek influence, but where Greek precedent has not sufficed, the architect has resorted to a modification of Italian Renaissance, supplemented by a certain amount of originality'. The Council Chamber, with a fine coffered ceiling, was converted into a theatre in 1971 by *W.I.N.G. Doig* (Borough Architect). Other rooms are now club rooms. A covered way under the Guild Hall leads to the large MARKET HALL of 1864, by *Thorburn* (altered by *Thompson*). It is 220 by 110 ft and has a tunnel-vault of iron and glass, supported on iron columns with a gallery all the way round.

COUNCIL HOUSE, Corporation Street. 1938–41 by *C. H. Aslin*

* 1660 is the generally accepted date, but the rainwater heads are dated 1659. The building must have been planned during the last years of the Commonwealth.

‡ Mr Peter Hogben kindly gave us these details about the County Offices.

(then Borough Architect). A poor design in an C18 style. Brick and stone dressings, with giant portico facing the roundabout at the meeting of two of the ranges. The building is of four ranges (one facing the river) round an internal courtyard. – PLATE. Great Mace, 1638; Common Seal, C15, with rebus: a deer.

CIVIC CENTRE. 1971–6 by *Casson, Conder & Partners* as executive architects in association with *W.I.N.G. Doig* (Borough Architect).* It comprises a multi-storey car park and two halls, the larger one tiered for concerts, facing each other across a small internal court. The façade to the Market Place is a brick screen wall with a first-floor passage glazed with tinted glass between irregularly spaced aluminium mullions supported on pillars. The façade continues in an L-shape on the E side of the Market Place, and unfortunately, being both bland in colour and rather featureless, fails to give the Market Place, as the centre of the town, any sense of visual climax.‡

LIBRARY AND MUSEUM, Wardwick. 1876 by *R. Knill Freeman* of Bolton. Brick in a Gothic style with a Franco-Flemish central tower (altered since 1897) and much decoration by means of those moulded tiles with diapered leaf and similar motifs which were so popular in the seventies. To the W an addition of 1915 and, set back behind an open court, a simple extension to house part of the Museum, 1963 by *T. W. East* (Borough Architect). At the back (facing the Strand) the ART GALLERY, 1883 by *Story* of Derby. To the r. of the front the IRON GATES of the old Silk Mill (*see* Perambulation below) have been re-erected (*Robert Bakewell* at his best, *c.* 1730: ES).§

COLLEGE OF ART (Annexe), Green Lane. Built by *F. W. Waller*

* The Civic Centre stands on the site of the ASSEMBLY ROOMS, gutted by fire in 1963. The façade, 1752–5, has been re-erected at the Crich Tramway Museum (*see* p. 157). It is a handsome five-bay stone-faced front with raised pedimented three-bay centre. Inside was a charming hall, 1773–4, with a coved ceiling. The architect is unknown, although *Washington Shirley*, fifth *Earl Ferrers*, a leading member of the committee, has been suggested (cf. Staunton Harold, Leics.; *see* E. Saunders, *Derbyshire Life & Countryside*, 1971, pp. 36, 64). *Joseph Pickford* was the contractor. In 1770, *James* and *Robert Adam* were asked to submit a design for the interior. There is no evidence that they did so, but the ceiling was probably the work of *Abraham Denston* of Derby, a plasterworker who had worked for Adam at Kedleston. Dr Gomme points out that the façade design is very retardataire, with motifs from buildings of the 1970s (e.g. Derby Cathedral and Sutton Scarsdale). 89

‡ At the time of writing (1977) just a shell.

§ They are to be re-erected at the Silk Mill.

of *Waller & Sons*, Gloucester, as the Municipal Technical College in 1876. Imaginative neo-Gothic. Additions 1899.

PLAYHOUSE THEATRE. *See* Perambulation, p. 179.

MECHANICS' INSTITUTION, Wardwick. 1882–3 by *Sheffield & Hill*, typical of the remarkably sober style of city architecture at the time in Derby. Heavily decorated classicism.

ST CHRISTOPHER'S HOME FOR THE CHILDREN OF RAILWAYMEN, Ashbourne Road. A large red brick château-style orphanage by *A. A. Langley* (Midland Railway Architect), 1887, set back in grounds.

GENERAL POST OFFICE, Victoria Street. 1869. *The Builder* in 1897 said: 'An admirable piece of dignified and restrained design in Classical Renaissance – somewhat cold perhaps.' A characteristic example of mid-C19 commercial architecture in Derby.

MIDLAND STATION. Incorporated into the building is the tower of *Francis Thompson*'s celebrated Trijunct Station of 1839–41, built jointly for three companies.* It had an immensely long, low, Italianate façade (1,050 ft long, 40 ft high) screening an equally long single platform and cast-iron shed by *Stephenson*. The polygonal former ENGINE SHED also survives. The MIDLAND HOTEL, also by *Thompson*, 1840, is still Late Georgian in style. It is important as the earliest surviving railway hotel built with a station. Round the station, houses for railway workers, *c.* 1840, in MIDLAND TERRACE, and the former RAILWAY INSTITUTE, 1894 by Mr *Trubshaw*, the Midland Railway's Chief Architect.

MIDLAND RAILWAY WAR MEMORIAL, Midland Road. 1921 by *Lutyens*. Stone catafalque on a pedestal.

ST MARY'S BRIDGE. Rebuilt in 1788–93 by *Thomas Harrison*. Three arches, each buttress with a pedimented niche. For the Chapel of St Mary *see* above.

EXETER BRIDGE. 1931 by *C. H. Aslin* (Borough Architect).

PERAMBULATION

The MARKET PLACE is the best centre to start from. (For Guild Hall and Civic Centre *see* Public Buildings above.) Otherwise a few C18 houses, especially Nos. 2–3 (early C18 and of imposing size) and 35–36. On the W side the former bank of Samuel Smith

*The North Midland, Birmingham and Derby Junction, and Midland Counties, amalgamated in 1844 to form the Midland Railway Co.

& Co. (now NATIONAL WESTMINSTER), a good, dignified early C20 classical structure.

N of the Market Place IRON GATE starts. At the corner of Sadler Gate, No. 43 (LLOYDS BANK), early C18, brick, with decorated keystones to the windows. Further N the NATIONAL WESTMINSTER BANK is a fine essay in severe Italian palazzo style, built in 1877–9 as Crompton & Evans Union Bank Ltd. Brick with stone facings to ground and top storeys and a Greek-key frieze at first-floor level. Also noteworthy No. 27, C18, brick, four-storeyed, with decorated keystones, and No. 22, mostly C17, timber-framed, now rendered, with oversailing upper storeys and two C18 oriels. (Good C17 staircase. DOE) Nothing old on the E side. The street was widened on this side in the 1860s.

Iron Gate is continued to the N in QUEEN STREET. Here the DOLPHIN INN, a timber-framed gabled C16 house, much restored (the licence dates from 1580: DOE). Off Queen Street to the E is FULL STREET. Behind the cathedral by the river stands the SILK MILL (now Derby Industrial Museum), on the site of the first mill in England built in 1702 (with mill work and machinery by the engineer *George Sorocold*) for Thomas Cotchett. It used the power of the river. It was superseded in 1717 or 1718* by Thomas and John Lombe's much larger mill, also with mill work by *Sorocold*.‡ By 1828 1,000 hands were employed there. Of this mill only some stone foundation arches and the (altered) tower survive. The present mill was rebuilt after a fire in 1910. For the fine GATES *see* Library and Museum, above.

To the NW the East Midland Electricity Board SWITCHING STATION (1963–9 by *Peter Coake*) with its undulating brick perimeter forms a surprisingly good group with the Silk Mill. Back to Queen Street and N, over ST ALKMUND'S WAY, part of the devastating inner ring-road, into what remains of BRIDGE GATE. Only one late C18 house, No. 11, survives.§

* The date is disputed. John Lombe had returned from Italy by 1717 but Thomas Lombe did not receive his patents securing to him the privilege of working the organization for the term of fourteen years until 1718. It is most probable that Thomas committed himself to the considerable financial outlay after he had the patent rights. (Information from Brian Waters, Keeper of Industry and Technology, Derby Industrial Museum.)

‡ Cotchett's mill may have been incorporated in it.

§ In Bridge Gate, which continued E to St Mary's Bridge (*see* p. 176), were several Georgian brick houses and picturesque gabled later C17 houses. St Alkmund's Churchyard was a more serious loss. In 1953 it was described

At the corner of KING STREET, ST HELEN'S HOUSE, an excellent stone-faced Palladian mid-C18 front of seven bays with a three-bay centre with an attached giant Ionic portico above a rusticated ground floor and crowned by a pediment.* The main first-floor windows have alternatingly triangular and segmental pediments. The stone string-course and cornice are carried round the now exposed side elevation to Bridge Gate. In the hall a staircase with a fine wrought-iron handrail.‡ On the W side of King Street, the SEVEN STARS INN, a small but interesting house. It is dated 1680 and has a narrow gabled front. The painted brick front is divided by four string-courses, a broad one above the low ground floor, a second at eaves level, and two more in the gable. It is this demonstrative emphasis on horizontals alone that indicates the date of the house. The few original windows still low and mullioned.§

Return via Queen Street to the cathedral in Iron Gate. Opposite the Cathedral is ST MARY'S GATE. Here again three remaining groups of Georgian brick houses, e.g. the group at the corner of Iron Gate, with Nos. 40–42 especially successful in a modest way, and No. 36 interesting as a transitional house of *c.* 1740: finely moulded doorcase and cornice but now with flat brick arches over the windows. On the W side of County Hall (*see* Public Buildings) at the corner of Jury Street the SUB POLICE STATION, an altered C18 inn with rusticated lintels and keystone. On the first floor the arms of William III. Just S of the W end of St Mary's Gate in BOLD LANE the former THEATRE, converted from a malthouse in 1773. An unobtrusive stucco front of three bays, the interior entirely remodelled.

At the S end of Bold Lane the road forks. To the l. is SADLER GATE. In Sadler Gate two interesting houses. One is No. 48,

---

as a 'survival of C18 Derby unmatched, a quiet oasis although close to the traffic of the town centre. No houses are especially noteworthy but the ensemble is very satisfying.' Enough is said.

* It is so good that it would be interesting to know the name of the architect. Mr E. Saunders suggests *Lord Ferrers*, a friend of the Gisbornes who built it (cf. Staunton Harold, Leicestershire, Lord Ferrers's own house). Dr Gomme agrees. It has the same retardataire tendencies as the Assembly Rooms.

‡ It is the same pattern as those at Okeover, Staffordshire, 1748; the Master's House, Hull, and Nuthall Temple, Nottinghamshire, *c.* 1754; Staunton Harold, Leicestershire, 1763; and the communion rail at Manchester Cathedral, 1750–1. That at Okeover is by *Bakewell*, the others are probably by *Yates* after his death (ES).

§ The interior is gutted, and the house is due to be moved back 100 ft for road widening.

later C17, with a heavy doorcase with a segmental pediment displaying the date 1675; the first floor has Georgian windows, but the second-floor windows are evidently C17 (mullion-and-transom crosses). The gable is at r. angles to the street (not visible from it) and still of the early C17 shaped kind. The other is No. 53, the OLD BELL HOTEL, an C18 inn, the Bell and Castle, transformed by fake timbering in 1929–30.*

At the E end of Sadler Gate turn r. into the Market Place. From the Market Place S CORNMARKET, with the remains of two stately C18 brick buildings. Nos. 37–38 are altered but were originally of five bays. The central bay is pedimented with a coach arch and above a Venetian and a semicircular window. Nos. 34–36 is all that remains of what is said to be the Duke of Devonshire's town house. It was of nine bays with a pediment over the three central bays. Five bays demolished for LITTLEWOODS store, 1968.

Cornmarket continues S into ST PETER'S STREET. On the r. is ST PETER'S CHURCHYARD and facing it, at the rear of No. 58 St Peter's Street, is the GREEN MAN INN. Fine C17 brick façade with a shaped gable surmounted by a pediment, pediments over the second-floor windows, and elaborate brick string-courses etc. At the W end of St Peter's Church, the former FREE SCHOOL, early C17, stone, with mullioned and transomed windows and gables. (It had several illustrious pupils, including John Flamstead, first Astronomer Royal.) Back into St Peter's Street.‡ At its S by THE SPOT is the entrance to the EAGLE CENTRE AND PLAYHOUSE, 1970–5, on a twelve-acre site between St Peter's Street/London Road and Morledge. It incorporates a pedestrian shopping precinct and open market by *Elsom, Pack & Roberts*, and to the SE, towards Traffic Street, the PLAYHOUSE, by *Roderick Ham*. The main route through the shopping centre from St Peter's Street is down a rather narrow and darkened covered street, opening first into a small top-lit square and then into the main two-storey Copecastle Square, light and bright in contrast, with dark red brick, white tiling, and a glass roof in pyramidal sections. The scale is claustrophobically small, but the layout

* (The rainwater-heads dated 1717 and an overmantel dated 1700 probably refer to two older inns, the Bell and the Castle, made into the present inn by one John Campion (see pump-head insribed JC 1774). Maxwell Craven.)

‡ At the corner of East Street a wonderful example of the old BOOTS' shops, originated by Jesse Boot and his architect *Morley Horder*. This one is no longer Boots' but it still has all the distinctive half-timbering, statues of famous local figures, etc.

echoes the earlier street patterns. Opening from the main square is the market, with a more complicated glass roof and polygonal islands of stalls. On one side the entrance to the Playhouse. The brickwork of the foyer is the main feature; the auditorium is conventional. Only the glass roof of the market and the brick fly tower etc. of the theatre are seen from the outside, from Morledge and Traffic Street.

Back to the S end of Cornmarket. On the W side, the NATIONAL WESTMINSTER (formerly the Derby and Derbyshire) BANK, stone and classical, with a heraldic device forming the pediment. Next to it, at the corner of VICTORIA STREET, the fine group of the ROYAL HOTEL, divided into two parts, the one at the corner rounded and stone-faced with giant Ionic demi-columns, the other long, stuccoed, and with a minimum of Grecian details. Originally the group was Hotel and Athenaeum. Inside on the first floor a fine, large, and well preserved dining room. The Bank, Hotel, and Athenaeum are all by *Robert Wallace*, who won the competition for this group of public buildings in 1837. The General Post Office, later rebuilt (*see* Public Buildings), once formed part of it. The Bank was altered in 1850 by *Thomson*. (As planned improvement this group can be compared with Foulston's Royal Hotel, Assembly Rooms, and Theatre at Plymouth, 1811–18 (*see The Buildings of England: South Devon*, pp. 238–9).) At the top next to the G.P.O. the STRAND begins. It was created, like Victoria Street, in 1878, when the Markeaton Brook was culverted. Nos. 2–40 are a continuous curved stone neo-classical-style range of 1881. On from Victoria Street into WARDWICK, where the WARDWICK TAVERN is a building of *c.* 1740 (cf. No. 36 St Mary's Gate). Quite a subtle design in which a non-existent order is implied by projecting sections of the parapet between the windows. Probably always an inn. Nos. 25–29 are also C18 but earlier, *c.* 1720.* The JACOBEAN HOUSE is a tall, two-gabled building, dated 1677 (rather than 1611?).‡ Brick and stone with mullioned windows. It was originally of five bays, but three of these, of two storeys with a balustraded parapet, were demolished in 1852 when Becket Street was made and were rebuilt at r. angles; so the house now has an L-plan.

90 The continuation of Wardwick is FRIAR GATE, the best street in Derby, although halfway down crossed by a RAILWAY BRIDGE (with the most fanciful lacy cast-iron balustrade and

* These C18 buildings were pointed out to us by Dr Gomme.

‡ See footnote on p. 37 of the Introduction.

spandrels, and arches of lattice construction), erected by *Andrew Handyside & Co.*, ironfounders of Derby, in 1878 for the Great Northern Railway Company, whose station still exists near by.* Many of the houses deserve attention. Most of them are Mid Georgian. On the N side the following are worth singling out: from E to W Nos. 16–17 (eight bays, four gables, C17, with early C18 glazing bars to the windows except in the gables, where they are still mullioned); No. 27 (five-bay, C18, red brick, Tuscan doorcase, the centre window on the first floor pedimented); and No. 32. No. 41 was built by *Joseph Pickford* for himself soon after 1768, when the land along this part of Friar Gate was sold for development. It is of three storeys and five bays, brick with stone dressings. The central bay recessed under a stone arch and crowned by an open pediment decorated with large ball heads. The second and fourth bays project slightly. Fine Roman Doric doorcase. In the centre of the entrance hall ceiling, a plasterwork cameo portrait surrounded by garlands. Next is No. 42, then Nos. 43–44, also possibly by *Pickford* and with a façade almost identical to that of Lloyds Bank at Ashbourne (*see* p. 65). Three bays, plus one recessed to the r., ground floor with two Venetian windows flanking a Roman Doric doorcase and first-floor windows under flat arches. Further W Nos. 47–51 (eleven bays, ashlar-faced, with double porches, l. and r., and a three-bay pediment in the middle, Late Georgian); Nos. 56 and 57 (both mid-C18, five bays, brick), etc., to No. 65 (eight-bay brick, Greek Ionic porch); CHESTNUT HOUSE (ashlar-faced, Greek Doric porch, i.e. *c.* 1825), and Nos. 66–66a, GEORGIAN HOUSE (three-bay, three-storey, brick, with tripartite windows, the top ones semicircular).

On the S side, also from E to W, Nos. 116–117 (Georgian brick); Nos. 114–115 (C17, two-gabled); FRIARY HOTEL (a fine detached seven-bay mansion of three storeys, elaborate window frames, giant angle pilasters, top parapet; a lower wing on the l. and a modern porte-cochère; good panelled room inside, also some stucco work); No. 102 (corner house with rusticated window lintels); and No. 99 (five bays, three storeys, Tuscan doorcase, lower window on the l.).

Off Friar Gate is VERNON STREET, with a nice ensemble of early C19 classical, stuccoed, detached, semi-detached and terraced houses. Closing the vista down Vernon Street, the forbidding

* Cf. Handyside's bridge for the G.N.R. at Little Chester, p. 184.

Greek Doric front of the former GAOL by *Francis Goodwin*, 1823–7, one-storeyed, broad, and long. (Alterations by *J. Mason* of Derby, *c.* 1840, and remodelled 1880.)

Friar Gate continues in ASHBOURNE ROAD with a few more notable houses, mostly early C19, stuccoed. Especially stately No. 34 (GEORGIAN HOUSE HOTEL) with a one-storeyed stone porch on Tuscan columns. No. 35 opposite is mid-C18, brick, of five bays with a pedimented doorway. The houses clearly show how consistently this residential suburb developed: from the C17 and early C18 in Wardwick up to the early C19 nearly a mile further on.

Off Bridge Street (N side of Friar Gate) in BROOK STREET is one of the most imposing industrial buildings in Derby, the RYKNELD MILLS, built *c.* 1830 as a silk mill. Seven- and five-storey blocks with cast-iron columns, iron beams, and brick arched floors.

OUTER DERBY

The city of Derby consists of the C19 and early C20 suburbs nearest the centre, and of the villages, much expanded by C20 housing, and mansions that are now within the city boundaries. It seems most satisfactory to describe firstly the inner suburbs and then the villages and mansions (*see* p. 189). The inner suburbs, which are bounded on the N, W, and S by Derby's outer ring road and on the E by the River Derwent and the railway line, are described topographically as below, with the inclusion of the industrial area (Osmaston Park and Sinfin) to the S of the ring road and the C20 housing estate (Mackworth) to the W of it. Churches and public buildings will be found in their appropriate sector. There are exceptionally few houses of any interest. C19 red brick predominates, the result of Derby's railway age prosperity.

(1) North	(a)	Little Chester
	(b)	Kedleston Road
(2) West	(a)	Ashbourne Road – New Zealand – Uttoxeter New Road – California – Burton Road
	(b)	Mackworth
(3) South	(a)	Rosehill and New Normanton
	(b)	Osmaston Park and Sinfin
(4) South-East		Osmaston Road – London Road – Osmaston

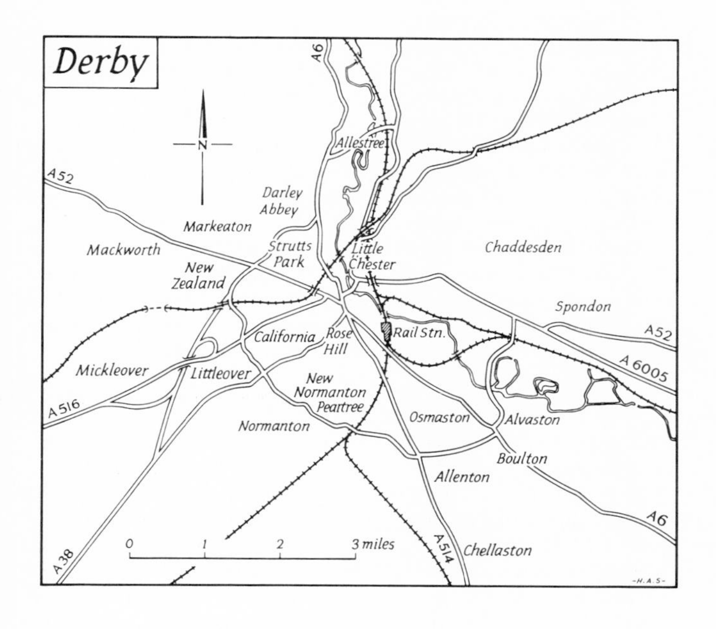

(1) NORTH

(A) LITTLE CHESTER

The Roman fort of DERVENTIO lies in the northern suburbs of the town. The outline of the defences can be traced on the N, E, and W sides. Excavation has shown that the place was occupied from the late C1 into at least the C3 and probably later. Saxon burials are known from the vicinity of the fort. A considerable extra-mural settlement lay to the N along the line of Ryknield Street and also to the E. Across the river at Strutts Park is the site of an earlier Roman fort, occupied from about A.D. 55 to 70. This site is now covered by a housing estate.

ST PAUL, Mansfield Road. 1849 by *Barry & Brown*. Aisle 1897 by *P. H. Currey* (GR). Quite a nice group, with a symmetrically placed tower and transeptal wings. – STAINED GLASS. E window 1849 by *J. J. Simpson* (TK).

In OLD CHESTER ROAD one or two old houses: SCHOOL FARMHOUSE, late C16, brick, with large medieval stone chimneys and l. wing dated 1597 (cellars said to contain Roman masonry: DOE); and opposite the handsome red brick mid to late C17 DERWENT HOUSE. Over the River Derwent, a RAILWAY BRIDGE by *Andrew Handyside & Co.*, 1878, for the Great Northern Railway Company. Very different in design to that over Friar Gate (*see* Inner Derby, p. 180). On the Strutts Park side of the river AUSTWICK, No. 144 DUFFIELD ROAD, is by *Parker & Unwin*, 1902–3. Its rectangular plan broken by mullioned corner bays is like that of Greenmoor, Buxton. The continuous mullioned window below the eaves may have its origin in the traditional Derbyshire weaving loft (Mervyn Miller).

(B) KEDLESTON ROAD

ST ALKMUND, Kedleston Road.* The replacement for Stevens's church (*see* Inner Derby, p. 171). Built in 1967–72 by *Naylor, Sale & Widdows*. Dark brick, oval plan, with sides composed of short walls placed at an angle and full-length stained glass panels (*John Hardman Studios*) between. On the SW a fibreglass spire rises over a stone believed to be part of St Alkmund's shrine, its concrete supports enclosed by the glass-fronted atrium leading to church (E) and parish hall and rooms (W). The interior of the church is of light brick with a curved organ recess and the low St Aidan's Chapel to the N. The following are from the medieval St Alkmund: FONT. C14, octagonal, with two simple blank arches to each side, badly preserved. – PLATE. Chalice, 1688. – MONUMENT (in the atrium). John Bullock † 1667, alabaster effigy, very long figure and extremely small head; on the tomb-chest much strapwork decoration.

(ST ANNE, Whitecross Street. A dark red brick, towerless, decidedly Butterfield-style church of 1871 by *F. W. Hunt*. The W elevation has five stepped lancets and roundels above them. –REREDOS. Late work of *George Walton*. Canopy by *P. H. Currey*, 1927. – STAINED GLASS. Some by *Clayton & Bell*. R. Hubbuck)

DERBY AND DISTRICT COLLEGES OF ART AND TECHNOLOGY, Kedleston Road. Built in several stages by the *Building*

* Information about St Alkmund from Miss Beadsmoore.

Design Partnership. The first stage (1956–61) comprises two tower blocks, nine and ten storeys high, at r. angles to each other and joined by a glazed staircase link. The construction is concrete H-frames with coloured panels in the cladding and V-shaped supports at ground level. Other buildings, including an administration block (1962–73), a six-storey tower for the College of Art (1964–6), and workshops, are arranged round a central concourse.

Off Kedleston Road in BROADWAY (outer ring road) the LEYLANDS ESTATE, an old people's estate, completed in 1955 by *T. P. Bennett & Son* and known as the Linen & Woollen Drapers Cottage Homes. Neo-Georgian brick cottages, flatlets, assembly hall, and rest home in the park of EBORN HOUSE (formerly Leylands), plain, early C19, and stuccoed.

(2) WEST

(A) ASHBOURNE ROAD – NEW ZEALAND – UTTOXETER NEW ROAD – CALIFORNIA – BURTON ROAD

ST BARNABAS, Radbourne Street. 1880 by *A. Coke-Hill*. – FONT. C18, cruciform.

(ST LUKE, Parliament Street. The masterpiece of *F. J. Robinson* of Derby, 1872. Wide nave with broad semicircular apsed chancel and narrow passage aisles. Each bay under a separate gable. Commanding saddleback roof to the SW tower. Impressive, spacious interior. – STAINED GLASS. Some by *Clayton & Bell*. R. Hubbuck)

CEMETERY, Uttoxeter New Road. 1842. Disused. A stone chapel with starved lancet windows by the entrance.

BEMROSE SCHOOL, Uttoxeter New Road. 1930 by *Macpherson & Richardson*. Neo-Georgian.

ROYAL SCHOOL FOR THE DEAF, Ashbourne Road. 1964–73 by *Naylor, Sale & Widdows*. A group of two-storey residential buildings in dark brick with low pitched roofs as a contrast to the flat-roofed school buildings in buff rustic brick. The roof over the nursery school is of butterfly form, those over the assembly halls are seesaw.

(B) MACKWORTH

For All Saints church and Mackworth Castle *see* separate entry, p. 269. The parish church and old village centre are outside Derby city boundary.

The Mackworth housing estate was begun to the E of the village in 1950, and by 1959 there was a population of 10,000. Housing, Mackworth Secondary School, and the shopping centre in Prince Charles Avenue are by *T. W. East* (then Borough Architect). The following churches serve the estate.

ST FRANCIS, Prince Charles Avenue. 1953–4 by *Milburn & Partners*. Very plain, brick, aisleless, with transepts. Windows very simplified Perp. – PLATE. Chalice and Flagon, 1725 by *Gabriel Sleath*; two Patens, 1725 by *William Spackman*.

CHRIST THE KING (R.C.), Prince Charles Avenue. 1971–2 by *Montague Associates*. A small, low brick church with a prominent slate roof sloping up from W to E. The plan is basically a rhomboid. Inside the altar (E) faces a sloping auditorium lit by continuous glazing round three sides. On the NE side of the rhomboid the Lady Chapel, on the SE side ancillary rooms and at the apex a clerestory-lit oratory with a separate E entrance.

MARKEATON PARK lies to the N of the Mackworth Estate, on the other side of the Ashbourne Road. The house, built for Wrighton Mundy M.P. in 1775, was demolished in 1964. Only a contemporary ORANGERY survives in the landscaped park.*

(3) SOUTH

(A) ROSEHILL AND NEW NORMANTON

ST AUGUSTINE, Upper Dale Road. By *Naylor & Sale*, 1897–1908. Brick with a little flèche and no tower. Two W porches into the aisles.

ST CHAD, Mill Hill Lane. 1881–2 by *H. Turner* (GR). E.E. style, rock-faced, with E bell-turret. A typical 'railway' church.

(CHRIST CHURCH, Normanton Road.‡ 1838–41 by *Habershon*. Plain ashlar-faced parallelogram. W tower with spire supported by flying buttresses. Lancet windows. Chancel added in 1865 by *Giles & Brookhouse* (GR).) – PLATE. Chalice and Paten Cover on knob foot, 1698; Chalice, 1798, Dublin made.

ST JAMES, Malcolm Street. 1867 by *J. Peacock*. High Victorian.

ST THOMAS THE APOSTLE, Richmond Road. 1881 by *J. Peacock*. Rock-faced, in the Norman style, with a silly conical

* The house was brick with restless stone dressings, rather ugly in design. The Torrington Diary of 1789 comments unfavourably on the 'flaming red' colour. The N front had five windows very close together and canted bays flanking them, the E front an asymmetrical canted bay, and the S front was nine windows wide with a five-bay pediment and a curved double staircase up to the main entrance.

‡ Made redundant in May 1976; in 1977 for sale as a site.

flèche. A low porch with a 'dwarf gallery' across the W front. – (STAINED GLASS. Chancel, two side windows, 1949–50 by *Nuttgens*. R. Hubbuck)

ARBORETUM, off Osmaston Road. 1839–40. Designed by *John Claudius Loudon* and given to the town by Joseph Strutt. It is the earliest public park of any English town. The size is moderate, the style mildly picturesque, with artificial undulation. The chief importance according to the donor was the large variety of different trees. Ornamental vases by *R. Blore* of Derby. The medieval CROSS shaft was removed from Friar Gate. The original lodges (by *E. B. Lamb*) are Elizabethan in style, but there was from the beginning a debased Italianate pavilion, one of a pair originally terminating a cross walk. The equally flabby Italianate gateway towards Arboretum Square was added about 1850 by *Duesbury*. The Rose Hill entrance lodge is also by *Lamb*, who was clearly following Loudon's *Encyclopaedia* style.

(B) OSMASTON PARK AND SINFIN

REGIONAL SWIMMING POOL, Moor Lane. By *W.I.N.G. Doig* (Borough Architect), opened 1974. The pool is well lit by long wooden mullioned windows away from the road. The almost windowless dark grey brick diving area contrasts with this.

On the industrial estate S of Osmaston Park Road are the buildings of ROLLS ROYCE (1971) LTD. The best are the Engineering Centre, Moor Lane, 1961–8 by *Fry, Drew & Partners* (seven three-storey office blocks with curtain walls linked at angles by brick-faced service blocks to form three parallel three-sided courts: very prestigious in appearance with facings of blue and brown brick, matching tiles, and polished slate); linked to it the Computer Centre, Moor Lane, 1965 by the same architects (a single block of two storeys with a basement to the N: aluminium sectional walling and Staffordshire blue brick); and the Precision Test Facility, Victory Road, 1968–70 by *J. V. Clifford*, Chief Company Architect (to the street a two-storey block with a curved façade and above it a four-storey steel-framed office block with red brick service tower).

(4) SOUTH-EAST

OSMASTON ROAD – LONDON ROAD – OSMASTON

ST BARTHOLOMEW, Nightingale Road. 1927 by *Currey & Thompson*. Large apse and vestry 1966–9 by *Humphreys &*

Hurst. A simple, towerless church but with the red brick, cream stucco, leaded windows, and steep tiled roof of contemporary suburban houses in the Arts and Crafts tradition.

ST OSMUND, London Road, Osmaston. 1904 by *P. H. Currey*. A pleasant brick church with lancet windows, transept, and a flèche. Low circular piers inside and a very tall, well-lit clerestory. – PLATE. Elizabethan Chalice; Paten on foot, 1702 by *Francis Garthorne*. – Sunk garden in front and a group of cottages on the N side of it as part of the composition.

BAPTIST CHURCH, Osmaston Road. 1971 by *C. Leech*. Small A-frame construction.

ST ANDREW, London Road. Demolished 1971 and replaced by St Andrew's House (Social Security Office).*

DERBYSHIRE ROYAL INFIRMARY, London Road. Founded 1810. Of that date a statue of Aesculapius by *W. J. Coffee*. Nightingale Wing 1869 by *H. I. Stevens*. The main part of the infirmary, built *c*. 1890 by *Young & Hall*, is gradually being demolished and the site filled in with new buildings: ACCIDENT AND EMERGENCY CENTRE and NURSES' SCHOOL AND HOME, 1970–4 by *Morrison & Partners*, both towers with concrete frames and facing. The Victorian hospital is red brick, Jacobean style, originally with a gabled central block with two detached wings faced with stone loggias, and corner towers with ogee caps.

BRITISH RAIL SCHOOL OF TRANSPORT, London Road, Osmaston. 1937–8 by *W. H. Hamlyn* in a friendly neo-Georgian style with a slightly Swedish angular lantern that goes well with it.

BRITISH RAIL TECHNICAL CENTRE, London Road. 1965–8 by *F. F C. Curtis* (British Rail Board). Near the road, three three-storey office buildings, each with a landscaped central courtyard. Stark black frame; blue brick and white vitreous panels. Completely regular and simple.

In OSMASTON ROAD, several large C19 villas and the CROWN DERBY CHINA WORKS, former Union Workhouse, 1839 and altered. In LONDON ROAD the LIVESAGE ALMSHOUSES, 1836 by *John Mason* of Derby. Brick and Gothic. At the end of London Road RAYNESWAY (inner ring road) runs NE. Next to it buildings by *Morrison & Partners* for ROLLS ROYCE ASSOCIATES, 1961–74. Large four-storey concrete-framed

* It was by *Sir George Gilbert Scott*, 1866, tower and spire after his death (1881). Big church in surroundings of no character; C13 detail. NW tower with broach-spire, apsidal chancel.

and glass blocks. The cafeteria (1961) is one-storey, with brick panels and a butterfly roof raised to admit a clerestory.

VILLAGES

The villages are described alphabetically. For their location in relation to the inner suburbs *see* map p. 183.

ALLENTON

(ST EDMUND, Sinfin Avenue. 1939 by *Eaton* of Derby in Gothic style.)

SHELTON LOCK PRIMARY SCHOOL. One of the post-war standard steel and brick schools erected by the County Education Department. (*See* Introduction p. 46.)

ALLESTREE

ST EDMUND. The church is of 1865–6 (by *Stevens & Robinson* of Derby), but has a good broad Norman S doorway, partly renewed. The inner jambs and inner arch have quadruple zigzag without intervening capitals. Then an order of colonnettes with beakheads biting into them and the same repeated in the roll-moulding of the arch. The outer label has partly upright stylized leaves, partly a kind of four-petalled flower with the petals of fern-like shape. The W tower is the other old feature, C13, with broad buttresses only at the foot, a treble-chamfered tower arch into the nave, two-light cusped bell-openings, and a C19 stair-turret.

ST NICHOLAS, Allestree Lane. 1957–8 by *Peter Woore*. Brick with stone dressings. Simplified Gothic.

ALLESTREE HALL, situated in the public Allestree Park to the N. It was begun in 1795 by *James Wyatt* (Colvin) and sold unfinished to John Charles Girardot in 1805. One stone bears the date 1802 and the initials JW. It is a plain five-bay, two-and-a-half-storey stone house, with a full-height central bow and three ground-floor windows divided by Ionic columns carrying an entablature. (Inside, a bowed entrance hall and two Adam-style ceilings which may be old. DOE)

Near the church there is some village atmosphere, although only No. 19 Cornhill (YEW TREE COTTAGE) is notable: probably C17, timber-framed, with a good E elevation. N of Cornhill off West Bank Road in LADYCROFT PADDOCK, a discreet one-storey house by *Diamond, Redfern & Partners*, 1966. Nothing much to see from the entrance but the outer brick walls of house, cottage, and garage grouped round a courtyard. The main walls of the house are glazed back and front, plus clerestory lighting. In the S of the village is the PARK FARM CENTRE, a district centre begun by *William Blair & Partners* in 1960, completed *c.* 1975 by *Montague Associates.*

ALVASTON

ST MICHAEL. The church is of 1855–6 by *H. I. Stevens*, but a Saxon coffin lid with a big primitive cross, and an extremely pretty, if somewhat rustic, piece of wrought iron with a figure of an angel and lambrequins and scrollwork speak of the existence of the preceding village church. (The ironwork was a reredos given by Charles Benskin (d. 1739) and may be by *Bakewell.* ES) – PLATE. Cup, 1633; Paten, 1735 by *Edward Pocock*, given by Benskin in 1736.

There are also a few village houses left in Church Street and Elvaston Lane in the middle of all the surrounding suburban Derby housing. Off Elvaston Lane in Ellastone Gardens THE POPLARS, early C19, with a columned porch and ornamental ironwork on the side.

ALVASTON AND BOULTON JUNIOR SCHOOL, Elvaston Lane. One of the standard steel and brick schools, built in 1951 for the County Education Department (*see* Introduction, p. 46).

BOULTON

ST MARY. Mostly C19 and C20 (W end 1840 by *John Mason* of Derby; N aisle 1870; enlarged *c.* 1960 by *Sebastian Comper*), but the S doorway is Norman (one order of colonnettes, zigzag arch, tympanum almost completely defaced), the N chancel doorway also Norman (similar but smaller), the S porch has a nice cusped outer doorway of *c.* 1300, and a few small Perp windows survive. – (STAINED GLASS. E window 1913 by *Walker J. Pearce.* R. Hubbuck)

OAKWOOD INFANTS SCHOOL, Waldene Drive. 1971–2 by *George Grey & Partners.* Simple steel-framed rectangle, mostly glass but with a deep, stained timber fascia, the rest brick.

(NUNSFIELD HOUSE, Boulton Lane. Early C19, ashlar, two storeys, Doric porch with triglyph frieze. DOE)

CHADDESDEN

ST MARY. Rebuilt as a college or chantry foundation *c.* 1357 by Henry Chaddesden, Archdeacon of Leicester, encouraged probably by the immediately preceding work at Sandiacre. Important as a dated example of church architecture before the advent of the Perp style. Nave and aisles and tall and wide chancel. The high chancel N and S windows of three lights have a star motif in the tracery, similar to so-called Kentish tracery, but with the three points of the star long and with concave sides (just as at Sandiacre). The E window is C19. The chancel was restored in 1857–8 by *G. Place*. The N aisle also has Dec windows (four lights in the E, three lights in the N). The S windows all new except the E and W ones, given flowing tracery by *Street* in his 1858 restoration in imitation of those in the N aisle.* Some more windows re-done Perp, the W tower (ashlar, with angle buttresses, big W door and W window, and concave chamfering of the tall arch to the nave) also Perp. When the tower was built the aisles were extended to the W (see W window, S aisle). The arcades inside (three bays) have tall octagonal piers with moderately finely moulded capitals and double-chamfered arches. At the E ends of the N and S aisles SEDILIA and PISCINA, with crocketed ogee arches and stone reredoses to the altars, just long sunk panels no doubt originally painted. – SCREEN and STALL ENDS (with figures of a monk and a deacon). The screen has one-light openings with ogee tops rising into an upper part with panel tracery. – LECTERN of stone built into the chancel N wall (cf. Crich, Etwall, Mickleover and Spondon (Derby), Taddington). – PULPIT. 1858 by *Street*.

(ST MARK, Francis Street. 1938 by *Naylor, Sale & Widdows*.)

ST PHILIP, Taddington Road. 1954–6 by *Milburn & Partners*. Simple church in concrete reinforced stone with very reduced Gothic features.

CEMETERY, Nottingham Road. Central gatehouse with a lodge either side all linked by a screen wall. E.E. style.

LEESBROOK SCHOOL, Morley Road. By the *Architects' Co-Partnership* in collaboration with *F. Hamer Crossley*. The best of the early 1950s schools and probably the most interesting building of its date in the county. Subsequently many schools have followed this type. The plan is broadly speaking cross-shaped, heights vary greatly, in part owing to the sloping

* The S aisle windows were square-headed like the SE one (information from the vicar, the Rev. John Parry).

ground. In the centre of the cross low entrance hall, W of it smaller one-storey block with assembly hall and gymnasium, to the E higher classroom wing, to the S yet higher and shorter block with classrooms (four storeys). Construction is with a light steel-frame to a 3 ft 4 in module. The façades are in large stretches completely of glass, constructed against other walls left entirely solid.

BRITISH OLIVETTI LTD, Meadow Road, on a barren industrial estate S of the Nottingham Road. Immediately identifiable by its big yellow plastic-clad roof. Like Stirling's Olivetti training school at Haslemere it is both stylish and expandable, here round three (eventually four) sides of a court. The offices and workshops are in an enclosed strip above an open car-park-cum-storage area, presenting a complete face to the road, with a smooth yellow roof pierced at the base by triangular windows, and continuous glazing to the embryo court. The Derby building (1970–1) is one of four built on the same principle but adapted to individual sites in Belfast, Carlisle, Dundee, and Derby. The intention is to create an oasis protected by the building itself in often inhospitable surroundings. Architects: *Edward Cullinan*, *Michael Chassay*, *Julian Bicknell*, *Julyan Wickham*, *Giles Oliver*, among a number of distinguished architects commissioned by Olivetti, including Eierman, Kahn, Stirling, and Tange. Sad to say neither the Derby building nor its landscaping have been maintained in the way they deserve.

CHELLASTON

Chellaston was famous in the Middle Ages for its quarries of alabaster which was used for figure carving chiefly by Nottingham and Burton artists.

ST PETER. Small church consisting of a W tower, rebuilt in 1842, a nave and S aisle, and a lower chancel. Three-bay arcade with the usual octagonal piers and double-chamfered arches. The window tracery mostly elementary late C13 (intersecting in the S aisle E window). The chancel is Perp. – FONT. Norman, plain. – (STAINED GLASS. E window 1919–20, a late work of *Holiday*. R. Hubbuck) – PLATE. Chalice and Paten. 1751 by *William Grundy*; Flagon, 1770. – MONUMENT. John Bancroft and wife † 1557, incised slab. Greenhill says by the *Royleys*.

1 *Scenery:* Dovedale

2 *Scenery:* High Tor, a limestone crag in Matlock Dale

3 *Scenery:* The Ridge t Lose Hill from Mam To in the High Peak

4 *Church Architecture, Anglo-Saxon:* Repton, crypt

5 *Church Architecture, Norman:* Melbourne, nave, early twelfth century

6 *Church Architecture, Norman:* Steetley, apse, mid twelfth century

7 *Church Architecture, Norman:* Ault Hucknall, tympanum, eleventh century

8 *Church Architecture, Early English:* South Normanton, vestry doorway, *c.* 1250–75

9 *Church Architecture, Early English:* Bakewell, thirteenth century, fourteenth-century spire, all much rebuilt

10 *Church Architecture, Early English:* Ashbourne, chancel, *c.* 1241

11 *Church Architecture, Early English:* Breadsall, thirteenth-century tower with early-fourteenth-century spire

12 *Church Architecture, Early English:* Dale Abbey, east end, late thirteenth century

13 *Church Architecture, Fourteenth Century:* Ashbourne, capital in the nave, *c.* 1300

14 *Church Architecture, Fourteenth Century:* Sandiacre, sedilia and piscina, *c.* 1342–7

15 *Church Architecture, Fourteenth Century:* Norbury, chancel, perhaps *c.* 1300–7

16 *Church Architecture, Fourteenth Century:* Tideswell, *c.* 1320–80

17 *Church Architecture, Fourteenth Century:* Chesterfield, nave, *c.* 1325–75

18 *Church Architecture, Early Sixteenth Century:* Derby Cathedral, tower

19 *Church Architecture, Georgian:* Derby Cathedral, nave, by James Gibbs, 1723–5

20 *Church Architecture, Twentieth Century:* Buxton, St Mary the Virgin, by Currey & Thompson, 1914–15

21 *Church Sculpture, Anglo-Saxon:* Wirksworth, coffin slab, *c.* 800

22 *Church Sculpture, Anglo-Saxon:* Eyam Cross, probably early ninth century

23 *Church Sculpture, Late Thirteenth Century:* Bolsover, Nativity

24 *Church Furnishings:* Youlgreave, font, *c.* 1200

25 *Church Furnishings:* Ashover, font, lead, *c.* 1200

26 *Church Furnishings:* Fenny Bentley, screen, wood, early sixteenth century

27 *Church Furnishings:* Ilkeston, screen, stone, early fourteenth century

28 *Church Furnishings:* Derby Cathedral, screen, by Robert Bakewell, *c.* 1730

29 *Church Furnishings:* Haddon Hall, chapel, wall painting, fifteenth century (*Copyright Country Life*)

30 *Church Furnishings:* Wilne, Willoughby Chapel, stained glass, 1622

31 *Church Furnishings:* Darley Dale, Gillum window, by Sir Edward Burne-Jones for Morris & Co., 1862–3

32 *Church Furnishings:* Buxton, St John the Baptist, flagon, by Edward Barnard & Sons, 1839

33 *Church Monuments:* Scarcliffe, probably Constantia de Frecheville, thirteenth century

34 *Church Monuments:* Bakewell, Sir Godfrey Foljambe †1377, carved in 1385

35 *Church Monuments:* Hathersage, Robert Eyre †1459 and Robert Eyre the younger and family, kneeling, *c.* 1500

36 *Church Monuments:* Norbury, Sir Ralph Fitzherbert †1483

37 *Church Monuments:* Norbury, Sir Nicholas Fitzherbert †1473

38 *Church Monuments:* Youlgreave, Robert Gylbert †1492

39 *Church Monuments:* Morley, Katherine Babington †1543

40 *Church Monuments:* Wirksworth, Anthony Lowe †1555

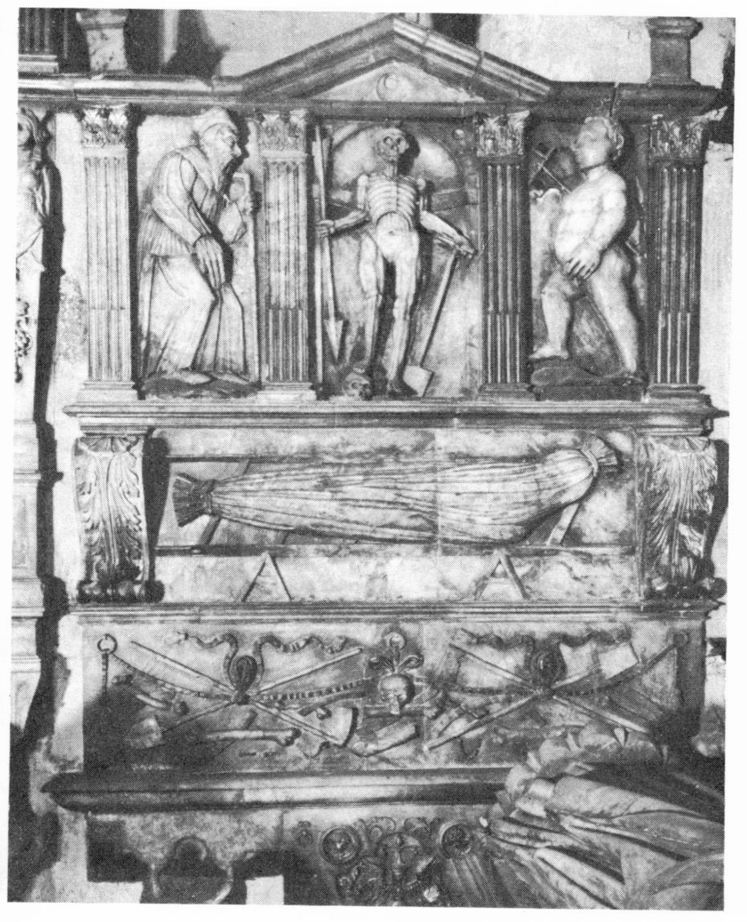

41 *Church Monuments:* Chesterfield, a Foljambe monument, *c.* 1580–90

42 *Church Monuments:* Chesterfield, Godfrey Foljambe †1594, erected 1592

43 *Church Monuments:* Fenny Bentley, Thomas Beresford †1473, erected late sixteenth century

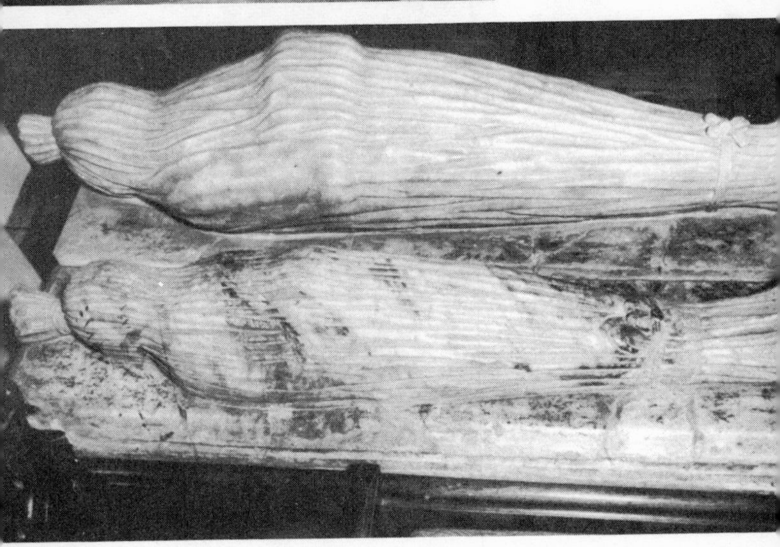

44 *Church Monuments:* Edensor, William, first Earl of Devonshire, †1625 and Henry Cavendish †1616

45 *Church Monuments:* Weston-upon-Trent, Richard Sale †1615

46 *Church Monuments:* Ault Hucknall, figures on the monument to Anne Keighley, first Countess of Devonshire, 1627

47 *Church Monuments:* Radburne, German Pole, by Grinling Gibbons, 1683

48 *Church Monuments:* Alfreton, George Morewood †1792, by the Fishers of York

49 *Church Monuments:* Ashbourne, Penelope Boothby, by Thomas Banks, 1793

50 *Secular Architecture:* Peveril Castle, 1176 and thirteenth century

51 *Secular Architecture:* Haddon Hall, twelfth to seventeenth centuries (*Copyright Country Life*)

52 *Secular Architecture:* South Wingfield, Wingfield Manor House, begun in 1439 or 1440

53 *Secular Architecture:* Haddon Hall, hall, *c.* 1370 (*Copyright Country Life*)

54 *Secular Architecture:* Haddon Hall, Parlour, *c.* 1500 (*Copyright Country Life*)

55 Hazelbadge Hall, 1549

56 Somersal Herbert, Somersal Hall, probably 1564

57 Snitterton Hall, Elizabethan

58 Ashbourne Grammar School, founded 1585

59 Hardwick Old Hall, 1580s

60 Barlborough Hall, 1583–4

61 Hardwick Hall, 1590–7

62 Hardwick Hall, High Great Chamber, completed 1599

63 Haddon Hall, long gallery, early seventeenth century (*Copyright Country Life*)

64 Haddon Hall, long gallery, early seventeenth century (*Copyright Country Life*)

65 Hardwick Hall, Withdrawing Room, relief of Apollo and the Nine Muses (*Copyright Country Life*)

66 North Lees, mainly late sixteenth century

67 Swarkeston, Summer House, early seventeenth century

68 Bolsover Castle, Keep, 1612–21

69 Bolsover Castle, Keep, interior

70 Bolsover Castle, the Gallery, *c.* 1617–30

71 Bolsover Castle, State Rooms, doorway

72 Derby, County Hall, *c.* 1660

73 Eyam Hall, completed 1676

74 Etwall, Sir John Port's Hospital, 1681

75 Sudbury Hall, exterior completed 1670

76 Sudbury Hall, long gallery, 1675–6

77 Chatsworth, 1687–1707, right wing begun 1820

78 Chatsworth, west front, 1700–3

79 Chatsworth, chapel, completed 1694

80 Chatsworth, Cascade House, by Thomas Archer, 1702, Cascade by Grillet, 1694

81 Melbourne Hall, the Arbour, by Robert Bakewell, 1706–11

82 Risley, Latin House, 1706

83 Sutton Scarsdale, by Francis Smith of Warwick, 1724

84 Melbourne Hall, east façade, by William Smith the Younger, 1744

85 Foremark Hall, by David Hiorns, 1759–61 (*Copyright Country Life*)

86 Kedleston Hall, south front, by Robert Adam, 1760–5 (*Copyright Country Life*)

87 Kedleston Hall, north front, by Matthew Brettingham, James Paine, and Robert Adam, 1758–65

88 Kedleston Hall, hall, by Robert Adam, *c.* 1770–80 (*Copyright Country Life*)

89 Derby Assembly Rooms, façade (now at Crich), 1752–5

90 Derby, Friar Gate, eighteenth century

91 Buxton, The Crescent, by John Carr of York, 1780–6

92 Tissington Hall, Gothick fireplace, *c.* 1750 (*Copyright Country Life*)

93 Cromford, Willersley Castle, by William Thomas, 1789–90

94 Renishaw Hall, by Joseph Badger of Sheffield, 1793–1808, the core Jacobean

95 Bretby Park, mainly by Sir Jeffry Wyatville, 1812–13

96 Edensor, by Joseph Paxton and John Robertson, 1838–42

97 *Industrial Architecture:* Cromford, Masson Mills, 1783

98 *Industrial Architecture:* Heage, Morley Park Farm, iron smelting furnace, 1780 and 1818

99 *Industrial Architecture:* Calver Mill, 1803–4

100 *Twentieth Century:* Tupton Hall School, Craft Centre, by George Grey & Partners in association with D. S. Davies, the County Architect, 1965–9

DARLEY ABBEY

DARLEY ABBEY was an Augustinian priory founded by Robert Ferrers, second Earl of Derby, *c.* 1146. Most of the canons were moved from St Helen, Derby, which became its cell. Very little of it survives, mainly in the rear elevation of Nos 7, 8, and 9 ABBEY LANE and in the OLD ABBEY BUILDING, Darley Street. On the Duffield Road is the GATE to DARLEY ABBEY PARK.* (*William Yates*, the son of Bakewell's assistant, supplied a gate in 1782. This is probably the one. ES)

In Old Lane, DARLEY ABBEY MILLS, cotton mills founded by Walter Evans in 1783. The oldest part (East Mill, Middle Mill, and West Mill) is five-storeyed, of brick, and has segment-headed windows. It dates from 1789–92; the rest is pre-1850. Also a finishing house, three storeys with sash-windows, and an octagonal toll house in the mill yard. Connected with the mill is early C19 industrial housing, mostly three-storey red brick terraces. The best perhaps are in BRICK ROW, but there are terraces also in Darley Street, West Row, Lavender Row, Poplar Row, Flat Square, Hill Square, and Mile Ash Lane. Also in Brick Row, the SCHOOL (C of E), built in 1826. Brick, of two storeys and nine bays, the end and central bays pedimented. The ground-floor windows are round-headed in arched recesses.

ST MATTHEW. 1818–19 by *Moses Wood* of Nottingham for Walter Evans. Stone, unaisled, of Commissioners' type, with tall slender windows with Perp tracery and angle pinnacles. The W tower is pinnacled too. Chancel 1885–91. – MONUMENTS. Arthur Evans † 1821 by *Sir Richard Westmacott*. – Walter Evans † 1839, tablet by *Joseph Hall the Younger* of Derby.

LITTLEOVER

ST PETER. Plain Norman doorway (with replaced shafts), now the entrance to the belfry originally in the W wall. Otherwise the exterior mostly over-restored. Bellcote and N aisle 1856, S aisle 1908. Enlarged at the W end by *Sebastian Comper* in 1959–61. – PLATE. Chalice, 1687. – MONUMENT. Sir Richard Har-

* The house called Darley Abbey was demolished in 1962. It was early C18, of seven bays with bays one and seven slightly projecting, the projections flanked by giant brick pilasters and the top parapeted. The central door with a Gibbs surround was reached by a pretty staircase with a wrought-iron balustrade. The S front was by *Joseph Pickford* of Derby, 1776, uncommonly well proportioned, with wide spaced windows.

pur † 1635 and wife, wall-monument with kneeling figures facing each other across a prayer desk. In the predella the children.

S of the church YE OLD COTTAGE, Upper Hollow. C16, timber-framed with brick-nogging, and thatched. NE of the church No. 17 SHEPHERD STREET is a small late C17 brick building with stone mullioned windows.

LITTLEOVER SCHOOL AND LITTLEOVER INFANTS' SCHOOL. Among the standard steel and brick schools provided by the Country Education Department about 1950 (*see* p. 46).

MICKLEOVER

ALL SAINTS. Low W tower with angle buttresses; chancel early C14, see the window with intersected tracery, priest's door, PISCINA, and stone LECTERN, cf. Chaddesden (outer Derby); Crich; Etwall; Taddington; Spondon (outer Derby). All much renewed in 1858–9 by *H. I. Stevens*, who extended the N aisle and rebuilt the nave arcade and chancel arch. Vestry and N aisle chapel 1965–7 by *G. I. Larkin* (*T. H. Thorpe & Partners*). – FONT. Octagonal, C14. – CANDLESTICKS, brass, by *G. F. Bodley*. – STAINED GLASS. In the E window, by *Charles Gibbs*. – PLATE. Chalice and Paten Cover (modern finial), 1606; Ciborium, 1968 by *S. A. Hall*.

The centre of the village is THE SQUARE, with All Saints church to the NW of it and next to it, dominating the N side, the early C19 red brick OLD VICARAGE. E of The Square, in LIMES AVENUE, the lodge to THE LIMES, an early C19 villa in its own grounds. Stucco, two storeys, five bays, with a central full-height bow window. The entrance front has a porch with Doric columns *in antis*.

OLD HALL, No. 5 Orchard Street. Inscribed on the two-storey porch 'Nisi Deus Frustra 1648'. Timber-framed with brick in-filling, the S side with twin gables. No fancy timber decoration. (Similar to the Old Hall is No. 4 THE HOLLOW. DOE)

WOODLANDS HOSPITAL, Etwall Road. An early model asylum designed on humane principles by *Duesbury*, 1849–51. It is a sober neo-Tudor structure with shaped gables and mullioned and transomed windows. Symmetrical S front formerly with three symmetrically placed thin towers.

NORMANTON-BY-DERBY

ST GILES. 1861 by *Giles & Brookhouse*. E window 1882. The

only fragment from the previous church is a Norman carved stone from a lintel, almost unrecognizable (S porch). – PLATE. Chalice and Paten Cover on knob foot, 1645.

(ST STEPHEN, Sinfin Lane. 1935 by *P. H. Currey*.)

SPONDON

ST WERBURGH. A largish church, well placed above the street. It would be architecturally unusually interesting if it had not been so thoroughly restored, first in 1826 and then again in 1891–2, by *J. Oldrid Scott*. It was completely rebuilt after a fire in 1340, in which year the inhabitants were granted exemption from taxes while the rebuilding went on. W tower with spire recessed behind battlements, as usual in Derbyshire. Large nave with three-bay arcades to the wide aisles. Octagonal piers, double-chamfered arches, fairly finely moulded capitals. The chancel has ogee-reticulated windows (E and S probably renewed), the aisle E windows have fanciful flowing tracery of different designs. All three are of five lights. The N aisle N windows again have reticulated tracery, the S windows of the S aisle flowing forms. In the chancel N wall a low recess for a tomb or Easter Sepulchre and a stone lectern built into the wall (cf. Chaddesden (Derby), Crich, Etwall, Mickleover (Derby), Taddington). In the S wall, SEDILIA and PISCINA. – STAINED GLASS. (E window inscribed 1892–3, by *J. Powell & Sons* of Whitefriars: an intricate design. R. Hubbuck) – SE window S aisle, 1904, also by *Powell*. – PLATE. Two Cups, 1624 and 1655; Paten, 1665.

Near the church, in Church Street, Potter Street, Park Road, and Sitwell Street, several good Georgian brick houses, the best THE HOMESTEAD, Sitwell Street, five bays, two and a half storeys, with quoins and a central 'Venetian' entrance with Doric columns and arched windows above it, the upper one reaching into the pediment. (Date 1740 on rainwater-head with initials I.A. Good staircase and contemporary panelling. DOE) (Fine Bakewell-style wrought-iron balustrades to the main steps. ES) Former COACH HOUSE, altered, but with an ogee-topped lantern.

In Park Road, a pair of C18 ashlar gateways with round-headed arches and rusticated walling, formerly the entrance to FIELD HOUSE (demolished) but now leading to SPONDON PARK and SPONDON HOUSE SCHOOLS, 1962 and 1964 by *F. Hamer Crossley* (County Architect) in association with *Grey, Goodman & Partners*.

DERWENT WOODLANDS *see* LADYBOWER RESERVOIR

3050

DETHICK

The parish is Dethick, Lea, and Holloway, three separate villages.

ST JOHN THE BAPTIST. In a fine position on a hill close to the buildings replacing the manor house of the Babingtons and the surviving big stone-built C16 BARN.* The view to the S across the valley is splendid. The church possesses, thanks to Sir Anthony Babington, a lavishly built W tower, dated 1530. It has diagonal buttresses and the unusual feature of a tall polygonal SE stair-turret. The windows are Late Perp, and a frieze with a proud display of the shields of Sir Anthony and his kinsmen runs below the bell-openings. Eight short pinnacles on the battlements. The tower arch towards the nave is surprisingly narrow for its height. The church itself is insignificant after this monumental tower, aisleless and without visible division between nave and chancel. Two lancet windows show that it is C13, and the difference in material shows that the clerestory was later. No furnishings of interest.

CHRIST CHURCH, Holloway. 1901–3 by *P. H. Currey*. With big crossing tower and freely Perp details. The position is as fine as that of the old church. – PLATE. Paten, *c.* 1782, Italian, parcel-gilt.

LEAHURST, in Holloway village. C17 gabled house with low mullioned windows, much enlarged in 1825 by Florence Nightingale's father to his own design.

LEA WOOD, W of Leahurst. By *Nesfield*, 1874–7, in the typical style of this architect and his partnership with young Norman Shaw. Many materials freely mixed: stone, fancy tiling, tall brick chimneystacks (tops gone), half-timbered gables, and plaster infillings with incised floral patterns and patterns in relief. Not at all connected with local traditions. Also by *Nesfield*, the lodge and remains of landscaping on which he consulted his father.‡

* (The barn belongs to CHURCH FARM. MANOR FARM, C17, incorporates earlier masonry and a massive chimneystack. The outbuildings of these farms and of BABINGTON FARM, C18, have fragments of medieval carbing set in. RE)

‡ Information from Mr Andrew Saint.

LEA HALL, in Lea village. An inscription reads PN (Peter Nightingale) 1754. The house is rather old-fashioned for this date. Georgian stone façade of five bays, the centre bay distinguished by Roman Doric giant pilasters. Door with pediment and Gibbs surround. Short brick side bays, slightly lower and set back. Some windows glazed with an unusual tracery pattern of quarter-circles. Parallel but longer vernacular rear range with mullioned windows. C18 staircase with turned and twisted balusters.

LEA MILLS. The original mills were built by Peter Nightingale, a rival of Arkwright, and bought by Smedley in the 1840s. The present buildings for worsted manufacture are C19, linked by a bridge across the road. Near by groups of workers' cottages and a branch, 1802, of the Cromford Canal built to serve Nightingale's lead-smelting mills at Lea.*

HIGH PEAK JUNCTION. *See* Cromford.

DINTING *see* GLOSSOP

DOLL TOR STONE CIRCLE *see* STANTON-IN-THE-PEAK

DOVE HOLES *see* CHAPEL-EN-LE-FRITH

DOVERIDGE

1030

ST CUTHBERT. The church was in the grounds of Doveridge Hall.‡ Now that the Hall has been pulled down, it lies in a happy green solitude close to the river Dove, although the developing village has crept towards it on the E. To its E a very old yew tree and a yew canopy. The building itself is distinguished by its broad and wide C13 chancel with fine long lancet windows and a S doorway with one filleted order, and a W tower in its lower parts Norman (see the corbel-table and arch into the nave), but remodelled in the C13. The tower windows are lancets and above coupled lancets with dogtooth decoration. The upper parts of

* The cottages bear a striking resemblance to housing in North Street, Cromford, which may imply a closer connection with Nightingale and Arkwright than is generally thought.

‡ It was begun in 1769 by *Edward Stevens*, a pupil of Chambers, for Sir Henry Cavendish. Very conventional Palladian mansion with hexastyle portico and pavilions, demolished 1934. (N of the church a red brick house which may have belonged to the Hall. RE)

the tower and the spire recessed behind the broad battlements are later. The aisles have Dec windows with flowing (S, renewed?) and reticulated tracery (N). The knave is very wide too, and the absence of a chancel arch (and of much stained glass) emphasizes the airiness of the interior. The N arcade is of three bays, the S arcade of four smaller ones. Both sides have octagonal piers and double-chamfered arches. The C13 W tower arch is very low and narrow; the clerestory and E window are C15. – STAINED GLASS. Jumbled fragments of medieval glass in the SW window. – Two N windows 1954 by *J. E. Nuttgens*. – PLATE. Chalice and Paten Cover, *c.* 1619. – MONUMENT. Incised alabaster slab to a priest, probably C14. – Ralph Okeover † 1487. Incised slab with a brass surround in front of a wall recess. – Big wall-monument to William Davenport † 1640 and his wife † 1639. Of her the inscription says:

Wearied with lingering motion drop erewhile
A star to rest under this quiet pile
Whose unstain'd lustre more adorned her sphere
Than all the glorious beauties sparkled there.

Thomas Milward † 1658. Wall-monument similar to one at Brampton with crudely carved Fames holding back curtains from the tablet.

(In the village several worthwhile brick and timber-framed houses, e.g. LOWERSTREET FARM, C16 timber-framed, THE GABLES, C17 and C18 brick, and the MANOR HOUSE, C18. RE)

BROCKSFORD HALL, 1 m E, S of the A50. A neo-Jacobean house of 1893 by *Douglas & Fordham* of Chester.* Brick with stone dressings and the brick diapering of which Douglas made such great use in his work for the Duke of Westminster on the Eaton estate. Five-bay entrance front, symmetrical in massing but not in detail, plus a further gable to the l. A half-timbered gatehouse leads to the stable court. The garden front of the main block is symmetrical in massing only, and to the r. is a pyramid-roofed tower. Inside, and said to have come from Fenton Hall, is some Jacobean woodwork, and an C18 staircase with turned balusters, a swept rail, and scroll enrichment on the stair ends.

(E of Brocksford Hall, LEY HILL FARM, N of the A50, brick, vernacular, but with a huge domed semicircular bay, and HOME FARM, S of the A50, C17 timber-framed. RE)

* Information from Mr Edward Hubbard.

DRAYCOTT*

4030

ST MARY (former Methodist Chapel). 1836.

(DRAYCOTT HOUSE, Nottingham Road. Late C18, red brick, three storeys, three bays with a projecting centre. Columned porch, Venetian windows to the first floor. Side elevation similar but with pediment to the centre.‡ Stable block in similar style with cupola. RE)

Dominating the village VICTORIA MILLS, a C19 tenement lace factory.

DRONFIELD

3070

ST JOHN THE BAPTIST. A dark grey church with a Perp W tower with spire, and a tall chancel, more ambitious than the rest of the church.§ Buttresses Dec, enriched with tracery. Its high and wide N and S windows have (renewed) early C14 tracery, intersected; but at the top the intersections are interrupted and replaced by a cusped quatrefoil. The E window is very odd indeed, of seven lights and only divided by mullions and transoms: no curve, no diagonal. Is it C16?* To the N of the chancel is a two-storeyed vestry. The S aisle has intersected E and W windows, also with the top intersections replaced by quatrefoils, but here within circles. The S doorway goes with that date. Inside, the tower arch tells of a date earlier than the exterior reveals. The imposts on the nave arcades look early C14. In the chancel an ugly modern roof, an ogee-headed doorway into the vestry, and SEDILIA with thin filleted shafts and thickly crocketed ogees and gables. The arches are double-cusped with small figures in the cusps. The PISCINA, against the custom quite away from the sedilia, is of two lights with ogee tracery. – STALLS. Some old parts; also poppyheads. – PULPIT. Jacobean, of very good quality, similar to that at Chesterfield. The columns are studded with small knobs all over. – STAINED GLASS. Fragments of C14 glass in two chancel windows and in the first window from the E in the nave. – PLATE. Paten of *c.* 1520; two

* The parish is Draycott and Church Wilne. For the medieval parish church, *see* Wilne.

‡ It is related in style to Long Eaton Hall about 3 m. away and, according to Mr Evans and Mr Saunders, may be by *Pickford* of Derby.

§ It should be compared with the C14 chancels at Chaddesden (Derby), Norbury, Sandiacre, and Tideswell (C. Wilson).

* The original tracery fell out in 1563.

Cups, 1601 and 1650; two Patens on feet, 1697 and 1714; Flagon, 1759. – MONUMENTS. Plate with brasses of two Priests, Thomas and Richard Gomfrey, 1399, the figures *c.* 33 in. long. – Sir Richard Barley, alabaster effigy of mid C15 date on a tomb-chest with angels holding shields. – Brass to John Fanshawe † 1580, wife and children.

THE TOWN. Dronfield must have been especially prosperous in the C18. The town and the outskirts have a remarkable number of sizeable mansions. At the far end of the High Street the MANOR HOUSE (Library), probably early C18, with upright windows of one mullion and one transom at the back, hipped roof, and Tuscan pilasters to the l. and r. of an arched doorway. In front of it the highly Gothic TOWN CROSS, erected in 1848 to commemorate the repeal of the Corn Laws. The UNITED METHODIST CHURCH, though dated 1863, is still Late Georgian in style with arched door, arched windows, and pediment. (Opposite, ROOKERY COTTAGE, one wing of a larger C17 house with hood-moulds on the side elevation linked to form a string-course; No. 21 also C17; and No. 19 (THE HALL), C18. Plain mullion-and-transom cross windows, open parapet with square balusters, segmental pedimented door. Crudely detailed but in advance of Chiverton House and Rose Hill (*see* below). RE) (Also on the N side a stone L-shaped BARN of five bays. Early C15 kingpost roof with braced principal post. Clearly a remnant of a two-storey dwelling converted to a barn. S. Jones). Opposite the church RED HOUSE, dated 1731 and built by public subscription for the usher of the GRAMMAR SCHOOL (No. 18 Church Street, built *c.* 1580 but with C19 windows). Red House is of brick with quoins, as is the neighbouring and contemporary OLD VICARAGE with two canted bay-windows. Also in Church Street the C17 GREEN DRAGON INN, rendered, with mullioned windows, and S of the church a CRUCK BARN with five trusses encased in a stone structure of no interest.

The other houses are farther away.* CHIVERTON HOUSE to the W, across the railway, just above Chesterfield Road, is dated 1712. It has a symmetrical front with the same cross windows as the manor house but still a middle gable. The door-head is depressed segmental and rusticated. Next to it ROSE HILL, in spite of its date, 1719, still with low mullioned windows and a thin semicircular door-head (like the Peacock at Rowsley, 1652). It combines two symmetrical outer gables with a balu-

* The Midland Railway, driven through in 1870 to reach Sheffield, effectively cut the settlement in two.

strade, between, i.e., the old and the new roof motifs (cf. Bagshaw Hall Bakewell, 1684). HALLOWES GOLF CLUB HOUSE lies on the hill to the SE. This, of H-shape, with gables on the wings, has a date-stone 1657 over the door and on the other side an C18 segmental pediment over the other door. The windows are low and mullioned, but their arrangement is symmetrical and they are tied to a long uninterrupted string-course. Barn of 1638, with six-bay queen-post roof.

About ½ m. E a feature once prominent in the county, i.e. a large group of C19 beehive COKE OVENS. These, about forty-eight arranged in banks of twenty-four, are associated with Summerley Colliery, of which a tall brick engine house survives.

BRONZE AGE BARROWS W of Dronfield Woodhouse.

DUFFIELD

3040

ST ALKMUND. Outside the village, to the SE. W tower with angle buttresses connected on top by a horizontal band below the battlements; recessed spire. Tower arch to the nave treble-stepped. All this looks C14, and probably early. The church is much restored (in 1846 by *St Aubyn*, in 1896 by *J. O. Scott*), and it is not certain how much of the detail is reliable. N aisle, E window, and N transept E window of three stepped lancet lights, i.e. *c.* 1300 or earlier. Chancel E window Perp of five lights with panel tracery. The other windows straight-headed (S aisle windows C19). The interior has three-bay arcades on both sides with octagonal piers and double-chamfered arches. The N chamfering seems earlier. The date is controversial. Dr Cox called the N arcade C17, Mr Ward thinks of a Norman core much remodelled. In the chancel N wall a broad, low, ogee-arched recess. – (WEATHERCOCK. 1719 by *Bakewell.* ES) – PLATE. Flagon, 1846 by *Francis Skidmore.* – MONUMENTS. Sir Roger Mynors † 1539 and wife, alabaster effigies on a tomb-chest with saints in round-arched cusped panels. – Anthony Bradshaw † 1614; a remarkably original standing wall-monument set up in 1600. No effigies; instead a frieze dividing the substructure with rusticated pillars and inscription tablets from the superstructure also with rusticated pillars. On top are inscription plate and obelisks and achievement. On the frieze incised demi-figures of husband in the middle, two wives at the outer corners, and twenty children between, four sons on the l. of the father, sixteen daughters in two tiers to the r. of the father. All figures have their initials to the l. and r. of their heads. Acrostic at the foot of the inscription below the figures.

DUFFIELD CASTLE, one of the most formidable Norman fortresses in England, was erected by the Ferrers, a leading family in the county. It had a keep of 95 by 93 ft with walls *c.* 15 ft thick. The size of this C12 keep was thus only matched by the White Tower in London and by Colchester. Only one course of the foundations is visible in two places, and only a small part of the motte survives to the S with a fragment of the ditch in the grounds of Castlehill House. Excavations in 1957 established that the first castle (C11) had a timber keep and dry ditch and that the site had been occupied first in the C3.

DUFFIELD HALL. The core is Elizabethan or slightly later. The mullion-and-transom cross windows, two bay-windows, porch, and lower wing on the main (E) front are of 1871. Of the original façade only the oval vents in the gables. In a ground-floor room a fireplace of *c.* 1600. House restored, and behind it a head office for the Derbyshire Building Society begun in 1975 by *George Grey & Partners.*

To the N of the Hall, TOWN STREET is particularly rich in Georgian houses. Note especially GERVASE HOUSE (No. 48, towards the N end), a three-bay brick house with tripartite windows and Adamish trim; THE FERNS (No. 56), brick, three bays, one-bay pediment, quoins at the angles and flanking the centre bay; on the opposite side THE MEADOWS with its stables (later Georgian, also brick, with full-height arched recesses and a pediment), and past the Hall the delightful BAPTIST CHAPEL of 1830 with brick front facing the little triangular graveyard to the S. A dwelling house is attached to the chapel. SW of the chapel, POTTERELL'S ALMSHOUSES, 1810.

Duffield is at the junction of brick and stone areas. Tamworth Street, off the W side of Town Street, is lined with fine stone walls and behind these two C18 stone houses: THE PARK, Late Georgian, large, with a balustraded Doric porch, the core said to be Tudor, and TAMWORTH HOUSE, early C18, with a rusticated plinth and angle pilasters ending in acroteria. A lost pumphead was dated 1714.

In Wirksworth Road one of the most effectively detailed modern buildings in the county, the BRANCH LIBRARY by *George Grey & Partners* in collaboration with the *County Architect,* 1963–4. Very simple rectangular system-built structure with blue brick and glass panels, clerestory lit and slightly raised on a recessed podium.

See p. 409

Medieval POTTERY KILNS at Burley Hill.

DUNSTAN HALL *see* CHESTERFIELD, p. 150

EARL STERNDALE

0060

ST MICHAEL. 1828–9 by *G. E. Hamilton*, chancel by *R. R. Duke*, 1877. Rebuilt and refurnished in 1950–2 after war damage. Stone, aisleless, with single- and double-light windows and a battlemented tower. – (FONT. Probably early C12. DOE) – PLATE. Jug, 1781 by *Hester Bateman*.

(GLUTTON FARM. Date-stone 1675. Fine example of a farmhouse with barn attached. J. B. Wright)

FOX HOLE CAVE, High Wheeldon Hill. This cave was occupied in the Upper Palaeolithic, Mesolithic, and Neolithic periods. Romano-British occupation is also attested.

EASTWOOD HALL *see* ASHOVER

ECKINGTON

4070

SS. PETER AND PAUL. A church of exceptional architectural interest for its contribution to the C12 and C13 styles in Derbyshire. The tower is the most impressive piece, big and square, with broad, flat buttresses, an ambitious picturesquely decayed W doorway of three orders with E.E. detail but a round arch, two large lancets on the stage above, then one small lancet, and then the bell stage with three lancets towards each side. All this can hardly be later than the first years of the C13. The spire (with one tier of dormer windows) is recessed behind a parapet (no battlements). It is relatively broad and may be early C14. The tower arch towards the nave rests on imposts with keeled demi-shafts; the arch is double-chamfered. There were originally lower double-chamfered arches on double-chamfered imposts to the N and S as well to connect the tower with former aisles projecting that far W. The uncommonly tall nave arcades link up with this story in an instructive way. They are of five bays, and the two E piers are evidently a little earlier than the rest. The E responds are keeled, the capitals waterleaf on the N side and some sort of crocket type on the S, i.e. late C12 rather than early C13. The piers are circular, the capitals moulded, the arches round and double-stepped. The two pairs of W piers are octagonal, the arches as before. So these bays are presumably of the time of the tower. The chancel arch goes with the E responds, but is near enough in style to the tower arch to show that building proceeded fast. The exterior of the church tells nothing of this interior story. The N aisle shows that the E parts are early C14 (see the E window, only visible inside), its W parts C15; the castellated clerestory is Perp too, and the S aisle and S porch were completely remodelled in 1763, in a not at all provincial style by *John Platt* of Rotherham. The porch is heavily rusticated, the aisle windows are arched. The W end of the S aisle was rebuilt again in 1802 by *J. Turner*. The chancel was treated similarly, but re-gothicized in 1907. An unusually elaborate squint connects N aisle and chancel. – COMMUNION RAIL. Handsome early C18 with foliated balusters. – ALTAR PAINTING. Said to be by one of the *Carracci*; bought in Spain by Sitwell Sitwell. – MONUMENTS. George † 1667 and Margaret Sitwell † 1658, wall-monument with two wildly gesticulating demi-figures. – Sir Sitwell Sitwell † 1811, tall Corinthian column embedded in the wall, carrying a small urn. It is by *White Watson*. – Several more Sitwell memorials.

RECTORY. Handsome Late Georgian stone front, five centre bays and two broad pedimented angle bays with Venetian windows and tripartite semicircular windows above. The present appearance of the house is due to the Rev. Christopher Alderson, who also improved the grounds. *The Gentleman's Magazine* of 1795 says that he was so renowned as a garden improver that he was employed at Windsor as well.*

(Former METHODIST CHAPEL, N of the High Street,‡ with a handsome mid-C19 classical stone façade. DOE)

MOSBOROUGH HALL, N of the village and now over the county boundary in Sheffield. Elizabethan or Jacobean house with two projecting wings and a recessed centre. Of the original date the only witnesses are some mullioned windows, now partly hidden inside the house, and some moulded beams and plasterwork. The entrance side was remodelled in the C18 and the centre between the wings filled in; see the doorway, the arched central window, and the characteristic oval window of the entrance side, and the broken pediment of the doorway in the centre of the main front. Now a hotel.

RIDGEWAY. *See* p. 309.

EDALE

1080

HOLY TRINITY. 1885–6 by *William Dawes* of Manchester.

* Information kindly given by Sir Osbert Sitwell.

‡ Demolished (1977).

Aisleless, with broach-spire completed in 1889. Bleak interior with some insipid STAINED GLASS by *Comper*. – PLATE. Cup, 1795, an oration prize from Trinity College, Cambridge.

EDALE MILL, towards Hope. Early C19 mill converted with their usual skill by the Landmark Trust (*George Robb*, architect).

EDDLESTOW

3060

½m. W of Ashover

The barn behind the house has two fireplaces, probably older than the house which, with the few surviving mullioned windows at the back and the gabled two-storeyed porch, appears Elizabethan or Jacobean.

EDENSOR

2060

The village of Edensor was removed from its original to its present site between 1838 and 1842. It was the wish of the sixth Duke of Devonshire to have it out of sight of Chatsworth, and the planning of the new site lay in the hands of his gardener *Paxton*. In 1840 he was joined in designing the village houses by *John Robertson*, a draughtsman (1829–40) to J. C. Loudon and responsible for several designs in Loudon's *Encyclopaedia of Cottage, Farm and Villa Architecture*, edition of 1846. The church came a good deal later, though it now dominates the picture. Its spire spoils the scale of the village.

96

ST PETER. 1867 by *Sir George Gilbert Scott*, who incorporated some old fabric. Tall E.E. tower and spire, E.E. interior with two aisles, circular and octagonal piers including four of the C13, clerestory, and chancel (typical, competent Scott). In the chancel SEDILIA in the best crocketed ogee style. In the C15 S porch a few Norman fragments from the old church and a foliated CROSS SLAB. In the chapel at the E end of the S aisle the vast MONUMENT to William, first Earl of Devonshire, and Henry Cavendish † 1625 and 1616. The two bodies under a low fourposter with black columns and black covering slab. Henry appears as a skeleton on a straw mat, William in his shroud with his face exposed. Extremely grand back architecture with two martial flanking figures, then arches with on the l. armour, on the r. purple, coronet, and sword hung up, and in the middle an angel holding the black inscription tablet and blowing a trumpet. The whole is surmounted by a big

44

broken pediment.* – STAINED GLASS. S aisle E window 1882 by *Hardman*. – PLATE. Chalice and Paten Cover on knob foot, 1661. – BRASS to John Beton † 1570, servant to Mary Queen of Scots. – In the CHURCHYARD *Paxton* † 1865 is buried.

At the foot of the churchyard a green with some older houses and Late Georgian stables on one side, close to it the castellated entrance lodge to the village, completed by *Robertson* in 1842, and a beginning of the typical architecture of Edensor. This is an attempt at making the Blaise Castle type of picturesque and fanciful artificial village respectable by good solid stone masonry and a display of more serious architectural styles: a Norman fountain by the side of the green, next to it a house, built as an inn in the C18 (see the inn sign staples in the wall), and given a Swiss *châlet* roof, and so on. Higher up the village street one can see the hideously elongated debased Italianate windows which Loudon liked so much in his *Encyclopaedia of Villa Architecture*, side by side with Jacobean gables, bargeboarding, Norman window surrounds, and Tudor chimneys. The best part of the design is the general loose and leafy layout, for instance the way in which the village street ends on top with a house with an octagonal turret and looks down from there across the valley to the Hunting Tower of Chatsworth. 'Everything', says Bagshaw's Gazetteer of 1840, 'tends to show his Grace's taste, good feeling, and liberal disposition towards those in humble circumstances.'

Outside the Edensor village gate and through the Buxton Lodge on the N a further, typically Loudonesque villa is preserved. The BUXTON LODGE itself is a design of *Wyatville*, dated 1837, a by-product of his vast work at Chatsworth (in a far more playful romantic spirit than Edensor village), half-timbered, with brick infillings and fancy bargeboards. Completed by *Paxton* in 1839 and illustrated by *Robertson* in Loudon's *Encyclopaedia* (Design X).‡ Opposite the EDENSOR INN, now Chatsworth Institute, a fine brick building of *c.* 1775, attributed to *James Paine*:§ five bays with projecting lower wings with Venetian windows. The big porch looks later. It was built to serve the needs of well-to-do travellers along the fourth Duke's new N-S road through the park.

Farther N on the way to Baslow on the W side is DUNSA HOUSE,

* Mrs Esdaile attributes the monument to *Colt*.

‡ No doubt an instructive example for the originators of the Domestic Revival style.

§ According to Mr P. Leach.

an Italianate villa built by *Paxton* *c.* 1848. On the E side was BARBROOK HOUSE (demolished), designed by *Paxton* for himself in 1842–7, extended in 1851–2. Also Italianate.

For other estate buildings *see* Baslow, Beeley, and Pilsley.

EDLASTON

1040

ST JAMES. Small and low. The distinguishing feature the extremely pretty bellcote of 1900, with two bells hanging exposed and all the details typical of the date. The architect was *E. Arden Minty* of Westminster. Chancel of the C14 with E window of *c.* 1870. The chancel arch also C14. The nave S side has a picturesque haphazard grouping of straight-headed windows. – PLATE. Chalice and Flagon, 1734 by *Thomas Evesdon*; Paten Cover on knob foot, *c.* 1734.

EDNASTON

2040

EDNASTON MANOR. Built in 1912–14 for W. G. Player and described by Butler as 'perhaps the most perfect country house that *Lutyens* designed'.* It is certainly extremely lucid in its planning. The style is Queen Anne, the plan is an H. Towards the curved entrance court (W) the two-storey, five-bay brick façade is divided by stone pilasters with monogrammed capitals. On either side is a windowless bay set back. The garden front to the S has the two projecting wings of the H. Here the pilasters and windows of the recessed centre are irregularly spaced, and to the E and W are garden pavilions with Tuscan columns. The E façade to the offices is plainer, the N façade of the servants' hall appropriately more domestic, with gables. Inside, the drawing room and staircase are in the W wing, the dining room and offices in the E wing, with the hall and servants' hall between. Only the staircase seems remote because the intended billiard room was not built to its N to balance the NE projection.

(HOME FARM and RUCK O' STONES COTTAGE are by *Lutyens* (N. Taylor), and a house in the village (S of the A52) bears many Lutyens hallmarks. RE)

ST MARY'S NURSING HOME. Attached to the house is a pavilion-like stuccoed chapel by *Montague Associates*, 1963–4. In the tall deeply recessed windows, STAINED GLASS by *Reyntiens*.

* A. S. G. Butler, *The Architecture of Sir Edwin Lutyens*, vol. 1, p. 50.

2020

EGGINTON

ST WILFRID. A small church mostly of *c.* 1300, see the W tower bell-openings (but the W window Perp), the N aisle windows, and the chancel windows, and inside both arcades. That on the S side has short quatrefoil piers, that on the N circular piers. Double-chamfered arches on both sides. In the chancel SEDILIA and PISCINA trefoil-headed. The S aisle windows from outside form a nice muddled group with a later Tudor window in the middle. Inside in the S aisle S wall an equally muddled series of recesses. Restoration 1891 by *Evans & Jolly*. – PULPIT made from panelling from Egginton Hall. – STAINED GLASS. Good fragments of Crucifixus, Virgin, St John, other figures, all small, dark colours, C13. – Other C13–15 fragments. – PLATE. Chalice and Paten, 1703 by *Jonathan Clifton*; Flagon, 1752. – MONUMENTS. Civilian, holding his heart in his hands, very damaged. – Francis Every † 1690, black medallion with white frontal bust, cheek propped up on the hand, badly done.

MONKS' BRIDGE. Medieval but widened in 1775. Four segmental arches, three with chamfered ribs. Beyond Monks' Bridge a brick AQUEDUCT carrying the Trent and Mersey Canal, engineered by *James Brindley*.

EGGINTON HALL was demolished in 1955.*

5070

ELMTON

ST PETER. Rebuilt completely in 1773. The W tower was left incomplete. Nave and lower apsed chancel. The windows are arched. On the N side no windows at all. – PULPIT, with tester: nice contemporary work. – PLATE. Cup, 1669; Paten, 1717.

MARKLAND GRIPS. Promontory fort, originally trivallate and covering 10½ acres in area. Both Iron Age and Roman occupation is attested. Near the E end of the fort, four Neolithic burials had been deposited in a cave.

* It was built for Sir Edward Every in 1782–3 by *Mr Wyatt*, probably *Joseph Wyatt*, and succeeded a house of 1758–61 for which the Wyatt family had been contractors. A finely detailed porch led into a circular room projecting as a bow in the middle of a nine-bay front. The other main front had two bows and a tripartite window between. All plain, of brick, two-storeyed, with top balustrade.

ELTON

2060

ALL SAINTS. Unbuttressed W tower with arched windows and battlements: 1812. The nave has lancet windows of two lancet lights with pierced spandrels and the chancel an E window with intersected tracery. These windows are slightly later alterations. Two N windows in the nave are simply arched. – FONT. Replica of the one taken to Youlgreave in 1838 (*see* p. 362).

In the village a number of worthwhile houses, especially the Youth Hostel, with a big semicircular pediment above the door, dated 1668 and 1715 on the S side, and a pair still with two-light low mullioned windows, dated 1717.

ELTON COMMON, ½m. S. Several Bronze Age barrows.

BORTHER LOW, ½m. W. Bronze Age barrow.

ELVASTON

4030

ST BARTHOLOMEW. In the grounds, close to the mansion. The Perp W tower of unusual design, tall, three-storeyed, with angle buttresses and on each side two tall two-light bell-openings placed under one ogee arch. Top with eight pinnacles, renewed in 1847. Nave and S aisle. The latter has a lancet W window and S windows with intersected tracery, i.e. late C13. The arcade piers (three bays) are octagonal and carry double-chamfered arches. The N nave windows with straight-sided arches. This and the clerestory Perp. Lord Mountjoy of Elvaston provided for the completion of the church in 1474. The chancel of *c.* 1200 restored and extended by *Bodley*, 1904–5. The sanctuary has Bodley's characteristic stencilled wall decoration and pretty roof. – SCREENS to chancel and E bay of S aisle. Both have ogee-headed one-light sections with panel tracery above; the rood screen with richer crocketing than the parclose screen. Behind the latter a Jacobean FAMILY PEW. – PAINTING. Virgin and Child by *Pasinelli*, 1693. – STAINED GLASS. (Chancel N surely by *Burlison & Grylls*. It replaces earlier glass by *Baillie*, hence the inscription dated 1853. R. Hubbuck) – Nave N by *Comper*, 1934–5. – PLATE. Slender Chalice and plain Paten, early C17. – MONUMENTS. Sir John Stanhope † 1610, standing wall-monument with alabaster effigies between coupled columns under a deep coffered arch. – Memorial to William Piggin, plasterer, 1621, handsome simple tablet with brass inscription. – Sir John Stanhope † 1638, the fragments reassembled in 1731; in a transeptal extension with a tall mullioned and transomed side-window, under a fine classical ceiling, typical of *c.* 1730–5. – Third Earl of Harrington † 1829, large wall-monument with musing allegorical figure by an urn on a tall pedestal against which leans a shield with the head of Medusa, one of only three monuments by *Canova* in England. The others are at Speen, Berks, and Belton, Lincs. – Algernon Russell Gayleard Stanhope † 1847, recumbent boy lying on a straw mat. Unsigned. – Fifth Earl of Harrington † 1862, recumbent effigy on tomb-chest, unsigned. The inscription says that the Earl 'was with Lord Byron in Greece' and there erected the first school and the first printing press, entirely at his own expense.

ELVASTON CASTLE. The grounds are more famous than the house. Derbyshire County Council with Derby Borough Council restored them in 1968–70 and opened them to the public as a Country Park. They were designed for the Earl of Harrington between 1830 and 1850 by *William Barron*, who came to Elvaston from the Botanic Gardens in Edinburgh, and they can boast long straight avenues as well as fine landscaping (with a wide selection of trees as in the almost contemporary Arboretum at Derby), a large serpentine lake, and also plenty of topiary. In the grounds, and all of 1830–50, a MOORISH TEMPLE, with a roof with convex slopes and odd fancy-shaped windows, the interior painted with Moorish twisted columns, the MOORISH ARCH, ALHAMBRA, SUMMERHOUSE, RACQUETS COURT, and elaborate GROTTOES on the N side of the lake. Associated with the lake, a small water-powered PUMP HOUSE containing an elegant four-cylinder table pump by *Harrison* of Derby, 1832. SE of the house STATUARY on pedestals including a fine lead Farnese Hercules, probably by *Nost*, and two vases by *Jacob Cresant* dated 1738. At the end of the S avenue the GOLDEN GATES, said to be of Spanish origin. (Apparently C19. DOE)

The house was remodelled in a castellated Gothick style to the designs of *James Wyatt*, executed after his death in 1817 by *Robert Walker*, a pupil of Thomas Leverton. It has a two-storey symmetrical entrance front (S) with a one-storey porch and two slightly projecting end bays with turrets. The r. one is the remaining part of the original house visible on the exterior, brick with a canted bay with mullioned and transomed windows. It carries the date 1633. Inside the E wing early C17 panelling. A cistern is dated 1705 and of that date is the drawing room inside. The C19 work, ashlar-faced, has also a symmetrical nine-bay E front with an emphasized centre by

L. N. Cottingham, 1830–40, and a stuccoed side to the stables court which formerly had a picturesque water tower in its centre. (On its W side the COACH HOUSE, also by *Wyatt*, ashlar, Gothic, with a central carriageway and a clumsy clock tower. The kitchen court has been enclosed by an arcaded stone building to house museum exhibits (*R. Kenning*, County Architect, 1970). RE)*

Inside, the ENTRANCE HALL is the best early C19 interior, jade green, dark red, and gold, with an elaborate tierceron-vault with pendants and niches for coats of armour. The LIBRARY, in a similar vein, has a fireplace carved with scenes of chivalry. (The spacious classical STAIRCASE is possibly by *Benjamin Dean Wyatt*.‡ RE) Apart from these the finest rooms are late C18, some with good fireplaces.

THURLESTONE GRANGE, 1 m. SE, on the A6. A handsome C18 brick house standing back from the road. Enlarged by one bay *c.* 1840.

END LOW *see* YOULGREAVE

ETWALL

2030

ST HELEN. Nicely placed between the village street and the almshouses. Short W tower with diagonal buttresses and low unembattled body. The windows all Perp or later. On the S side they are of an unusual design, perhaps late C17 or C18. The only external feature telling of a greater age is the S doorway, round-headed, C13. But inside the N arcade of three bays is Norman. The piers are circular, the capitals scalloped, and the arches unmoulded and unchamfered. The fourth arch taller, wider, pointed and double-chamfered. Restoration 1881 by *F. J. Robinson*. – SEATING. Port (N chancel) Chapel: Elizabethan. – SOUTH DOOR. C17, handsome. – LECTERN. Stone, built into the N chancel wall (cf. Chaddesden (Derby), Taddington, Spondon (Derby), Crich), probably C13, i.e. a proof that the chancel wall is as old as that. – PLATE. Paten on foot, 1691, Chalice, 1708, by *Daniel Sleath*. – MONUMENTS. Incised alabaster slab of a civilian † 1503, wife, and children, badly preserved. – Brass

* A barn (post and truss with purlins, arcaded on the N side) from Church Farm, Sandiacre, is to be re-sited at Elvaston.

‡ The Architectural Publications Society Dictionary gives the names of both *James Wyatt* (1813) and *Benjamin Dean Wyatt* (1812) as architects of the remodelling.

to Henry Port † 1512 and wife and children; his brass lost. – Top of tomb-chest with civilian and two wives, the heads broken off. Probably Sir John Port † 1541. The figures in sunk relief so that a broad band can run across their bodies at the level of the border of the slab. The canopy may belong to the early C19 restoration. – Sir John Port † 1557. Brasses of husband, wives, and children kneeling, against the back wall of a finely carved straight-topped recess in the chancel S wall.

JOHN PORT SECONDARY SCHOOL (1955–70 by the *County Architect*) stands on the site of Etwall Hall, demolished in 1954. It was early C18, stone-faced, the S front of five bays and two storeys with a top balustrade and to l. and r. two-and-a-half-storey projections, also top-balustraded. The wrought-iron GATES by *Bakewell* of *c.* 1730 have been re-erected (1976).

74 ETWALL HOSPITAL. Almshouses founded in 1550 by Sir John Port, who also founded Repton School. Rebuilt in 1681. Of this date only the central frontispiece gives evidence by its scrolly pediment. The rest of the large composition might well be considered much older. It is a brick structure on three sides of a courtyard with an E wing, the ground floor with four-centred doorway and two windows for each little house, all these features stone-framed. Plain gables and massive chimneystacks.

ETWALL LODGE, S of the village. 1812 for the Master of the Hospital. Two-storey brick house with a stone pilastered doorcase and the Port arms in the parapet.

Several nice houses in the village, notably the early C18 RED HOUSE facing the Longford road (five bays, two and a half storeys) and its Late Georgian neighbour THE LIMES, built as an extension to the Red House, and ETWALL LAWN, C17 in origin, with a pretty early C19 *cottage orné* garden façade and half-timbered C17 building in the grounds. In MAIN STREET No. 42 is the former Post Office (front with three neo-Jacobean shaped gables, probably Early Victorian, though the house itself is older).

2070

EYAM

ST LAWRENCE. C13 chancel with lancet windows, C13 N arcade of three bays with one circular pier and one quatrefoil pier keeled. The arches are double-chamfered, but one of the two chamfers is slight. The S arcade has octagonal piers and seems to be C15. The clerestory and nave roof probably of the same time. The W tower also appears Perp, though it has a tower arch to the nave which seems C14. It was rebuilt in 1618 (datestone). The N aisle and chancel were restored by *Street* in 1868–9, the S aisle and porch rebuilt by *J. D. Webster* in 1882–3.* – PAINTINGS. Between the clerestory windows, six cartouches of a series with the signs of the twelve tribes of Israel, second half of the C16, repainted in the early C17. Over the chancel arch a detached fragment with the Creed from a scheme, dated 1645, painted over the earlier work. – FONT. Norman, circular, with blank arches on columns (cf. Hognaston; found in a garden at Hathersage). – PULPIT. Plain C18. – SCREENS to chancel and tower, made of parts of the former Stafford Pew, Elizabethan or a little later. – MOMPESSON CHAIR. A chair was given to the church by a former rector which has on its back a very crude representation of the Virgin and above it the inscription MON 1665 EYAM. It records William Mompesson, the quiet hero of Eyam who shut the village off from the outer world in 1666 when the plague had been brought in from London, and went on ministering amongst the dying and holding services in the open. His wife was amongst the victims and is buried in the churchyard. – STAINED GLASS. S aisle W window 1911 by *Geoffrey Webb*. – PLATE. Chalice, Paten Cover, and Flagon, 1719 by *William Fawdrey*. – In the churchyard a SAXON CROSS, notable for the survival of the cross head. 22 Defaced figures in the head, coarse vine scrolls and interlace on the shaft, of which unfortunately the top two feet or so are missing. The date is probably early C9.

Nice houses around the churchyard. The RECTORY, built *c.* 1768 for the Rev. Thomas Seward, has been demolished (Cox attributed it to *Paine*: *see* note to Stoke Hall, p. 329). The C17 E wall, staircase, and Mompesson study have been incorporated in the modern building.

EYAM HALL. Dated 1676 on a rainwater-head.‡ The date goes 73 with the front towards the formal trimmed garden and its central gateway to the street. That is, it would be very late in counties of the South, but corresponds to other later C17 houses of Derbyshire. The front is a half-H with the sides projecting far. It is three storeys high with string-courses sharply dividing the storeys from each other and a straight top interrupted by three small gables above the centres of the wings and the centre of the recessed part. The windows are low and mullioned of

* Information from Paul Joyce.

‡ This must be the date of completion. Described in November 1672 as 'that messuage house in Eyam newly erected' (Miss Sinar).

three and four lights, symmetrically arranged, and touch the string-courses with their tops. This latter feature as well as the comparatively classical door surround tally with the date 1676. The E front is different, with three gables and windows with individual hood-moulds not quite symmetrically arranged. At the back two projecting parts show earlier masonry. In one of them the staircase, said to have come from Bradshaw Hall (the earlier manor house),* but appearing in its right place and of a date, probably Late Elizabethan or Jacobean, which might well be that of the masonry. The hall could also be Elizabethan in position, but the central entrance from the S which makes it into an entrance hall instead of a hall in the medieval and Tudor sense must be a contribution of 1676. Older parts to the W.

EYAM MOOR, to the N. Several Bronze Age barrows.

ROUND HILLOCK, 1½ m. N. Large Bronze Age cairn.

LEAM MOOR, to the NE. More than a hundred cairns, many of them very small, are visible on this moor.

WET WITHENS MOOR, 1¾ m. ENE of Eyam. Bronze Age ring-cairn. Twelve stones stand within a circular earthen bank, the whole work measuring about 10 ft across.

0070

FAIRFIELD

Now part of Buxton.

ST PETER. 1839, built from plans by *William Swann*, the village schoolmaster. W tower with quoins, battlements, and pinnacles. Windows of a characteristic pre-archaeological shape: Late Perp arches, but late C13 tracery. No aisles; W gallery on cast-iron columns. S porch 1897. Transepts and chancel 1901–2 by *Garlick & Flint*. – PLATE. Chalice and Paten Cover, 1595; Paten on foot, *c.* 1710.

THE FRONT, i.e. the houses alongside the green or common. Among them OLD HALL COTTAGES, dated 1687, but still with gable and low, hood-moulded, mullioned windows, and YHELT COTTAGE, earlier C17.

FAIRFIELD LOW. Large Bronze Age cairn.

COW LOW, 1¾ m. SW. Bronze Age barrow with Anglo-Saxon secondary burial.

FANSHAWGATE HALL FARM *see* HOLMESFIELD

* It collapsed in 1962.

FENNY BENTLEY

1050

ST EDMUND. Spire added to the W tower in 1864 by *Stevens & Robinson*. N aisle 1847–50 by *Stevens*. S side of the nave with one intersected and one coarse Dec window, the latter probably C19. The chancel E window of five lights, an odd design, but possibly *c*. 1300. Nothing remarkable in the interior architecture. – SCREEN with two-light openings with very cusped ogee tops and no panel tracery. The groining is preserved. Probably from the former Beresford Chantry, founded in 1511. – PARCLOSE SCREEN, with single-light openings and very Flamboyant tracery. Said to date from 1519. – CHEST with elementary ironwork (C13?). – STAINED GLASS. E window 1877, five big figures, good work, by whom? – PLATE. Paten on knob foot, 1712 by *Thomas Parr*; Chalice, 1721 by *Thomas Morse*. – MONUMENT. Thomas Beresford † 1473 and his wife; Elizabethan. The two effigies shrouded and completely bundled up (cf. Chesterfield). Against the tomb-chest the children upright and equally bundled up: a weird, grotesque idea.*

26

43

CHERRY ORCHARD FARM (OLD HALL). Square medieval tower with small openings except for one large, partly blocked low seven-light window with one transom, and attached to the tower a gabled house, also with mullioned and mullioned and transomed windows.

FERNILEE *see* TAXAL

FIN COP *see* ASHFORD-IN-THE-WATER

FINDERN

3030

ALL SAINTS. 1863–4. From the previous Norman church a tympanum survives, very raw, with two small figures standing l. and r., and, in the centre, two rows of saltire crosses and above a large cross with chequerboard patterns l. and r. – FONT. The characteristic type of 1662; small (*see* Weston-on-Trent, Southwell Notts., etc.). – PLATE. Chalice with a band of engraved strapwork decoration and Paten of 1565. – MONUMENT. Isabella de Fynderne † 1444, incised slab.

* But presumably for the same reason as the similar tomb at Chesterfield, i.e. there was no likeness of an ancestor who had died so long before the tomb was erected.

Neolithic CURSUS, 1½ m. S of the village, at least 1600 ft long. Round barrows occur between its ditches and in the vicinity.

FIVE WELLS *see* TADDINGTON

THE FOLLY *see* HOPE

1070

FOOLOW

OLD HALL. Small, C17; in the centre of the front a canted bay with mullioned windows.

CHAPEL, next to the equally small C19 church. 1836, yet still with a heavy Tuscan porch and thin lancet side windows, as if the date were thirty years earlier.

CROSS. Medieval, base 1868.

TUP LOW, NW of the village. Bronze Age cairn.

LONG LOW, ½ m. NW. Cairn built of limestone blocks set in a circle. It contained 90 inhumations in all.

0080

FORD HALL

1¼ m. NE of Chapel-en-le-Frith

A *mixtum compositum* of one remaining gabled bay of early C17 date with mullioned window, a C20 neo-Georgian bit in replacement of the remainder of the Jacobean house, a genuine Georgian front of *c.* 1727 (five bays, central pedimented ground floor windows), and mid C19 additions. Much altered since 1970. Outside the grounds by the main road SLACK HALL, dated 1727, still with low two-light windows, although these are now symmetrically arranged and 'hanging' from a string-course. Two gables, and in the middle between them a giant recess.

3020

FOREMARK

ST SAVIOUR. An uncommonly interesting building, in so far as it was built completely in 1662 (by Sir Francis Burdett) and has kept most of its original furnishings intact. The style of the exterior is still entirely Gothic: embattled W tower and embattled nave without aisles; Perp windows (five lancet lights under a depressed arch). Where the real date comes out is in the following features. First of all the nave has a central buttress and the two windows are placed symmetrically to its l. and r.

with stretches of bare wall further out. So the wall is a completely symmetrical composition. Also the windows have hoodmoulds on the typical square stops of the C17. Finally above the E window is some strapwork decoration with two small figures. The interior has a rich rood screen, still wholly Jacobean in character, except that the steep big central pediment (with a panel of C17 stained glass) is characteristic of the mid C17. The wooden frames of the stone altar-mensa and the box pews are also original. Three-decker pulpit. The communion rails are of iron, early work (*c.* 1710) of *Bakewell* of Derby, very like the rails by him in St Anne's, Manchester. – PLATE. Chalice, Paten Cover on knob foot, and Flagon, 1771 by *John Parker & Edward Wakelin*. – Also probably an early work by *Bakewell* the GATE to the avenue which leads from the E end of the church to the mansion.*

FOREMARK HALL. Built in 1759–61 by Sir Robert Burdett, M.P. The architect was *David Hiorns* of Warwick, the contractor a *Mr Pickford* (probably *Joseph Pickford*). The style is the correct Palladian of the period, the design a smaller and simplified version of Isaac Ware's Wrotham Park, Hertfordshire, of 1754. It is of seven bays' width plus broad canted bays with cupolas at the angles. The garden front (N) has as its centre a giant detached portico of four unfluted Ionic columns with pediment, the side towards the original drive (S) a simple doorway. Large outer staircases lead up to this and the portico. The elevation of the house is of basement plus one-and-a-half storeys. The only criticism of the composition is that the cupolas come rather near the pediment, so that the effect is somewhat tight and compact. There are curved screens on both sides connecting them with tiny inaccessible pavilions – a miniature version of a favourite Palladian motif ('Venetian vanities', wrote Torrington, in 1790. He found the house 'of vile architecture'). Inside, the entrance hall goes across and has a handsome staircase to one side and a large saloon beyond, filling the W side entirely. N lodge with excellent iron GATE, also presumably by *Bakewell*.

85

ANCHOR CHURCH, N of Foremark. This is not a church but caves in the cliff of the escarpment S of the river Trent traditionally connected with an anchorite. (In their present form probably C18. DOE)

FOSTON HALL *see* SCROPTON

* Bakewell's patrons, the Cokes of Melbourne, were cousins to the Burdetts (ES).

FOX HOLE CAVE *see* EARL STERNDALE

FOX LOW *see* BURBAGE

FRITH HALL FARMHOUSE *see* BRAMPTON

FROGGATT EDGE *see* CURBAR

GALLY LOW *see* BRASSINGTON

GANTRY'S HILL *see* CHAPEL-EN-LE-FRITH

GIB HILL *see* YOULGREAVE

3080

GLEADLESS

Now over the county boundary in Sheffield.

CHARNOCK HALL JUNIOR SCHOOL. 1949–51. One of the standard steel and brick schools set up by the County Education Department (*see* Introduction, p. 46).

0090

GLOSSOP

ALL SAINTS. The parish church of Old Glossop. Of the medieval church no more remains than one arch (N aisle E end) on two head corbels not originally part of it. The W tower is of 1853, the nave of 1914–15 (by *C. M. Hadfield*), the chancel of 1923 (also by *Hadfield*). – PLATE. Paten, 1698; Cup, 1750; Chalice, 1786. – INCISED SLAB. William Dewsnape † 1572.

Behind the church in Church Street South an exceptionally well and completely preserved group of C17 cottages with low mullioned windows and gables. One of them is dated 1638.

Also close to the church was GLOSSOP HALL, a mansion of 1850, once the Duke of Norfolk's, demolished in 1960. (No. 82 Norfolk Street was a gate lodge.) From the Howard time dates the church of

ALL SAINTS (R.C.), Church Terrace. 1836 by *Weightman & Hadfield*, severely neo-Greek, or rather neo-Etruscan (cf. Hassop). Heavy front of Tuscan pilasters with pediment. Coved ceiling and shallow apse inside. Opposite another lodge.

The centre of new Glossop (or Howard Town) is NORFOLK SQUARE with the TOWN HALL of 1838 by *Weightman & Hadfield*, an unusually well and quietly designed building with a central lantern (added 1897) and slender arched windows. The shops to either side are part of the original design, which had domed pavilions at either end. One was never built, the other demolished earlier this century. The central arcade (re-opened 1977) leads to the MARKET HALL built in 1844. Beyond this lie the MUNICIPAL BUILDINGS of 1923, neo-Georgian, with wide gabled wings, facing the spacious Market Ground. On the E side of Norfolk Square the LIBERAL CLUB of 1914 by *Paul Ogden*, tall and fanciful, in a kind of free neo-Tudor, and the NATIONAL WESTMINSTER BANK, 1897, in similar vein. The RAILWAY STATION was also provided by the Duke of Norfolk in 1847 – see the Howard Lion over the entrance.

Of early industrial architecture in and around Glossop the following deserve notice: WOOD'S MILL, in Victoria Street, *c.* 1850 with additions of 1910, and classical gatehouses; WREN NEST MILLS, High Street West, of *c.* 1800–10 plus small extension of 1815 plus extension with polygonal tower of 1818 (?) plus newer additions; LOGWOOD MILL of 1804; and GNAT HOLE MILL, Chunal, of *c.* 1800.

On the outskirts of new Glossop, to the W, HOLY TRINITY, Dinting, 1875, by *Mills & Murgatroyd* (GR). Over Dinting Vale a VIADUCT, 1845, carrying the Sheffield and Manchester railway at great height. Arches spoilt by reinforcement.

(To the SW, HALL FARM, Simmondley. Stone, gabled, with six- and seven-light mullioned windows. DOE)

ST JAMES, Whitfield, to the S. 1844–6 by *E. H. Shellard* (RE), chancel enlarged in 1897 by *Naylor & Sale* (GR). Big spire. – STAINED GLASS. S aisle window 1930 by *Morris & Co.*, design by *Burne-Jones*.

In Hague Street, Whitfield, the JOSEPH HAGUE SCHOOL, 1779, with pointed windows, and several C17 and C18 houses.

HADFIELD. *See* p. 229.

MELANDRA CASTLE. *See* p. 275.

GORSEY BANK *see* WIRKSWORTH

GRANVILLE PITHEAD BATHS *see* SWADLINCOTE

GREAT HUCKLOW

1070

UNITARIAN CHAPEL, S end of the village. 1796, of stone, with round-arched windows. S extension with bellcote 1901.

(METHODIST CHAPEL. 1800. Plastered gabled front with round-headed door and windows in stone surrounds. RE)

BURR TOR, ½ m. N. Iron Age hill-fort, oval and bivallate.

ABNEY LOW, 1½ m. NE. Bronze Age barrow, now destroyed. Five other barrows on Abney Moor, and a further four on Smelting Hill.

LITTLE HUCKLOW. *See* p. 263.

2070

GREAT LONGSTONE

ST GILES. N aisle lancet windows C13. Of the same century the S doorway. W tower early C14, unbuttressed and with an ogee-headed lancet window on the W side. Perp battlements and pinnacles. Perp clerestory and other windows. The church was restored, it is said very carefully, by *Norman Shaw* in 1873.* His are the tower battlements. C14 six-bay arcades inside. The chief pride of the church is its Perp woodwork. Original ROOFS with bosses in nave, chancel, and aisles. The aisles of lean-to type, nave and chancel simply braced, without tie-beams. – PARCLOSE SCREEN in the S aisle with a broad flat top frieze of not at all usual design. – Excellent STALLS, ORGAN CASE, PULPIT, and REREDOS by *Shaw*. – STAINED GLASS. The Wright Memorial (E) window 1873 by *Heaton, Butler & Bayne*, who executed windows in the S aisle to *Shaw*'s designs, 1897 and (E) 1907. – BRASS. Roland Eyre, 1624, two small kneeling figures facing each other across two prayer-desks.

VILLAGE CROSS. Late medieval.

LONGSTONE HALL. 1747. Extremely attractive, completely plain brick house with stone quoins and parapet. The windows are widely spaced, and the effect is entirely due to proportions. (The use of brick, probably for prestige, is very early in this stone area, cf. Parwich Hall, also 1747, and Sycamore Farm, Hopton. RE) On the l., part of the earlier house, stone with mullioned windows and, inside, a fine panelled room.*

GILD LOW. Built *c.* 1927 by *Sir Hubert Worthington*. Stone, neo-Georgian, with a central canted bay on the garden façade.

STATION (disused) of *c.* 1861, with steep gables and traceried bargeboards.§

CRESSBROOKE. *See* p. 155.

* Information about Shaw's restoration from Mr Andrew Saint.

‡ Says Mr J. Barron Wright.

§ Designer unknown. D. Lloyd suggests *Edward Walters* (as at Rowsley). G. Biddle's suggestion is *William Barlow*, the railway company engineer.

THORNBRIDGE HALL. *See* p. 339.

ROLLEY LOW, on Longstone Moor. Bronze Age barrow, containing several inhumations. The central circular chamber was divided into four segments.

LONGSTONE EDGE, ½ m. N. Several barrows and cairns, probably of the Bronze Age.

LONGSTONE MOOR. Large cairn, possibly dating from the Bronze Age.

GREAT ROWSLEY *see* ROWSLEY

GREEN HALL *see* ASHBOURNE, p. 65

GREEN LOW *see* BALLIDON

GREY DITCH *see* CASTLETON

GRIN LOW *see* BURBAGE

GRIND LOW *see* BAKEWELL

HADDON HALL

2060

51 Haddon Hall is the English castle *par excellence*, not the forbidding fortress on an unassailable crag, but the large, rambling, safe, grey, lovable house of knights and their ladies, the unreasonable dream-castle of those who think of the Middle Ages as a time of chivalry and valour and noble feelings. None other in England is so complete and convincing. It is set in gentle green surroundings, with woods above and lush fields and the meandering river below. The river in its winding course enhances the charms of the W as well as the S side. The slope up to the house on the W is steep but not high, and grassy not rocky. The towers and turrets and crenellations look exactly as if they were taken out of the background of some C15 illuminated manuscript. There is any amount of variety and no architectural system whatsoever. The architectural critic and historian would indeed be hard put to it if he were asked to define what in the sensations of a first visit to Haddon Hall is due to aesthetic and what to extraneous values.

There is first of all the approach, across the broad bridge of 1663 to the C16 stables (with their odd decoration by a sheila-

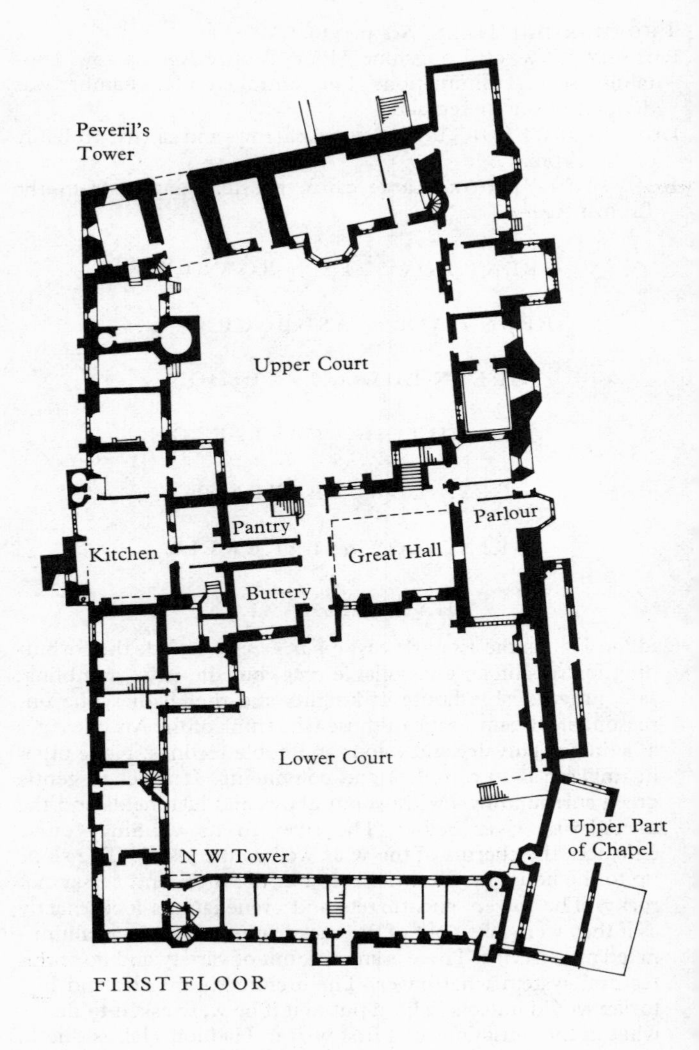
Peveril's Tower
Upper Court
Pantry
Kitchen
Great Hall
Parlour
Buttery
Lower Court
Upper Part of Chapel
N W Tower

FIRST FLOOR

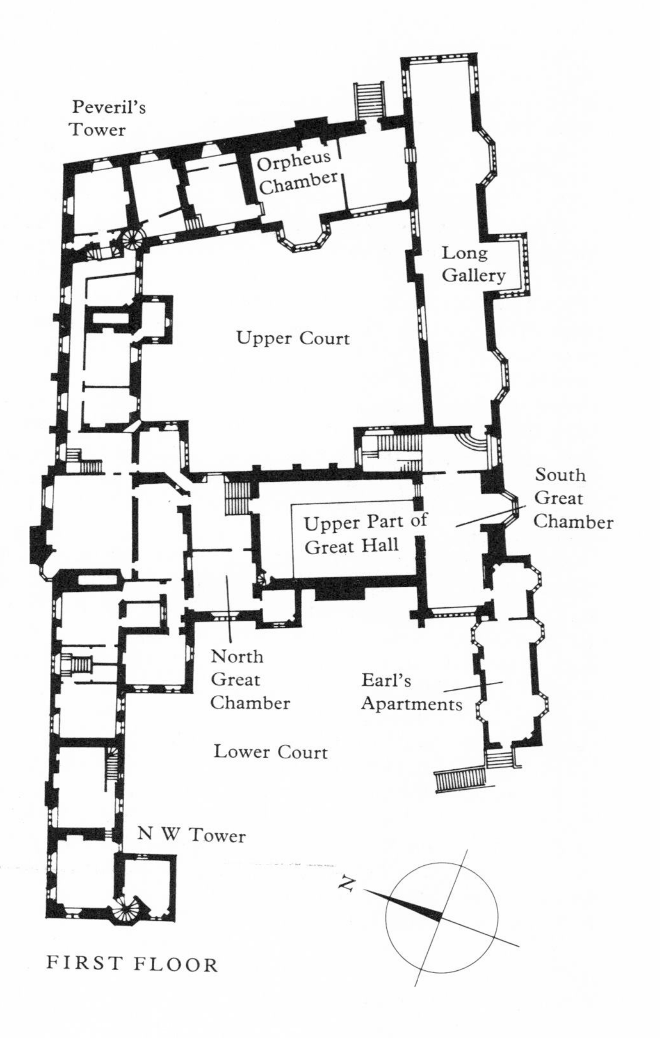
Peveril's Tower
Orpheus Chamber
Long Gallery
Upper Court
South Great Chamber
Upper Part of Great Hall
North Great Chamber
Earl's Apartments
Lower Court
N W Tower
N

FIRST FLOOR

na-gig) and to the NW gate tower, the highest element in the whole agglomeration of parts, and placed in the lowest position. This, however, became the main access to the Hall only in the early C16, and it is usable only on foot, having steps to connect it with the courtyard. So its use demands the stables below and testifies to a time when fortification did not much matter any longer.

Access in the earlier Middle Ages was at the highest level of the site by Peveril's Tower close to the NE corner. The other sides were defended by nature. Here masonry of the C12 is most clearly discernible. There is a document of 1195 allowing Richard de Vernon to fortify 'domum suum de Heddon muro exalto XII pedibus sine kernello'. The tower, it is true, has crenellations, but they are of the C14. The Vernons had come into Haddon by marriage about 1170 and kept and developed it until, again by marriage, it passed to the Manners family in 1567, the marriage this time being that of Dorothy Vernon to John Manners after their celebrated (but historically unproven) elopment in 1558. The Manners family has held it ever since. It ceased to be inhabited about 1700, and was left alone for two hundred years.

But while, as the Torrington Diary says, the house had an 'awful and melancholy look', walls and roofs remained sound, and when restoration started in 1912 and was carried on slowly and carefully for some twenty years, nothing drastic had to be done. The house is in its whole extent in remarkably genuine and good condition. Its whole extent is about 220 by 110 ft; and that area must already have been covered one way or another by the Norman stronghold. For there is masonry attributed to the C12 not only in Peveril's Tower, the lower bastions flanking it (and originally connected on the E side by a passage-way on corbels which are still visible), and the wall to the S of that group, but also all along the S wall, the centre of the W wall, and in the chapel* W and S walls (in the latter with small lancet windows with deep inner reveals). There is no evidence, however, for a cross-wing nor for a keep.

This cross-wing, which divides a lower from an upper court-yard, was the creation of Sir Richard Vernon IV about 1370‡ and is the architecturally most important part. It contains the

* Originally the parish church of Nether Haddon.

‡ P. Faulkner (*Archaeological Journal*, CXVIII, 1961, p. 188) suggests an earlier date, between 1330 when a licence to enclose the park was given and 1357 when Sir Richard Vernon went to the Holy Land.

hall, parlour, kitchen, and offices in their familiar arrangement, very similar in many ways to Penshurst in Kent begun about twenty years earlier. At about the same time the chapel S aisle was widened and a N aisle created. The lower parts of the long gallery range (upper courtyard S range) also belong to this period.

During the C15 and earlier C16 the lower courtyard assumed its present form. The NW gate tower dates from *c.* 1530, the apartments to its E from the same time, those to its S towards the chapel from a few years before.* The chapel received its new chancel in 1427, the hall its porch, chimney, and battlements about 1450. Contemporary internal alterations will be mentioned later.

As to the exterior, Elizabethan and Jacobean improvements show themselves towards the courtyards only in windows, bay-windows, and such-like additions (especially the staircase cube to the SE of the hall and the canted bay-window to the S of Peveril's Tower), but towards the outside the whole S front was radically modernized about 1600, when John Manners built his long gallery with its three broad well-spaced bay-windows, 64 stimulated no doubt by Hardwick, completed in 1597. He also added oriel windows of similar type but smaller size to the W, to what had been the long gallery before his time.

Before entering these various rooms, architectural details may be examined, first the late C12 lancets of the chapel S wall, already mentioned, and then the characteristic hall windows of *c.* 1370, almost identical with those at Penshurst (tall, of two lights, with steep two-centred arches, one transom, and tracery consisting of the cusping of the two lights and an ogee quatrefoil in the spandrel). The E doorway is contemporary. A porch was apparently not yet regarded as necessary. The buttery N of the porch is again of the C14, as is proved by its excellent gargoyles (gargoyles also on the E side of the hall range). Of the early C15 are the big five-light chapel E window with its conventional Perp panel tracery, and the chapel S and N windows, straight-headed, of three and two lights, with arched cusped heads to the individual lights. These windows date from 1427, the picturesque octagonal chapel turret from *c.* 1450. The window shapes of the

*This difference in time and the fact that the W range stands on Norman walls account for the odd and ingenious way in which the new gateway could find an entry into the courtyard without running against the E wall of the W range. The wall was canted back, and complicated squinches above bring it back to the line along which the rest of the wall runs.

sides of the chapel remained in fashion for another century. They are the same in the broad W window of Sir Henry's Parlour of *c.* 1500 (ogee-headed lights), the W range of the lower courtyard (depressed heads), and in the three upper storeys of Sir George's NW gate tower of *c.* 1530 (depressed heads). Here, however, they have those hood-moulds to which minor Derbyshire manor houses were to stick for another 150 years. The earliest example at Haddon of the 'Elizabethan' mullioned window with straight-headed lights seems to be the S bay-window of the parlour. There is no accurate date for it, but it is clearly later than the room itself (*c.* 1500) and earlier than the Elizabethan Age. The panelling inside (cf. below) is indeed dated 1545. Elizabethan and Jacobean detail is plentiful, and no one would not recognize the twice-transomed windows of the long gallery, the staircase from the hall to the Great Chamber (facing E), and the Great Chamber itself (facing W).

It is now time to examine the INTERIOR of Haddon Hall so far as it is open to the public. The public entrance is by the NW tower.

The CHAPEL is the first room shown, and rightly so; for it affords, small as it is, a cross-section through all the building periods of the house. Nave of two bays with circular pier on the S, octagonal pier on the (later) N side, double-chamfered pointed arches. The clerestory belongs in date to the more spacious chancel of 1427. – FONT. Plain, circular, Norman, with Jacobean cover of double-curved scrolls meeting below a central knob. – WOODWORK remarkably well preserved, of the same date as the roof-beams which bear an inscription G.M. 1624. – SCREEN still with a broad band of Flamboyant Gothic tracery like the dado; above widely set slim balusters; straight cornice. – Three-decker PULPIT, PEWS. – PAINTING. The grisaille or almost grisaille wall decoration of the chapel has come out wonderfully in the C20 restorations. Nave clerestory: large figure of St Christopher with scrolly waves, and plenty of fishes and plants, and to the l. and r. extensive areas of verdure; C15. Nave W wall: the Three Quick and the Three Dead. Chancel: lives of St Nicholas and St Anne, and a simple, extremely pretty all-over pattern. – SCULPTURE. Reredos of Nottingham alabaster, bought in the C20, with the familiar scenes in the familiar renderings. – STAINED GLASS. E window (Christ Crucified, Mary, St John, and smaller figures, e.g. the Annunciation, in the tracery), and, in very good preservation, N window (St Michael, St Anne and the Virgin, St

George). In the S window, an incomplete Apostle series. The inscription which runs across the whole E window dates the glass and the chancel: Orate pro animabus Riccardi Vernon et Benedicte uxoris eius qui fecerunt anno dni 1427.

[53] HALL. The roof was renewed in 1923–5; otherwise there is nothing here less than 350 years old. On the other hand, none of the furnishings is of the date of the structure, i.e. *c.* 1370, except perhaps the stone flooring. Part of the structure are the E doorway and the three doorways behind the screen to buttery, kitchen, and pantry. – SCREEN, *c.* 1450, and one of the best early hall screens in the country. Note the shapes and mouldings of the panels and the blank tracery identical with what one finds in church screens. – PANELLING of *c.* 1600. – EAST GALLERY also *c.* 1600, incongruous and picturesque; inserted to make communication from W to S less cumbersome. The meaning of domestic comfort had dawned upon the English in the time of Queen Elizabeth. – TABLE. Elizabethan. – The exquisite armorial millefleurs TAPESTRY behind the table is of the C15 and may well form part of the remodelling of the hall under Sir William. – Jacobean DOG GATES to the staircase.

The KITCHEN belongs to the same building phase as the hall. It was originally higher, probably free-standing, and may have had a louvred roof. The low ceiling was put in in the C16. The surviving fitments are unique in number and variety, grates and baking ovens, entrance door with serving-shelf, log-box, wooden salting bath, carving table, and stone troughs for water storage.

[54] S of the hall on the ground floor is the PARLOUR (now called Dining Room), altered *c.* 1500. It has its original W window and, *mirabile dictu*, its original painted ceiling decoration (restored by Professor *Tristram*). This consists of diapers half white and half red and heraldic shields. The moulded beams are also painted. The panelling, covering the whole walls, with its ornamental top frieze, has a date 1545, and this probably refers to alterations which comprised the addition of the exceedingly pretty S bay-window. As an example of dated panelling prior to 1550, it is of great historical importance. Above the parlour is the solar or GREAT CHAMBER reached from the hall by a staircase which is in exactly the same position as the C14 staircase at Penshurst, but in its present form Elizabethan or Jacobean. The roof of the solar is a splendid example of domestic joinery of *c.* 1500. The blocked window in the S wall belongs probably to the same date. Above the bay-window of the

parlour is an identical one in the solar, though its mullions have been removed at a later date. The plasterwork inside the bay, and the quadruple frieze all along the wall of the chamber, are Elizabethan; earlier, that is, than the panelling which goes with the renewal of the W window and is probably early C17.

A door from the solar leads to THE EARL'S APARTMENTS, a room which receives its name from a time in the C17 when it was subdivided into three chambers. It was made, it seems, about 1500 out of earlier medieval masonry and some also slightly earlier timber-framing. So presumably there were here no rooms for family use before Sir Henry created his 'long gallery'. The ceiling is good and sturdy and very similar to that in the solar. A door from its W end led to an outer staircase, the easiest access to the chapel.

63 The LONG GALLERY is undated, but no doubt earliest C17. The room lies to the E of the solar and rests partly on Norman masonry. It is 110 ft long and only 15 ft high; that is, much shorter and lower than the gallery at Hardwick. But from Hardwick Sir John Manners probably caught the ambition of having such a gallery at Haddon and the idea of enriching it by three bay-windows. Their beautiful spacing and proportions, however, are his, and the atmosphere of the Haddon gallery is indeed as different from Bess of Hardwick's as was her character from Sir John's. The Haddon gallery has none of the demonstrative grandeur of Hardwick. It is intimate and warm, with the sunlight reflected on its exquisite panelling. Its panelling is indeed its finest feature; for the plaster ceiling is modest, though graceful. High dado, pilasters with scale pattern carrying arches. A specially attractive touch is the introduction of two N windows throwing light on those parts of the S wall between the bay-windows which would otherwise appear to the eye as expanses of darkness. At the E end the ORPHEUS CHAMBER, originally the State Bedroom, reached from an anteroom. In it a crude plaster overmantel showing Orpheus charming the beasts, far removed from the refinement of the gallery.

From the same anteroom a door and an outer staircase of a dozen steps lead into the terraced SOUTH GARDEN. This is also one of the glories of Haddon. It was made early in the C17, although gardens no doubt had existed before. In fact the narrow doorway just W of the early C16 gate tower, which is of the same date and decorated with a coat of arms and a quatrefoil frieze, leads one to believe that here was one of the ways of access to it. But as the gardens are at present, they are C17, with their typical top balustrade and lower down their formidable-looking substructures with a strong batter. A long staircase leads down from the S side of the chapel to the river, which is here crossed by a PACKHORSE BRIDGE (Dorothy Vernon's way of escape, we are told, and ready to believe).

HADFIELD

0090

ST ANDREW. 1874 by *M. & H. Taylor*, enlarged in 1923 by *C. M. Hadfield* (GR).

ST CARLO BORROMEO (R.C.). 1858 by *Weightman, Hadfield & Goldie* (GR).

OLD HALL, Old Hall Square. T-shaped, with two- to five-light mullioned windows under hood-moulds on heavy square stops. The date is 1646.

HADYHILL *see* CHESTERFIELD, p. 151

HAGGE FARM *see* STAVELEY

HALTER DEVIL CHAPEL *see* MUGGINTON

HANSON GRANGE *see* ALSOP-EN-LE-DALE

HARBOROUGH ROCKS *see* BRASSINGTON

HARDWICK

4060

Bess of Hardwick was born at Hardwick Hall some time after 1520.* Her father, John Hardwick Esq., owned the manor, a minor manor, and lived in a minor manor house, where Bess grew up until her marriage to a cousin, Robert Barley, who died in 1544. She then married Sir William Cavendish, Treasurer of the Chamber to the King. He was not a Derbyshire man and had properties in five counties. Bess induced him to sell his Suffolk properties and buy, in 1549, the Chatsworth estate (still in the possession of her Cavendish progeny) and settle down in her county. Here Bess could for the first time indulge in what was to become her master passion, a building mania, nobler no doubt than her other passions. For she appears from her actions and from contemporary records and accounts as a

* Information about Bess's life from Mr D. Durant, who advises scepticism about most of the usually accepted facts, especially ages and dates.

grasping and intriguing, if undeniably able, woman. The new Chatsworth was begun in 1552. Sir William Cavendish died five years later leaving Bess a woman of considerable wealth. Although it appears from her portraits that she was no longer physically attractive, she soon found a third husband in Sir William St Loe. He, however, died in 1565. Bess was now in her forties but instead of resigning herself to a comfortable widowed retirement, she set out to find yet another husband. She was successful, and it turned out to be the greatest *coup* of her life. Her second and third husbands had been rich, and much of their wealth had been conducted by her into her hands. The fourth was richer and more powerful than either: George Talbot, sixth Earl of Shrewsbury. Their marriage took place in 1568, and in the same year (a characteristic touch) she made her position trebly sure by arranging for two of the Cavendish children to marry two of his. Talbot proved to be almost as enthusiastic about building as his wife, and began Worksop Manor, Nottinghamshire (destroyed by fire in 1761), in the early 1580s possibly in conscious rivalry with Bess. The story of the Earl's guardianship from 1569 to 1584 of Mary Queen of Scots, of her intrigues, of Queen Elizabeth's intrigues, and of Bess's intrigues does not concern us here. The Earl died in 1590, seven years after he had separated from Bess. In that year she had deliberately created a rumour of a liaison between him and Mary. That she had also called him 'knave, fool, and beast' to his face was a minor point.

After their separation Bess began converting the old manor house she had inherited from her own family into a large mansion, now known as HARDWICK OLD HALL and in ruins. The irregular gabled part probably incorporates the earlier house. To this Bess added two wings at either end each, like Worksop, with balustraded parapets and each with top-floor state rooms, as at both Chatsworth and Worksop. One had a six-storey tower, the other full-height shallow projecting bays. Several features of the New Hall are adumbrated here: the large top-floor windows with two or even three transoms, the two-storey axially placed hall, and the style of plasterwork by *Abraham Smith* in the Hill and Forest Great Chambers. There was one Great Chamber in each wing. Bess also duplicated the state rooms in her New Hall. But the Old Hall, despite all the lavishness bestowed on it, was not built from the beginning to one design, and the irregular planning of rooms and façades (see the S front) was the result of adding and adjusting as the work progressed.

59

So directly the Earl died and Bess was free and much wealthier, she embarked on a new venture, more ambitious than any previous one. She started to build a NEW HALL at Hardwick, close to the old but on virgin ground, to a new and entirely up-to-date plan and at a rate of employment that enabled her to finish the job in seven years. She was about seventy when the foundations were laid in 1590 and in her late eighties when she died in 1608, eleven years after moving in.* 61

Hardwick Hall is basically H-shaped in plan, like say Montacute, but with a double-stepped extension at each of its shorter ends. This motif of stepping Bess's architect may perhaps have taken from Wollaton Hall in Nottinghamshire completed five years before she started. There, however, it is used for a square, not an oblong mansion. In elevation the most original feature at Hardwick is that it is of two storeys, but the projecting arms of the H and the centres of the stepped-forward additions are carried up to form three-storey pavilions, or square towers. That motif originated at the Earl of Shrewsbury's Worksop Manor and is seen again at Barlborough, begun in 1584, which has four polygonal relatively slender towers. Whereas the effect of the Barlborough towers is rather like that of the raised turrets of a Tudor gatehouse, the six towers of Hardwick are four-square and massive. Four-square is the whole house, and in this is unlike the irregular Worksop. There are no curves anywhere, save in the rather niggly strapwork frills of the tower balustrades which frame Bess's proud and ostentatious initials, E.S., E.S., E.S., E.S., four times along each of the long fronts and three times along the short ones. The stepping on the l. and r. moves in hard r. angles, a colonnade with a straight entablature runs along the ground floor between the towers of the main façades,‡ a balustrade finishes the composition at the top. The roof is flat, the central bay-window only slightly canted on the second upper floor, and all the windows are transomed as well as mullioned. 'Hardwick Hall more window than wall'; it is indeed the size and rhythm of the windows that distinguish Hardwick from all other Late Elizabethan houses. The close grid of the mullions and transoms sets the pace: one transom

* Hardwick was not in fact her last project, for in 1593 she began Oldcotes, near Sutton Scarsdale, for, and at the expense of, her son William Cavendish. This with Chatsworth and Hardwick is recorded on her tomb.

‡ It was originally meant to run all round the building, but the idea was given up during erection. A line of rough stone can be seen where the roofs were to be tied in.

on the ground floor which is treated as a basement, two transoms on the first, three on the second, and two on the third.* No obstacle gets in its way. Some windows in the towers are false with chimneypieces behind, others serve two storeys where a mezzanine is inserted, and even the chimney flues go up through internal walls. It is of a consistency and hardness which must have suited the old woman entirely. And as the house stands on the flattened top of the hill, there is nothing of surrounding nature either that could compete with its uncompromising, unnatural, graceless, and indomitable self-assertiveness. It is an admirable piece of design and architectural expression: no fussing, no fumbling, nor indeed any flights of fancy.

There is plenty of circumstantial evidence to suggest that the design was made by *Robert Smythson*, the architect of Wollaton. One of Bess's chief sculptors, *Thomas Accres*, and the masons *John* and *Christopher Rodes* came to Hardwick from Wollaton. Moreover an unspecified payment to 'Mr Smythson, the surveyour, and his son' was made in 1597, and either *Robert* or his son *John* drew a design for Bess's tomb in Derby Cathedral (*see* p. 170) some years before her death. All three generations of the *Smythson* family spent much of their careers working for members of her family; for her husband at Worksop, for her youngest Talbot son at Pontefract, and for the Cavendishes at Bolsover, Slingsby, and Welbeck. The most persuasive evidence is the existence of a ground-floor plan (RIBA I/8) very close to what was built.

Inside, the style is very different from that of the severe exterior. Here a show of luxury was aimed for and at once it becomes coarse, as it does so often in the art of decoration in Elizabethan England. We shall take the rooms in the order that the visitor sees them (1977).‡

The ENTRANCE HALL is from the planning if not from the decorative point of view the most remarkable room in the house. The hall of Elizabethan houses is still in the position in which it had been ever since the Middle Ages: in the middle. But while in the Middle Ages it extended asymmetrically along part of the front and was approached at one end by a door leading in-

* The heightening of the turrets was an afterthought. It was resolved in 1594.

‡ It must be remembered that *The Buildings of England* do not discuss movable furnishings in houses. Hence neither the magnificent old oak nor even the needlework will be mentioned. Many of these furnishings were brought to Hardwick by the sixth Duke of Devonshire from other houses.

to the screens passage, at Hardwick the entrance is central and the hall is central and has its axis not parallel with the front but at r. angles to it, going right across the middle of the house. The only known earlier example of this arrangement is at Hardwick Old Hall. The reason for its use is not known (it may have followed the arrangement in John Hardwick's manor house), but here it fits in with similar experiments with the same purpose of getting away from the traditional, asymmetrical and therefore no longer satisfactory placing of the hall.* The chief examples are those by Smythson which had to be mentioned in comparison with the Hardwick elevations. Barlborough has no proper hall at all, and Wollaton has a hall right at the centre of the square block and rising higher than the rest. Hardwick is in line with these developments of the eighties and makes its own contribution. It has a screen, as earlier halls had, but it now runs across forming a kind of lobby by separating an area of moderate size by the chief entrance from the rest of the hall. A dais and high table can never have existed. The screen, carved by *William Griffin*, has remarkably correct Roman Doric columns, and supports a gallery on the first floor, the only connexion between the rooms of the N and S halves. The fireplace is adorned with rather flat strapwork, but the overmantel with the Hardwick crest introduces us to the bold and always rather gargantuan displays of *Abraham Smith*, Bess's chief plasterer, coarse but jolly work.

From the screens passage or lobby the pantry was reached on the S, the buttery and kitchen on the N. Doors in corresponding positions near the E end of the hall lead to the main stairs on the S, the secondary stairs and so-called lower chapel on the N. This was made into a steward's room *c.* 1800, but it originally went through two floors (as in medieval episcopal chapels and, for instance, at Versailles), the ground floor for the servants, and the upper-floor gallery at first-floor level for the mistress and her family and guests. What has happened, if anything, to the staircases we do not know. They are remarkably dramatic it is true, but I cannot believe them to be Elizabethan. The sixth Duke of Devonshire between 1820 and 1858 did so much ingenious adjusting and heightening of effects at Chatsworth

* Sir John Summerson (*Architecture in Britain: 1530–1830*, 5th (1st paperback) ed., p. 71) suggests that Smythson may have been looking at Palladio's *Quattro Libri*. If so, he is the first English architect known to have done so.

and did it so often to his own idea that he may have been the designer of the two staircases as we now see them.*

The main stairs lead up to the DRAWING ROOM (originally the Withdrawing Room). Over the door outside a crude plaster relief with an *all'antica* bust of a man in armour and inside an overmantel similar to that of the entrance hall but more modest. It is one of the suite of family rooms on the FIRST FLOOR. The other rooms of this suite, the dining room (originally the Low Great Chamber) and chapel, are on the N side of the hall, connected by the gallery or balcony above the screen with the S half. They are seen on the descent from the second floor. The stairs lead on up to the STATE ROOMS on the SECOND FLOOR: the long gallery and the High Great Chamber, the one running all along the E front to a length of a full 166 ft, the other placed at the SW corner so that the W tower window belongs to it. The HIGH GREAT CHAMBER is one of the most impressive and characteristic rooms of its date in England, large, light, and broad in treatment. Broad indeed is *Abraham Smith*'s coloured plaster frieze, forest scenes (the Hunt of Diana)* with plenty of animals and figures of divers sizes. It must have been a monstrous show in the eyes of a visitor from Fontainebleau or Florence, barbaric in the extreme. The same comment would have been made of the Elizabethan furniture such as filled and now fills Hardwick. The bay-window walls are panelled to the top cornice and on the panelling coloured engravings of emperors and philosophers by *Peter de Coster* of Antwerp are stuck and varnished over. Some are painted in imitation on to the panels, by Bess's painter *John Ballergons* (or *Ballechonz*), a Fleming previously at Chatsworth. The fireplace, attributed to *Accres*, is of alabaster, Derbyshire marble, and touch, with the Royal Arms by *Smith* over it breaking into the frieze. The tapestries in the style of Michael Coxie are part of the original scheme completed in 1599, two years after Bess moved in. The great sensation of the GALLERY is its three bay-windows, each the size of a C20 council house. On a sunny day the gallery is as light as a factory in the International Modern style. Let

* It should be noted that the sixth Duke does not record any major alterations in his 'Handbook' and that both Walpole in 1780 and Torrington in 1789 remarked on the stairs. They seem to be an integral part of Smythson's planning. If not arranged in this way they would have come up in the middle of the long gallery. Their precedent is the long staircase of two dog-leg flights in the Old Hall.

‡ After Martin de Vos and Nicholas de Bruyn.

nobody say that C20 fenestration is alien to this land. Along the back wall facing the windows between the bays are two large fireplaces, clearly more architectural than Abraham Smith's and therefore probably by *Accres*. They are in fact loosely based on designs by Serlio and both have coupled banded pilasters below and black columns above, and in the middle, surrounded by strapwork of far more vigour and tension than Smith's, small figures of Justice and Pity in oval frames. The figures, probably inserted in the C17, are obviously by the same hand as the Charity in the Best Bedchamber. Could the hand be that of *Maximilian Colt* (cf. his work at Hatfield)? The tapestries of the gallery must have one word: for they too are part of the original furnishing scheme. Bess bought them in 1592 from the heir of Sir Christopher Hatton, Queen Elizabeth's Lord Chancellor. She paid £326 15*s*. 9*d*. for them, an enormous sum, as will be realized if one compares it with the £600 which Sir William Cavendish had paid for the whole Chatsworth estate.* Above them a frieze by *John Ballergon*. In the WITHDRAWING ROOM, in the middle of the W front, next to the Great Chamber, is the best piece of sculpture at Hardwick, a large alabaster relief of Apollo and the Muses by an unknown sculptor who without doubt was neither English nor Flemish. It does not belong to the house but was brought over from Chatsworth by the sixth Duke.‡ N of the Withdrawing Room are a number of bedrooms, lower so that another set could be housed on top of them, the two tiers behind one set of three-transom windows. (The Withdrawing Room was lowered later.) The chief thing to mention in these bedrooms is again the mantelpieces. In the GREEN VELVET ROOM (originally the Best Bedchamber) the fireplace, with a central figure of Charity, was carved and inlaid by *Nayll*, *Mallery*, and *Accres*. The overmantel in the BLUE ROOM (which was originally called the Pearl Bedchamber) may have been made for Chatsworth. In any case it is unlike any other carving at Hardwick. It shows one of Bess's favourite themes, the Marriage (one of many) of Tobias. The wooden stairs in the N tower descend to the first-floor DINING ROOM, which has an overmantel with unimaginative strapwork and two stiff, elongated, female nudes. The inscription says: 'The con-

65

* Also bought from Hatton's heirs, the Abraham set in the Green Velvet Room and the set that has always hung in the Drawing Room.

‡ It was probably made for the 'Muses' Chamber', which was either the High Great Chamber or the Earl of Leicester's Withdrawing Chamber according to the 1601 inventory.

clusion of all things is to fear God and keep his commandments.' Bess might well have felt guilty about the ninth. Next to the dining room is the PAVED BEDROOM, the former Little Dining Chamber, with an overmantel relief of Ceres made by *Smith*, no doubt from a Flemish engraving. The figure is like those on late C16 monuments, the execution far from elegant. In the CHAPEL the most interesting features are the C17 pulpit brought up from the chapel below and the wooden screen which originally separated the Countess's gallery from the open area. The screen is very simple, as if the panels were taken out of Elizabethan wall panelling. There are no Gothic reminiscences at all. In the late C17 matching apartments consisting of withdrawing chamber, bedchamber, and closet were made out of the rooms on this floor. The Withdrawing Room, bedchamber, and inner chamber on the S side formed one suite, the Low Great Chamber, Ship (now Cut Velvet) Bedchamber, and Tobias Chamber the other on the N side. All have richly moulded late C17 overmantels, doors, and chimneypieces.

Bess of Hardwick's GARDENS have disappeared (*Lady Louisa Egerton*, daughter of the seventh Duke, created the present S garden), but Bess's madly crenellated garden wall and gateway, triangular lodges, and triangular bastion-like banqueting house with the crazy headgear are all miraculously preserved. In the E colonnade, *Westmacott*'s statue of Mary Queen of Scots, commissioned *c.* 1825 by the sixth Duke for Queen Mary's Bower at Chatsworth but placed here instead.

HARLAND EDGE *see* BEELEY

HARTHILL *see* ALPORT

1060

HARTINGTON

ST GILES. High up above the little town. Perp W tower of red ashlar sandstone with set-back buttresses, gargoyles, battlements, and pinnacles. The body of the church is distinguished by the presence of transepts (cf. Ashbourne, Wirksworth), that on the S side with a W aisle. This plan dates back to the late C13 or a little later: see the arcades between nave and aisles exactly as at Wirksworth (quatrefoil piers with fillets and the E responds slimmer with shaft-rings), the lancet windows in the chancel N wall and N transept W wall, the two S windows of the S transept, especially the large one which is worth some study (a five-light window of intersected tracery cusped but with the very top quite illogically interrupted to leave space for a quatrefoil with a pointed, elongated lower lobe), the S transept E window, the chancel E window (five-light intersected), the N transept windows, the S doorway, the PISCINAS in the two transepts, and the low, finely moulded arch of a tomb recess in the S transept. The two-storeyed porch is a picturesque and felicitous addition of the late Middle Ages with its W wall in line with the S aisle W wall, broadening the aisle for the eye, and with its embattled parapet sloping up towards the transept. One feature at Hartington differs from Wirksworth: the S transept has a W aisle (octagonal piers, C14 capitals). (Restoration 1858 by *H. Currey*. R. Hubbuck) – FONT. Perp, octagonal, with divers tracery panels (similar to Darley Dale). – GAUNTLET, mid C17, made for funeral use, provenance the Bateman family. – PLATE. Chalice, Paten on foot, and Flagon, 1756 by *John Richardson*. – MONUMENTS. Several top parts of lids with foliated crosses, probably C13. – Effigy of a lady under a trefoiled arch. She is visible only to the height of her folded hands; the rest is hidden by the slab as if she were tucked in under a blanket. C13.

HARTINGTON HALL (Y.H.A.). Above the church to the SE. 1611, with three gables, two of them on l. and r. symmetrical projections. Three- to five-light mullioned windows with hood-moulds. Minor plaster ceilings.

In the village, Market Place with cottages of C18 and C19 dates (1777, 1828) and a classical MARKET HALL of 1836 with a ground floor of three rusticated depressed arches.

To the NE of the village the impressive portals of the NEWHAVEN TUNNEL, which carries the Cromford and High Peak Railway beneath the Ashbourne to Buxton road.

(WOLFSCOTE GRANGE, 1 m. SE. Irregular plan, mullioned windows, gabled porch dated 1649, one panelled room. DOE)

CARDER LOW, 1½ m. N. Bronze Age barrow, containing at least two inhumations, one accompanied by a bronze dagger and a stone axe-hammer.

PARSLEY HAY (earlier PARCELLY HAY). Beaker barrow, the central burial a contracted inhumation, accompanied by a bronze dagger and a stone axe.

BENTY GRANGE, 3 m. NE. Small Anglo-Saxon barrow, surrounded by a ditch. The grave-goods included the famous Anglo-Saxon helmet of plates of horn over an iron framework, and surmounted by a bronze figure of a boar. To the nose-guard was affixed a small cross. The burial also contained a hanging bowl, a leather vessel, various iron objects, and other ornaments.

PILSBURY CASTLE, 2½ m. NNW. Small motte and bailey castle, perhaps erected over the site of earlier earthworks.

DOWEL CAVE, 2 m. NW. This cave contained ten Neolithic inhumations.

HARLEY HILL, 3 m. NW. Large barrow originally containing seven Romano-British cremation burials.

THIRKELL LOW, 4 m. NW. Bronze Age cairn erected over a crouched inhumation burial accompanied by a battle-axe.

FRANK I' THE ROCKS CAVE, 1½ m. S. Roman and Anglo-Saxon burials have been found in this cave.

HARTSHORNE

ST PETER. 1835, with Perp tracery of cast iron in the lancets, and a W gallery on cast-iron columns; medieval (C15) only the W tower with battlements and the chancel. – FONT. Octagonal, tapering, plain, probably C14. – PLATE. Paten of *c.* 1500 with a face of Christ, one of the oldest pieces of plate in Derbyshire; Chalice of 1611; pewter Flagon dated 1638. – MONUMENT. Humphrey Dethick † 1599 and wife, recumbent alabaster effigies; on the tomb-chest the six children, standing up, in two panels, each with a triple arch.

(OLD MANOR HOUSE, SW of the church. Fine timber-framed building with decorative diagonal work unusual in Derbyshire. Jettied upper floor; upper parts of wings rebuilt or brick-faced. RE)

HASLAND *see* CHESTERFIELD, pp. 150, 151

HASLING HOUSE *see* BUXTON

2070

HASSOP

ALL SAINTS (R.C.). 1816–18 by the Roman Catholic architect *Joseph Ireland* for the Eyre family, a family with distinguished Catholic traditions. Building was supervised by Ireland's 'pupil-clerk', *J. J. Scoles*. The design is in the severest Classical Revival style: a correct Etruscan temple front, tetrastyle, prostyle. Five Grecian side windows and Tuscan pilasters at the back. The interior has a coved coffered ceiling. – PAINT-

ING. Large Crucifixion with the Virgin and St John said to be by *Lodovico Carracci*. – MONUMENT. Thomas Eyre † 1833, tablet with figure of Faith and portrait medallion on a pedestal, by *J. E. Carew* of Brighton.

Opposite the church, the entrance to HASSOP HALL. It incorporates an earlier house, probably that built in the early C17 by the Eyres of Padley. Of this period a blocked mullioned window and plaster overmantel in an upper room and apparently the N side; limestone with two string-courses. In 1827–33 Thomas Eyre, seventh Earl of Newburgh, modernized the house. He moved the entrance from the S to the W and classicized both façades. The main S front is stone, of three storeys, with a top balustrade and four full-height canted bays, the centre only slightly emphasized by an elaborate doorcase with a pedimented window over. Between the bays *œil-de-bœuf* windows above plain sashes and, on the ground floor, niches. The details are neo-classical and more competent than the overall design. The architect of these improvements is unknown as yet, but the sort of architect the Earl employed is perhaps indicated by his social position, as son-in-law of the Marquess of Ailsa, who was a friend of William IV, and as a friend himself of the Duke of Devonshire. The interiors are early C19 with chimneypieces by *White Watson* of Ashford-in-the-Water. In the dining room heraldic glass from Warkworth Castle, Northamptonshire, and in the NW wing a crude carving with the date 159(6), found bricked up in this part of the house.

To the N a ballroom of 1827–33, raised above the dairy, with a shaped gable, and reached from the house by a vaulted passage and stairway. Other subterranean passages, reminiscent of the later ones at Welbeck, lead to the lake, church, and extra cellarage in the park. On the E, an Italianate garden with a sham-Tudor gazebo near the gate.

Below the house towards the road, the DOWAGER HOUSES, a plain, quite big late C17 house divided into three, with three gables and two intermittent string-courses to which the (altered) windows are tied.

STATION (now Fearn's Depot). An elegant station built in 1863 by *Edward Walters* to serve the Duke of Devonshire.

CROCKENDALE PASTURES, 1 m. SE. Unusually constructed Beaker period cairn, in which three projections radiated from the central mound.

2080

HATHERSAGE

ST MICHAEL. High up at the end of the little town; a typical Derbyshire sight with its castellated aisles, porch, and clerestory, its gargoyles and its spire. Good Perp W tower with diagonal buttresses, and traceried W window. The spire is recessed behind the battlements and crocketed. The tower arch to the nave is tall and has the unusual feature as part of its capitals of a broad band of big leaves, embattled. The arcades are of four bays, that on the N side with very odd capitals on its octagonal piers. They are mostly renewed (restoration by *Butterfield*, 1849–52), but what is old seems to have a kind of upright leaf of *c.* 1200. The church is supposed to have been built in 1381. The S arcade might correspond to that date and the chancel; see the SEDILIA and the N window, cut into by the Eyre monument (cf. below). The *Kempe* STAINED GLASS in the E window was put in only in 1949. It comes from Derwent church and was transferred when that church was submerged in the reservoir. Of the C15, besides the tower, the clerestory and the N chancel chapel. This was added as an Eyre chantry in 1463. – ROOFS, PULPIT, ALTAR RAILS, and BENCHES by *Butterfield*. – PLATE. Flagon, 1718 by *Richard Green*. – MONUMENTS. Remarkable set of Eyre brasses. Tomb-chest with foiled 35 panels and on it the excellent brasses of Robert Eyre † 1459 in armour and his wife and, below, their children. The chest stands between chancel and chancel chapel and has above a big heavy ogee-headed recess with very curious tracery below. There are tomb recesses of this type in Ireland, cf. Kilconnel Friary and Galway church. This was restored by the Countess of Newburgh in 1852. – Robert Eyre, *c.* 1500, wife and children, kneeling figures, placed comparatively recently against the back wall of the recess just mentioned. – Ralph Eyre † 1493 and wife, standing figures. A fragment of two daughters above. – Sir Arthur Eyre, *c.* 1560, kneeling, with wife.

ST MICHAEL (R.C.). 1806. Plain parallelogram with altered interior. The outside surprisingly heavily detailed, with big quoins, a broad doorway on big corbels, and arched windows with thick frames. The nave is probably the remains of the Mass House erected in James II's reign and sacked in 1688. The features described support a late C17 date.

Two early C19 MILLS, one by the Derwent Bridge, the other at the head of the town (which incidentally is the Morton of *Jane Eyre*). With the latter mill ROCK HOUSE seems to be connected, a neurotic attempt to use the extremely heavy rustication of Paine's Chatsworth stables for modest domestic purposes. All windows and the door of the two-storeyed house of five bays have colossal rock-faced frames as if they were at Mantua and by Giulio Romano.

THE HALL. Two-storeyed front of *c.* 1820 and three-storeyed back with remains of the late C16 or C17.

NETHER HALL was built *c.* 1840 for J. A. Shuttleworth of the Hall.

HIGHLOW HALL. *See* p. 244.

HAZELFORD. *See* p. 242.

BROOKFIELD MANOR. *See* p. 111.

LONGSHAW LODGE. *See* p. 268.

PADLEY HALL. *See* p. 296.

STANAGE EDGE, 2¼ m. N. There are well preserved remains of the Roman road from Templeborough to Brough-on-Noe on the Edge.

HAYFIELD

0080

ST MATTHEW. 1817–18 by *Bradbury & Rangeley* (GR).* Characteristic of its date, with arched windows and windows with intersecting tracery. The tower is of 1793, raised by a clock stage in 1894. Inside, galleries on three sides on thin iron columns. (The church was built on the foundations of a medieval predecessor. The floor is supported on the bases of the nave arcades with the lower part of the columns intact and visible in the crypt. DOE) – BOX PEWS. – PLATE. Paten on foot, 1707 by *Andrew Raven*; two Chalices, 1784 by *Thomas Chawner*; Paten on foot, 1823 by *Robert Hennell*. – MONUMENT to Joseph Hague † 1786 (from Glossop church). Wall inscription tablet with a fluted superstructure diminishing in size and ending in a big full-round bust by *Bacon*.

ST JOHN'S METHODIST CHAPEL. Stone, 1782, round-arched windows. Porch and window above it later. C. Stell) The galleried interior is 42 ft by 35 ft, i.e. the proportions favoured by Wesley, who was a friend of the vicar.

(FOX HALL, Kinder Road, is dated 1625 over the main door,

* According to the Rev. Roger Castle there is no mention of Bradbury in the accounts. The faculty plans (1817) are signed *John Day*, who was apparently paid only £16 for 'expenses for plans and planning'. One *Dennis Rangeley* was paid £370 for work unspecified. Only one man was paid more, £452 for the pews, and since the total cost of the church was £2,458 it seems that Rangeley may have been a contractor rather than an architect.

but the three-gabled elevation may be later C17. Low-pitched gables with arched attic vents. Long, low mullioned windows with hood-moulds returning in labels. The barn on the N has much smaller mullioned windows and crude door openings – C16 perhaps. RE)

PARK HALL, 1 m. N. 1811. Two-storeyed, seven-bay house with one-storeyed Ionic entrance colonnade. Fine semicircular stables with end pediments.

(KINDER UPPER HOUSE, 1¼ m. NE. Big quadrangular stone house, mostly C20 but of various dates since the C16. Fine medieval wooden roof in an outbuilding, said to come from a Cheshire church and certainly of that type. DOE)

KINDER LOW, 2 m. E. Well preserved Bronze Age cairn.

1080

HAZELBADGE HALL

¾ m. S of Bradwell

55 The coat of arms of the Vernon and Swynnerton families and the date 1549 appear in the W gable of a rectangular building whose windows are on the side with the date, still six-light and five-light mullioned with depressed pointed arches to each light. On the S side they are normal, straight-headed, and mullioned. The SW room has moulded ceiling beams. The entrance is through a lobby, not a screens passage – i.e. a type of plan usually found in hunting boxes or retreats used by only a few people (cf. Old Hall Farm, Kneesall, Notts; Bolsover Keep). (Barns probably C16. DOE)

Large cairn, containing many inhumations, N of the Hall.

2070

HAZELFORD

1 m. S of Hathersage

C17 house, L-shaped, with porch, gables with ball finials, and four- and five-light mullioned windows.

3040

HAZELWOOD

ST JOHN. 1840 by *Stevens* (restored after a fire in 1902 by *Naylor & Sale*). Stone nave and chancel, bellcote, lancet windows.

3050

HEAGE

ST LUKE. The church has a T-plan owing to an addition of 1826 to an earlier building. The plan turned out (by chance probably) to be one of those specially recommended for Protestant worship from early days. The only part of the medieval church to survive the furious storm of 1545 was the E window of three stepped lancet lights cusped. The rest of the old part (now the chancel) was rebuilt in 1646–61 and has small straight-headed side windows. The new part is taller and has the typical early C19 lancets of two lancet lights with pierced spandrels. Over the entrance a polygonal bell-turret (1896?). The date 1752 on the door lintel does not refer to either main building period.

(HALL. C16 to C17, gabled, with mullioned windows. DOE)

(CROWTREES, Ripley Road. 1712 but still with mullioned windows. Inside three good crucks, and a timber-framed rear wall, heavily restored. RE)

WINDMILL, Dungeley Hill. Mid-C19 sandstone tower mill, the only such in Derbyshire with complete sails and machinery. (*See* Dale Abbey for a complete post mill.) Ogee cap and six sails a reconstruction of 1894. Restored in 1972–4 by Derbyshire County Council.

MORLEY PARK FARM, ¾m. S. The remains of two early iron blast furnaces, one of 1780, the other of 1818. They were built by Francis Hurt and are steeply pyramidal truncated structures with brick linings. The outstanding monument to the production of cast iron in Derbyshire since the last remaining C20 furnaces at Stanton Ironworks were demolished in 1976.

98

HEANOR

4040

ST LAWRENCE. 1866–8 by *Stevens & Robinson*, except for the dark grey Perp tower with angle buttresses. It has on each side two large two-light bell-openings with transoms (altered in the C19). – PLATE. Chalice and Paten Cover, 1663. – MONUMENT. John Sutton † 1803, by *White Watson*, the descendant of Samuel Watson † 1715, the chief woodcarver at Chatsworth whose epitaph is in the church. ('Watson is gone, whose skilful Art display'd/To th' very life whatever nature made/View but his wondrous works at Chatsworth Hall/Which were so gazed at and admired by all.') He was born at Heanor.

WILLIAM GREGG V. C. SWIMMING BATHS. 1968–70 by *Rex Savidge* of *Gelsthorpe, Savidge & Simpson*, simpler than the same architect's baths at Ilkeston. Rectangular, red brick, with black-stained timbering to the windows.

LOSCOE. *See* p. 269.

4060

HEATH

ALL SAINTS. 1853 by *Stevens* (GR). Rock-faced, with spire. Restored in 1882–6 by *Butterfield*, who added the screen. – PLATE. Chalice and Paten Cover, 1698. – In the porch COFFIN SLABS, one (C11 or C12) with a cross and figure group (Resurrection, Betrayal, etc.). They come from the old church, fragments of which can be seen ¼ m. down the hill.

(HIGH HOUSE, ¾ m. WNW of the church. A handsomely dressed farmhouse of *c.* 1725 with moulded window architraves and doorcase, pilasters at the angles, and a moulded cornice. Five bays, two storeys, all of stone. Almost certainly by a mason from Sutton Scarsdale. A. Gomme)

HERMITS CAVE *see* YOULGREAVE

3050

HIGHAM

(An attractive estate village on Ryknield Street, with a number of old cottages, sympathetically improved by the Turbutts of Ogston Hall in the late C19. No. 22, Bull Farm, the Crown Inn, and Higham Farm contain crucks. Nos. 77 and 79 STRETTEA LANE are a curious pair of C18 houses with classical façades to the back gardens. Ashlar, fluted Doric pilasters, pedimented doorways to each house, and a central passage with Gothick-glazed window over on the otherwise windowless street front. RE)

2080

HIGHLOW HALL

1¼ m. SW of Hathersage

Small manor house built by the Eyres, probably C16, the front crenellated, with a square porch projection. (The hall has moulded timber beams, oriel, and open fireplace. Good C17 staircase. DOE) Contemporary barns and a C17 gateway and garden house survive.

OFFERTON HALL, entrance facing Highlow Hall, *see* p. 293.

Group of about twenty CAIRNS W of Highlow Hall.

HIGH PEAK JUNCTION *see* CROMFORD

HILTON

2030

OLD HALL (or WAKELYN). Pretty half-timbered C16 house. Symmetrical front, gables of equal size l. and r. The timberwork with various ornamental motifs, lozenge in square, oval in square within square, ogee lozenge in square.

HIPPER HALL *see* WALTON

HOB HURST'S HOUSE *see* BEELEY

HOGNASTON

2050

ST BARTHOLOMEW. Amazing Norman doorway. The tympanum shows incised pictures of a bishop with a crook, the lamb with cross, two fishes, a hog (?), and several other beasts. What on earth did our forebears mean by such representations? And how can one account for this total absence of a sense of composition and this utterly childish treatment? The subject is thought to be the Agnus Dei, cf. Parwich.* The doorway has one order of colonnettes with very stylized beakheads, no more than tongue shapes. The label has head stops and a head at the top. The W tower is C13, square and unbuttressed, with small lancet windows. The ground floor is of stone different from the first floor (broad low buttresses). The ground floor opens into the nave in a three-stepped arch on the simplest imposts. The first floor, however, also has lancets. The top is Perp, with battlements and C19 pinnacles. A big buttress up the middle of the W side. Inside, the chancel arch is early C14; see the keeled shafts and the moulded capitals (cf. Bradbourne). The rest of the church was rebuilt in 1879–81 by *F. J. Robinson.* (A design by *Street* of 1876 was rejected.) – FONT. Norman, tub-shape, with short stumpy arcades.

In the village a few good C17 and C18 stone houses, e.g. the OLD HALL, opposite the church, and CHURCH FARMHOUSE, with a stair window over a door with a segmental pediment.

HOLBROOK

3040

ST MICHAEL. Plain parallelogram with broad angle pilasters;

* For a discussion of the Agnus Dei theme in the C11 see Michael Dolby: 'The nummular brooch from Sulgrave' in *England before the Conquest: studies in primary sources presented to Dorothy Whitelock*, ed. Peter Clemoes and Kathleen Hughes, Cambridge, 1971.

rebuilt in 1841. On the N side still long arched windows and a pedimented porch which probably go back to the previous building of 1761. S aisle, chancel, and NE porch added in 1907–8 after a fire. – PLATE. Chalice and two Patens, 1765 by *Thomas Whipham.*

HOLBROOK HALL. Five-bay, two-storey stone house with quoins, a segmental pediment above the doorway, another above the middle window going up into the roof. The date is 1681, surprisingly early for such details in Derbyshire.

HOLLINGTON BARN *see* TISSINGTON

HOLLOWAY *see* DETHICK

HOLME *see* BAKEWELL

3070

HOLMESFIELD

ST SWITHIN. 1826. W tower with odd battlements and crocketed pinnacles. Nave with long slim arched windows, with frames of rusticated blocks of alternating size. The chancel was added in 1897–8, enlarged in 1963. – PLATE. Continental Chalice and silver-gilt Paten, C17.

HOLMESFIELD HALL. Dated 1613 inside. Mullioned windows with straight hoods. The front redone in the C18 with a doorway with open pediment and swagger coat of arms. The windows still mullioned, but unmoulded frames and mullions.

CARTLEDGE HALL. Asymmetrical gabled Elizabethan or Jacobean farmhouse. Inside panelling, a carved fireplace with a relief of the Fall of Man, and rich plaster ceilings (those in the parlour and N bedroom from Greenhill Hall, Sheffield, demolished 1964). There are similar ceilings at Renishaw and Brampton Hall and were others in several now demolished houses in the Sheffield area.

FANSHAWGATE HALL FARM, ½ m. NW. Two pairs of elaborate C17 garden gateposts now lead only to a farmhouse with low mullioned windows, probably an outbuilding of or successor to the former Hall which was apparently dismantled in 1636. To its E a pretty dovecote.

(OLD HORSLEYGATE HALL, ½ m. SW. A C17 L-shaped house. Mullioned windows with plain chamfers to the lane, ovolo-moulded at the side. Tall BARN and outbuildings behind with some C17 mullioned openings. Bob Hawkins)

WOODTHORPE HALL, ½m. N. Sizeable L-shaped C17 manor house, much renovated. Some materials said to be from Fanshawgate Hall (*see* above). The front with three gables of which that on the r. is larger than the others, the side with two gables. Of the two porches one incorporates the original main doorway, the other was brought from Owlerton Hall, Sheffield. (The roof is made up of cut-down cruck trusses, some inverted together with their purlins. S. Jones)

(UNTHANK HALL, 1 m. SW. C16 or C17, a big gabled house with mullioned windows. Cruck barn and C17 stables. RE)

TOTLEY MOOR, BROWN EDGE, 1¾m. N. Small cairn surrounded by two concentric banks of rubble. It contained three Bronze Age cremations.

RAMSLEY MOOR, 2m. SW. The moor is famous for the huge number of mainly Bronze Age cairns which still survive here. About 130 are still in evidence.

HOON MOUNT *see* SUTTON-ON-THE-HILL

HOPE

1080

ST PETER. Early C14 W tower with angle buttresses, rebuilt in 1728. Heavy, i.e. early, broach-spire on it starting direct from the top of the unembattled tower. All tower and spire windows are Dec (bell-openings C19). The chancel was rebuilt in 1881–2, but incorporates PISCINA and SEDILIA of *c.* 1300 or the early C14. Another PISCINA with trefoil head in the S aisle. N and S aisles, clerestory, and S porch all Perp and unusually complete, obviously a rapid and steady rebuilding job. Battlements everywhere and oversized gargoyles on the S side. The aisle windows of three lights with panel tracery, the arcades of four bays with tall slim octagonal piers and moulded capitals of a section which one does not meet often. The S porch is two-storeyed with a good front with ogee niche between two windows. – PULPIT. 1652, on a later base. – FONTS. One early C12 bowl, another of 1662 from Derwent church. – STALL BACKS. Made up from parts of the former box pews (cf. Castleton). Dates 1587, 1632, 1658, 1690. – STAINED GLASS. In the chancel by *Kempe & Co.*, 1908; two in the Lady Chapel by *F. C. Eden*. – PLATE. Chalice and Cover, 1662; Paten, 1665; Flagon, 1715. – MONUMENTS. Two C13 foliated cross slabs to Forest officials (see the horns), N aisle W end. – Brass to Henry Balguy † 1685. – In the churchyard Saxon CROSS SHAFT with interlace and on the E and W faces pairs of figures, badly preserved, perhaps C11.

(DAGGERS HOUSE, E of the church, built as the Cross Daggers Inn. C18, stylish, with pilasters and semicircular attic windows.)

Near Hope are the large CEMENT WORKS of the Blue Circle Group, sited away from the village, and disguised by planting.

To the W of the works, the former engine house and chimney of the PINDALE LEAD MINE. Early C19, stone.

THE FOLLY, ½ m. SW. Rather flat Bronze Age barrow.

PIKE LOW, 3½ m. NNE of Hope. Large Bronze Age cairn.

2050

HOPTON

HOPTON HALL. An Elizabethan house with two gabled projections, redone in the later C18, when the garden front received Venetian windows, the centre between the projections was filled in and crowned by an oversized heavy segmental pediment (cf. Brizlincote), and the entrance side completely Georgianized by the Gells.* In the gardens a brick forcing wall for fruit made into a handsome composition early in the C18. In the centre a tower (summer house?); to the l. and r. the wall makes three segmental curves (i.e. crinkle-crankle).

SIR PHILIP GELL ALMSHOUSES. 1719–22, for two men and two women. One-storeyed, central gable, the windows still mullioned.

(In the village several attractive buildings, e.g. a BARN of *c.* 1780, TUDOR COTTAGES, C17, next to the almshouses, and WOODBANK, picturesque, with wide Gothick windows. RE)

(SYCAMORE FARMHOUSE, ½ m. E. C18, stone, with a brick front for prestige (cf. Parwich Hall and Great Longstone Hall, both 1747). Central bow with Venetian windows. RE)

HOPTON WOOD QUARRIES
see MIDDLETON-BY-WIRKSWORTH

4030

HOPWELL HALL

The Hall was demolished after a fire in 1957. It was a five-bay, two-and-a-half-storey brick mansion with broad giant angle pilasters. The bulgy top cornice, the moulded stone window frames, and the doorcase with open segmental pediment and

* Probably *c.* 1780 when *Thomas Gardner* made (unexecuted) designs for 'improvements' (ES).

pilasters with sunk panels all characteristic of the inscribed date 1720. A lower three-bay wing to the W. In Borrowash church is a wrought-iron balustrade said to have come from here.

HORSLEY

3040

ST CLEMENT. A fine all-embattled church with a spire on a hill. The spire is broached and not high (two tiers of dormer windows), but the view of the E end is quite splendid. The interior is wide and light with N and S aisles, the S arcade on tallish circular piers, the N arcade octagonal. The arches are double-chamfered, the whole looks early C14. Of the same date probably the S doorway and the tower (see the tracery of the bell-openings and the S doorway with head-stops to the label). The tower has angle buttresses. Most of the windows are Perp, segment-headed, of two and three ogee-arched lights, including the clerestory windows. A two-light window opens above the chancel arch, an unusual feature. All this Perp work and the whole of the crenellating is connected with a rededication in 1450. SEDILIA C14 or C15, with cusped ogee arches and plain shields in the spandrels (cf. Breadsall). – FONT. Big, Perp, octagonal. – PLATE. Elizabethan Chalice.

ST SUSANNA. Horsley Woodhouse. 1878 by *Robinson* (GR). – STAINED GLASS. E window by *Burlison & Grylls*.

(HORSTON (or HORSLEY) CASTLE, 1 m. SW. C12, built by Hugh de Buron, passed in 1198 to King John, who did substantial rebuilding in 1200–3. The ashlar N wall of the keep survives, with a fragment of the W wall showing the sloping plinth of corner towers, together with a square mural chamber. The rest destroyed by quarrying in the C18.)

(COXBENCH HALL, NW of the castle, off the A61. C18, stucco, with Doric porch and iron balcony over. Stables dated 1774. DOE)

HULLAND

2040

CHRIST CHURCH. 1838 by *John Mason* of Derby. Neat rectangle with embattled W tower. No aisles. All windows lancets of two lancet lights with the spandrel pierced. E window three-light intersected. Box pews, two-decker pulpit, W gallery on cast-iron columns, flat ceiling, whitewashed – i.e. nothing altered. – PLATE. Brass Almsdish with St George and the Dragon, probably German, *c.* 1600, given to the church in 1936; Paten, 1705 by *Humphrey Payne*.

(HULLAND HALL, hidden from the road by a stable block with turret and lantern. Red brick house built in 1777 to replace the OLD HALL which is farther down the hill. Main façade of three storeys and three bays, with a long two-storey wing at r. angles, its E façade divided by chimneystacks.)

HULLAND WARD *see* MUGGINTON

2040

IDRIDGEHAY

ST JAMES. 1844–5 by *Stevens* (GR).

SOUTH SITCH. An uncommonly good timber-framed house with closely set uprights and no decorative bits. The date 1621 on the house probably refers to an alteration of an earlier building. (It shows signs of having been an open hall-house. DOE) The interior well preserved too. (Rare timber-framed chimney. DOE)

ALTON MANOR, ½m. N. Elizabethan-style stone house built in 1846 by *Sir G. G. Scott* for James Milnes. L-shaped, with a lantern over the entrance bay. (Matching lodge. RE)

(ALTON HALL FARMHOUSE. C17, L-shaped, and interesting because like two separate houses with arched doorways in both wings. RE)

4040

ILKESTON

The town, with its spacious market place crowning a steep hill, is more topographically than architecturally attractive.

ST MARY. A big stately church now, but chiefly owing to a bold enlargement of 1909–10 which made out of a nave three bays long one of double that length and shifted the W tower to a new position at the same time. Of the original building of *c.* 1200 there remain the three E piers between nave and S aisle, circular with transitional capitals with small upright leaves and chevron-moulded pointed arches. When the N arcade was built in the C14 with octagonal piers and double-chamfered arches, the authorities wanted their church to be considerably higher than the Norman church had been, and so about 5 ft were added to the Norman piers and the new N piers were made that much longer. A clerestory was not found necessary. But before then the W tower* was built, as its rather low arch towards the nave

* The tower was rebuilt in 1723, the top classical in style. This was remodelled in 1853–5. Originally the church had a spire.

with semicircular responds and dogtooth ornament shows. That must have been early in the C13. It was followed by the chancel; see the excellent SEDILIA and DOUBLE PISCINA which are datable *c.* 1280 by the foliage capitals, head label-stops, and the bar tracery of the piscina (with a quatrefoil in a circle). The exterior of the church is terribly over-restored – the E window, for example, is entirely of 1853–5 by *T. L. Walker* (a pupil of the elder Pugin) – but the tracery of the original (E) parts of the two aisles, though renewed, represents what was there: fine three-light windows, the three lights lancet-shaped and stepped, with pointed trefoils in the heads and much cusping, i.e. typical of the early C14. Of the late C14 the N chancel chapel (Chantry of St Peter) with a delicate arcade. Its piers and arches are delicate and many-shafted. The capitals are small and decorated with bossy leaves. N and E walls rebuilt by *Walker*. – SCREEN. Remarkable early C14 stone screen, each division of one light only with a cusped ogee arch and a large quatrefoil in each spandrel. Very light and transparent. – (STAINED GLASS. E window 1910, probably by *Burlison & Grylls*. – N aisle, third from E, an Edwardian window by *Jones & Willis*, commemorating the visit of George V and Queen Mary in 1914 and including their portraits. R. Hubbuck) – PLATE. Chalice given in 1622; Chalice, 1759 by *Charles Woodward*. – MONUMENT. Fairly well preserved effigy of a cross-legged knight, presumed to be Sir Nicholas de Cantelupe † 1272. 27

ST BARTHOLOMEW, Hallam Fields. 1895 by *Currey*. Brick, a pretty composition with an almost detached NW tower with saddleback roof. Now used (1977) by the St John Ambulance Brigade.

ST JOHN EVANGELIST, Nottingham Road. 1894 by *Currey*. Brick with lancet windows, no tower but a turret in the angle between nave and N transept.

ST ANDREW'S METHODIST CHURCH, Wilmot Street, replaces six chapels including the Primitive Methodist Chapel of 1849 which stood here until 1971/2. 1973–5 by *Terry Bestwick*, and cleverly fitted on to an oddly-shaped site. The façade to Bath Street (really the E end of the church) is a plain red brick wall, with a glass roof above set back on a sloping brick basement.

UNITED REFORMED (formerly Congregational) CHURCH, Wharncliffe Road. 1905 by *H. Tatham Sudbury* of Ilkeston. Huge brick Art Nouveau Gothic church with tall tower and copper spire. Extensive basement where the hill slopes down the back.

(GENERAL BAPTIST CHAPEL, Queen Street. 1858, round-ended, with tall arched windows. C. Stell)

TOWN HALL, Market Place. A red brick 'palazzo' of 1867–8 by *R. C. Sutton* of Nottingham. Extension 1974.

COURT HOUSE, Pimilico. By *R. W. Kenning* (County Architect), 1974–6. A plain red brick building in landscaped surroundings, in keeping with the residential area and quite unlike the jazzy Court House at Chesterfield.

CARNEGIE LIBRARY, Market Place. 1904 by *Hunter & Woodhouse* of Belper. Large and red brick with full-length stone-mullioned bay-windows at each end and, under the eaves, small windows with decorative Art Nouveau stone panels between. A good period piece.

GRAMMAR SCHOOL, King George Avenue. By *G. H. Widdows* (former County Architect), opened 1914. It has a plan like New Mills Grammar School (*see* p. 287) with a quadrangle of class-rooms round a central domed hall. Here the details are classical and the exterior rendered. In the hall glass painted by *Stodart* of Nottingham.

CHAUCER PRIMARY SCHOOL, Cantelupe Road. 1973–5 by the *County Architect's Department* in association with the Department of Education and Science.

SWIMMING BATHS, Victoria Park. 1967–72 by *Rex Savidge* of *Gelsthorpe & Savidge*, in association with *A. S. Martin* (Borough Engineer and Surveyor). Rather brutal red brick exterior of two irregular polygons linked by an L-shaped wing. Inside, the large pool area, completely tiled in white with windows overlooking the trees of Victoria Park, is altogether very successful.

To the E of St Mary's Church in HIGH STREET is ST GEORGE'S HOUSE,* C18, brick, with semicircular windows over Venetian windows. To the NE BALL'S FACTORY, Burr Lane, built in the 1840s but still in the Georgian idiom. Red brick with cast-iron windows. In the SW of the town towards Kirk Hallam are two interesting houses. On LITTLE HALLAM HILL, THE GABLES, early C18 brick with dentillated string-courses and a two-storey porch. Off the road, LITTLE HALLAM HALL with an C18 brick wing similar to The Gables and behind it the original C16 timber-faced house with a recessed brick porch

* Formerly Dalby House.

to the former hall. (Good interiors with C16 and C17 panelling and Early Georgian features. DOE)

Spanning the Erewash valley NE of the town, the wrought-iron BENNERLEY VIADUCT by *Handyside* and *Eastwood & Swingler* of Derby, 1876–7. It is 500 ft long and at the maximum 60 ft high. Disused.

For COTMANHAY *see* p. 155.
For KIRK HALLAM *see* p. 260.
For SHIPLEY *see* p. 317.

INGLEBY

3020

(INGLEBY TOFT is said to have been built by the Burdetts of Knowle Hill as a dower house. Early C18, brick, two storeys, three bays, with a slightly projecting central bay crowned by a pedimented attic. Hipped roof with dormers behind a brick parapet which curves up to meet the pediment. Doorcase with a segmental pediment, Venetian windows to the ground floor. RE) (Inside, a hall with a Doric columned screen, arched in the centre. DOE)

HEATH WOOD. Some sixty burial-mounds are situated here, the excavated examples being apparently Scandinavian. Others in the vicinity may belong to earlier periods.

IRONVILLE

4050

Built by the Butterley Iron Company between 1834 and 1850. There was well-spaced factory housing, long rows of plain brick cottages, but the last unaltered housing in the axial King William Street, built in 1834, was demolished in 1977. At the end of it a late C18 bridge over the Cromford Canal. There are also quite an ambitious church of 1852, a school of 1841, enlarged in 1857, and a monument of 1854 in the recreation ground. Along the canal to the W at GOLDEN VALLEY some early Butterley Company stone housing built between 1797 and 1813.

KEDLESTON

3040

ALL SAINTS. In spite of its Norman S doorway (one order of colonnettes, with beakheads biting into them, arch with zigzag, and defaced tympanum with traces of beasts) this is essentially a late C13 church, cruciform with crossing tower, which is rare in Derbyshire. The transepts have their original N and S windows of three stepped lancet lights, the chancel new windows, except for one small cusped lancet, but original S doorway, PISCINA, and the springers of the arch of a recess replaced by a Perp one. The top parts of the crossing tower are Perp. The E end was classicized late in the C17; see the pedimented sundial and the two vases to the l. and r. The N aisle was added by *Bodley* in 1907–13 as a memorial to the wife of Lord Curzon of Kedleston, Viceroy of India. Sumptuous wrought-iron GRILLES by *P. Krall* inside, STAINED GLASS by *F. C. Eden*, and a MONUMENT of gleaming white marble with two recumbent effigies and an elegant white woman, life-size, standing at the head end. By *Sir B. MacKennal*. – FONT, BOX PEWS, COMMUNION RAILS, all *c.* 1700, the font baluster-shaped on four scrolly feet. – FAMILY PEWS in the chancel, *c.* 1700. – COMMUNION RAIL, *c.* 1700. – PAINTINGS. Holy Family by *Giampetrini*. – Madonna by *Pier Francesco Mola*. – Baptism of Christ by *Correggio*. – PLATE. Fine silver-gilt Cup, 1601; two Patens, 1671; C17 Paten Cover; Flagon, 1765 by *Fuller White*.

OTHER MONUMENTS. Coffin-shaped slab with foliated cross, C13. – Twin quatrefoils with large heads of a knight in chain mail and a lady wearing a wimple, sunk in the oddest way into the floor of the crossing. Really part of a grave slab under the present floor. – Effigy of Sir John Curzon † 1406, in a recess in the chancel S wall. – Excellent alabaster tomb-chest for Sir John Curzon † *c.* 1450, effigies of husband and wife, against the front wall of the chest five figures, three of them seated saints, the other two standing angels. – Brass to Richard Curzon † 1496, and wife. – William Curzon † 1547, incised slab. – Sir John Curzon † 1686, large wall-monument erected in 1664, shockingly bad. The main part divided into two panels by a black column. Flanking columns as well. In the panels frontal demi-figures, each accompanied by an angel in whole figure. In the predella seven frontal busts of children between draperies. – Sir John Curzon † 1727, obelisk with portrait medallion surrounded by a wreath of cherubs' heads. Standing putti l. and r. – Sir Nathaniel Curzon † 1737, an ambitious composition by *Peter Scheemakers*. Standing wall-monument with obelisk and at its foot husband and wife in Roman attire seated with an urn between. – Sir Nathaniel Curzon, 1765 by *Rysbrack* to *Robert Adam*'s design. Yet not very satisfactory. Rusticated pyramid, and in front of it the upright figures of Sir Nathaniel, his wife, and two sons.

KEDLESTON HALL. The most splendid Georgian house in Derbyshire, in extensive grounds with a long serpentine lake to the N, and to the S the slope upwards of a hill which tends to deprive the house of some of its effect on that side. (It was begun early in 1759, very soon after the death of Sir Nathaniel Curzon I, by his son, another Nathaniel, created Lord Scarsdale in April 1761. *Matthew Brettingham* provided the basic plan with quadrant colonnades, following Palladio's Villa Mocenigo. Building began with the NE (family) wing to *Brettingham*'s design. The existing early C18 house, probably by *Smith* of Warwick,* was demolished in stages and replaced by the new central block from late 1759 until a general state of completion was reached in 1765. The NW wing was built *c.* 1760–2 and supervised by *James Paine*, who made some new designs for the two principal fronts. In December 1758 Sir Nathaniel Curzon II had consulted *Robert Adam*, inviting his opinion on Brettingham's designs and commissioning designs for garden buildings (*see* below). However, by early 1760 *Adam* was in full charge of all designing work for the main building with, at first, *Abraham Swan* as clerk of works. By mid 1760 the latter was replaced by the young *Samuel Wyatt*. The initial team included *John Chambers* and *Joseph Hall* for bricklaying and masonry with *Jason Harris* for carpentry. By 1761 there were changes leaving *Hall* in charge of the masons and carvers and *James Denston* of the bricklayers; *Wyatt* retained direct control of the carpenters. *Abraham Denston* dealt with plain plastering, and *Joseph Rose* was responsible for ceilings etc. LH‡)

Adam built the NORTH FRONT to a modified version of Brettingham's or Paine's design, more or less as shown in *Paine's* engraving (*Works*, ii, 1783). The main block derives from Campbell's Wanstead. It is oblong, of eleven bays, with a great N portico raised above a rusticated basement storey and reached by a double staircase. It has six Corinthian columns, a commanding if not especially imaginative motif, and in the portico blank niches and medallions (Vintage, Pasturage, Ploughing, and Bear Hunting) by *Collins*, paid for in 1769. Two

87

* There is a plan at Kedleston showing a rectangular house with corner projections inscribed 'Built by Smith'.

‡ We must thank Mr Leslie Harris for providing us with so much unpublished information. His contributions are acknowledged in the text either by his initials or in footnotes. A full account of the building history will appear in his forthcoming book.

quadrants of one tall storey with attached colonnades above an arched basement project from the NE and NW angles to link one-and-a-half storey pavilions, each with four attached Ionic columns supporting a pediment. These two above a rusticated basement. The NW pavilion houses kitchens, etc., the NE the private apartments. The much more original SOUTH FRONT is entirely by *Adam*. It has as its centre motif, derived from the Arch of Constantine, four detached Corinthian columns standing close to the wall and each carrying its own piece of projecting entablature. Above this is an attic with the date plate of 1765 and statues on the four pieces of entablature. The motif, combined with the curves of dome and staircase, possibly possesses just that 'diversity of form' and 'advance and recess' of which Adam wrote in 1773 that they 'add greatly to the picturesque' of an architectural composition. Between the columns also the motifs are more varied than in the centre of the N front. The less emphasized parts to the l. and r. of the centre have only window pediments on brackets, whereas Paine had given them attached columns. Adam is unquestionably less grand, but he is more elegant, and despite the great size of the block more intimate.* The intended SE and SW wings, never built, would have completed a layout reminiscent of Paine's uncompleted plan for Nostell Priory, begun *c.* 1733. ‡ Inside, the scheme of an axially placed rectangular hall lined with detached columns and with a saloon behind derives principally from Holkham. Perhaps *Brettingham*, who was clerk of works there *c.* 1734, initiated the idea at Kedleston, an idea subsequently developed by *Paine* and *Adam*. Ranged along each side of hall and rotunda are three major rooms.

86

The HALL of Kedleston is one of the most magnificent apartments of the C18 in England, about 67 ft by 37 ft in plan, and 40 ft high, with fluted columns of pink Nottinghamshire alabaster and a generously coved ceiling with stucco decoration. Round the walls are niches with casts of antique sculpture (by *Matthew Brettingham Jun.* and others: LH); above them grisaille panels of Homeric subjects, a scheme inspired by Palladio's illustration of the Temple of Mars. Below are sarcophagus

88

* *Paine*'s design for the S front shown in his *Works* is also more imaginative than that for the N front, with a domed saloon projecting in the centre surrounded with a semicircular portico. Flanking this and repeated in the pavilions, Venetian windows, and, on the balustrade, statues.

‡ Mr Harris thinks that Sir Nathaniel Curzon may have suggested the plan to avoid resiting the church.

benches. The stucco of the ceiling was executed in the mid seventies by *Joseph Rose* to a design by Adam's chief draughtsman, *George Richardson.** The fireplaces have elaborate overmantels by *Rose*, incorporating roundels after *Gravelot* and *Domenichino*. (Magnificent firebaskets by *Adam*. LH) The character of this stucco is somewhat different from that of the architecture which is, like all early Adam work, just a little more robust than his later designs. Giant columns so consistently used would have appeared too massive to Adam in the seventies. From the far end of the hall the ROTUNDA is immediately reached,‡ the room replacing *Paine*'s projected staircase (Adam's is W of the hall and less conspicuous) and saloon. The hall and rotunda lie in the relationship of 'atrium' and 'vestibulum', a theme expounded by Adam in his book on the *Ruins of Spalato* published in 1764. The rotunda is fitted into the square outer walls by means of corner niches, again a typical motif of Imperial Roman architecture. The room is domed, and the coffering of the dome and its central skylight are also clearly of Roman derivation.§ The spatial effect of moving from the hall into the rotunda is delightful, for the rotunda is considerably higher (62 ft high; diameter 42 ft). The paintings of ruins are by *Hamilton*, the grisaille panels with scenes of British worthies between them by *Rebecca*. In the niches are cast-iron vases on pedestals disguising Adam's heating arrangements, and seats to his design. The pilasters flanking the doorways are of blue scagliola. The decoration was not completed until late in the 1780s.

To the l. (W) of the hall and rotunda are, taken from N to S and also order of completion, the MUSIC ROOM (with an organ, the case designed by *Adam* and made by the carpenters and carvers, and a fireplace with a tablet by *Spang*);** the DRAWING ROOM, 44 by 28 by 28 ft (with a gorgeous Venetian window of alabaster, alabaster doorcase, a fireplace flanked by large standing female figures by *Spang*, *c*. 1760, and settees with gilt merfolk supporting the arms by *John Linnell*, *c*. 1765);** and the LIBRARY (more severe in its architecture, with a massive Doric doorcase leading to the rotunda and bookcases designed

* Richardson exhibited this design in his own name in 1776. In 1774 he had dedicated his *Book of Ceilings* to Lord Scarsdale. Mouldings of the entablature carved by *George Moneypenny* (LH).

‡ The normal route for visitors is via the Music Room, etc.

§ And in fact the dome on the outside was originally stepped like that of the Pantheon (LH).

** Information from Mr Harris.

by *Adam* and made on site).* To the N on the other side of the hall and rotunda is the DINING ROOM‡ with an apse at the W end into which fit curved tables designed by *Adam* in 1762 and inspired by *James Stuart*'s design of early 1757 for interiors presumably meant for Kedleston.* Flanking the apse, stucco medallions by *Collins*. The ceiling, coloured as in *Adam*'s drawing, has panels by *Zucchi* (continents), *Hamilton* (seasons), and *Morland* (centre). The original wall panels are paintings by *Zuccarelli*, *Snyders*, *Claude*, and *Romanelli*. The fireplace has termini caryatids by *Spang*, *c*. 1760, and the design of the monumental wine cooler of jasper is attributed to *Stuart*. To the S are the STAIRCASE (with stucco of 1924),* seen from the STATE BEDROOM (with its fantastic bed, the four angle posts of which are carved in the form of palm trees; probably not by *Adam* but possibly inspired by his design for a barge).‡ Next to it, the STATE BOUDOIR (originally designated principal dressing room),* spatially the most complex room in so far as the part nearest the rotunda is divided off by a wall opening in the middle in a somewhat lower tripartite screen with pierced segmental arch above the entablature, a very characteristic Adam motif. This room and the bedroom were completed with ceilings of the flatter and slightly later style. Below the hall and rotunda at ground level are a low double-aisled hall (the inner columns are modern)* and a tetrastyle hall. The interior was in general complete by 1765, except the State Bedroom and Boudoir which followed in 1768 and the decoration of the hall and rotunda which dragged on until the 1770s and 1780s.*

(In the GROUNDS several buildings to *Adam*'s designs: the NORTH LODGE (1761–2, with gates by *Benjamin Yates*) set in a screen of Doric columns with a pediment over; and N of the North Lodge a GOTHICK TEMPLE of 1759–60 with a façade with three ogee arches, traceried windows, shields, and a pierced parapet. An elegant three-arched BRIDGE (built 1769–70); to the E of it the BATH HOUSE (*c*. 1761); to the S of it the LION'S MOUTH (*c*. 1763); and to the W of it a combined FISHING- and BOATHOUSE with a central Venetian window (*c*. 1770). SW of the house a fine VASE; a LION on a pedestal; and the ORANGERY. W of the house the STABLES (1767–9).*)

The SOUTH LODGE (NW of the house), possibly also by *Adam*, leads to the VILLAGE. To the N the former VICARAGE, 1771–2 by *Samuel Wyatt*. Brick, with a big arched recess on the garden

* Information from Mr Harris.

‡ Visitors go first into the State Boudoir.

elevation containing the central window. Returning S past the SCHOOL (late C19 and picturesque with fretted bargeboards) and a similar house opposite, at the junction with the main road is SMITHY FARMHOUSE, a two-storey whitewashed brick building with Gothic windows. Further S along the main road is HOME or IRETON FARM, an C18 model farm, mainly brick with a stucco front to the courtyard with pilasters, pediment, and sunk oval panels in the attic. At the S end of the park in Quarndon parish is the KEDLESTON HOTEL, C18, built as an inn by the Curzons. Brick and three-storey with single-storey wings. The central feature with Doric columns, now a staircase hall, was originally a porte-cochère.

See p. 409

KILBURN HALL

3040

Partly Jacobean and partly dated 1712. The latter work is remarkably conservative, still with gables. Quoins and stone lintels to the windows. Much renewed and added to after 1900. (The stables incorporate a five-bay cruck building. RE)

KILLAMARSH

4080

ST GILES. The interest of the church is the Norman S doorway (one order of colonnettes, capitals with leaves, arch with zigzag on intrados and extrados). The Late Perp S window should also be noted in which all curved forms of Gothic arches have gone straight. W tower Perp (diagonal buttresses, battlements, pinnacles). (N aisle and vestry added in 1895 by *J. M. Brooks*, son of James Brooks. R. Dixon) – STAINED GLASS. C15 Virgin in a chancel S window. – Chancel E window by *Warrington*, 1845 (TK). – PLATE. Elizabethan Chalice.

KINDER *see* HAYFIELD

KINGS NEWTON

3020

One of the most attractive village streets in Derbyshire, with several C18 houses and two ranges of timber-framed cottages on the S side.

HALL. A C17 H-plan stone house (modern date 1560) fairly accurately rebuilt in 1910 after a fire in 1859. (Fine Bakewell-type wrought-iron gates. ES)

KINGSTERNDALE *see* p. 409

4040

KIRK HALLAM

Part of Ilkeston

ALL SAINTS. Two Norman beakheads preserved in the porch; the FONT also Norman, tub-shaped, with an arcade of intersecting arches. Small, aisleless church with Dec chancel windows (straight-headed) and SEDILIA and PISCINA. Perp W tower, short and ashlar-faced. (Minor restoration by *G. E. Street* in 1859. P. Joyce)

INFANTS' SCHOOL. 1953–4 by *Morrison & Partners* in association with *F. Hamer Crossley* (County Architect). One of the standard brick and steel schools provided by the County Education Department in the early 1950s (*see* Introduction, p. 46), and one of the most successful.

2050

KIRK IRETON

HOLY TRINITY. C18 gateway into the churchyard. Embattled W tower low, broad, and unbuttressed: obviously early. Blocked W doorway. Small low church with Norman S doorway, two-bay Late Norman S arcade (piers circular and with simplified leaves, arches lopsided two-stepped, quite illogical) and slightly later N arcade (piers circular with moulded capitals, arches single-chamfered). Chancel arch Perp. Arch into the chancel chapel one huge ogee. These parts are embattled on the S side, the nave and aisles are not. The only more ornate detail in the church is the C14 doorway from the chancel into the vestry, with thin shafts and the voussoirs decorated with big fleurons. – PLATE. Chalice, 1755 by *Thomas Whipham.*

(A very good stone-built village with a homogeneous character. Starting at the NE end worth noting are: CHURCH FARMHOUSE (C17 with tiny mullioned windows indicating an early date); a FARMHOUSE W of the church, the one exception to the rule of stone but blending happily; the fine C18 group of NORTHFIELD FARMHOUSE and MANOR HOUSE, some way up the hill; BUXTON HALL FARMHOUSE with a cruck truss, further up; and the BARLEY MOW INN of 1683, a good example of the late Derbyshire Jacobean style (gabled dormers with ball finials, mullioned windows and door still with a slightly arched head). In Coffin Lane, the tiny early C19 METHODIST SUNDAY SCHOOL. RE)

BLACKWALL HOUSE, ¾ m. S. Built by the Blackwalls before 1623. L-shaped, made into a square in 1736 (date on the basement

W door). S façade refaced and heightened in the late C18 and early C19, and given four Venetian windows, a gabled porch with steps to the terrace, and a pedimented shaped gable between the main gables. C19 road elevation. Opposite, an outbuilding with mullioned windows.*

KIRK LANGLEY

2030

ST MICHAEL. Early C14 chancel (SEDILIA with pointed trefoiled heads, lancet window, N doorway). N aisle also early C14 (windows, arcade). W tower Perp, ashlar-faced, with angle buttresses connected at the top, below the battlements, by a horizontal band. Restoration, including S aisle windows and clerestory, by *Bodley & Garner*, 1885. – TOWER SCREEN. Apparently *c.* 1300, see its simple geometrical tracery. – PARCLOSE SCREEN. Perp, with original tracery motifs. – PLATE. Silver-gilt Set consisting of Chalice of Gothic shape, Paten, and large Flagon; London-made, 1640, the gift of Lady Frances Kniveton (*see* Bradley, Kniveton, Mugginton, Osmaston for identical sets). – MONUMENT. Henry Pole † 1559 and wife, tomb-chest with twisted columns and incised slab.

Several good brick houses in the village, e.g. the Georgian Langley House and the Meynell Arms on the main road, with broad doorway with attached Tuscan columns and stone-dressed window above.

(MEYNELL LANGLEY, 1 m. NE. A late C18 house, remodelled from 1806 (staircase), refronted by *Francis Goodwin* in 1829. Stone, two-storey, nine-bay façade with a central portico on coupled Ionic columns.)

(LANGLEY HALL, ½ m. NW. Rebuilt in 1836, it is said to designs by *Pugin*, incorporating parts of a C16 house. Brick, gabled, sash-windows with hood-moulds. DOE)

KNIVETON

2050

ST MICHAEL. Small; just nave and chancel and W tower. The latter C13, unbuttressed, with small lancet windows, battlements and a short spire. S doorway Norman, on the plainest imposts. Label with two stops (one of them a beakhead). The keystone a bear, the whole evidently tampered with (cf. Hognaston). All windows are renewed. – FONT. Of the Ashbourne type, but the trefoil motif pointed. – PLATE. Silver-gilt set (Chalice,

* Information was kindly supplied by Mr Anthony Blackwall.

Paten, and Flagon) given by Lady Frances Kniveton in 1641 (*see* Bradley, Kirk Langley, Mugginton, Osmaston for identical sets).

(BROOK HOUSE. Dated 1695 in the pediment over the door. Still Jacobean in detail but prophetic of the C18 vernacular, especially the big gap between the upper windows and the eaves. RE)

(Also in the village two early C19 CHAPELS, and 1 m. S two C17 houses, WOODHEAD and AGNES MEADOW. RE)

KNOWLE HILL *see* TICKNALL

1080

LADYBOWER RESERVOIR

The name applies to a group of connected reservoir lakes which form a splendid enhancement of the natural beauties of Derbyshire. The purpose of the reservoirs is to supply water for Derby, Leicester, Nottingham, Sheffield, and some smaller local authorities. They consist of the two upper NE parts with their two forbidding castellated dams, Howden Dam and Derwent Dam, begun in 1906 and 1907 and completed with their respective reservoirs in 1912 and 1916. These were followed by the Ashop Diversion or Compensation Works (1921–30) and finally the Ladybower proper, with its grass-embanked dam (1935–45). The filling of the reservoir submerged DERWENT WOODLANDS Church and DERWENT HALL. A PACKHORSE BRIDGE was re-erected just to the N of it.

LADY LOW *see* CHAPEL-EN-LE-FRITH

LANGLEY HALL *see* KIRK LANGLEY

LAPWING HILL *see* TADDINGTON

LATHKILL DALE *see* MONYASH

LEA *see* DETHICK

LEAM MOOR *see* EYAM

LID LOW *see* THORPE

LIFFS LOW *see* BIGGIN-BY-HARTINGTON

LITTLE CHESTER *see* DERBY, p. 183

LITTLE EATON

3040

ST PAUL. Built 1791, enlarged 1837, but all that is visible now is a modernization in the Norman style of 1851 (with embattled W tower).

The village has a neat little centre with rows of stone cottages on three sides. SW of the church in Station Road, THE POPLARS, a handsome Mid Georgian brick house of three bays and two and a half storeys, with quoins, rusticated lintels, a pedimented doorway and l. and r. of it Venetian windows.

LITTLE HALLAM *see* ILKESTON

LITTLE HUCKLOW

1070

OLD HALL (now part of the Bull's Head Inn) with date-stone 1661. Yet the windows are low and mullioned and have hood-moulds, oddly double-stepped (cf. Unstone 1657). At the back is a projecting spiral staircase; so the structure of the house is older. (Inside two open fireplaces with cambered heads and stone bracketed hoods. Exposed ceiling beams and some internal timber-framing. DOE)

GREAT HUCKLOW. *See* p. 219.

LITTLE LONGSTONE

2070

(HALL or MANOR HOUSE. Built *c.* 1700, but the plan with recessed centre and gabled wings is still C17. RE)

(THE STOCKS. The date 1575 on a gable may be authentic. T-shape, with small mullioned windows. Coped gable with a ball finial. RE)

(MONSAL DALE RAILWAY VIADUCT, ½m. W. Handsome stone arches spanning the dale. Built in the 1860s and denounced by Ruskin. The railway has now gone. RE)

NW of the village, HAY TOP HILL. Cairn over cist containing a crouched inhumation. Another cairn contained a cist with four inhumations.

½m. N, two BARROWS, probably Bronze Age.

LITTLEMOOR *see* CHESTERFIELD, p. 148

LITTLEOVER *see* DERBY, p. 193

1070

LITTON

(CHRIST CHURCH. 1926–7 by *W. H. R. Blacking* in a traditional style using local materials. – FONT. C18 baluster type, brought from elsewhere. – Other fittings by *Blacking*.)

Those interested in the development of the architectural style in Derbyshire houses will find one of 1723 (Clergy House), still with the old low two-light windows, but with a doorway with pediment on corbels and regular quoins, and another of 1768 (Hammerton Hall Farmhouse) with a segmental pediment to the doorway and an arched window above it, but the other windows even now still of the three-light mullioned type.

4030

LOCKO PARK*

Large stone mansion approached from the S through a pair of pretty C18 LODGES, and overlooking a park with an ornamental lake, landscaped in 1792.‡ It is nine bays wide, three storeys high, with emphasis on the rusticated giant pilasters at the angles and at the angles of the five-bay centre. Top balustrade, lettered like Felbrigg ('Dulce est dicipere in Loco'), originally ornamented with urns. At either end one-storey projecting wings, that on the W older than the main house and containing the CHAPEL, built in 1669. Refurbished in 1882 by *F. J. Robinson* and again in 1899, with STAINED GLASS by *Powell*. It retains its original coffered wooden ceiling and PULPIT and contains an unusual C17 wooden FONT, C17 PLATE (Chalice and Paten, 1670; Tankard by *John Jackson*, 1688; Paten on foot, 1694), and a *Schnetzler* chamber ORGAN of 1779, brought from the Music Room in the other, mid-C18, wing. This wing was probably added in the interest of Palladian symmetry after William Drury-Lowe bought the estate in 1747. Inside, of the early C18, a fine staircase, with two turned and one twisted baluster per tread and tread ends identical to those that used to exist at Wingerworth Hall,§ in a very narrow staircase hall. (Probably altered in the C19, it now rises to the top of the house.)

* This description has been revised by Mr G. Hughes Hartman.

‡ Probably by *William Eames*, a pupil of *Capability Brown*, whose design for Locko Park is dated 1792. The house as seen from the S was built *c.* 1725–30 for Robert Ferne and is attributed to *Smith* of Warwick (cf. his demolished part of Alfreton Hall) by John Cornforth (*Country Life*, CXLV, 1969).

§ According to Dr Gomme.

Of the same date doorcases, panelling, and an elaborate *ex-situ* carved architrave to the boudoir. Interior of the r. wing remodelled *c.* 1779 when the dining room became a music room. Fireplace mid C19. At the back a plain mid C18 service wing, and behind the chapel a W wing of 1804, built after designs by *William Wilkins* had been rejected in 1803. Much internal remodelling of that date.

Large additions were made in a restrained Italianate style by *Henry Stevens* of Derby, starting with the bell tower in 1853–6 and following on the E side in 1861–4 with a new entrance porch, hall, and dining room, all clearly showing the influence of William Drury-Lowe's Italian travels. They enclose a top-lit picture gallery, built to accommodate Drury-Lowe's collection of Italian paintings. E front extended in 1896 by a billiards room. Inside, ceilings painted by Italians: in the picture gallery and dining room by *A. Romoli*, in the entrance hall by the *Brothers Andreotti* of Florence, and in the billiards room (1906) by Cavalieri *G. Bacci Venuti* and *P. F. Santini*, who also painted in the upper hall and boudoir of the old house.

At Locko in the Middle Ages (*c.* 1297–1347) was the only preceptory of the Lazarite order in England.

LONG EATON

4030

ST LAURENCE. Behind the Market Place. The low and broad church makes a pretty picture, with its separate N aisle and nave roofs and its SW tower. This picture is C19. It belongs to *Street*'s rebuilding of 1868. He made the old nave his S aisle and thereby displaced the old W tower. The tower is ashlar-faced with diagonal buttresses and has the recessed spire behind battlements which is so frequent in Derbyshire. The old nave has a Norman doorway with one order of colonnettes and in the voussoirs an inner order of beakhead and a second order of large chain-links. In the chancel also a few Norman fragments of a doorway (zigzag, shaft). The windows are of the C14, straight-headed. The old church had been restored in 1831. In 1868 the old chancel became *Street*'s organ chamber, connected with his new chancel by a two-bay arcade of interesting design. (The organ is now over the new vestry of 1905.) Chancel roof decorated in 1936 by *Wystan Widdows*. – (FONT by *Street*. Paul Joyce) – (STAINED GLASS. In the Norman window of the S aisle, the best in the church. Undated. It looks like *Hardman*'s work. R. Hubbuck)

ST JOHN THE EVANGELIST, College Street. By *Sir Charles Nicholson*, designed 1916, begun 1922. Brick (English bond) with stone dressings. The SW tower was never built, and the E end was completed simply, with tile-hanging and a bell canopy, and the interior modernized by *Montague Associates* (re-opened 1972).

BETHEL METHODIST CHURCH, Derby Road. By *Brewill & Bailey*, 1903–4, in the enterprising and fanciful style of these architects and of Methodist architecture about 1900.

TRINITY METHODIST CHURCH, Cross Street. 1880. Classical, with a columned portico and nice lettering.

THE HALL (Erewash District Council Offices), The Green. Built in 1778 and attributed* on stylistic grounds to *Joseph Pickford*. Handsome three-storey, three-bay red brick house with a slightly projecting pedimented central bay and a stone Doric doorcase. (Inside all that remains of note is the staircase and a chimneypiece by *George Moneypenny*, identical to one in the demolished Egginton Hall. ES)

TRENT COLLEGE, Derby Road. 1866–8 by a Mr *Peck*, red brick and in castellated Tudor style. On the r. projects the CHAPEL of 1874 by *Robinson* of Derby, remodelled inside by *Sir Albert Richardson* in 1949. (STAINED GLASS. Apse windows by *Francis Spear*, 1949. R. Hubbuck) Many later buildings, including the MAY HALL, *c.* 1964 by *J. W. Wilcox & Partners*.

GRAMMAR SCHOOL, Tamworth Road. 1911 by *G. H. Widdows* (County Architect). A near relation of Widdows's St Helena School, Chesterfield (*see* p. 145), also a mixture of Tudor and Baroque styles. Some glass painted by *Stodart* of Nottingham.

LONGMOOR PRIMARY SCHOOL. One of the standard schools built after 1945 by the *County Architect's Department* (*see* Introduction, p. 46).

CARNEGIE LIBRARY, Tamworth Road. 1906 by *Gorman & Ross*. Arts and Crafts style with shallow pitched roof and bay-windows flanking an elaborate doorway with a mosaic in the tympanum. Inside, painted glass by *Stodart*. Red brick extension to the N (Stevenson's Gallery and Elder Citizens' Centre) by the *Borough Engineer's Department*, 1964–5. The library has a Continental, possibly Secessionist, flavour.

SWIMMING POOL, Wilsthorpe Road. 1972–4 by *Vincent, Gorbing & Partners*.

The town has been a lace-making centre since the 1830s. The earliest factory is HIGH STREET MILLS (1857). The largest

* By Edward Saunders.

tenement lace factories are W of the Green in LEOPOLD STREET (1880s); BRIDGE MILL, Derby Road (1906), was the last of this type. Although industrial, Long Eaton is not unattractive, with plenty of green spaces and trees near the centre. In the MARKET PLACE, two extraordinary Arts and Crafts style buildings by *Gorman & Ross*: YORK CHAMBERS (built in 1903 for the Midland Counties Bank Ltd), of three storeys, roughcast, with half-timbering, brick-nogging, and a shaped gable with a tympanum of coloured tiles; and No. 38, the architects' own office, with a round gable flanked by brick turrets. (To the W in DERBY ROAD, two houses for lace manufacturers: No. 150 by *Gorman & Ross* (note the battered chimney and stair projection); and No. 170 (RED COURT), 1910, by *Osbourne Moorhouse Thorpe*, another local architect. A Y-plan house, altered but still unusual).* Off Derby Road at the top of CURZON STREET, a suburban house by *Diamond, Redfern & Partners*, 1961–2. Two storeys, with vertical panels of buff brick and olive-brown glass.

SAWLEY. *See* p. 313.

LONGFORD

2030

ST CHAD. Close to the house. The oldest part is the Norman three-bay N arcade with circular piers, many-scalloped capitals, and unchamfered two-step arches. The fourth arch is early C14, as is the chancel, see the tall two-light windows, the SEDILIA and PISCINA, and the low N recess. The E window, however, dates from 1843. The S and N aisles are *c.* 1300 (see the windows, lancets of two-lancet lights with pierced spandrel, also three-light intersected). At the same time the S arcade was altered. Its piers are still the Norman ones, but the arches are double-chamfered, and the capitals are an ugly makeshift. The clerestory with battlements is C15. So is the fine ashlar-faced W tower with angle buttresses and two large two-light bell-openings on each side (cf. Youlgreave and North Wingfield). – CHANCEL SEATS with a few old poppy-heads. – PLATE. Chalice and Paten Cover on knob foot, *c.* 1660; Paten, 1666; Flagon, 1739 by *Thomas Whipham*. – MONUMENTS. A whole alabaster corner in the S aisle, with effigies laid on the floor: Sir Nicholas Longford † 1610 and wife. – Then three Knights, one of them under a recess in the S aisle, the latter Sir Nicholas Longford † 1357, the others probably Sir Nicholas III † 1402 and Sir Nicholas

* Information from Keith Reedman.

IV † 1429. – Mutilated effigy in the chancel recess. – Sir Edward Coke † 1733, plain large pyramid in relief. – Thomas William Coke, Earl of Leicester, † 1842, tall wall-tablet with Dec canopies, by *Joseph Hall the Younger* of Derby, and marble portrait bust by *John Francis*. – Anne Amelia Countess of Leicester † 1844, large marble wall-tablet with angel taking her to heaven; unsigned.

LONGFORD HALL. Brick with stone dressings. Burnt out in 1942 and partially reconstructed. The main façade (S) very peculiar. Evidently a Tudor front (similar to the former Risley Hall) was remodelled about 1720. The result is a façade fifteen windows long and between them symmetrically arranged four big projecting chimney-shafts carrying Tudor chimneys. The work of 1720 consisted of the introduction of sash-windows, quoins, and top balustrade with vases. The E front has two far-projecting wings and a recessed one-storeyed range to connect them. The former courtyard behind this is now partly pulled down and the main entrance moved from the cross-wing to the rear of the main front. The E gates probably by *Bakewell* of *c.* 1730. Nothing seems known of the building history of the house (except that *Joseph Pickford* of Derby was working here in 1764. What did he do? ES) (The Stables, Almshouses, and Rectory (now Longford Grange) are Georgian and associated with the Hall. MILL, C19 estate building, brick with lattice windows. RE)

LONG LEE *see* ROWARTH

LONG LOW *see* FOOLOW *and* TIDESWELL

2070

LONGSHAW LODGE

1¼ m. SE of Hathersage

Built as a shooting box for the Duke of Rutland *c.* 1827. A long, rather uneven façade of five gables, unequal in size. Rectangular and lancet windows with emphatic hood-moulds. Battlemented tower to the rear, a separate chapel, extensive stabling and servants' quarters.*

LONGSTONE *see* GREAT LONGSTONE *and* LITTLE LONGSTONE

* Information and description kindly supplied by Mr J. Barron Wright.

LORD'S SEAT *see* CASTLETON

LOSCOE

4040

ST LUKE. 1936–7 by *Bernard Widdows*. Large brick church, imposing from the W. Square tower, coupled lancets with triangular heads to the nave, round W window. Light plastered interior with contemporary fittings.

LOW LEIGHTON *see* NEW MILLS

LULLINGTON

2010

ALL SAINTS. Old only the W tower with diagonal buttresses and a broach-spire with two tiers of dormer windows, one low down, one high up. The spire was taken down and rebuilt in 1776. The rest is of 1861–2. – (STAINED GLASS. E window 1862 by *Capronnier*. R. Hubbuck) – PLATE. Elizabethan Chalice.

MACKWORTH

3030

ALL SAINTS. On its own in a field. W tower ashlar-faced, Perp, with angle buttresses connected at the top below the battlements by a horizontal band. Recessed spire with one tier of dormer windows. The bell-openings altered in the C19. S aisle with two-storeyed porch and Perp windows, N aisle windows also Perp except for the W window which is typical of *c*. 1300 (lancet consisting of two lancet lights with pierced spandrel). The W tower is supposed to have had defensive purposes, as it has provision for barring the door into the nave (see holes in the stonework into which timbers were inserted) and no door to the outside, and also very small openings in its lower stages. N and S aisles, both C14; that on the S side has characteristically earlier capitals than that on the N. The approximate date of the S aisle is indicated by the finely moulded low recess in the S wall: early C14. In the chancel the plain SEDILIA prove that it is also no later than the early C14. The niches at the E end of the N aisle and the canopy in the same aisle are supposed to be old but altered in the restoration of 1851. – Lots of lavish Victorian and later alabaster decoration, e.g. the neo-Dec vestry door surround of 1886 and the fantastic LECTERN of 1903 with its vine twining round the stem and ending in leaves and grapes below the bible support, provided by the Mundys. –

MONUMENT. Edward Mundy † 1607, alabaster effigy on a tomb-chest with figures of children on the front wall.

CASTLE. Only the front wall of the GATEHOUSE survives, erected between 1495 and 1500. The gateway has a four-centred arch. Above, one upper storey with cusped straight-headed two-light windows under hood-moulds. Above the upper storey battlements and gargoyles. No turrets.

MACKWORTH ESTATE. *See* Derby, p. 185.

MAM TOR *see* CASTLETON

1040

MAPLETON

ST MARY. An C18 stone building with a W tower crowned to one's shocked surprise by an octagonal dome with a lantern. The W porch was originally more ornate and attached to the S wall. The nave has arched windows. The interior is disappointing. – PLATE. Chalice, two Patens, and Flagon, 1751 by *Benjamin Cartwright*.

CLERGYMEN'S WIDOWS' ALMSHOUSES, W of the church. 1727. A fine brick house with ample stone dressings. Five bays, two storeys, hipped roof, quoins. The centre bay projects and is flanked by giant rusticated pilasters. Doorway with Gibbs surround and triangular pediment. Windows with stone frames. Connected with Okeover Hall across the river in Staffordshire and probably contemporary with the original work there.*

(MANOR HOUSE. Stylish C18 house similar to the Almshouses. DOE)

(CALLOW HALL. 1852 by *H. I. Stevens* of Derby for Mr Goodwin Johnson. Elizabethan style, similar to the demolished Osmaston Manor of 1846, and built of the same stone from Kniveton. Stevens's first design was more ambitious, with three storeys, conservatories, and a big tower. As built the house has a big bay-window on the S front and a small turret with concave pyramidal cap where the service wing joins the main house.)

MARKEATON PARK *see* DERBY, p. 186

MARKLAND GRIPS *see* ELMTON

* According to Dr Gomme.

MARSTON-ON-DOVE

2020

ST MARY. C13 chancel, wide, with lancet windows and small S doorway with one order of colonnettes. Early C14 S aisle, windows with flowing tracery, two-bay arcade with tall quatrefoil pier and double-chamfered arches. Ashlar-faced C14 W tower, no battlements, recessed spire with three tiers of dormer windows. The N side of the nave altered in the C15, when the clerestory was built. – The church possesses the oldest BELL in Derbyshire (1366; cast by *John of Stafford* at Leicester). – ORGAN. C18, in original case, from Sudbury Hall. – PLATE. Chalice, *c.* 1625.

MARSTON MONTGOMERY

1030

ST GILES. Nave with pyramidal bellcote by *St Aubyn* dating from 1875–7. Beneath it in the W wall of the church a small Early Norman window. On the S side of the church the S doorway Norman with one order of colonnettes and a tympanum with an incised cross. The S chancel doorway also Norman. The chancel windows and the nave S window late C13, lancets or intersected tracery. Inside, the chancel arch is Norman, plain; the N arcade has circular piers with plain moulded capitals and still single-chamfered arches. – FONT. Plain Norman. – PLATE. Chalice and Paten Cover, 1606.

MANOR FARM. Half-timbered with huge stone chimneystack, not outstanding and spoilt by a modern addition. (Inside panelling dated 1670 and a splat baluster staircase. NMR)

(MARSTON PARK FARMHOUSE, ¾ m. N via Thurvaston. Mostly C17, perhaps with earlier stonework in the S gable. L-shaped. The N wing is of C18 brick except the N wall, which is still timber-framed. Stone plinth all round. Two panelled rooms in this wing, one dated 1695 over the fireplace. The S wing has a stone gable and mullioned windows. Side walls of red brick, English bond. RE)

MATLOCK

3050

Matlock consists of a group of hamlets (The Matlocks), chiefly old Matlock village, Matlock Green, Matlock Bridge, the main centre Matlock Bank, and some distance away the spa Matlock Bath. The old village, Matlock Bank, and Matlock Bath are still distinctly separate.

(*1*) *Old Matlock*

ST GILES is the church of old Matlock, on a bluff with the village street on one side and the river making one of its frequent bends to the NW of it. The church itself has a Perp W tower with diagonal buttresses but the rest was rebuilt in 1859 (chancel) and 1871 (nave in Dec style by *Benjamin Wilson* of Derby; S chapel added in 1898 by *P. H. Currey*: GR). – FONT. Norman, very big, ribbed at the angles and with little crescents along the upper border. – STAINED GLASS. E window 1969 by *Lawrence Lee*; two-light chancel window by *Heaton, Butler & Bayne*, 1920. – PLATE. Chalice, Paten, and Flagon, given 1791. – MONUMENTS. Anthony Woolley † 1576; by the *Royleys*?

The RECTORY to the W of the church is late C18, of irregular plan. Between it and the church WHEATSHEAF HOUSE, 1681, with a symmetrical front with windows of mullion-and-transom crosses. Church Street bends prettily round by the church, but further up the hill is very ordinary modern housing.

(*2*) *Matlock Green*

Below the old village to the N. In KNOWLESTON PLACE, directly below the church, a good group of different periods overlooking riverside gardens: No. 3 (Derwent House) is C17 (moved datestone, 1621) and C18; No. 5, stone with one part of 1753 and flanking bay of 1772; Nos. 7–13, a big stone terrace of 1857 in the Georgian tradition but with Gothic details, including Gothic glazing bars, pointed arches, gables with fretted bargeboards, and in the garden a stone post with a Gothic top; and No. 15 (Knowleston House), early C19, ashlar, with a Doric columned porch. On the S side of Matlock Green itself, SWISS COTTAGES, 1839 by *Paxton*, a pair of stone houses in the Edensor manner.*

Further E, HUNTBRIDGE HOUSE, mid C18, stone doorcase with an open pediment. Further E still and N of the main road, in THE CLIFF is a good early industrial group: a mid-C18 stone corn mill (with C19 wings), malthouse (altered), and house (St Andrew's House) dated 1757 on a rainwater-head. Three storeys and attics with a pilaster doorcase.

(*3*) *Matlock Bath*

Matlock Bath lies about one mile SW of Matlock Village. The old

* Paxton owned land here including the old mill. The two houses on Matlock Green (Paxton House and Paxton Tor) are not by him (Chadwick).

bath of wood lined with lead was made in 1698. Before 1725 a new stone bath was constructed and the Bath House was 'a handsome house' according to Bray in 1777. Torrington in 1789 complains of the growing popularity of Matlock: 'The quiet and society of the place is lost.' Lysons in 1818 calls it a favourite summer resort. By then a road had been blasted from Cromford through Scarthin Nick, the NEW BATH HOTEL, Derby Road (for fifty visitors), and the TEMPLE HOTEL, Temple Road (originally an annexe to the Old Bath), existed, and a Museum Parade or SOUTH PARADE was probably just about being built, a row of honest, solid, attractive houses along the road by the River Derwent.* HODGKINSON'S HOTEL of *c.* 1790 at the N end is perhaps the best. Building was continued *c.* 1840 with NORTH PARADE, which has several good classical stone terraces of shops and the semi-detached FOUNTAIN VILLAS, rendered, with Roman Doric doorcases. The former Methodist Chapel is also classical. The spa gained even greater popularity after the Ambergate to Rowsley railway line opened in 1849. The STATION has two of its original five buildings in Swiss chalet style, half-timbered, with overhanging eaves, to complement the Alpine atmosphere of the Derwent gorge. The date is uncertain. The line opened in 1849, but the buildings look considerably later. (Biddle says *c.* 1880.) Later a PAVILION was provided in the unimaginative and none too costly spa architecture of *c.* 1885.

The church of HOLY TRINITY was built in 1842 by *Weightman & Hadfield*; S aisle and enlargement of the chancel 1873–4 by *T. E. Streatfield.*

Above Matlock Bath, several picturesque villas, notably LOWER TOWERS, Waterloo Road, and UPPER TOWERS, Upperwood Road, both Strawberry-Hill-Gothic castles built in association with the HEIGHTS OF ABRAHAM pleasure grounds laid out in the early C19. At the summit a PROSPECT TOWER, built in 1844 to provide work for unemployed stonemasons. Also on the hill, a BARROW, possibly of the Bronze Age.

Matlock Bank is reached from Matlock Bath by DALE ROAD. Here HIGH TOR HOTEL, early C19 *cottage orné* style with ornamental bargeboards and complicated Gothic glazing. Standing separately the former servants' hall. Further N DALE

* It was built as the Great Hotel. It was probably complete by 1818, but the scheme failed and the property was subdivided into museums and shops displaying curios, and Hodgkinson's Hotel. (Information kindly given by Barry Joyce.)

COTTAGE, 1820, and on the cliff above, in ST JOHN'S ROAD, THE ROCKS (formerly Rock Villa), another *cottage orné*, and the CHAPEL OF ST JOHN, 1897 by *Guy Dawber*. Very picturesque, built into the side of the cliff. Stone with simple mullioned windows, an oriel to the chancel, and a tiny pyramid-roofed turret. Inside, the fittings and the plasterwork have Arts and Crafts touches. At the end of the road CLIFF HOUSE, a prominent landmark. Mid-C18, rendered, with ground-floor Venetian windows and a wrought-iron porch.

(4) *Matlock Bridge*

At the N end of Dale Road, BANK HOUSE (Williams and Glyn's Bank). Late C18, ashlar, of two storeys and three bays divided by plain pilasters. Over the door a segmental pediment. To the l. a later wing with elaborate doorcase, to the r. a sympathetic modern wing. In the station yard, a COTTAGE apparently of *c.* 1850 by *Paxton* (Chadwick). W of the station up SNITTERTON ROAD, THE SHAWS, another early C19 cottage, and two small houses by *Parker & Unwin*: one of 1907–8, typical of their Letchworth years, the other, CAWDOR COTTAGE, of 1898–9, below it in Cawdor quarries (Mervyn Miller).

(5) *Matlock Bank*

Over the medieval stone BRIDGE (C15, four pointed arches, massive breakwaters, widened 1904) the modern town rises up the hill to culminate in SMEDLEY'S HYDRO, the hydropathic establishment started by John Smedley in the 1850s and closed down a century later. The buildings were bought in 1955 by Derbyshire County Council for use as their headquarters. It is a large group of buildings, with a castellated half of *c.* 1867 and a larger Italo-Frenchy part of 1885 with some good interiors, the latter by *Statham*.* Of *c.* 1900 are at one end the WINTER GARDEN and at the other the COLONNADE (now County Library) built as a covered exercise area. The hydro had its own private church, demolished in 1958–9. The success of the hydro was enormous. In 1867 Smedley treated 2,000 patients and there were another nine competitive establishments at Matlock Bank.

The church up here is ALL SAINTS, 1883–4 by *Healey* (GR). It has an E window by *Morris & Co.*, 1905, three lancets with a rose above, the saints and prophets to *Burne-Jones*'s designs.

* The earliest part, *c.* 1855, on the N side of the street behind the main buildings.

Below in Bank Road is the TOWN HALL, Italianate, with a tall piano nobile, 1899.

The continuation N of Bank Road is RUTLAND STREET. Here, the TRAM DEPOT, 1893 by *J. J. Turner* for the steepest-graded cable tramway in the world. At the top in WELLINGTON STREET is one of the rivals to Smedley's Hydro, ROCKSIDE (now College of Education), built in 1903–6 by *Parker & Unwin*. Lofty stone tower with two turrets with strange, slightly oriental-style roofs: concave copper roofs topped by spires, conservatory of 1923. Disappointing interiors but still with Parker's original fittings.* Some stone vernacular buildings still remain. Off Rutland Street WELLFIELD COTTAGE, dated 1667; WOLDS FARMHOUSE, Cavendish Road, E part 1634, W part C18; and DIMPLE FARMHOUSE, Hurds Hollow, C17.

DARLEY DALE. *See* p. 163.
TANSLEY. *See* p. 339.

MELANDRA CASTLE

0090

¾m. WNW of Glossop

Ardotalia was a Roman auxiliary fort. First occupied *c.* A.D. 75–80, it was rebuilt early in the C2. It was still occupied in the reign of Hadrian (117–37) and was eventually evacuated between 140 and 150. A timber *mansio*, or official lodging-house, lay to the S. The entire site has been damaged by erosion and by indiscriminate early excavation.

MELBOURNE

3020

ST MICHAEL AND ST MARY. The church is one of the most ambitious Norman parish churches of England, and its interior is as impressive and as well preserved as any. ‡But its exterior is unfortunate: not only does a TITHE BARN stand within a few yards of the W front, but the two W towers are incomplete, and rise no higher than the ridge of the nave roof. That in itself is far from handsome, and it is made worse by the excessive heightening of the crossing tower which was carried out after 1602. As has come out in these preliminary remarks, the church

* (The existing building is only one wing of the original design of 1901–2. *Parker* also designed houses in Cavendish Road (Nos. 79–81, with *Unwin*, 1903–4, and No. 87, 1928–9, all with some original fittings), and the layout of the Wolds Estate, NE of Rockside (1933). Mervyn Miller)

‡ It was restored by *Sir G. G. Scott* in 1859–62.

possesses a two-tower façade, a unique feature amongst Norman parish churches, and a crossing tower as well. It has in addition a nave of six bays and aisles and transepts. All this is Norman with the exception of the Perp aisle windows and the Perp E window. This is due to an alteration of the chancel which originally ended in an apse. The transepts also had apsidal E chapels of which the entrance arches remain. But there were no chancel aisles, with or without apses, i.e. the plan was not that of so many Romanesque churches of Normandy and England (with a stepped E end) – the plan usually known as Cluny II and first transferred to Normandy with the Cluniac reform at Bernay – but rather that of the Romanesque style of the German C10 and C11 (e.g. Gernrode and Goslar in the Saxon territory and St Pantaleon at Cologne, Hersfeld, and Laach farther W). It is not entirely absent in Normandy (Domfront, *c.* 1050), but rare, and its existence at Melbourne may be one of the several C10–11 survivals of architectural connexions between the Holy Roman Empire and England.*

No building dates are known for Melbourne and most of the details look C12, but the plan may well have originated before 1100. The living of Melbourne went to the Bishop of Carlisle when the see was founded in 1133. The sumptuous interior of the nave and the W parts are certainly younger than that date.

5 The nave has tall circular piers of four feet diameter, standing so close together that the arches are strongly stilted to give sufficient height. The bases have angle-spurs (usually a later C12 motif), and the capitals are many-scalloped.‡ The arches are thickly zigzag-decorated, a somewhat barbaric but very strong effect. On the capitals stand coupled wall shafts as if transverse arches and perhaps vaults had originally been intended.§ If so, they were not carried out; but there is a clerestory with small arched windows (with nook-shafts on the exterior) and a wall-passage with tripartite stepped openings towards the nave: again a motif familiar from cathedrals and large collegiate churches, but unique in parish churches. This upper part is

* Closer parallels are Carolingian (Steinbach, Celles-lès-Dinant, and Einsiedeln) and in Normandy (Sequeville-en-Bessin, Ouistreham, and Bourg-Dun), all towerless and without W galleries – closer in scale and in date; see C. McAleer, *Norman Façades*, Ph.D. thesis, 1963.

‡ Except for the last four to the W on the N side and the W respond on the S side which have embryonic volutes as well.

§ Which is no necessity; for such shafts with no other motif but to articulate a wall had been quite usual in C11 Normandy (cf. e.g. Jumièges as early as *c.* 1030–60).

preserved only on the N side. On the S side there are C13 pointed twin openings instead and twin pointed windows.

The crossing again is most remarkable. It has arches to all four sides, standing on twin demi-shafts. Most of these have broad cushion capitals, but some on the E side are enriched by capitals with flat foliage scrolls interspersed with grotesques and human figures. The capitals of the E transept apses also had flat decoration. Inside the crossing tower above the arches are three tiers of openings. The lowest of them opens into nave and transepts, and to the E this and the higher ones opened into an upper storey of the chancel: once more an extremely unusual motif. The three tiers of openings are vertically connected by attached shafts, as if here also vaulting had been intended. Outside, the Norman parts of the crossing tower, the broad buttresses, are also shafted. The chancel windows have nook-shafts inside as well as outside. Outside, the chancel still reveals the beginning of the former apse, and also the beginning of blank arcading outside the former upper storey.

As for the exterior of the aisles, the most noteworthy features are the two small doorways, both with one order of colonnettes, but that on the N side with more elaborate moulding of the voussoirs. The aisle windows, as has already been said, are Perp replacements, but the lower parts of the broad Norman buttresses survive.

The W front would be impressive, no doubt, if it had been completed. It has a central W portal of four orders of colonnettes with zigzag voussoirs,* a window above converted in the C15, and the two W towers with very broad flat buttresses. The inside arrangements of the W parts deserve special notice. Immediately behind the front are three very roughly groin-vaulted rooms, two square underneath the towers and one rectangular between them. The latter carries on a broad arch with rich zigzag voussoirs, open to the nave, a gallery or balcony also open to the nave. This is a motif known from C11 buildings in Normandy and elsewhere in France but unique in England. The three vaulted rooms are interconnected by arches on coupled shafts, and the square ones communicate with the aisles by pointed arches on very simple imposts. The whole W bay is separated from the nave by immense compound piers.

ROOF. Chancel, C16. – PAINTING. On the NW tower pier, a large horned devil with outspread wings, holding a scroll, and

* The capitals have grotesques and very unusual sunk diamond motifs on the abaci.

two women in C14 costume, each with a smaller devil on her back. On the opposite pier, traces of a Passion series (Crucifixion, Flagellation), probably also C14. – FONT. Norman; simple bowl on four squat columns. – (STAINED GLASS. Chancel windows: E to a person † 1867 and S of 1869, both by *Hardman*, the latter especially good of its kind. – N lancet 1869 by *Clayton & Bell*. This was a good year in this firm's High Victorian period. R. Hubbuck) – N transept N window 1865 by *Powell & Sons* with a medallion of Moses and the Tablets by *Henry Holiday*. – PLATE. Chalice, 1606. – MONUMENTS. In the S transept, now vestry. C13 slab with foliated cross. – Early C13 effigy of a knight, damaged, wrongly placed in a C15 arched recess. – One C16 and three crude C17 alabaster slabs, to Henry Hardie † 1613, Anne Harding † 1673, and Sir Robert Harding † 1679.

In the CHURCH CLOSE, the VICARAGE, 1863 by *Joseph Mitchell* of Sheffield, stone and Tudor, and CLOSE HOUSE, C18 brick.

MELBOURNE HALL. Immediately E of the church, a big stone mansion, rather forbidding-looking, except from the E. The architectural details reveal at least four building phases. The house is said to incorporate part of the medieval residence of the Bishops of Carlisle, but the oldest fabric visible (on the N and W sides) is evidently C16 or early C17, with mullioned and transomed windows on the N side. The N and W wings are in fact the remains of an L-shaped manor house, with the hall (now dining room) in the N wing, leased from the Bishops in 1628 by Sir John Coke, Secretary of State to Charles I. Of the early C17, panelling in the hall and first-floor rooms of the W range. (The dining room overmantel, dated 1596, is a recent importation.) Between 1708 and 1710, the DOVECOTE (altered in the C18 and now the muniment room) and the LAUNDRY (two storeys with wooden mullion-and-transom cross windows) to the N of the house were built. Also of this period, the W front of the W wing, also with cross windows. (Of the interior alterations made in 1706–8, and again in 1721–2 by *William Gilkes* of Burton-on-Trent, is 'an iron collom to support ye stares', made for the back stairs by *Bakewell* in 1722. ES) The E wing of big rough stonework was added in 1725–6 by *Francis Smith* of Warwick, making a deep *cour-d'honneur* to the W, somewhat reduced in depth by the small room (now inner hall) built at its N end. (The *cour* was partly glazed over in the early C20 to make a billiard room.) S front of the W wing Georgianized to match and, facing the *cour*, two blocked classical doorways. The

E façade is the show front, built in 1744 by *William Smith* the younger. It is of seven bays with a three-bay pediment, and door and windows on the ground floor with rusticated surrounds. The outer door of the inner hall received a Gibbs surround.* 84

The GARDENS on the E were first extended about 1690, and then extended to the S and laid out by the Royal Gardeners, *London* and *Wise*, before the house was remodelled. In 1699, Thomas Coke, Vice-Chamberlain to Queen Anne and George I, chose a plan from Mr Wise 'to suit with Versailles', but work did not begin until 1704 under a local contractor, *William Cooke* of Walcot. The garden is not at all big, but its composition makes it appear larger. It is divided by three main avenues leading down gently with some broad staircases to a Great Basin, converted from the moats and basins of the previous garden. At the far end of the basin, as a focal point, an exquisite wrought-iron ARBOUR of 1706–11 by *Robert Bakewell* of Derby. (Also probably by *Bakewell*, the lyre pattern balustrade at the end of the terrace.) There are many contemporary lead figures by *Jan van Nost*, 1699–1700, in the angles of the yew hedges. To the S of the composition a long yew tunnel, and further S the GROVE, with stands and circular fountain pools, like those by Le Nôtre at Marly. At the top of the slope, *Nost*'s Four Seasons Vase of 1705, given by Queen Anne. The stone pedestals are by *Devigne*. Also by him the stone baskets in front of the Hall.‡ To the SW a large serpentine lake, the POOL, with a C17 WATERMILL, made picturesque in the C19 and now a house, on the E side. The waterworks at Melbourne are by *Sorocold*. 81

MELBOURNE CASTLE lies along the E side of Castle Square, no doubt at the centre of the medieval village. It was built by Thomas, Earl of Lancaster (died 1322), and later became a royal possession of Henry IV. In 1562 it was still in good condition, having undergone extensive repairs in 1483–5. James I sold it in 1604 to the Earl of Nottingham. When it was engraved in

* According to Dr Andor Gomme, *William Smith* was possibly completing work left unfinished by his father at Sir Thomas Coke's death in 1727. Dr Gomme dates the interior and staircase of the E wing to 1725–7 (cf. the staircase at Stoneleigh Abbey, 1714–26), in which case the arrangement of the E front windows, at least, must have been decided then. However, rainwater-heads on the S front dated 1744 may either denote the completion of all the work or indicate that *William Smith* was responsible for a substantial remodelling of the whole wing.

‡ There are several vases in the garden that could be by *Samuel Watson*, who supplied designs in 1706.

1733 it was a many-towered group of structures. Now only an ivy-grown wall, thought to be C14, stands high up behind the buildings of CASTLE FARM, a good gabled brick house, partly C17 and partly *c.* 1800, and most of its ground area lies under the orchard or is covered by CASTLE MILLS of 1857.

Several pretty brick buildings in the main streets of Melbourne, domestic and commercial. A PERAMBULATION can begin NW of the church in CHURCH STREET, with OUR LADY OF MERCY AND ST PHILIP (R.C.), 1906, broad, low, and of very red brick, and CHANTRY HOUSE, with a handsome late C18 to early C19 garden front attached to an older part by the street. HIGH STREET leads NE from the Market Place at the top of Church Street. Here a cruck building (Nos. 11–13), thatched, with one cruck frame visible. In BLANCHCROFT, the SICK CLUB BUILDINGS No. VIII of 1795, a group of three-storey industrial dwellings. Back towards the church, in PENN LANE, the NATIONAL SCHOOL, 1831–2, brick, with pointed arched windows and cast-iron tracery, and PENNFIELD HOUSE, an C18 brick house, raised in the C19, with an industrial block on the E and a Gothic iron porch on the garden façade. Opposite, Nos. 51–57, a row of C18 stone-fronted cottages. Back to the Market Place. N of it, in CHAPEL STREET, the BAPTIST CHAPEL of 1750, enlarged in 1833, stucco-fronted and pedimented. To the E, in POTTER STREET, a long timber-framed thatched cottage and a second, smaller, earlier one. (Also the ATHENAEUM AND SAVINGS BANK (now Wesley Hall), built in 1853–4 by *H. I. Stevens* of Derby in an Italianate style of which Palmerston, who laid the foundation stone and opened the building, would have approved. RE) Further out to the S in Robinson's Hill, SHAW HOUSE, another fine C18 house.

KINGS NEWTON. *See* p. 259.

ST BRIDE'S FARM. *See* Stanton-by-Bridge.

MEYNELL LANGLEY *see* KIRK LANGLEY

MICKLEOVER *see* DERBY, p. 194

MIDDLETON-BY-WIRKSWORTH

2050

HOLY TRINITY. 1844 by *Newton* (GR). No tower, no separate chancel. Stone. Castellated gabled porch. Perp straight-headed windows.

Between Middleton and Wirksworth are the HOPTON WOOD QUARRIES, which were amongst the most exciting pieces of rock-scenery in the county. Sheer walls of great height rising quite close to the road. Now mostly quarried away.

Phillip Gell of Hopton Hall created the VIA GELLIA (a stretch of the A5012) to give access to his quarries. On it the remains of his waterworks and a villa built of solid tufa.

MIDDLETON TOP ENGINE HOUSE, at the top of the Cromford and High Peak Railway Middleton incline. Two storeys, grit-stone, round-arched windows with cast-iron Gothick tracery. Attached a boiler house with two horizontal boilers. The beam winding engine, made by the *Butterley Ironworks* in 1829, was in use drawing trains up the incline until the line closed in 1963. On the road to Middleton a very early (1828?) railway over-bridge.

MIDDLETON-BY-YOULGREAVE

1060

Just behind the Gothic style CONGREGATIONAL (now United Reformed) CHAPEL of 1826 is the tomb of Thomas Bateman † 1861, a C19 gentleman of means and indefatigable excavator of Derbyshire's innumerable barrows. The tomb is cutely surmounted by a stone model of a Bronze Age cinerary urn. Bateman's collections and his beautifully written and illustrated MSS. are now housed for the most part in Western Park Museum, Sheffield. He lived at LOMBERDALE HALL on the road to Youlgreave, a house of 1845 with prominent Gothic windows.

(At CASTLE FARM, fragments and foundations suggesting a fortified house rather than a fortress. DOE)

Many barrows in the area. On SMERRILL MOOR five barrows can still be traced of the many that formerly existed.

MILFORD

3040

Milford owes its fame to Jedediah Strutt, who founded a mill here about 1780 and lived at MILFORD HOUSE (a seven-bay stone house with a three-bay pediment, altered). Almost all the mill buildings were demolished between 1952 and 1964, including the Old Mill (1780 and 1806) and the Cruciform Warehouse of 1793, the second of Strutt's fireproof buildings with brick arch floors, timber beams, and iron pillars. The pretty, airy suspension bridge of 1826 has also gone. The principal features from Strutt's time are now the WEIRS, downstream from the stone BRIDGE of 1792 (widened 1906) with its two elegant segmental arches, and the industrial housing in HOPPING HILL (two-storey stone terraces, with full-width garrets), built in 1793–4 with much ironwork from Strutt's own Milford foundry. Also of interest the former WESLEYAN CHAPEL of 1842, the BAPTIST CHAPEL of 1849 (both stone and classical), and the church of HOLY TRINITY by *Moffatt*, 1848 (E.E. style, lancet windows, SW turret).

MILLER'S GREEN *see* WIRKSWORTH

MILLTOWN *see* ASHOVER

MINNING LOW *see* BALLIDON

MOAT LOW *see* ALSOP-EN-LE-DALE

MONSAL DALE *see* LITTLE LONGSTONE

1060

MONYASH

ST LEONARD. In a dip between exposed high moors. Founded *c.* 1198. Of the earliest building period the SEDILIA and PISCINA with segmental arches decorated with dogtooth, the shafts with crude stiff-leaf or crocket capitals. The chancel arch is contemporary. The imposts rest on stiff-leaf capitals and these on head corbels. In the chancel, lancet windows, renewed. Also of about the same time the S doorway and the lower parts of the tower, see the tower arch towards the nave. The tower is unbuttressed and has lancet windows. The tower stair starts in a most unusual way from the S aisle. The tower battlements and the spire with two tiers of dormer windows are later. The church has S and N transepts (cf. Ashbourne, Bakewell, etc.). The former was founded as a chantry in 1348, the latter was rebuilt on the old foundations in 1887 as part of *Butterfield's* restoration of 1884–7. The windows of the transepts and the aisles are mostly straight-headed. Yet their tracery is still essentially Dec, see especially the one big four-light window in the S aisle and the smaller N aisle windows. Their date may well be as late as *c.* 1375. Of the same time probably the nave arcades. Pretty timber tracery in the outer walls of the S porch, built by *Butterfield*. – SCREEN, PULPIT, ALTAR RAILS, and BENCHES all by *Butterfield*. – FONT. C15. Octagonal bowl on quatrefoil stem decorated with animals. – PARISH CHEST. Big, iron-bound, perhaps as old as the C13. – PLATE. Chalice, 1726 by *Jacob Margas*.

(Former FRIENDS' MEETING HOUSE. Stone, 1711, tiny. C. Stell)

HADDON GROVE FARM, LATHKILL DALE. Bronze Age barrow.

A sector of the parish boundary on the W side is formed by the ROMAN ROAD from Little Chester to Buxton.

MORLEY

3040

ST MATTHEW. The church is important in several ways, for its architecture, its monuments, and its stained glass. It stands away from the village, but close to the large stone TITHE BARN and DOVECOTE of the former Hall (with mullioned windows and four-bay tie-beam roof) and not far from the handsome early C18 former RECTORY. The oldest part of the church is the Norman S arcade of two bays with circular pier with scalloped capital and unmoulded arch. The E respond has sparse leaves in the capital. The N arcade has the same piers but very elementary moulded capitals, probably of the early C13. The chancel seems to be early C14 (see the renewed E window and the S window high up). The chancel arch is tall and of fine proportions (double-chamfered). The S porch with its handsome external doorway also seems to be early C14. The rest of the building history is exceptionally well documented by brass inscriptions. The N chancel chapel with its four-centred arch to the chancel was added by Ralph de Stathum, who died in 1380, the W tower by his widow Goditha and her son, who died in 1403 (inscription on their brasses in the S chancel floor: 'qui campanile istud et ecclesiam fieri fecerunt'), the S chancel chapel by John Stathum who died in 1453. The W tower has a round SW stair-turret, angle buttresses with many set-offs, Perp detail, and a recessed spire, the S chancel chapel an irregular arch to the chancel. C15 also is the clerestory. The windows of N and S aisles are straight-headed of three and four ogee-arched lights. – TILES. Many original floor tiles in the N chancel chapel which was built *c.* 1370. – STAINED GLASS. This came to Morley from Dale Abbey at the time of the Dissolution, according to documents in the church. It had there been used to glaze the new cloister of 1482. The glass was repaired and much added to in 1847 by *William Warrington*, but enough remains of the original work to make Morley the most rewarding place in the county to study late medieval stained glass. Most of the glass is in the N chancel chapel, in the two N windows. The more westerly one has chiefly scenes from the legend of St Robert of Knaresborough, the other stories from the Invention of the Holy Cross. In the E window an original figure of St Ursula, the rest Victorian. – (S aisle S window by *Hardman*, 1860s. – Several windows by *Burlison & Grylls*, some rather dull. The best is the E window to a person † 1896. Others, S aisle W, 1905; N aisle, both W windows;* N aisle NW, 1908, R. Hubbuck) – PLATE. Chalice and Paten Cover on knob foot, 1663. – MONUMENTS. A larger number of medieval monuments than in most Derbyshire churches. They are the following in chronological order: John Stathum † 1453 and wife, brasses, kneeling; above their heads a St Christopher (N chapel). – Thomas Stathum † 1470 and two wives, brasses of the three figures with scrolls leading up to figures of St Christopher, St Anne, and the Virgin with Child. On a tomb-chest (S aisle, N side). – Henry Stathum † 1480, and three wives and children, brasses on tomb-chest under a cusped depressed arch between chancel and S chapel. – John Sacheverell † 1485 on Bosworth Field (see the inscription) and his wife, the Stathum heiress; brasses also of the children (S wall of the S chapel). – Henry Sacheverell † 1558 and wife, brasses on tomb-chest (between chancel and N chapel). – Katherine Babington † 1543, tomb-chest with recumbent effigy and kneeling figures against the tomb-chest (N chapel), aesthetically the best monument in the church. The effigy as well as the kneeling figures are competently and sensitively carved. The monument might well be in Westminster Abbey. – Four incised slabs to Sacheverell children, in the N chapel floor, 1625, 1626, 1638, 1639. – Jacynth Sacheverell † 1656 and wife, recumbent alabaster effigies, kneeling children against the big tomb-chest (N chapel). – Henry Sacheverell † 1662, big tomb-chest with polished black marble top; no effigies (N chapel). – Jonathan Sacheverell † 1662 and wife, wall-monument (S chapel) with two frontal demi-figures holding hands; two Fames pull away draperies from them; very poor workmanship (cf. Kedleston). – William Sacheverell † 1691, big tomb-chest with polished black marble top; no effigies (N chapel). – Robert Sacheverell † 1714, big pedestal

39

* These, of *c.* 1875, should be noticed for their careful historicism. They cleverly match the C15 glass in the N chancel chapel (R. Hubbuck).

with free-standing urn, urns at the angles, etc., very Baroque and not at all elegant (N chapel).

In the churchyard a small CHAPEL (1897, Bateman Mausoleum)* and a SUNDIAL, 1762 by *Whitehurst* of Derby.

(SACHEVERELL ALMSHOUSES, Morley Moor. 1656, single-storey, stone, with mullioned windows and arms in the central gable flanked by Ionic pilasters under a broken pediment. RE)

MORLEY MANOR (formerly Hayes Lodge) is an asymmetrical neo-Tudor house of moderate size, by *Bodley*, 1900.

A large MOUND on the outskirts of the village may be a medieval moated site, but its true character is unknown.

MORLEY PARK FARM *see* HEAGE

MORTON

4060

HOLY CROSS. Perp W tower with diagonal buttresses and eight pinnacles on the battlements. The rest 1850 by *T. C. Hine* except for the N arcade of circular piers with double-chamfered arches. The capitals as well as the filleted E and W responds are typical late C13. – PULPIT. 1635. – STAINED GLASS. E window 1854 by *Warrington*. – PLATE. Chalice and Paten Cover, 1727 by *William Darkeratt*.

Close to the church the handsome C18 stone RECTORY with a central Venetian window.

MOSBOROUGH HALL *see* ECKINGTON

MUGGINTON

2040

ALL SAINTS. The W tower is Norman, unbuttressed, but for one big buttress placed at a later date against the middle of the W wall. It half-covers traces of a round-headed doorway also visible from within. The tower arch to the nave had semicircular keeled responds and a pointed unchamfered arch, i.e. early C13. But above this is a small, deeply splayed, evidently earlier window. It may well be of the C11. On the upper floor on the N side bell-openings with Norman arches but C13 twin openings underneath them. Norman corbel-table above. The top later. S doorway and W window of the S aisle look C18. The small SE doorway is late C13 and the S doorway early C14. The S arcade need not be later. Perp S chancel chapel; the piers and responds

* Mr Hubbuck thinks by *Bodley*.

have their capitals decorated with big individual leaves, heads, and shields. Perp roofs. – FONT. Perp, hexagonal, with pointed quatrefoils; re-tooled. – PEWS. Plain and honest, dated by an inscription 1600. Some later box pews. – SCREEN. C15, of single-light openings with ogee arches and between them and the straight tops of the individual divisions Perp panel tracery. – PLATE. Set (Silver-gilt Chalice, Paten Cover on knob foot, and Flagon) of 1640, given by Lady Frances Kniveton (*see* Bradley, Kirk Langley, Kniveton, Osmaston for identical sets). – MONUMENTS. Good large brasses on a tomb-chest to Nicholas Kniveton † 1400 and wife. The brass figures of *c.* 1475.

HALTER DEVIL CHAPEL, Hulland Ward, 1½m. N. 1723, enlarged in 1890. Attached to a farmhouse. Stone-faced, with doorway, two arched front windows, and parapet. The chapel was built by Francis Brown, a farmer, who one night swore he would ride into Derby even if he had to halter the Devil. When he found his horse in the field and tried to halter it in the dark, he found that it had horns. Brown fainted and the Devil disappeared in a flash of lightning.

NAT LOW *see* ALSOP-EN-LE-DALE

2010

NETHERSEAL

ST PETER. Mostly 1877 by *Blomfield*. But Perp N tower with diagonal buttresses, and inside the following C13 features: a four-bay arcade with octagonal piers, double-chamfered arches, and very elementary moulded capitals, and two-light chancel windows with nook-shafts placed high up in the wall. – MONUMENT. Incised slab to Roger Douton † 1500, rector of Netherseal.

(BAPTIST MEETING HOUSE. Brick with iron-framed windows; 1840. Box pews and gallery inside. C. Stell)

NETHERSEAL HALL. Plain, nicely proportioned parallelogram, two-storeyed, with mullion-and-transom-cross windows. The window frames finely moulded, the door frame also. The date seems *c.* 1700; yet the date 1751 displayed on the façade may be correct. (According to the DOE the date-stone was moved from elsewhere. The hexagonal red brick dovecote bears the date 1686.) Much C19 addition.

NETHERTHORPE *see* STAVELEY

NEWBOLD *see* CHESTERFIELD, pp. 148, 150

NEW BRAMPTON *see* CHESTERFIELD, pp. 150, 151

NEWHAVEN

1060

NEWHAVEN HOUSE HOTEL. Quite large, with a five-bay front, a nicely unexpected porch, and a big canted bay-window round the corner. Painted white with black quoins and window frames. According to *The Beauties of England and Wales* (1802) the inn had been built 'lately' by the Duke of Devonshire.

NEW MILLS

0080

ST GEORGE, Church Road. 1829–30 by *R. D. Chantrell*. Chancel 1897–8 by *Preston & Vaughan*. Big church with wooden galleries inside, thin lancet windows, and a W tower with spire. – ORGAN CASE. 1835 by *Samuel Renn*.*

ST JAMES THE LESS. 1878–80 by *W. Swinfen Barber* (GR). (Stone, with a deep three-sided apse and lancet windows. Complete contemporary interior, decorated by *Powell* (GR), with a painted timber roof, monochrome mural paintings set in lancet shapes on the windowless N wall, and original furnishings – note lectern and altar rails. T. Cocke) – STAINED GLASS. Crucifixion by *Kempe*, 1880, four Evangelists, 1888. – (Also by *Swinfen Barber*, INGRAMS ALMSHOUSES, linked to the W end of the church. Three pairs round a three-sided courtyard, each pair sharing a porch with two pointed arches. T. Cocke)

CONGREGATIONAL PROVIDENCE CHAPEL, Mellor Road. 1823, with a broad gabled front and arched window. The centre window of the Venetian type.

GRAMMAR SCHOOL. By *G. H. Widdows* (County Architect), *c.* 1915, with the same plan as Ilkeston Grammar School, i.e. classrooms round an open quadrangle with a central domed hall. Tudorish in detail. Extensions 1961.

In St George Road is a group of characteristic C17–18 cottages. The HIGH STREET starts from here into the centre. In it the BULLS HEAD, with a typical symmetrical C18 front (low mullioned windows) and the WESLEYAN SUNDAY SCHOOL, 1844, with arched windows.

LADYSHAW HOUSE, dated on the barn 1759. In spite of this date, the windows are still low and mullioned, but they now

* Information from Michael Sayer.

have broad unmoulded frames and are arranged symmetrically, and the door frame is arched and of blocks of alternating size.

(FRIENDS MEETING HOUSE, Low Leighton. 1717; single-storey, stone, plain. RE)

OLLERSET HALL, Low Leighton. The usual L-shape, with gable and low mullioned windows of four lights. Date-stone 1529 renewed, perhaps for an original 1629.

NEW NORMANTON *see* DERBY, p. 186

2020

NEWTON SOLNEY

ST MARY. Plain Norman N doorway and bits from a more decorated Norman doorway built into the tower N wall. N aisle with lancet windows. On the N side they are coupled and have heads inside at the springer between the two. W tower short with recessed spire with one row of dormers. The interior mostly C14 (low octagonal piers, double-chamfered arcade arches). Perp the straight-headed chancel windows and the clerestory. Restored by *F. J. Robinson* in 1880. – PLATE. Paten, *c.* 1670; Chalice and Paten Cover, 1757. – MONUMENTS. Headless Knight of mid C13 date. – Cross-legged Knight, very effaced. – Alabaster Knight of *c.* 1375. – Sir Henry Every † 1709, very well carved semi-reclining figure in Roman attire, originally with a pyramid behind, by *Thomas Carter* the elder. Erected *c.* 1734. – Tombstone in the churchyard to Thomas Gayfere † 1827, mason in London who restored Westminster Hall and Henry VII's Chapel.

BLADON CASTLE, ¾m. SW. A large brick-built house overlooking the valley with a long crenellated front. All windows pointed. Walls with little bastions. This front was built *c.* 1790 entirely as a sham (known as Hoskins's Folly). Converted in 1801–2 by Abraham Hoskins into a house. The tall octagon tower, central block of rooms, arcade of Tudor windows, and the round tower behind the earlier wall are all of this date. All now derelict except a small wing of 1890 on the gatehouse side. The architect may have been *Wyatville* (cf. Bretby Park), who was paid in 1799 for a design for 'Bladon Hill, Burton on Trent, for A. Hoskins'.*

To the N of the castle other early C19 buildings, including Bladon Castle LODGE, picturesque with fretted bargeboards, Gothic

* Information from Mr Frank Ward.

windows, etc., NEWTON PARK (remodelled in the mid C19), THE CEDARS, and THE COTTAGE.

NINE LADIES *see* STANTON-IN-THE-PEAK

NORBURY

1040

ST MARY. Norbury church is one of the most rewarding of Derbyshire because of its wooded position, because of the variety of its parts, and because of the noble grandeur of its chancel. 15 The rest of the church is comparatively small, and especially short. The chancel is 46½ ft long, the nave 49 ft. Width and height and the absence of a chancel arch towards the nave also contribute to create an impression of splendid breadth. The windows are tall and large, three-light on the N and S sides and five lights at the E end. Their tracery is entirely out of the ordinary, with a stylized flower at the main meeting point in each window, both on the inside and the outside. The tracery is based on intersection and pointed quatrefoils and trefoils, i.e. Early Dec motifs; but it has (in the E window) just a few hard Perp uprights. There are no flowing forms. Below the windows runs blank arcading, without any ogee motifs. These tracery designs are consistent with a date within the first three decades of the C14. The evidence of the armorial glass is suggestive of an early date, *c.* 1300–7* Externally the chancel has saw-teeth-like crenellations and big buttresses. Do these in conjunction with the shafts (triangular section) running up to the roof inside (a timber roof of the later C15) tell of a projected vault? The S tower and nave were erected by Nicholas Fitzherbert († 1473). He also built the chapel E of the tower. The N aisle was added either by Nicholas or his son Ralph († 1483). This has octagonal piers and double-chamfered arches. His grandson John Fitzherbert († 1513) erected the SW chapel, finished in 1517. The nave has a Perp clerestory. The whole S side of the church is embattled, the N side, less of a show-front, is not. The C15 and C16 windows are of three lights, consisting of cusped lancets under a four-centred arch. – FONT. Bowl on clustered shafts; E.E. – SCREEN. Badly restored: original parts consist of the

* *See* P. A. Newton, *Schools of Glass Painting in the Midlands* (1961) PhD Thesis. Mr Newton disagrees with Mr St John Hope's dating of 1300–27 (*Arch. Jnl.* LXXI) because of the appearance of the arms of Grandison, who left England in 1307, and of Bruce, at war with England from 1306–29. The medieval glass is being restored by Mr Dennis King of Norwich (1977).

misused fenestration tracery, some with traces of colour. – CHANCEL SEATING. With poppy-heads; the fronts with blank arches with Perp tracery also some elementary Flamboyant motifs. – Excellently preserved fragments of two SAXON CROSSES, mainly crisp interlacing, but also one small figure. The work belongs to an C11 group which includes Two Dales (now at Bakewell) and Hope. – STAINED GLASS. An uncommonly large amount of C14 and C15 glass survives. The earliest is in the side windows of the chancel (q.v.). Geometrical ornaments and shields of arms only. The colour is disappointing, all grisaille save the borders. The C15 figure glass in the E window was originally in the nave and N aisle. The large and small figures are also mostly colourless. There are smaller more colourful figures in the SE chapel (three saints and kneeling family of donor below). – PLATE. Chalice, Paten Cover on knob foot and Flagon, 1773, by *Charles Wright*. – MONUMENTS. Incised slab to Alice, wife of Sir Nicholas Fitzherbert, *c.* 1460. – Incised slab to Elizabeth, wife of Ralph Fitzherbert, † 1491, shrouded figure. – Incised slab to Henry Prince, Rector of Norbury, † 1500 with a chalice. – Stone effigy of a cross-legged Knight, Sir Henry Fitzherbert, † 1315. – Nicholas Fitzherbert † 1473, good alabaster effigy on alabaster tomb-chest with standing figures under ogee arches. – Sir Ralph Fitzherbert † 1483 and his wife, another big alabaster tomb-chest, this one with standing figures holding shields which stand on the ground; also under ogee arches. The feet of Sir Ralph rest on a lion, but under one of his soles crouches the tiny figure of a bedesman (cf. e.g. Strelley, Nottinghamshire). – Brasses to Sir Anthony Fitzherbert † 1538 and wife, their children kneeling below.

37 36

NORBURY MANOR, in an exquisite group with the church. The façade is brick with quoins and segment-headed windows. It was built *c.* 1680 on the site of a Tudor manor house and incorporates panelling and stained glass roundels of *c.* 1480 from it.* Behind to the NE Upper Hall House of *c.* 1250, enlarged *c.* 1305 by Sir Henry Fitzherbert (restored 1970 by *Lawrence Bond*). The main room on the upper floor has original blocked C13 windows in the W wall and an original entrance to the N. The two openings in the E wall, the fireplace, ceiling beams, and S entrance are all later, probably late C15 or early C16.‡

* Scenes from the Labours of the Months – a precious survival (R. Hubbuck).

‡ Information from Mr Stapleton Martin.

NORMANTON-BY-DERBY *see* DERBY, p. 194

NORTH LEES

2080

1¼ m. N of Hathersage

Impressive, small, towering manor house. The front belongs to the late C16. It is three-storeyed above a basement on sloping ground, with a chimney in the centre and four-light mullioned windows on the l., three-light mullioned and transomed windows on the r. The latter belong to the principal rooms of the house, which lie above each other and face S with six-light mullioned and transomed windows. At the back an (older?) tower rising into a turret with a newel staircase and Perp doorcases, and four storeys of smaller rooms. The house is embattled with semicircular merlons. The plan may owe something to *Robert Smythson*, cf. his design for a tower house (RIBA II/22). Similar in type is the Turret House at the Earl of Shrewsbury's Manor Lodge, Sheffield. Inside, the main rooms have elaborate plasterwork (restored in 1965 by Lt.-Col. *G. G. Haythornthwaite*), dated 1594 in the ground-floor room. Here the frieze bears the arms of the Rodes of Barlborough Hall, but the house was occupied from 1580 by a recusant, Richard Fenton, and from the mid 1590s by William Jessop, both men, like Rodes, within the Earl of Shrewsbury's circle.* Attached to the tower, a two-storey wing, probably later. North Lees plays a part in *Jane Eyre* (as Marsh End or Moor House).‡ 66

Across two fields a ruined building, once thought to be the Roman Catholic chapel built at Hathersage in 1688 (*see* p. 240), now thought to be pre-Reformation, if a chapel at all.

NORTH WINGFIELD

4060

ST LAWRENCE. The best piece of the church is the big, tall, Perp W tower with angle buttresses, two two-light bell-openings on each side, a frieze of shields above, and then battlements. The most interesting piece is the Norman N transept E window, big, with quite elaborately moulded jambs and voussoirs and odd, very sparsely decorated capitals. The arcade to the aisles consists of two circular piers with plainly moulded

* Miss Meredith considers that the ground-floor room ceiling may be Fenton's. Incorporated in the design are the *fleur-de-lis* motifs he bore on his seal.

‡ There is a cruck BARN at the N end of the farmyard, according to Bob Hawkins.

capitals and double-chamfered arches (the arch to the transept similar) and then two more Perp bays, their capitals with large shields set upside down, a very odd thing, as the tower arch has capitals of the same kind with the shields set correctly (the arch with concave chamfers). The chancel dates from the C14 (E window with ogee reticulation, ogee-headed recesses inside and outside). So does the N vestry, which has a window of unusual tracery (exactly as at Whitwell). The body of the church was embattled in the C15; the aisle windows are all Perp too (but S aisle rebuilt 1860, N aisle heavily restored 1872, clerestory windows 1872, general restoration 1879 by *R. H. Carpenter*). The Perp S porch is covered by a pointed tunnel-vault with transverse arches (cf. Ault Hucknall, etc.). The nave roof has old tie-beams and broad trefoil tracery above, C14 according to Cox (cf. Ault Hucknall). – FONT. 1662, with scarcely any decoration. – SCULPTURE. Defaced relief of the Martyrdom of St Lawrence, under a cusped broad flat ogee arch, C15 (S aisle. – STAINED GLASS. E window, some shields of arms and geometrical fragments, C15. – PLATE. Paten Cover, 1633; Cup, 1654; Paten on foot, 1701 by *Anthony Nelme*; Flagon, 1741 by *T. Gladwin*; Paten C18. – Many MONUMENTS, throughout in a very bad state of preservation: foliated cross slabs in the S porch; fragmentary stone effigy of a knight in the chancel recess (late C13?); priest, *c.* 1300, S porch; knight in the outer chancel recess.

BLUE BELL INN (CHANTRY HOUSE), S of the church. One end has an exposed Gothic archway and a buttress with two offsets. A chantry was founded in 1488.

MANOR HOUSE (former RECTORY), W of the church. Five-bay Georgian, stone, with segmental pediment above the central doorway.

(ELM FARM, Bright Street. C18, three storeys, with stone pilasters and a rusticated doorcase. Good staircase; some panelling. RE)

WILLIAMTHORPE COLLIERY, ¾ m. NE. Pithead baths of the 1940s by *J. W. M. Dudding*, in that sound contemporary style which was favoured by the Miners' Welfare Committee.

NORTON

3080

Church and Hall are across the border in Yorkshire. THE OAKES was in Derbyshire until the 1967 boundary change. It was built in the C17, but has a plain nine-bay, two-and-a-half-storey façade with Tuscan porch of 1827. Some C18 features inside, including an apse-ended dining room similar to that at Renishaw.

OCKBROOK

4030

ALL SAINTS.* The chancel of the old church was rebuilt by Thomas Pares in 1803. He also added the Pares vault to the N of the chancel. Above the vault (now organ chamber) were the family pews. His MONUMENT and, as a symmetrical group, those of Mary Pares † 1823 and Thomas Pares † 1824 are on the S wall. Mary Pares's is above a doorway and crowned by a female figure. The three monuments are by *Westmacott*. The chancel windows have typical neo-C13 tracery of the period about 1800. The E window is of three lights, intersected and with STAINED GLASS of 1968 by *Edward Payne*. The nave was widened to the N in 1814–15, to the S in 1835 and given a flat ceiling and a W gallery in two parts, on cast-iron columns.‡ – FONT. Norman, tub-shaped, with interlaced arches. – SCREEN, early C16, from the Wigston Hospital at Leicester, fine, slender, delicate workmanship, with tall one-light openings, ogee tops with much crocketing, and panelled tracery in the spandrels. The top part was removed in 1967 and converted into a communion rail, possibly its original use. The W tower is the only other medieval survival, C12, with a somewhat later plain broached spire and huge NE buttress. – CHEST, 1662.

MORAVIAN SETTLEMENT. Founded 1750. The chapel of 1751–2 and the adjoining houses are of brick, a neat, very handsome group. The chapel is of five bays and has three arched windows and two arched entrances to the l. and r. Pediment and white timber cupola above. (Interior refitted in the late C19. C. Stell)

OFFCOTE *see* ASHBOURNE, p. 65

OFFERTON HALL

2080

$1\frac{1}{4}$ m. W of Hathersage

Interesting house, partly C16 and partly 1658. Note the difference between the three-light mullioned window still with arched tops to the individual lights and the upright windows with mul-

* Mr John Harnan kindly provided much additional information about the church.

‡ *John Mason* of Derby was responsible for the later work.

lion-and-transom-cross, also the difference between the windows under individual hood-moulds and under continuous string-courses.

OFFERTON MOOR. Fifteen cairns, presumably mainly of the Bronze Age, can be traced on the moor.

3050

OGSTON HALL

½ m. NE of Brackenfield

An exceedingly instructive building, more composite than any other of its size in the county. A parallelogram with an irregular inner courtyard, Victorian at first sight. In fact there is a low W range wholly pre-Reformation, probably of *c.* 1500, according to the evidence of the moulded beams. At its S end was the hall. At the N end of this range a few C16 windows (mullioned, but no arched cusped lights). The N range has, it seems, masonry of the same early period, and in addition a gateway; but this is not *in situ*. Then on the S side a further building went up in the C17, see the four-light window with a transom which appears above a Victorian bay-window. It has a straight hood and should in Derbyshire be dated *c.* 1650. There is indeed in the garden a date-stone, obviously not in its original position, which carries a date 1659. Inside, contemporary panelling on the ground floor, and on the second floor a former external window, an oval of a type found in other places in Derbyshire in the C17. Against it an Elizabethan staircase which can hardly be *in situ*. The next stage in the building history is represented by a bit just N of the previous building, with windows still mullioned, but now of upright shape, i.e. late C17. The N wing ends on the E with a coachhouse extension dated 1694. Again two generations later, after the estate had passed from the Revells to the Turbutts, it was felt that the C17 house was no longer serviceable, and a completely new house was erected in the SE corner facing E. This was of five bays and two storeys with a hipped roof and is dated 1768 (architect *Joseph Pickford* of Derby, building supervised by *E. Stanley* of Chesterfield). This seems at first no longer to exist, but it is all there, only hidden by a Victorian veneer. Even the doorcase with Tuscan columns and a metope frieze survives behind a Victorian porch. The quoins can also still be seen without difficulty. Between 1851 and 1864 the whole house was Victorianized for Gladwin Turbutt by the addition, besides the porch, of bay-windows, a piece between the ancient hall and the 1659 block, a Gothic tower, etc. The architect was *T. C. Hine* of Nottingham. Further amendments were made between 1900 and 1913 by *G. M. R. Turbutt* (battlements, garden balustrade, etc.). The whole is an ideal object lesson in dating.*

The garden parterres were laid out by *Nesfield c.* 1865, with a conservatory (now in ruins) by *Hine*.‡

OLD BRAMPTON *see* BRAMPTON

OSMASTON

1040

ST MARTIN. 1845 by *Stevens*. Big and solid, inside correct and rather cold. The facing material is smallish rock-faced stones. – PLATE. Set (silver-gilt Chalice, Paten Cover on knob foot, and Flagon), 1640, given by Lady Frances Kniveton (*see* Bradley, Kirk Langley, Kniveton, Mugginton for identical sets); Chalice, 1773. – In the churchyard a WAR MEMORIAL, 1921 by the eleventh *Earl Ferrers*, praised by Goodhart-Rendel for its well detailed Dec style.

OSMASTON MANOR (demolished 1966). Of the large stone neo-Tudor mansion of 1846–9 by *Stevens* only a tower survives. The main staircase is now at Wotton Lodge, Staffs. It had extensive Italianate gardens and glasshouses on which *Paxton* is said to have advised.

In the village the lords of the manor of Osmaston have apparently done a good deal of building, notably a number of picturesque brick cottages with thatched roofs and bargeboards. In the park a Swiss-style saw mill with original water wheel.

OSMASTON-BY-DERBY *see* DERBY, p. 187

OVERSEAL

2010

ST MATTHEW. 1840–1 by *Thomas Johnson* (GR). Aisleless stone building with W tower, lancet windows, and five-light E window with Late Geometrical tracery.

In the village some nice brick houses; one with a pediment is OVERSEAL HOUSE, Accresford Road, another with a nice porch is GRANGE FARM (No. 8 Accresford Road).

* Additional information kindly supplied by Mr Gladwin Turbutt.
‡ According to Mr J. Bartlam.

3060

OVERTON HALL

The country house of Sir Joseph Banks. Datestones read 1699. On the E side there are still the typical C17 windows with mullion-and-transom cross. On the S side segmental door pediment. The S front is of five bays and two and a half storeys with parapet. Some medieval masonry in the W wing. The house is not specially shapely. Stables, etc., further SW. On the boundary wall a datestone: 1693.

2070

PADLEY HALL

2 m. SE of Hathersage

This was a quadrangular house of the C14 and C15. The foundations of the N and W ranges and, above ground, the chapel (S) range survive, the latter converted in 1933 into a Roman Catholic chapel (to commemorate the arrest in 1588 of two priests hidden in the manor house. This belonged at the time to the Fitzherberts to whom it had come by marriage from the Eyres who had built it). Now a single space, the original chapel lay above the main entrance and offices on the ground floor. Two ancient doorways remain and parts of the hammerbeam roof with angels against the hammerbeams. The windows much renewed. (The W part of the upper floor may have been the solar. DOE)

PADLEY HALL *see also* RIPLEY

4070

PARK HALL

Handsome C17 house of three storeys with three straight gables on each side. It was built by the Pole family and looks mid C17. Three castellated bays (W) and a central castellated porch (S) were added in the early C18. C18 interior with a Rococo chimneypiece and fielded panelling. (Also a remnant of the C17 staircase. Ruined STABLE WING with mullioned windows.)

PARK HALL *see also* HAYFIELD

1050

PARWICH

ST PETER. 1873–4 by *Stevens & Robinson*. In the tower the original N doorway and chancel arch. Norman tympanum with various animals, the lamb carrying a cross, and a stag, each standing on a serpent. Above the lamb a bird, above the stag a pig and a lion. The subject may be the Agnus Dei (cf. Hognaston). – PLATE. Elizabethan Chalice; Paten on foot, 1699.

PARWICH HALL. Five-bay house of three storeys with the centre bay projecting. It is said to have been completed in 1747. The fashionably brick-faced façade (cf. Great Longstone Hall; Sycamore Farm, Hopton) has a stone basement with mullioned windows, i.e. the remains of the previous manor house. An outer staircase leads up to the doorway, which has Tuscan pilasters and rustication of alternating size. Segment-headed windows, except for the first-floor middle window, which has a pediment. Quoins at the angles and at the angles of the centre projection. Edwardian l. wing.

HAWKS LOW. Large cairn.

PARWICH MOOR. A group of over seventy embanked circles, ranging from 12 to 50 ft in diameter, lies on the moor. They appear to date from the Bronze Age, but their function is unknown. They seem not to be funerary monuments.

PEAK CASTLE *see* PEVERIL CASTLE

PEAK FOREST

1070

KING CHARLES THE MARTYR. 1876–7 by *H. Cockbain* (GR) for the seventh Duke of Devonshire on the site of a C17 chapel. Dec, with a tower. – PLATE. Chalice, 1780.

READING ROOM. Built in 1880 with fabric from the C17 chapel. The Venetian window towards the road is its former E window.

PENTRICH

3050

ST MATTHEW. The arcades late C12 or *c.* 1200 (circular piers, single-chamfered round arches), the tower ground floor of the same date. The rest essentially Perp: embattled W tower, nave, S aisle, and S porch. All windows Perp, in the chancel more elaborate than otherwise (E window of five lights). – FONT. Rather puzzling. The foot is dated 1662; the top is of different stone and with an unusual motif of low arches. Is it really Norman, as Cox says? – MONUMENT. Edmund Horn † 1764, graceful Rococo wall-monument without effigy; trophies of cannon, anchor, etc., signed *A B fecit*.

PENTRICH CAMP. A small Roman fort set close to Ryknield Street. It probably dates from the late C1. It was later apparently replaced by a small fortlet, centrally placed within the earthworks of the earlier work.

1080

PEVERIL CASTLE

50 By far the most important castle in the county – in fact the only one of importance. William the Conqueror made William Peverel bailiff of the Royal Manors in NW Derbyshire and gave him the land for Peveril Castle. The castle was built by Peverel, at once, it seems, of stone, which is unusual. The strength and scale of the work are explained by the wealth of lead in the neighbourhood. Of the C11 work the N curtain wall towards Castleton survives almost complete, though much repaired. Its characteristic Early Norman herringbone masonry can easily be detected. It is understandable that this wall was the chief concern of the early builders; for Peveril Castle is wonderfully protected by nature towards the whole E (Cave Dale) and W (Peak Cavern) and a large part of the S. The N slope is steep enough, but not rocky. So attacks were expected from here or a narrow ridge at the back, where now the keep is, but where originally probably a bridge and the gateway had been built. Also of the C11 seem to be an orientated building in the SE corner of the steeply rising site, *c.* 36 by 25 ft, which may have been the chapel, and some older structures to the W of the chapel, comprising probably the original hall. The W curtain wall is attributed to the early C12.

The KEEP was erected by Henry II in 1176, about twenty years after the Peveril estates had been confiscated. There are documents to ascertain the date of the erection of the keep. It stands on the highest point of the site, in a splendidly commanding position, and its walls survive to the top. They were ashlar-faced inside and out. They are strengthened by the typical angle and middle buttresses of the time of Henry II. Access was by an outer wooden staircase. The main room was on the upper floor, with relatively large windows and two mural recesses. One of these contains a garderobe. The hall had an open timber roof. The roof-line against the outer walls is clearly marked. The walls are carried up higher and ended with a wall-walk and parapet and one angle turret which carried the staircase up.

Of the same date as the keep is probably the new GATEWAY in the NE angle. At present only its double-chamfered arch can be recognized, but it originally had zigzag decoration in the arch similar to that of Castleton church below. Of C13 additions only two need mention: the new HALL in the NW corner, which has an open hearth as well as a fireplace at the dais end, with angle colonnettes; and two circular towers on the S side visible from below the castle. Their interest lies in the fact that Roman brick (probably from Brough) is extensively used.

During the C14 the castle lost its importance, and in the C17 it was in ruins.

PIKE LOW *see* HOPE

PILSBURY CASTLE *see* HARTINGTON

PILSLEY

2070

Chatsworth estate village with C18 and early C19 cottages and some housing, 1838–9, and a school, 1849, by *Paxton.*

PINXTON

4050

ST HELEN. Of the medieval church only the unbuttressed C13 W tower and the very beginning of the nave remain (on the N side one small lancet window). On the S side of the tower a two-light Dec window has been incongruously inserted. (The top half of the tower was rebuilt in 1897.) In 1750 a large church was built at r. angles to the old one, with arched windows and a plain Venetian E window. To this in 1939 an aisle and a porch were added. – PAINTING. Annunciation attributed to *Guido Reni*. The painting was presented by the Pope to General Manley, who commanded his guard, and given in 1902 to the church by General Coke of the Coke family of Brookhill Hall. – STAINED GLASS. S transept window (behind the organ) by *Cook & Co.*, some of the figures rather Pre-Raphaelite. – PLATE. Chalice, Paten Cover, and Flagon, 1738 by *Richard Zouch.*

CASTLE WOOD, ½ m. N. Medieval moated site. Inside the surrounding bank, traces of C14 timber buildings have been recovered.

BROOKHILL HALL. *See* p. 111.

PLEASLEY

5060

ST MICHAEL. Norman chancel arch with double billet frieze on the label and two roll-mouldings in the arch. The rest mainly

C13; long aisleless nave. – FONT. Norman, circular, with seated figure. (Virgin?) – PLATE. C17 Chalice.

Dominating the valley 1¼ m. NE of the village are stone-built textile mills, mid-C19 successors to those founded *c.* 1780 by William Hollins of Viyella fame. Also late C19 company housing and amenities.

(PARISH HALL, S of the old A617. 1905–6 and typical of *Parker & Unwin*'s small village halls of about this date. Roughcast, on a sloping site, with an undercroft away from the road. Pantiled roof with dormers and diagonal brick chimneystacks. Inside, an elaborate inglenook fireplace opposite the stage, in detail similar to the almost contemporary Mrs Howard Memorial Hall at Letchworth. Mervyn Miller)

PRATT HALL *see* BRAMPTON

PRIESTCLIFFE *see* TADDINGTON

3040

QUARNDON

ST PAUL. 1874 by *Giles & Brookhouse* (GR), tasteless and restless, rock-faced, with SW broach-spire. – PLATE. Chalice, 1787.

Of the old church farther S nothing remains but an ivy-covered crag of tower-walling.

(CHALYBEATE WELL HOUSE, by the road. A small stone embattled structure.)

KEDLESTON HOTEL. *See* Kedleston.

2030

RADBURNE

ST ANDREW. In the grounds of Radburne Hall, with a fine spreading-out yew tree to the W. The chancel SEDILIA are early C13, the nave and N aisle windows early C14 (nave S side one three-light intersected and cusped window, and two small pretty Tudor windows higher up to its l. and r.). NW tower Perp, ashlar-faced, with diagonal buttresses. (*Bakewell* was paid 2*s.* 6*d* for the weathervane. Probably a piece by one of his apprentices, undated. ES) The N arcade of three bays has hexagonal piers and double-chamfered arches. – BENCH ENDS and BENCHES from Dale Abbey with poppy-heads with faces and tracery; late medieval. – WEST PEW. Front of linenfold panelling with motif of big grapes and vines. – PLATE. Cup and Flagon, 1759 by *William Bagnall*; Paten, *c.* 1759. – MONUMENTS. Coffin-shaped C13 slab with foliated cross. – Incised slab to Peter de la Pole † 1432 and his wife, quite good in the draughtsmanship. – Alabaster tomb-chest with recumbent effigy of John de la Pole and wife † 1491. – Incised slab to Ralph Pole † 1455 and wife. – Standing wall-monument to German Pole, erected 1683, with big sarcophagus in relief and big urn on it, under a segmental pediment with putti; no effigy. By *Grinling Gibbons*. 47

RADBURNE HALL was begun for German Pole in 1739, probably by *William Smith* the younger.* Red brick, placed on an eminence. Seven bays, stone-faced basement storey and two main storeys. The central, slightly projecting, three bays crowned by a carved stone pediment.‡ An open staircase leads up to the main doorway with a segmental pediment on attached Corinthian columns. The first-floor windows with alternating segmental and triangular pediments. The E and W sides of three bays with a central Venetian window. The entrance hall has at the back a screen with a pair of single and a pair of coupled columns, a fine fireplace with caryatids on one side, and a large niche for a statue opposite. Behind the hall, in the middle of the other side, an oblong saloon with Rococo decoration except for the positively Jonesian but no doubt contemporary overmantel. The paintings, commissioned late in 1770, are by *Mortimer* (Roman scenes and the sopraporta of the hall door, *c.* 1770 and 1774) and *Joseph Wright* of Derby (portraits of 1771 and 1772 and four 'candlelit' sopraporte). In the dining room a fine gritstone table with wrought-iron legs, apparently by *Bakewell*. On the ground floor much re-used C17 panelling from the former house. Main staircase with fattish balusters on a continuous string (cf. Catton), the bulgy bits resting in little fluted cups; basement stair with an iron rail writhing in serpentine curves at the turns.§ The house was restored in 1958–60 in exemplary fashion (architect *Frank Scarlett*, decoration by *John Fowler*).

RAIN'S CAVE *see* BRASSINGTON

* An entry in a diary written in 1803 by Edward Sacheverel Chandos-Pole (1769–1813) reads 'Smith of Warwick was his architect and he completed it for five hundred pounds under his estimate which he had the honesty to return'. (Francis Smith died in 1724; so the *Smith* referred to must be his son.) Information from Major J. W. Chandos-Pole and Dr A. Gomme.

‡ By *Henry Watson*.

§ According to Dr Gomme.

RAINSTER ROCKS *see* BRASSINGTON

RAMSLEY MOOR *see* HOLMESFIELD

RAVEN HOUSE *see* ASHOVER

4070

RENISHAW HALL

Built about 1625 by George Sitwell, made famous by the literary 'trio', and still the seat of the Sitwells. The original house survives as the core of a much larger structure chiefly the work of Sitwell Sitwell about 1800. (Some alterations had already been made in 1777 by *Platt* of Rotherham.) The Carolean core is entirely in the Jacobean style, in plan of H-shape. It is clearly recognizable on the S (garden) side. In the middle of the recessed centre is (oddly) a chimneystack. On the N side, the area between the two arms of the H has been filled in by an entrance hall of 1798 with a Gothic porch. The additions of 94 1793 to 1808 by *Joseph Badger* of Sheffield converted this small compact house into one that is long, rambling, and castellated, in spite of its Georgian windows. Inside, the library, formerly the Great Parlour, still has its original plaster ceiling with thin ribs and designs of lions' heads, squirrels, dolphins, and mermaids. But the most handsome of the rooms decorated before the present generation of owners are the dining room of 1797, oblong with an apsed end, the drawing room of 1803, and the ballroom of 1808, the two latter rooms connected by an anteroom remodelled with somewhat formidable formality as a billiard room by *Lutyens* in 1909. The chimneypieces in all these rooms are fine: those in the drawing room and ballroom by *Chambers*, c. 1772, taken to Renishaw from Albany in London, that in the dining room probably by *Platt*, 1795.*

The gardens were re-made with the greatest application and cost by Sir George Sitwell about 1890. Of the time of Sitwell Sitwell the STABLES of 1794 by *Badger*, which, as is so often the case, are, with their broad Tuscan archway, more monumental than the house to which they belong. In the vicinity several Reptonian buildings (by *Badger*?), built between 1804 and 1808, including the ROUND HOUSE or DAIRY and the garden side of the agent's residence, COLDWELL HOUSE, both

* The stucco ceiling in the ballroom with its Prince of Wales feathers is attributed to *Chantrey*, who came from the neighbouring village of Norton and visited Renishaw with his master Robert Ramsay.

with rustic wooden columns and both of them thatched; the GOTHIC TEMPLE, a ruined polygonal aviary; and, less ambitious, the KENNEL COTTAGES in the Park and STATION COTTAGES near the Golf Clubhouse.* The GOTHIC ARCHWAY on the Renishaw Drive was designed by *Sitwell Sitwell* himself as the E entrance in 1805. The GOLF CLUBHOUSE, a group of the C17, C18, and C19, was remodelled by *Lutyens* in the 1930s and again after 1945. Behind the clubhouse, MILL FARMHOUSE, with one wing of a C17 H-plan and the other side an enchanting *cottage orné*. ‡

REPTON

3020

Repton (Hrewpandum) was the capital of South Mercia under King Peada, who Christianized the Mercians. A double monastery was founded at Repton in the second half of the C7, for it was here that St Guthlac received his tonsure from Abbess Aelfthryth (*c.* 698). Two Mercian kings were buried here: Aethelbald in 757 and Wiglaf in 840. The church is dedicated to St Wystan, Wiglaf's grandson, murdered in 849 and buried in his grandfather's mausoleum. His body was the chief object of veneration until its translation to Evesham by King Cnut (1016–35). In 874 the Danes overwintered in Repton and were probably responsible for the destruction of the abbey. How much of the church now standing dates from before 874 is a matter for debate (*see* below). It stands close to the Augustinian priory, which was founded in 1172 and whose fragments have become part of the school.

ST WYSTAN. The Anglo-Saxon church was cruciform, with a central 'crossing', possibly supporting a tower. The chancel, NE and SE angles of the crossing, part of the N transept, and the crypt form one of the most precious survivals of Anglo-Saxon architecture in England. The NE angle of the crossing stands out boldly; on the S a straight vertical joint shows where the later medieval S transept has been built against the early work. Part of the N transept survives as the E wall of the N aisle and the lowest three courses of the E part of the N wall. The external walls of crypt and chancel show that the building

* Repton worked for Sitwell Sitwell's youngest brother at Ferney Hall, Shropshire (demolished), in 1789.

‡ I am grateful to Mr Reresby Sitwell for providing much additional information, in particular about the park buildings.

is of more than one date. The lower walls of the crypt, now being exposed from within a 4 ft deep trench round the E end, are of fine masonry, the lowest courses forming a plinth of four steps each projecting a few inches from the one above. Each internal wall of the crypt has a shallow recess, but outside on the S side two large blocks of stone projecting about 2½ ft from the wall suggest that there was an external projection, probably gabled. The projection to the N may have been swept away when a staircase was constructed in the C14. Between the lowest walls and the sill level of the C14 window is a section of walling of roughly squared blocks of brown stone with massive flat quoins, unique to Repton. Above this the masonry changes again to smaller whitish blocks, with pilaster strips running up from a string-course to end in curious splayed capitals below eaves level. The N and S windows are lancets, the latter made in 1940, but incorporating fragments of a blocked C13 original.

Inside, the crypt is reached by two contemporary staircases from the transepts, and in the E trench are the remains of another very different flight. The crypt is a small chamber (16½ by 16½ by *c.* 10 ft) of nine almost square bays covered by domical vaults carried on cross-ribs which spring from two pilasters on each wall and rest on four central columns. All the capitals are grooved, and the columns decorated with spiral fillets. The pilasters are decorated with blank arches. A double cornice runs along the top of the E, N, and S walls but not into the recesses, which may have housed tombs. Only the W recess has a cornice, and above it a partly filled-in triangular recess. The vaulting system is structurally independent. The pilasters are addossed against the outer walls, the cornice of which runs behind them. Saxon walling, with a string-course, also survives in the nave, above the E arches of both arcades. In 1854 the E arches were built to conform with the rest of the arcade. They replaced two arches on each side: the E arches contemporary with the wall above (see the columns, with capitals like those of the crypt pilasters, in the porch and the bases *in situ*) and the W arches probably knocked through the original fabric in 1792.

Interpretation of the Anglo-Saxon features varies. Clapham placed the church stylistically (pilaster strips etc. as at Bradford on Avon and other supposedly late Anglo-Saxon churches) in the late C10. He assigned the basic structure of the crypt to pre-874 and the recesses and vaulting system, with its sophisticated decoration, to the C11. This dating was challenged in 1971 by

Dr H. M. Taylor, who has been conducting excavations with Mr and Mrs Biddle since 1974.*

The aisles were rebuilt in the C13 (SW lancet, traces of a NW lancet). In the early C14 they were widened (octagonal piers and double-chamfered arches with only small chamfers, windows, also chancel E window). Of the same date the W tower and spire, completed in 1340. The tower has angle buttresses, battlements with tiny pinnacles, and a recessed spire rising with two tiers of dormer windows to a height of 212 ft. The C15, however, altered the tower windows. Also C15 the castellated clerestory, the timber roof, and the two-storey porch. A curious piece of tracery design is the four-light straight-headed S window of the S transept. Its upper part consists of a row of lozenges: that is straight-sided, and thereby a really un-Gothic motif. – (STAINED GLASS. Many windows by *Powell*. R. Hubbuck) – PLATE. Elizabethan Chalice and Paten Cover; Chalice and two Patens, 1713 by *Richard Green*. – MONUMENTS. Alabaster effigy of a knight, *c.* 1400. – Incised alabaster slab to Gilbert Thacker † 1563 and wife. – Francis Thacker † 1710. Tablet with frontal bust between columns carrying a scrolly pediment. – William Stevens † 1800 by *E. F. Evans* of Derby, better than his average. – John Macaulay † 1840 by *Joseph Hall* the younger of Derby.

THE PRIORY consisted of the church, the cloister, the ranges round the cloister containing in the usual way the chapter house on the E side, the refectory on the far or N side, and the prior's lodgings and hall with cellars beneath on the W, and in addition various buildings a little away from this compact group. It deserves special notice how close the priory buildings were placed to the old church. The priory buildings were taken over by REPTON SCHOOL, which was founded by Sir John Port in 1557. He left money for it as well as for the hospital at Etwall and lies buried there. The school is now entered through the PRIORY GATEWAY, not a proper gatehouse, but simply an arch in a buttressed piece of wall. Adjoining the precinct wall, a medieval outbuilding (the ART SCHOOL) with a five-bay tie-

* *See* H. M. Taylor, 'Repton Reconsidered', in *England before the Conquest: studies in primary sources presented to Dorothy Whitelock*, ed. Peter Clemoes and Kathleen Hughes, Cambridge, 1971. According to Dr Taylor the church is also pre-874. He proposes that the core of the crypt, entered from the E, was the burial chamber of Aethelbald and Wiglaf, *c.* 757, and that this was vaulted when a sanctuary with a central tower, porticus, and westward extension of at least 20 ft was built above it *c.* 827–40. W stairways were cut afterwards, *c.* 850, probably to facilitate access to a major relic (St Wystan?).

beam and queen-post roof. To find one's way through the remains of the priory one must remember that the range immediately to the E of the church is the W range of the CLOISTER, the War Memorial Garth is the cloister, and the Pears Memorial Hall stands in the place of the nave of the church. The W range was the first part of the cloister group converted by the school for its use and now appears C16 and C17 in character. It is of two storeys plus an attic with mullioned and mullioned-and-transomed windows and a ramped walk at the S end leading to a four-centred doorway and C16 door. On the cloister side the central bays projecting over an open arcade are C17. Excavations and research have shown the survival of characteristic bits of the first work, i.e. the work of 1172–*c.* 1200 untouched by the new Gothic style. Most of the W range undercroft houses the school MUSEUM.* Its circular piers are a replacement of the original ones. The room as far as one can see was never vaulted. To the S of it, between the undercroft and the church, is a tunnel-vaulted corridor, the SLYPE or outer parlour. By it (W wall) the remains of deeply splayed windows. At the N end a room with part of a C12 rib-vault and (E wall) two lancet windows. Above the undercroft, in place of a number of schoolrooms and the library (the original schoolroom with C 17 headmaster's desk), was the PRIOR'S HALL or Great Hall, rebuilt *c.* 1400 and with a fine open timber roof of which fragments still exist. At its S end the so-called Prior's Bedchamber. N of the hall were no doubt kitchens strategically placed between it and the REFECTORY. The latter room also stood on an undercroft which seems to have been unvaulted, but had to its E a small rib-vaulted room and then a slype. The wall which now represents this range is a C16 construction.

The most interesting remains are those of the CHURCH : lower masonry courses of the E and S wall of the outer S chancel chapel and the N chancel aisle as well as of the solid pulpitum erected at the W end of the choir under the E arch of the crossing tower. In addition there are stumps of piers of varying and characteristic sections, all clearly belonging to the C13. They are all based on the quatrefoil but vary the type imaginatively, in chronological order thus : nave E half main thick shafts keeled and in each of the diagonals a cluster of three thin shafts, nave W half main shafts unkeeled and only one (detached) shaft in each of the

* At one end is the Masters' Common Room, lined with re-used C16 and C17 panelling.

diagonals as if the core of the pier were an octagon, choir main shafts attached and unkeeled. All these forms are not connected with local Derbyshire traditions.

Of the buildings away from the cloister the most important is REPTON HALL, to the N, built about 1680 as a private house independent of the school. It has a nine-bay, three-storey façade with wooden mullion and transom casements, a segmental pediment over the door, a slightly later four-bay extension to the E, and fine gatepiers. On the river front is that part of the hall known as PRIOR OVERTON'S TOWER. It is in fact of an importance considerably more than regional. It represents the remains of the prior's new lodgings to replace the inadequate accommodation of an earlier age. Overton was made prior in 1437. The tower contained his STUDY on the first floor. It is built of brick with two corbelled-out angle turrets, and can be called one of the most ornate pieces of early domestic brick architecture in England. The style is more Hanseatic than English, with its two very tall, blank, cusped two-light arches into which the one-mullion one-transom windows on two floors are let in. The top cornice is of typical billet kind. The study has fine carved beams with ornamental bosses. (A notable later addition is the staircase window with enamelled armorial glass by *Eginton* of Birmingham, 1813. DOE)

The main changes to the school took place only in the C19 – the usual pattern of the English public schools which, for all their venerably remote foundation dates, were as a rule of very inconsiderable size before the Victorian era (Repton *c.* 100 scholars early C19, *c.* 50 before 1850). The rapid growth of the school under Dr Pears (1854–74) and after is not matched by buildings of high architectural merit. Names of architects and dates will be sufficient: CHAPEL (to the SW across the Willington Road) by *Stevens* of Derby, 1857 (apse 1867, N aisle, N transept, and antechapel 1904–5, S transept and porch 1929); PEARS MEMORIAL HALL by *Sir Arthur Blomfield*, 1883–6, and decidedly pretty with its open arcades on the lower floor, its neo-Tudor windows, gables, tower, turrets, and rock-faced surfaces; the unexceptional NEW HOUSE (outside the school precincts on the l., going up the Burton Road) by *Forsyth & Maule*, 1909; THEATRE (neo-Georgian) and CHEMISTRY BLOCK, 1957 by *Marshall Sisson*, opposite the gateway on the other side of Willington Road.

THE TOWN forms a pleasant background to the school, though it has few individual buildings calling for special notice. The wide main street runs from the church and priory gateway S towards the restored CROSS. It then splits, and on one branch, HIGH STREET, two houses may be noted: TUDOR HOUSE, a symmetrical timber-framed house with central porch, and THE GRANGE of 1703, a five-bay, two-and-a-half-storey brick house with stone trim, pedimented doorway, and original iron garden gates. (In the Pastures on the W side of High Street, EASTON HOUSE, 1907 by *Lutyens*. An interesting, well-detailed, transitional work with an irregular, Arts and Crafts entrance side, but a Queen Anne garden front, symmetrical with projecting wings. This front has no door, which gives an oddly dull appearance. RE) Further out, in BURTON ROAD, No. 31 is one of *Parker & Unwin*'s most originally planned small houses, with an abstract spatial quality (probably due to Parker) quite removed from their earlier Arts-and-Crafts-based buildings. The plan is two rectangular blocks, one a living area, the other a service wing, pulled apart on the long sides. Irregular exterior with an overhanging roof, eyebrow dormers, roughcast walls.*

3050

RIBER

High above and to the E of Matlock RIBER CASTLE formed an ideal eyecatcher for the poetical visitors to the baths. But the embattled castle with its four angle towers and its embattled curtain walls with its own angle turrets was built as late as 1862–8 – a surprising case of posthumous romanticism, due to Mr Smedley's unerring sense of publicity values. The castle was built to his design as his residence, though it is now derelict and used as a British fauna zoo and reserve. Its size is 145 by 110 ft.

After the ostentatious picturesqueness of the castle RIBER HALL and the MANOR HOUSE are happy surprises, both of the genuine, unselfconscious picturesqueness of minor Elizabethan and early C17 architecture in the county, stone, with low mullioned windows, and gables. The Manor House especially makes a most felicitous picture. It has a date-stone 1633. (The Hall, similar to the Manor in some details, is dated 1661 over a basement door in the SW wing. Original staircase and some plasterwork. Divided into two since 1724. RE)

RICK LOW *see* SHELDON

* Description provided by Mr Mervyn Miller.

RIDDINGS

4050

ST JAMES. 1832 by *Francis Bedford* (who built some of the Waterloo churches in London). A handsome building for its date. Stone, narrow W tower with spire, nave with buttresses carrying pinnacles, and coupled lancet windows. Straight-ended chancel. White interior, no aisles. W gallery on cast-iron columns.

(ESTATE COTTAGES, SCHOOL, and MODEL FARM (with octagonal feed-store) all erected *c.* 1880 by the ironmasters, Oakes of Riddings House (early C19, ashlar). RE)

RIDGEWAY

3050

ST JOHN. 1838–40 by *Woodhead & Hurst* (Colvin), tower 1883–4.

WESLEYAN CHAPEL. 1806; later porch. Stone with pinnacled gables. Round-headed windows with Gothic tracery.*

WESLEYAN SUNDAY SCHOOL. 1823, Gothick.

ST CROSS HOUSE, Sloade Lane. 1826, built by Joseph 'Blade' Hutton, a local scythe manufacturer and convert to Catholicism. The plan is an orientated cross (obscured by a SW angle addition of 1910). *Cottage orné* style, lower floor stone, upper floor fake timber-framed. Highly ornamented inside and out.

KENT HOUSE. Early C17, H-plan, some windows altered but still an impressive house of the period.

RINGWOOD HOUSE *see* BRIMINGTON

RIPLEY

3050

ALL SAINTS. 1820–1. Commissioners' type with aisleless interior and SW tower. Baptistery 1921.

TOWN HALL. Built in 1880 as a market hall, originally open on the ground floor. Upper floor Queen Anne-ish, with three tall windows on each side rising above eaves level and ending in fanciful gables.

BUTTERLEY HALL (Derbyshire Constabulary H.Q.). C18, altered in 1792–1800 for Benjamin Outram, one of the founders of the Butterley Company. Offices (1971–4, 1975–7) by *R. W. Kenning* (County Architect) in a park setting.

* This entry and the remainder of the Ridgeway entries were provided by Mr Roger Evans.

(PADLEY HALL, to the NW near Hammersmith, has a beautiful mid-C17 garden front with three gables, mullioned and transomed windows, continuous string-courses, and a two-storey porch with parapet. RE)

RISLEY

4030

ALL SAINTS. Built by Michael Willoughby in 1593; see the date above the S doorway. Consecrated only in 1632. N aisle 1841. The doorway still four-centred, with a hood-mould. The S windows interestingly posthumous-Gothic, i.e. with intersected tracery but round-headed. The W tower unbuttressed, of two stages only, with round-headed two-light bell-openings, the two lights of lancet shape. – FONT. Alabaster, octagonal, on a tapering shaft, with strapwork decoration. – SCREEN. Plain rectangular openings; cherubim on the cross beam. – PLATE. Chalice, Paten Cover, and two Patens, 1632.

In 1593 a school was founded here by Katharine Willoughby. Her descendant, Elizabeth Grey, provided the LATIN HOUSE to accommodate pupils, master, and usher. It stands to the E of the church and is one of the best buildings of its date in the county. Dated 1706 above the door in the big segmental pediment on big acanthus brackets. The house is of brick, in chequerboard pattern, with blue bricks on the ground floor, simply red brick on the upper floor. Generous stone trim. The ground-floor windows have wide eared frames, big keystones with female faces, and an entablature projecting above the keystones. The upper floor is similar, though more delicate. Stone quoins and hipped roof.

82

In her will of 1720, Mrs Grey endowed a Latin and girls' school. It was built in 1724 to the E of the Latin House. In 1758* an identical English school for boys was built further E. The Latin House seems then to have become the house of the Latin master and his boarders.

The SCHOOLS form a delightful group. The English master's house built in 1771* stands back in the middle (five-bay, two-storey, with a shell-hood over the door). The two schoolrooms are to the l. and r. nearer the street but parallel to the master's house. They are identical in design, each with four tall windows with one wooden mullion and two wooden transoms. The only decoration is simple brick friezes.

* According to the *V.C.H.*, vol. II, pp. 267–8. The schools and English master's house all look exactly contemporary, i.e. very early C18.

RISLEY HALL. Of the original residence of the Willoughbys nothing remains but an Elizabethan or Jacobean gateway with crowstepped walls on a terrace by the moat. The Hall itself is of several different dates. The oldest part, facing the entrance gate, is a long stone building (the old coach house) dated 1695. At r. angles to it, the stone W front is late C19 Jacobean. On the other (E) side of this range the façade is Late Georgian, of pinkish brick with two stone canted bays and a Doric columned porch. To the r. of the earliest part, a red brick courtyard and stables of 1908. Extensions completed 1975 by Nottinghamshire County Council.

ROAD NOOK FARM *see* BRACKENFIELD

ROSEHILL *see* DERBY, p. 186

ROSLISTON

2010

ST MARY. Tiny unbuttressed W tower with plain broach-spire. The door and windows ogee-headed. The church itself is of 1819, aisleless, with the typical lancet windows, a lancet porch, and the larger windows equally typically lancet-shaped with two lancet lights and pierced spandrel. An unusual addition is a transom at the springing points of the arches of the two lights. The E end and a group of two single- and one two-light lancets under a pediment-like gable.

ROUND HILLOCK *see* EYAM

ROWARTH

0080

LONG LEE. An exceptionally fine farmhouse, in the original C17 state, with all its farm buildings. The house itself is dated 1663 on the porch. It is of T-shape and has low, long, mullioned as well as mullioned and transomed windows. A barn-cum-shippon with similar windows has the date 1679. No signs yet of a move away from Tudor traditions. In fact rather a primitive design reflecting Lancashire standards. The tombstone of the builder, 'John Hyde, gentleman' † 1703, is in one of the outbuildings.

LITTLE MILL INN. This is dated 1781. Now at last windows of Georgian shape without mullion and transom have become accepted.

2060

ROWSLEY

ST KATHERINE. 1855 by *Salvin Jun.* (GR), in the Norman style. N aisle 1859. – Anglo-Saxon CROSS HEAD with curling ends, an interesting specimen dated to the mid C9 by Sir Thomas Kendrick. – PLATE. Chalice, C17, continental make. – MONUMENT. Tomb-chest with the recumbent effigies of Lady John Manners † 1859 and a child, by *Calder Marshall* (NE chapel).

PEACOCK HOTEL. 1652, but still entirely in the Jacobean tradition, with symmetrical gables l. and r., and mullioned and transomed windows. The door has a semicircular pediment.

(Great Rowsley is an impeccably maintained estate village of the Duke of Rutland with C17 and C18 stone houses. RE)

CAULDWELL'S MILL. Stone flour mill of 1875, still powered by a water turbine, first installed in 1898.

ROWSLEY BRIDGE. C15, widened in 1925 from 16 to 40 ft. Five pointed arches.

OLD STATION, across the river in Little Rowsley. 1850 by *Paxton*. Italianate single-storey block, originally the terminus of the Midland line before the Dukes allowed it to cross their estates in the 1860s. Then superseded by *Edward Walters*'s passenger station (now demolished).

To the E, four cottages probably by *Paxton*, 1850, on either side of the A6.

ROWTOR ROCKS *see* BIRCHOVER

ROYSTONE GRANGE *see* BALLIDON

ST BRIDE'S FARM *see* STANTON-BY-BRIDGE

4030

SANDIACRE

ST GILES. The most interesting church in its neighbourhood, with remarkably rich pieces of the Norman as well as the Dec style. Of the Norman church the S doorway, the chancel arch, and two windows remain. The S doorway is of three orders with capitals with volutes and scallops and an arch with three roll-mouldings. The two windows are big and curiously high up, so that they were later lengthened below. They have nook-shafts inside and out. The chancel arch has thick semicircular responds as well as several orders of shafts. The capitals have leaves, heads, scallops, and volutes. The frieze also has upright leaves and a diaper band above and extends along the E wall of the nave. To this Norman nave of quite sizeable proportions a taller chancel was added, only 6 ft shorter than the nave. This was presumably a gift of Bishop Norbury of Lichfield, who held the prebend of Sandiacre from 1342 to 1347. The chancel is buttressed with big crocketed pinnacles on the buttresses, and a quatrefoil frieze above the tall windows. These are of three lights on the N and S sides, of six on the E side.* The tracery is manifold, but on the S chiefly of three odd three-pointed stars similar to the so-called Kentish tracery but characterized by the points being specially long and concave-sided. The N windows have flowing leaf shapes; the E window tracery also consists of them, but they are multiplied by necessity of the greater width. In the nave at the time when the chancel was built a four-light S window was opened out to give more light to the Norman nave.‡ In date between the nave and the chancel lies the W tower, short and unbuttressed, with small lancet windows, no battlements, and a spire with low broaches. The date of this is C13. The Perp style added the small clerestory. In the chancel triple SEDILIA and PISCINA under matching crocketed canopies. Very splendid. – FONT also of high quality and unusual design. – STAINED GLASS. Medieval fragments (chancel, N side).

14

Below the church in BRIDGE STREET, backing on to the Erewash Canal, a huge tenement LACE FACTORY of 1888.

SANDYBROOK HALL *see* ASHBOURNE, p. 65

SAWLEY

4030

ALL SAINTS. Norman chancel arch with much wall exposed above. Very wide nave. Arcades of octagonal piers with late C13 to early C14 capitals and double-chamfered arches. Late C13 chancel with typical tracery (lancets of two lancet lights with pierced spandrel); especially fine the five-light E window (arches upon arches; cf. e.g. Lichfield chancel aisles).§ The N

* According to Christopher Wilson the N chancel windows are identical to the E windows of the transepts at Tideswell.

‡ Christopher Wilson points out that this window is far more rustic than its suave contemporaries in the chancel. He also draws attention to the details in the chancel: good head stops (those outside are replicas), and a nice imp on the S capital of the chancel arch. Also a priest's door.

§ But from the Rawlins manuscript it looks rather as if this were a C19 alteration.

aisle has windows of three lancet lights, the middle one higher than the others. The S aisle has a single smallish lancet as its W window; the other windows have elongated ogee reticulated tracery. This is Dec. Perp clerestory, embattled, as is the S aisle. Perp W tower (different stone). Angle buttresses and the spire recessed behind battlements. Inside, the tower is open to the nave in an opening not larger than a door. Inside the chancel there are two specially noteworthy features – a solid stone screen just W of the E wall separating a back vestry (cf. Tideswell), and a kind of bay-window, deep and with panelled sides and a four-centred vault. It is a CHANTRY CHAPEL and holds the alabaster effigy of John Bothe † 1496, Treasurer of Lichfield Cathedral (cf. the similar recess in the S chancel aisle at Lichfield).* Other Bothe MONUMENTS. Ogee-headed recess in the chancel N wall (panelled back wall) with tomb-chest with small brasses of Roger B. † 1467 and his wife and children. – Under the chancel arch big tomb-chest with larger brasses of Robert B. † 1478 and his wife. – At the E end of the N aisle brass to Richard Shylton † 1510 and wife. – Next to this stone effigy of a priest taken in from a tomb recess outside. – (Also fragments of a very important monument, dismantled in the 1830s: in the N aisle a censing angel from the canopy, and other pieces in the porch. C. Wilson) – PULPIT. 1636, still in the Jacobean tradition, with handsome tester with pendants. – SCREEN. Perp, with single-light openings. Also fragments from two other screens. – ROOFS and STALLS, partly old. – PLATE. Elizabethan Chalice and Paten Cover.

BAPTIST CHURCH, Wilne Road. 1800, enlarged in 1845. Handsome brick front with a classical stone doorcase.

BOTHE HALL, Tamworth Road. Refronted in the C18 with sash-windows etc., but still with the proportions and some mullioned and transomed windows of the original C17 house. Stone.

(RYE HILL CLOSE, No. 194 Tamworth Road. 1895–1900. Domestic Revival style with Dutch gables and some interesting stained glass. No. 196 similar but slightly later. K. Reedman.)

A small, square EARTHWORK with a single entrance in the N side lies close to the bridge over the Trent. Its date is uncertain, but may lie within the Roman period.

4060

SCARCLIFFE

ST LEONARD. Norman S doorway with one order of colonnettes,

* The one at Lichfield is by *James Wyatt* (Christopher Wilson).

one roll-moulding in the arch, and a lintel with ill-assorted wheels, stars, saltire crosses. Norman chancel doorway renewed. C13 W tower rebuilt in 1842. The detail not reliable. C13 lancet windows in the chancel N and S walls. Embattled nave S side with late C16 or C17 windows (the tall one C19). The windows on the N side of the same style but smaller. – FONT COVER. 1686. – Large medieval parish CHEST. – PLATE. Cup, 1599; Elizabethan Paten with sun face. – MONUMENT. A beautiful C13 effigy of a woman (probably Constantia de Frecheville † 1175) with a child in her arms, her head resting on a lion, with a long scroll of Leonine verse. 33

SCARCLIFFE PARK WOOD, 1 m. E. Two Romano-British enclosed settlements containing hut circles lie in the woodland. Associated with them are traces of a field system and clearance cairns.

SCROPTON

1030

ST PAUL. 1855–6 by *Ferrey* (GR). The W tower has the alien motif of a pyramid roof. – MONUMENT. William Schower † 1495, incised slab. – Nicholas Agard and his two wives, *c.* 1510. On the front wall of the alabaster tomb-chest angels holding shields under ogee canopies, and plain panels with shields.

FOSTON HALL, to the NNW, on the A50. A very red brick Jacobethan house of 1863 by *Hine* of Nottingham. (C18 pedimented stone archway to the kitchen yard, with a wrought-iron gate. RE)

SHARDLOW

4030

ST JAMES. 1838 it is said, by *Stevens*. Stone-faced. Aisleless interior, tall lancet-like windows with Perp tracery. Embattled W tower without pinnacles.

SHARDLOW HALL. Fine seven-bay garden front, of brick, bays one and seven quoined l. and r. Doorway with Gibbs surround and pediment. The date according to rainwater-heads is 1726. But the entrance side is dated 1684 and is stone-faced, very severe, with a receding centre and projecting side parts. The windows still have hood-moulds, and these are connected by horizontal courses. Heavy parapet, no visible roof (cf. Eyam). To the l. and r. of this main block stone-faced Palladian wings, three-bay, one-storeyed, with arched windows, and then two-storeyed pavilions with pediments, evidently late C18 (the W one altered). The odd thing is that the garden front is not also stone-faced. (Inside a staircase and some panelled rooms of *c*. 1684. DOE)

SHARDLOW CANAL PORT. This is a rare example of an inland canal port, one of the two recognizable survivals in the country (the other being Stourport). The Trent and Mersey Canal was known as the Grand Trunk, and was akin to the modern motorway, for it connected canal systems throughout the Midlands. Shardlow became important soon after the opening of the Grand Trunk, built by the engineer *James Brindley*, in 1777. Much of the character of the port area is generated by the mingling of industrial, commercial, and domestic buildings, and by the existence of a working boatyard still within the complex. BROUGHTON HOUSE, London Road, a handsome early C19 ashlar house, was built by one of the canal carriers and is linked to the CANAL BASIN, where there is much of interest. The warehouses are called mills as a result of more recent industrial use. The best is MILL NO 2, S of the A6, dated 1780. Three storeys, brick, projecting pedimented centre with wide segmental arch below spanning a canal inlet. Wings either side with small openings. N of the A6 there are other WAREHOUSES, those near Broughton House with semicircular windows, another with similar windows near the Maltshovel Inn. Some interesting houses on the WHARF, e.g. Nos. 9–17 Woodland Terrace and No. 47, WHARF HOUSE. In Wilne Lane, SHARDLOW LODGE (The Lady in Grey Restaurant), another handsome C18 canal carrier's house, brick, pedimented centre. On the other side of the road the remains of a rope walk.

SHARP LOW *see* TISSINGTON

SHEEPBRIDGE *see* CHESTERFIELD, p. 150

1060

SHELDON

MAGPIE MINE is one of the most completely surviving sites of the Derbyshire lead-mining industry, with the remains of a Cornish engine house, chimneys, an ore-crushing circle, and a large stone-lined drain along which the water obtained from the workings was raised from the site. Restored by *Montague Associates* for the Peak District Mines Historical Society.

½ m. to the NW of the village lie two undated BARROWS.

DEMONS DALE. Several Beaker burials were found in a natural rock-fissure.

RICK LOW, 1½m. S of Sheldon. Much denuded barrow.

RINGHAM LOW, ¼m. NW of Rick Low. Chambered Neolithic tomb, now largely destroyed. It contained the remains of some twenty individuals.

SHIPLEY

4040

SHIPLEY PARK. Opened as a Country Park by Derbyshire County Council.* Within it, a MODEL FARM, 1860–1 by *W. Eden Nesfield* (his earliest work) for A. M. Mundy. Described as an ornamental farm and dairy by Eastlake. Brick; an enclosed courtyard with a cart entrance flanked by a romantically baronial tower partly of stone; tiled conical roof. At the far end, a house with a low square tower and some brick banding. Beyond is the DAIRY, like a medieval baptistery, but sadly stripped of its tiles and stained glass.‡ The central font has been saved. Near by THE GARDENS, 1880, a house in the manner of Norman Shaw. Brick with a jettied upper storey and half-timbering. LODGES, stone, early C20. To the W the SMALLEY LODGE, 1861. One of the lodges referred to by Eastlake and the only other building by *Nesfield*, with many characteristic details and a charming well in the garden on the other side of the drive.

SHIRLAND

3050

ST LEONARD. Essentially a C15 church. W tower with diagonal buttresses and eight pinnacles on the battlements (cf. Morton), embattled clerestory with pinnacles, embattled aisles, windows Perp throughout, that at the E end of the chancel quite unusual (if correctly renewed): three lights under a four-centred arch with the centre light reaching up higher than the side lights, and a little panel tracery above all three. S porch vaulted, with pointed transverse arch (cf. Ault Hucknall, etc.). – PAINTING. Crucifixus and Magdalen, small in original altar frame; looks North Italian, mid C15. – STAINED GLASS. Some old fragments in nave windows. – MONUMENTS. Big ogee-headed recess in the chancel N wall with tomb-chest with many

* The Hall has been demolished. It was built in 1700, enlarged in 1788, extended again and faced with stone in 1895. *Walter Tapper* worked here from 1904 to 1914 according to *Who's Who in Architecture* (1926). (Information about the Hall, Model Farm, etc. kindly supplied by Mr Roger Evans and Mr Andrew Saint.)

‡ The glass (four quatrefoil panels depicting the seasons, thought to have been painted by *H. J. Westlake*) will be returned after restoration.

shields with the Grey arms;* the effigy has disappeared. – From another tomb-chest only an alabaster panel with four thin long kneeling figures remains (chancel S wall). – Tomb-chest in the N aisle with three fine large cusped and embellished quatrefoils and on the top incised slab of John Revell † 1537 and wife and children (attributed by Greenhill to the *Royleys* of Burton on Trent). – John Revell † 1699, and his son William † 1706; sumptuous wall-monument of wood with fruit, flowers, etc., and many cherubs' heads.

(SHIRLAND LODGE, 1 m. S. C17 (probably 1658). Unusual because of red brick with some diapering in the gables. Stone quoins, mullioned windows, two-storey porch. RE)

(1¼ m. S, at Toadhole Furnace, former FRIENDS' MEETING HOUSE of 1743. Tiny stone building attached to an altered cottage. It consists of two blocks with a stairway between, the outer one being the schoolroom over a stable. Also FURNACE HOUSE, 1787, and AMBER MILL HOUSE, an impressive late C18 stone house with a Doric doorcase.)

2040

SHIRLEY

ST MICHAEL. W tower and N aisle 1861 and 1842 respectively. C14 chancel (with Perp E window), C14 S aisle (with an arcade of octagonal piers and double-chamfered arches; the windows C19). The W gallery on cast-iron columns and the box pews no doubt of 1842. – In the N aisle E wall outside a badly preserved carved STONE from a Norman lintel (beasts and birds). – PLATE. Paten of 1491, parcel gilt; Elizabethan Chalice; Flagon, 1675. – MONUMENT. Late medieval incised slab to a priest.

SIMMONDLEY *see* GLOSSOP

SINFIN *see* DERBY, p. 187

SLACK HALL *see* FORD HALL

SLIPER LOW *see* BRASSINGTON

SLIPPER LOW *see* TADDINGTON

* According to Mr Gladwin Turbutt the tomb is believed to belong to Henry, fifth Lord Grey of Wilton, † 1396.

SMALLEY

4040

ST JOHN THE BAPTIST. Of the building of 1793 nothing survives. Additions and alterations 1844 (transepts), 1862, and again (the pretty, nearly detached, short W tower with pyramid roof) 1912. – Radford memorial window, 1882, with good STAINED GLASS. – MONUMENT. Anthony Woodward † 1803, terracotta tablet by *T. Moore* of Normanton.

STAINSBY HOUSE. *See* p. 324.

SMISBY

3010

ST JAMES. Small church with W tower, nave and S aisle, and chancel. The aisle arcade has three bays with circular piers hardly taller than four and a half feet. Double-chamfered arches. The chancel E window is of three lights, broad, with rather coarse Dec tracery. Most of the other windows are C16 or C17, straight-headed, with one mullion or one mullion and one transom (S aisle E). – PANELLING of the E end, linenfold pattern, from Ashby-de-la-Zouch Castle. – MONUMENTS. Alabaster effigy of Joan Comyn of Smisby, mid C14; it must originally have been of good quality. – Incised alabaster slab to W. Kendall † 1500 and his wife. – Wall-monument to Henry Kendal † 1627 and wife, with large kneeling figures facing each other across a prayer desk. Kneeling children below (nine sons and seven daughters, the swaddled babies upright and incongruously mixed up with the kneeling figures).

LOCKUP, close to the Tournament Field. Brick, polygonal, with spire and ball on top.

SNELSTON

1040

ST PETER. Only the NE tower is old, with diagonal buttresses, battlements, and pinnacles. The church, of nave and chancel only, was almost completely rebuilt in 1825, and again in 1907 (by *Hodgson Fowler*: DOE). – (STAINED GLASS. W window 1907, a stock composition by *W. E. Tower*; N chapel N window 1949 by *Nuttgens*. R. Hubbuck) – PLATE. Chalice designed by *Cottingham*.

SNELSTON HALL, a spectacular piece of romantic Gothicism by *Cottingham*, 1827, was demolished in 1951. Only the ruins of the gateway, part of the W wing, the landscaped setting, and some of Cottingham's estate buildings survive: the brick Tudor-style Snelston Arms and School Farmhouse, and the ornate half-timbered Lodge and Bailiff's Cottage (now Post Office).

2060

SNITTERTON HALL

$1\frac{1}{4}$m. W of Matlock

57 A gem of an Elizabethan manor house. Symmetrical front, embattled and gabled, with broad shallow projections on the sides and six-light and four-light mullioned and transomed windows. The doorway asymmetrically placed, flanked by crude fancy Ionic pilasters and with a lintel decorated with flower motifs. In front of the house a small formal garden. The garden wall with its arched door was flanked on the l. and r. by square pavilions or summer houses. The one on the r. has gone. At the back wings of *c.* 1695 and 1908. Roof pitch lowered and interior altered in 1747 (rainwater-heads).

4050

SOMERCOTES

ST THOMAS. Chancel, side chapel, and vestry 1854. The rest of 1902, by *P. H. Currey*. Handsome E front, the four-light window with a big mullion running right to the top. Angular bell-turret to the r., on the aisle.

METHODIST CHURCH, Birchwood Lane. 1853. Brick, with a pretty embattled tower and lancet windows. Not at all Nonconformist in appearance. The church was given by John Smedley (*see* Matlock).

1030

SOMERSAL HERBERT

ST PETER. 1874 by *C. J. Neale* of Mansfield, of good solid design. (W tower 1912. DOE) – FONT. Norman, tub-shaped, with blind arcade of intersecting arches and above a border of lozenges overlaid with intermittent circles. – STAINED GLASS. N chancel window by *Kempe*, 1896. – PLATE. Cup, 1678. – MONUMENT. Priest with chalice in his lap below his folded hands.

56 SOMERSAL HALL. A most felicitous picture of Elizabethan half-timbering. The entrance side in particular has four gables grouped so that a broad low one on the l. is matched by two small ones on the r., higher by one overhanging half-storey. The fourth gable in the middle of intermediate height and width. The timbering chiefly narrow uprights. More decorative

motifs in the gables. In the entrance two inscription tablets of 1564. The builder was John Fitzherbert. SW block of brick, 1712. Much added in 1850. Porch, 1899.

(In the village two timber-framed cottages. RE)

SOMERSALL HALL *see* CHESTERFIELD, p. 151

SOUTH NORMANTON

4050

ST MICHAEL. Perp W tower with diagonal buttresses (cf. South Wingfield). Nave with N and S aisles, the S aisle 1878, the N aisle with a three-bay arcade on thin, coarse octagonal piers. Late Perp N windows. N chancel chapel opening by one arch into the chancel. In the chancel N wall (originally S wall) is the only interesting piece of architecture in the church, the head of the vestry door, pointed trefoiled with dogtooth decoration and the two cusps in the shape of a kind of stiff-leaf fleurs-de-lis. The shafts in the jambs of the doorway are filleted. Its date must be *c.* 1250–75. – FONT. Probably C14. Octagonal, with simple tracery. – PLATE. Chalice, Paten on foot, and Flagon, 1713 by *John Jackson*; two Patens, 1713 and 1714, by *Gabriel Sleath*. – MONUMENT. Robert Revel † 1714, wall-monument with two standing putti, not good.

8

CARNFIELD HALL. *See* p. 122.

SOUTH WINGFIELD

3050

ALL SAINTS. The church lies on its own, half a mile E of the village and a mile NNE of the Manor House. The body of the church is C13, see the arcade of five bays with circular piers, characteristic capitals (occasional nailhead decoration), and a keeled respond. The W tower is of different stone and Perp (diagonal buttresses). In 1803 the windows of nave and aisle were all re-done, arched and unmoulded. The chancel, except for the bare masonry of the walls, dates from 1877. – FONT. Plain, big, Norman, of tub-shape. – PLATE. Cup, 1609.

WINGFIELD MANOR HOUSE. Neither the picturesque nor the strictly architectural traveller should miss Wingfield Manor House. Its tall ruins, with the chief tower standing to a height of 72 ft, are an extremely dramatic sight. It is a larger complex of buildings than Haddon Hall, and it was all built within fifteen years and never much altered after. The manor came into the hands of Ralph Lord Cromwell in 1439 or 1440. He was ex-

52

tremely rich, Lord Treasurer, Warden of Sherwood Forest, Constable of Nottingham Castle, and had already begun Tattershall Castle, Lincs, in 1434. He began building at Wingfield immediately and on the largest scale. It is 416 ft long and over 256 ft wide. Like Haddon it consists of two courts.

Of the outer court the GATEHOUSE with a large and small entrance survives in the SE corner, and next to it the only roofed building of the Manor, a two-storey aisled building with massive timbers, now called the BARN but probably originally the servants' quarters above offices. What we see today of the E and W ranges is their inner and outer walls respectively. The range dividing the S from the N court has a S front towards the outer court which is more or less symmetrical although there is a modern farmhouse to the E side of the gateway. The gateway, again with one large and one small entrance, is flanked by square turrets. At about equal distances from these follow big projecting chimneys. A second chimney on the l. is balanced by the porch of the farmhouse on the r. The symmetry is, however, in the end effectively overturned by the Great Tower riding on the W extremity of this range.

The W range of the INNER COURT is destroyed except for the outer wall with its groups of fireplaces etc. showing it was divided into lodgings on two floors over a basement, reached by staircases in octagonal turrets. The E range was apparently never built, but a parlour and chapel may have been intended here. The N range contains the STATE ROOMS, the HALL with bay-window at the dais end and porch, and to the l. of this an apartment as large as the hall but placed at r. angles so that it projects far to the N. This apartment was the GREAT CHAMBER block with a basement, service floor, and above it the Great or Audience Chamber. At its N end was an inner chamber. The range ends to the l. (W) with the KITCHEN facing the court. Between it and the hall was a small open court and covered alley, behind it a suite of private chambers linked with the hall.

The architectural details deserve as much notice as the planning. The hall rests on a vaulted undercroft with five octagonal piers along its centre line and heavy ribs with typical Perp mouldings (wavy curves). The hall is 72 by 36 ft in size, of finer workmanship than the rest of the Manor, and conforms exactly to the specifications of the contract summarized in the building accounts. The PORCH leading into the former screens passage was originally fan-vaulted. It has fleuron decoration in the jambs of the arch, an upper chamber, and battlements decorated with shields above a quatrefoil frieze. The bay-window tracery is remarkable in that it still preserves some traces of the Dec past (ogee and leaf shapes): a warning to those who try to date church windows on insufficient evidence. To the N the original windows were altered in the late C17, when a first floor was inserted, into two tiers of mullion-and-transom cross windows. The greatest surprise is the S window of the Great Chamber, a very large four-light transomed window with panel tracery, the arched panels starting higher for the inner than the outer lights. Above it an oculus window with three cusped spherical triangles with tracery. Perp three-light and two-light windows with a minimum of panel tracery W of the Parlour on the first floor and simpler Perp windows in the same part of the range to the N. Similar windows in the outer court on the E side and in the tower.

A building account for the period 1 November 1442 to Christmas 1443 sheds much light on the building of the inner court, which was begun in 1439 or 1440 and was nearing completion in 1443; it may have been ready when Lord Cromwell visited the house at the end of the year. There is no reference to the outer court, implying that it had not yet been begun. All Cromwell's craftsmen were English, the chief masons being one *John Entrepas*, who drew up the contract for the hall, and *Richard North*, who supervised the construction of the undercroft.

The estate was sold after Ralph Cromwell's death in 1456 to the second Earl of Shrewsbury, whose descendants often resided at Wingfield. The fourth Earl died here. The sixth Earl accommodated Mary Queen of Scots at the manor house three times in 1569, and again in 1584. In the Civil War it was badly damaged. After the Restoration Immanuel Halton occupied it, but in the 1770s masonry from the house was used in the building of WINGFIELD HALL, N of the old manor house which was abandoned until a farm was built into it in the C19.

(STATION.* 1839–40 by *Francis Thompson*. The design was later used by Loudon as a villa in the Supplement to his *Encyclopaedia of . . . Villa Architecture* (1846). Classical in an original mode with shallow hipped roofs, wide-spreading eaves, and

* This and the slight remains of the Trijunct Station at Derby alone survive of the early stations built by Thompson for the Midland Railway.

large Jacobean-style chimneys. Also a stationmaster's house by *Thompson*. DOE)

SPARROW PIT *see* CHAPEL-EN-LE-FRITH

4070

SPINKHILL

MOUNT ST MARY'S COLLEGE. The nucleus is a house of the C17, much altered for the school in 1842 (*A. Hansom*). Wings were added in 1859. The R.C. CHURCH is of 1844–6 by *J. A. Hansom, à la* Pugin, with a broach-spire. The new school was built in 1876 by *Clutton*. Further enlargements 1902 and 1912 (*C. & C. M. Hadfield*). The War Memorial Chapel is by *Adrian G. Scott* and was completed in 1930: pale brick with a dome over the crossing.

PARK HALL, ½m. E. *See* p. 296.

SPONDON *see* DERBY, p. 195

STADEN LOW *see* BUXTON

4040

STAINSBY HOUSE

Near Smalley

The plain nine-bay, two-and-a-half-storey late C18 and mid C19 stucco and stone house with a three-bay pediment has been demolished (1971–2) and replaced by a Spanish-style ranch, odd-looking in the Derbyshire landscape (architect *David Shelley*, 1972–4).

STANAGE EDGE *see* HATHERSAGE

4040

STANLEY

ST ANDREW. Small Norman doorway on the S side; E of it a small C13 lancet window. The chancel E window of three stepped lancet lights is early C14. The rest mostly 1874, by *Evans & Jolly*. Nave, chancel, bellcote. – (Jacobean PULPIT and ALTAR RAILS. DOE) – PLATE. Paten on foot, 1719; Chalice, *c.* 1719.

3020

STANTON-BY-BRIDGE

ST MICHAEL. Small and low, with a C19 bellcote. Interesting

Saxon remains, especially the long-and-short work at the SE angle. Norman S doorway (one order of colonnettes, and zigzag in the arch), Norman W window and wall, Norman chancel arch. The rest is later C13, see the chancel S window (bar tracery with quatrefoil in circle) and the N aisle windows. The arcade inside is of three bays, low, with octagonal piers and double-chamfered arches. – MONUMENTS. Recess with effigy of a Priest, *c.* 1400. – Incised alabaster slab to William Sacheverell † 1558 and separate slab with kneeling children (from the front of the tomb-chest). – A second badly preserved incised alabaster slab to Richard Francis † 1530.

ST BRIDE'S FARM, 1½ m. S. In the outer wall next to the door a tiny Norman tympanum with a quadruped in profile, not an unusual representation. (Part of remains from a cell, grange, or chapel attached to Burton Abbey. DOE)

SWARKESTON BRIDGE. *See* p. 337.

STANTON-BY-DALE

4030

ST MICHAEL. Chiefly *c.* 1300, see the chancel windows (with three stepped lancet lights), the N aisle N and W windows, and the three-bay N arcade. The S doorway has a tympanum with a rude cross which may be Norman. The W tower with buttresses covering the angles, battlements, and crocketed pinnacles. Handsome S porch, tunnel-vaulted with thick transverse arches (cf. Ault Hucknall, etc.). – PLATE. Cup, 1629.

VILLAGE CROSS. Slim, octagonal, on a substructure.

ALMSHOUSES, E of the church. 1711, extended to the S in 1735, and again in the same style in the early C19. With their plain brick gables they look a good deal older.

STANTON HALL. C18. Three-bay centre with rusticated stone lintels to the windows and giant angle pilasters. Other parts castellated.

STANTON-IN-THE-PEAK

2060

HOLY TRINITY. 1839, with spire and transeptal chapels. Inside, as gifts of members of the Thornhill family, a HOLY WATER STOUP, Italian, bronze, dated 1596, and a TABERNACLE, of very good Florentine Quattrocento style, with praying angels in three tiers above each other, used to hold a dedication inscription of the church. – PLATE. Chalice, C17 Spanish, parcel gilt; Paten on foot, 1710. – MONUMENT. Henry Bache Thornhill † 1822, an imitation of the Florentine Quattrocento, very skilfully done, probably *c.* 1860–70.

STANTON HALL. A composite building with one gabled bay remaining of the C16 or early C17, then a broad, fine, eight-bay, one-and-a-half-storey house with original sash-windows and top balustrade, dated 1693, and then an addition of 1799 by *Lindley* of Doncaster with a semicircular porch and a three-bay pediment above, five by five bays.

STANTON OLD HALL, now a farmhouse. Still gabled and with mullioned windows, yet dated 1667.

STANTON WOODHOUSE, 1 m. E. C17 or a little earlier. Much altered. But the two-, three-, and four-light windows with the individual lights ending triangularly instead of in pointed arches are apparently original. (Inside, Manneristic wall paintings, quite good for the remote situation, over a close-studded partition. S. Rigold)

DOLL TOR. Stone circle with two cairns in association.

STANTON MOOR. A large group of barrows and cairns, about seventy in all, still stand on the moor. Approximately half have been excavated. The largest measures 54 ft in diameter and now stands 5 ft high. It contained two concentric rings of large stones. Within these lay twelve cremations. Three other monuments consist of circular banks of stones with entrances. The best known of these is the circle known as the NINE LADIES, now surrounded by a modern wall. The isolated KING STONE stands near by. Most of the other funerary monuments here are small barrows and cairns.

TOWER on Stanton Moor Edge. Erected in 1832 in honour of Earl Grey to commemorate the Reform Bill.

4070

STAVELEY

The village, with its large, friendly C20 housing estates, winds along to the S of the large Staveley Iron Works.

ST JOHN THE BAPTIST. C13 W tower with W door, tall W lancet window, tower arch to the nave with keeled semicircular responds. The upper parts are Perp (different stone), the battlements and pinnacles of 1681. The doorway also C13, with one stiff-leaf capital and renewed arch. The S aisle Perp, see its arcade and windows. The N aisle of 1865–9 by *Sir G. G. Scott.* In the N aisle a curiously crude ogee-headed recess, from the nave N wall, with figures above each other in the flanking buttresses and fragments of painting on the back wall. Possibly an Easter Sepulchre. The style is Perp. The most interesting part of the church is the Frecheville Chapel (S chancel aisle), slightly earlier than the glass (cf. below) dated 1676: two bays, latest Perp windows. The chancel clerestory is a C17 addition. – FONT. Apparently Norman; it may be an assembly of fragments. – STAINED GLASS.* A splendid window of heraldic display, big, fat, scrolly foliage and cherubs. By *Henry Gyles* of York for Lord Frecheville, Governor of York, whose tomb is in front of it. – (S aisle, scholarly pastiche of a C15 window, *c.* 1927, by *F. S. Eden*, a writer on stained glass. R. Hubbuck) – MONUMENTS. On the N side of the chancel two memorials, one to Peter Frecheville, *c.* 1480, a tomb-chest with brass effigy in armour, the other to Piers Frecheville † 1503, a coarse Perp wall recess with kneeling figures of brass against the back wall. – On the S side of the chancel incised alabaster slab to John Frecheville, 1510. – In the Frecheville Chapel large wall-monument with semi-reclining figure of Christian Frecheville, who died in childbed in 1653. She is shown contemplating her baby. Two putti pull away curtains to the l. and r. – John Lord Frecheville † 1682, standing wall-monument with a big bulgy base and a bulgy sarcophagus with two putti on it. No effigy.

DISTRICT COUNCIL OFFICES. Originally Staveley Hall, later the Rectory. Built in 1604, although the exterior tells little of that. (The exterior was made classical about 1710 by the Cavendishes, who acquired the house from the Frecheville family in 1681. From this period date the pedimented windows on the garden front and two panelled rooms inside. Partly demolished in the early C19, then further remodelling, more nearly Jacobean, by *Scott* in 1867. Presumably his the impressive staircase with stone arches. Massive early C18 stone walls round what was presumably once a formal garden. RE)

To the W of the church the former SCHOOL with octagonal master's house. The style is typical of the 1840s. The school was indeed established in 1844 by the Duke of Devonshire and is very much in *Paxton*'s manner.

(Former RECTORY (Nos. 7 and 8 Church Street). Dated 1719 on a rainwater-head. Double-gabled house with recessed centre, stuccoed and gothicized *c.* 1820. Brick at the back, an early example of brick in this area. Good original staircase. RE)

(THE CHANTRY (No. 39 High Street). Medieval, said to have been a chantry or chapel originally. The interior has indications

* C14 fragments in the E windows of the N aisle and the S chancel chapel. W window by *Stammers*, *c.* 1963.

of massive timbering, particularly in the roof, where the timbers are oddly spaced out. DOE)

GRAMMAR SCHOOL, NETHERTHORPE, ½ m. E. Founded in 1591. Probably not the building that still exists, gabled, with an asymmetrical porch and three-light mullioned and transomed windows. (Sundial over the porch dated 1697. The building could well be of this date. Lysons says it was rebuilt in 1698. RE)

HAGGE FARM, 1 m. NW. Small, very tall symmetrical house with square porch projection between two gabled bays. Built according to White in 1630 for Sir Peter Frecheville.

BARROW HILL. *See* p. 84.

5070

STEETLEY

STEETLEY CHAPEL is by far the richest example of Norman architecture in Derbyshire. Yet it is only 52 ft long and 15 ft wide. The lavish, almost ostentatious display of mid C12 decoration must be connected with some special purpose of the chapel; but manorial history has not so far yielded an answer. The chapel consists of a nave, a slightly narrower and lower chancel, and a yet a little narrower and lower apse. The nave is oblong, the chancel square, the apse provided with a short oblong W bay. There are elaborately ornamented arches between nave and chancel and chancel and apse, and the apse is in addition vaulted, a tunnel-vault over the oblong bay and a hemisphere over the apse proper. The two parts are separated by a transverse arch of relatively complex profile (three roll-mouldings and two ridges between) and two ribs of the same profile run against it. There is no keystone or boss where they meet. The arch and the ribs are strengthened (or emphasized) outside by buttresses. The apse receives its light through three windows with nook-shafts outside. At the height of their sill a band of scrolly ornament runs round the apse. A corbel-table supports the roofs of apse, chancel, and nave.

6

The nave and chancel were roofless right through the C19 and probably earlier. A restoration took place in 1880 (designed in 1876–80 by *J. L. Pearson*), and although it was careful, a certain amount of what we see at present is Victorian and not Norman. That applies in particular to the S portal. Of its four orders of colonnettes, two were at the time of Lysons' *Magna Britannia* of 1818 so completely defaced that he does not illustrate them. Of the inner orders one has medallions, the other foliage scrolls. The corresponding arches are decorated with zigzag and simplified beakhead. The gable dates from 1880. The nave has two very narrow W windows and one on the S side, and a small and insignificant N doorway.

Much better preserved naturally are the two chancel arches and the apse. The chancel imposts have four shafts each. The capitals display, besides the usual scallops, foliage scrollwork, animals (a double-headed lion), and scenes (St George and the Dragon, Adam and Eve). The chancel W arch with zigzag and crenellation and a kind of crescent-motif on the label is more elaborate than the E arch, which is plain except for a billet frieze on the label.

There are few Norman churches in England so consistently made into showpieces by those who designed them and those who paid for them.

GRAVE SLAB. Anglo-Norman, with a representation of a chalice and paten resting on an altar and a blessing hand.

STOKE HALL

2070

1½ m. NW of Curbar

Quite a stately stone mansion, five by five bays, two and a half storeys. W doorway with Tuscan columns, the head connected with the frame of the window above. E door with a pediment and shallow round-headed arch. Dated 1757 on rainwater-heads and built for the Rev. John Simpson, who subscribed to James Paine's *Plans, Elevations and Sections of Noblemen's and Gentlemen's Houses* (1767). Some features are reminiscent of *Paine*; floating cornices to some of the windows, splayed architrave surrounds to others, ball machicolation on the parapet, etc.* Fine fireplaces inside. Coach house and stables across the road, round three sides of a court with two pyramid-roofed towers.

STONE EDGE SMELT *see* ASHOVER

* According to Mr Peter Leach, who gives the following information. Cox attributes the design of Stoke Hall to *Paine*, together with Stony Middleton Church, Eyam Rectory, the stables at Chatsworth, and the stables at Buxton. In fact, the Chatsworth stables are by Paine, those at Buxton by Carr, but *William Booth* of Stony Middleton was the mason responsible for both and this suggests that he may have designed Stoke Hall and Eyam Rectory (possibly with Paine's co-operation) and Stony Middleton Church. Eyam Rectory (demolished) was built *c.* 1768 for another subscriber to Paine's volume, the Rev. Thomas Seward.

STONEGRAVELS *see* CHESTERFIELD, p. 148

2070

STONY MIDDLETON

ST MARTIN. A rarity, if not a visually very satisfying one. To the low unbuttressed Perp W tower (C19 doorway) in 1759 a new church was added which is octagonal with an ambulatory and a lantern storey on piers (*see* note to Stoke Hall). The roof of the lantern unfortunately is almost exactly the height of the tower. The ambulatory has circular windows, the lantern tripartite semicircular ones, the chancel a tall arched window with two mullions and one transom continuing the string-course round the building which also runs above and below round the circular windows. The open timber roof is C19. – PLATE. Cup, 1638; Flagon, 1772 by *William* and *John Priest*, given by the Rev. John Simpson of Stoke Hall.

STONY MIDDLETON HALL. Elizabethan or Jacobean, with a symmetrical front with two gables; much remodelled, probably early in the C19.

In the village the style of the C18 windows of the church can be found in several houses.

3060

STUBBING COURT

1½ m. W of Wingerworth

Seven-bay, two-storey stone house with central pediment and pedimented doorway, and with older portions at the back. The date of the remodelling is said to be *c.* 1700, but it looks later, after *c.* 1725, when Henry Gladwin acquired the house, and most probably as late as 1735–40 (cf. the reduced Palladianism of the E front of Melbourne Hall and Radburne Hall).

STYDD HALL *see* YEAVELEY

1030

SUDBURY

ALL SAINTS. Over-restored. Low W tower with diagonal buttresses and a top C17 balustrade with short pinnacles. Norman S doorway and small window in the Vernon Chapel, both renewed. Inside, arcades of three bays, on the N side on circular piers, on the S side on octagonal ones. Capitals with nailhead decoration. Double-chamfered arches, i.e. *c.* 1300 and a little later. Of about the same time the opening from the chancel into the Vernon Chapel (octagonal pier without capital). Perp clerestory. Other Perp windows date from *Devey*'s restoration of 1874–5. – STAINED GLASS. E window 1850, given by Queen Victoria and Prince Albert and made, it is reported, by a German artist. – Memorial windows to the sixth Lord Vernon, 1885 (and many other windows), by *Burlison & Grylls*. – PLATE. Chalice and Paten on knob foot, 1678; two Flagons, 1775 by *Matthew Boulton* and *James Fothergill*. – MONUMENTS. Two defaced effigies of women with their hearts in their hands, *c*. 1300. – John Vernon † 1600 and wife Mary (inscription; *see* p. 332); alabaster; she lies on a tomb-chest, he behind and above her under a shallow arch rising between baluster columns. – Margaret Vernon † 1675; urn on a free-standing pedestal.* – George Vernon † 1710, wall-monument by *Edward Stanton*. – George Charles Lord Vernon † 1835 and his wife, Grecian twin stelae in relief, with profile heads and drapery over the stelae. By *John Francis* of London. – Two Vernon children † 1862, wall-monument with pretty oval showing the two asleep and a few trails of blossom around them. – Augustus Henry Lord Vernon † 1885, elaborately neo-Quattrocento wall-monument.

SUDBURY HALL is uncommonly satisfying to the eye both outside and inside and at the same time uncommonly interesting in its architectural history. The building dates from the C17 and is of comfortable moderate size, brick-built, with diapering in dark brick on both storeys. The plan is of a usual Elizabethan and Jacobean type, the E-type with central porch and somewhat projecting wings. On the E side is a mezzanine in the Smythson manner (cf. Hardwick). On the garden (S) front the wings do not project but are marked by bay-windows. To the W is a lower wing by *Devey*, 1876–83, well matched to the main house.‡ 75

The windows are mullioned, of two, three, and four lights and with two transoms. The quoins are flat below, in relief above. The window tracery has in some upper windows been replaced by an odd design, in its very oddity typical of the mid-C17 transition. Each light ends in a round arch above which runs a transom, and above the transom is a horizontal tracery oval. It is evidently an attempt at achieving novelty without abandoning tradition entirely. Tracery as such is traditional;

* In November 1674 *Edward Pierce* was paid 'in pt for monument'.

‡ *Salvin* had made plans for turning the house into another Harlaxton. They were fortunately rejected. In the early 1870s *E. M. Barry* made more enlargement plans, but *Devey* succeeded him before they were carried out.

the round arch and the oval are classical. The mixture resembles contemporary work at Oxford, and identical fenestration is recorded in a painting of William Sacheverell's C17 house in Derby. The hipped roof, which originally had a top balustrade and a cupola, is more uncompromisingly of the new style in domestic architecture, similar to Coleshill (begun 1650), Clarendon House, London (1664–7), and other such buildings.* The most conspicuous innovation is in the style of the frontispiece of 1670 marking the two-storey porch, although as a feature it was out of date. It has coupled columns and broken pediments on two floors and is of a decidedly Baroque depth of relief and liveliness of contrast. The carving, and the similar carving on the S front, is the work of *Sir William Wilson* (1641–1710), born in Leicester and later sculptor and architect of Sutton Coldfield near Birmingham.

The conservative E-plan, the mullioned windows, the diapering, and, inside, the long gallery have been interpreted as the result of building the house in two stages: the basic plan and ground floor with its flat quoins begun by Mary Vernon *c.* 1613, left unfinished at her death in 1622, and continued by her grandson, George Vernon, in the mid 1660s with more progressive features such as the tracery and the frontispiece. However it has been plausibly argued ‡ that George Vernon was responsible for the whole house. The main arguments are: that Mary Vernon is stated in a MS. poem and on her tomb to have built and not just begun the manor house (until 1613 the Vernons lived in the rectory); that this house is the more modest house shown on George Vernon's estate map of 1659 to the E of the present house and marked as the site of the Manor House; and that the conservative features of the house are quite normal for Derbyshire, remote from the centre of architectural development in the 1660s (cf. County Hall, Derby, *c.* 1660, Locko Park Chapel of 1669, and Longford Hall). Even the diapering may be an allusion to the fret on the Vernon coat of arms. The hipped roof and the cupola (carved by *Wilson* in 1670) are possibly modifications of the design while building was in progress, and a gabled silhouette like that of the even more old-fashioned Vernon Arms, built by Vernon in 1671, may have been intended. George Vernon's complete accounts from 1659 to 1701 are preserved. He began building on the estate with Park Gates

* The roof was altered in 1872 by *E. M. Barry*, who removed the top balustrade and added the one above the cornice.

‡ By John Cornforth in *Country Life*, vol. 149, to June 1971, pp. 1428–33.

in 1660, then built a barn (demolished) in 1661 and STABLES, with mullioned windows and gables in the Tudor tradition, in 1664 before beginning work on the house *c.* 1665. A clerk of works is recorded in the accounts but not an architect, and it is possible that *Vernon* acted as his own architect and surveyor (H. M. Colvin doubts this). Mr Cornforth suggests that the change of style on the exterior and the change *c.* 1675 from provincial to London craftsmen working on the interior may indicate Vernon's evolving taste, his growth in fortune (through his mother and his first wife) and in rank (in 1670 he became M.P. for Derby and in 1674 High Sheriff of Derbyshire), and his subsequent friendship with the Cavendishes, rather than a long pause in the building. The change in the colour of the brickwork ten courses up on the S front could have been due to a break in building, or equally well to the use of several brickmakers, recorded in the accounts.

On the interior, begun after the outside had been finished in 1670, the provincial craftsmen were first employed, with *Samuel Mansfield* of Derby (1672–5) and *Sir William Wilson* as carvers. They were replaced *c.* 1675 by the carvers *Edward Pierce* and *Grinling Gibbons* and the plasterers *Robert Bradbury* and *James Pettifer*, all London men and all except Bradbury involved with the rebuilding of the City churches. Pierce was a contractor and designer as well as a carver and was the sculptor of the best known bust of Christopher Wren. About 1690, soon after Vernon's third marriage, 'Mr *Young*, ye carver', who went on to Chatsworth (*see* p. 135), appears in the accounts, and in 1691 *Laguerre* arrived from Chatsworth.

The house is entered through a passage and entrance hall, originally one large room (the great hall), but divided by *Salvin* in 1850. The doorway to the passage is a copy of the original doorway at the W end; the ceiling is by *Samuel Mansfield* (1675) and the overmantel by *Laguerre* (1691). In the projecting NW wing is the gorgeous STAIRCASE, with its white-painted balustrade with luxuriantly carved foliage by *Edward Pierce*, and an equally luxuriant, breathtakingly skilful plaster ceiling by *Pettifer* (1675). The ceiling paintings are by *Laguerre* (1691) and the more delicately carved doorway to the Parlour is attributed to *Young*. The state rooms are all on the W side of the house. In the PARLOUR, S of the staircase, *Bradbury* and *Pettifer* decorated the ceiling, *Laguerre* painted the shallow dome, and *Pierce* carved the panelling in 1678, possibly following for the outlines a design by Jean Barbet. It was altered *c.* 1736–

41 to take the portraits and painted in the C19. The original overdoor is a portrait of George Vernon. The fine giltwood chandeliers are of *c.* 1740. The DRAWING ROOM follows E of the Parlour on the S front. This and the library were made into one room by *Salvin c.* 1850, but reconverted and redecorated in 1970. Here also a *Bradbury* and *Pettifer* ceiling, but Pierce was replaced by *Grinling Gibbons* himself. His overmantel (an early work of 1678) is miraculous, but so are Pierce's carvings in the Parlour. The ceiling painting, on canvas not plaster and not by Laguerre, is probably early C18. In the LIBRARY a ceiling by *Mansfield* (1672) and late C17 or early C18 bookcases made for the room. On the upper landing two doorcases carved by *Pierce*, one leading to the QUEEN'S ROOM (State Bedroom), one of the first rooms to be finished. The plasterwork, simpler and more Jonesian than Bradbury and Pettifer's, is by *Mansfield*; similarly Jonesian the alabaster fireplace by *Wilson* (1670). Note how its cornice breaks into but continues the design of Mansfield's plaster cornice. Filling the whole S front 76 is the LONG GALLERY, a very conservative feature with a magnificent ceiling, completed in 1676 by *Bradbury*, and simple bolection-moulded panelling painted in the C19. The E side of the house was altered in the 1870s, probably by *E. M. Barry*, and the State Rooms restored and redecorated (by *John Fowler*) from 1967 to 1970.

In the C18 the formal gardens of *c.* 1690 were swept away and the lake was formed. The present terraces which descend gently to the lake are the remains of formal gardens created by *W. S. Gilpin* in the 1820s.* To the N some distance away a deer park was laid out in the C18, its main feature being a DEER-COTE. Built before 1751 (in 1723 according to tradition), it is a brick parallelogram with angle turrets, originally with ogee caps, and an early C19 turreted sham gatehouse. (LODGES. 1787 by *Thomas Gardner* of Uttoxeter. ES)

The village is of brick houses and unusually pretty. It consists chiefly of one long street. The VERNON ARMS, built by George Vernon in 1671, is a symmetrical composition with slightly projecting outer bays, straight gables, and a segment-headed central carriageway. The windows are mullioned in the Tudor tradition. Several ranges of contemporary cottages near by. (In School Lane, the disused GASWORKS, brick with a diaper pattern like the Hall, for which it supplied gas. Mid C19; is it by *Devey*? Also in School Lane the SCHOOL, 1831. The

* In 1850 *W. A. Nesfield* produced a scheme for a vast Italianate garden.

schoolroom is clerestory-lit with Gothic tracery in the windows. At either end are screen walls with strange Soane-like finials, and at one end the master's house with a central pedimented bay with lower flanking wings. RE)

SUTTON-ON-THE-HILL

2030

ST MICHAEL. C14 W tower; the spire rebuilt in 1841. The rest of the church was rebuilt in 1863, save for the C14 aisle arcade with octagonal piers and double-chamfered arches. Heads and leaf motifs on the label-stops. – PLATE. Paten Cover on knob foot, 1647; Chalice, Paten Cover on knob foot, and Flagon, 1748 by *John Swift*. – MONUMENT. Judith Sleigh † 1634, standing wall-monument with, instead of an effigy, a coffin carved in black stone, complete with its handles. Back architectural with arch.

SUTTON HALL was built as the vicarage *c.* 1820. Castellated front with two canted bays and Gothic sash-windows. Behind, a courtyard with a mock-fortified gateway. The towers have rose windows. (Inside, a vaulted dining room and other Gothick features.)

HOON MOUNT, 1 m. S. Bronze Age barrow.

SUTTON SCARSDALE

4060

SUTTON HALL. Now a ruin, facing the depressing untidiness of open-cast coal mining. A C17 house was remodelled by *Francis Smith* of Warwick in 1724 for Nicholas, fourth Earl of Scarsdale. *Edward Poynton* of Nottingham was the carver. It was made into easily the grandest mansion of its date in the county. Stone, two-storeyed, with giant fluted pilasters throughout. The straight main front, to the E, has a pedimented centre where the pilasters are replaced by attached columns and angle pavilions where the pilasters are coupled.* The principal entrance was on the N. The doorway has a Gibbs surround. On that side some of the rooms still show traces of their once gorgeous decoration (plasterwork by *Artari* and *Vassalli*), a delight which people elderly now can still remember *in situ*.

83

* Dr Gomme remarks on the richness of the design; on the fluted Corinthian pilasters (which incidentally incorporated the Vitruvian basket – a learned architectural joke) against the banded rustication all round; on the curious aprons from the cornice above the upper windows of the W front; and on the windows with richly carved volutes above segmental pedimented doorcases in each angle pavilion of the E façade.

To see some of it now, one must go to the Philadelphia Museum. The back (to the W) has two projecting wings with a relatively narrow courtyard between (cf. Melbourne Hall). There are visible remains of the C17 house and to the W an outbuilding (called the OLD PRIORY) of C17 date.

ST MARY. Incongruously and picturesquely close to the Hall. Poignant contrast between the low embattled and pinnacled E parts of the church and the desolate grandeur of the Hall. Perp W tower with diagonal buttresses. Some C14 windows (the two-light S window however is C19), a C14 S porch, and a C14 N arcade to aisle and chancel aisle. – COMMUNION RAIL. C17. – PLATE. Chalice, 1774. – MONUMENTS. John Foljambe † 1499, incised slab. – Samuel Pierrepont † 1707, wall-monument with bust in roundel, not good.

3010

SWADLINCOTE

EMANUEL CHURCH. 1848 by *Stevens*. Aisleless stone building of modest size. No tower, polygonal apse, lancet windows. – PLATE. Chalice, 1791 by *James Young*.

The distinctive industrial features of the Swadlincote area are the kilns of the potteries and brick and pipe industries. In ALEXANDRA ROAD the town's last surviving kiln of traditional bottle shape.

GRANVILLE PITHEAD BATHS. 1941 by *J. W. M. Dudding*, one of the many modern structures erected by the Miners' Welfare Committee.

4050

SWANWICK

ST ANDREW. 1859–60 by *Benjamin Wilson* of Derby (GR). Large SW tower by *Naylor, Sale & Woore*, 1902, with ugly pinnacles and gargoyles. – Inside, vivid STAINED GLASS. E window by *Martin Travers*, a war memorial, 1921–3. – W window 1953 by *J. E. Nuttgens*.

SWANWICK HALL GRAMMAR SCHOOL. The hall is mid-C18, three storeys, three bays, stone doorcase with pediment on Tuscan columns. Lower C19 wings. At the back 1930s school building by *G. H. Widdows* (then County Architect), who combined red brick with steeply pitched tiled roofs and wooden verandas. Further extensions by *F. Hamer Crossley* (County Architect), completed in 1959.

SWARKESTON

3020

ST JAMES. So much restored by *F. J. Robinson* in 1874–6 that only the SW tower and the Harpur (SE) Chapel are now worth recording. The chapel contains two alabaster MONUMENTS consisting of tomb-chests with the recumbent effigies of Richard Harpur † 1573 and his wife, and Sir John Harpur † 1627 and his wife, the effigies of the former supplied by the *Royleys* (Jeavons), the latter of much superior workmanship. In addition in the chancel tomb-chest with effigy of John Rolleston † 1482 and his wife; against the front wall of the chest two angels and between them two attractive panels with the kneeling children. – FONT. Norman, plain. – HELMET of *c.* 1580, decorated for the funeral of Sir John Harpur † 1627. – PLATE. C17 Paten Cover. – A few small Norman fragments built into the E aisle wall.

SWARKESTON BRIDGE. Though much restored, still a remarkable example of medieval public works. The bridge and causeway, altogether three quarters of a mile long, probably date from the C13 and C14. Seventeen old arches remain, depressed-pointed and ribbed underneath. The part actually crossing the river is a fine C18 classical design (span 414 ft) with five round-headed arches, by *Thomas Harrison.*

SWARKESTON HALL. Rectangle of stone, with a front of three gables and a central doorway with four-centred head. The windows symmetrical and mullioned. The date may be *c.* 1630.

67

SUMMER HOUSE. An extremely odd structure, probably of Jacobean date, connected with the big Harpur mansion which stood at Swarkeston. The function of the building is not clear.* It overlooks THE CUTTLE, a kind of rectangular enclosure with a low wall. The Summer House is also known as the Grandstand (cf. The Stand at Chatsworth), and it is assumed that bull-baiting and similar sports took place in the arena. The house has two angle towers with bulbous tops and a crenellated three-bay centre with a loggia on the ground floor (Tuscan columns, and, strangely enough, depressed ogee arches). The first-floor windows have one mullion and one transom each. The large room behind them is in ruins. The mansion was demolished after the Civil War when the Harpurs moved to Calke, though Swarkeston Hall is no doubt connected with it.

* Dr Girouard (*Robert Smythson*, p. 198) suggests that it might be the 'Bowle Alley House' paid for in 1631–2. He attributes it tentatively to *John Smythson.*

(Parts of the garden wall are remains of the mansion. One stretch has three fireplaces and a doorway. DOE)

SWARKESTON LOWS, ½m. N. A group of presumably Bronze Age barrows. Others in the vicinity have now been ploughed down. One was a bell barrow over a cremation burial. It also contained two Anglo-Saxon secondary inhumations.

SWINE STY *see* BASLOW

SYCAMORE FARMHOUSE *see* HOPTON

SYDNOPE HALL *see* DARLEY DALE

1070

TADDINGTON

ST MICHAEL. Not large, but in a fine position, with its N side overlooking the high country around, and of some architectural interest. The W tower early C14 throughout; the arch towards the nave with double-chamfered imposts and double-chamfered arch without any intervening capitals, the windows small and ogee-headed, the spire broached, with big broaches starting directly on the tower without any battlements. The dormer windows altered in 1891. The rebuilding of the rest of the church followed, inspired perhaps by Tideswell. Nave with tall four-bay arcades. Octagonal piers, E responds on head corbels. The chancel arch exactly contemporary with these, and the chancel, if smaller than Tideswell, yet clearly of the same type, i.e. tall straight-headed N and S windows, and a very large E window with elaborate flowing tracery. The aisle windows also with flowing tracery, though of course more modest. No battlements at all. The whole considerably restored in 1891 by *Naylor & Sale*. – BIBLE SUPPORT (chancel); cf. Chaddesden (Derby), Crich, Etwall, Mickleover and Spondon (Derby). – PLATE. Small Chalice and Cover, 1568. – CROSS SHAFT in the churchyard with zigzag and saltire cross decoration. Is it Norman? – BRASS to Richard Blackwall † 1505, wife and children.

(TADDINGTON HALL. Plain two-storey, six-bay C18 house, plastered, with an ashlar parapet surmounted by urns, and a Venetian window over the modern porch. DOE)

FIVE WELLS, 1½m. W. Neolithic chambered tomb, some 70ft in diameter and carefully built in coursed rubble. At the centre were two burial chambers, now roofless, although the portals of the E chamber still survive. Twelve inhumations were found in the chambers and several secondary cremations elsewhere in the monument.

SLIPPER LOW. Anglo-Saxon barrow covering a rock-cut grave.

LAPWING HILL, 1 m. N. Anglo-Saxon barrow.

PRIESTCLIFFE. A fine series of strip lynchets lies SE of this hamlet. Unusually in this landscape, they run down the slope and not along it.

TANSLEY

3050

HOLY TRINITY. 1839–40 by *John Mason* of Derby. N aisle 1869 (GR). (Simple little stone church in E.E. style with a miniature tower. RE)

TANSLEYWOOD MILL. Dated 1799 by coins found buried in the walls. Big and tall. Unarched casement windows, cast-iron pillars, timber beams.

(KNOLL HOUSE, The Knoll. 1788, three storeys, with an elaborately carved doorway, niche in the attic, and acorn finials. Several other good C18 houses, e.g. GROVE HOUSE and the plainer BROOK HOUSE in Church Street. RE)

TAPTON GROVE *see* BRIMINGTON

TAPTON HOUSE *see* CHESTERFIELD, p. 150

TAXAL

0070

ST LEONARD (now called ST JAMES). C16 W tower with later C17 pinnacles. The body of the church 1825, restored 1889 (chancel enlarged). Aisleless, originally with galleries. The windows have Y-tracery. – (ALTAR RAILS. Early C18; turned balusters. – MONUMENT. Tablet to Michael Heathcote † 1768 'Gentleman of the Pantry and Yeoman of the Mouth to his late Majesty King George III'. T. Cocke)

(HOLY TRINITY, Fernilee (S of Taxal). 1904–5 by *Currey & Thompson*, chancel 1922–3 (GR). Stone, in a free Gothic style.)

THORNBRIDGE HALL

1070

½ m. S of Great Longstone

A Georgian T-shaped house extensively altered in 1871. In 1897 *Charles Hadfield* designed its spectacular neo-Tudor exterior.* Castellated, with a tall asymmetrically placed tower. In the Grand Hall a double-flight staircase of *c.* 1910 and a large window with *Morris & Co.* stained glass (top lights, Griselda, Dorigen, Constance, and Cressida by *Burne-Jones*, 1876; middle tier, minstrels by *Morris*, 1876; bottom tier, Luna, Earth, Morning and Evening Star by *Burne-Jones*, 1885, originally in a billiard room window). Other rooms have fireplaces, panelling, etc., brought from various country houses between 1930 and 1945, e.g. fireplaces in the dining room from Harlaxton Manor, woodwork from Derwent Hall and church. In the entrance hall the grand Buffet Fountain from Chatsworth, by *Samuel Watson*, 1709.

In the same style, WOODLANDS, built in 1903–4 as the railway entrance. Originally one large recreation room over the archway.

1050

THORPE

ST LEONARD. The church marks the entrance to Dovedale. It overlooks a hilly skyline and manifold green slopes. Short Norman W tower, unbuttressed, with big quoins. The W doorway blocked, the twin bell-openings badly preserved. Corbel table and later battlements. The nave of Norman masonry too, see a small lancet in the S wall. Another small window C13 of two lights. Perp window in the chancel. The E window is new (chancel rebuilt 1881). – FONT. Plain Norman. – COMMUNION RAIL. Elizabethan. – STAINED GLASS. (Chancel E window 1893 by *Powell*. R. Hubbuck) – Chancel S window by *F. C. Eden*, 1930. – PLATE. Chalice, Paten on knob foot, and Flagon, 1709 by *Philip Rollos Jun.* – MONUMENT. John Millward † 1632, badly preserved, with standing figures against the tomb-chest. – In the churchyard a SUNDIAL, 1767 by *Whitehurst* of Derby.

LID LOW, ½ m. NE. Bronze Age barrow, now largely destroyed.

THURLESTONE GRANGE *see* ELVASTON

4060

TIBSHELF

ST JOHN THE BAPTIST. On a hill overlooking the surrounding

* Information about Thornbridge Hall from Mr C. G. Cutts.

mining scenery. W tower with diagonal buttresses Perp. The rest by *Bodley & Garner*, 1887–8.

(SAPA LTD ALUMINIUM EXTRUSION PLANT. 1972–3 by *Foster Associates*, intended to be purely functional, with an infinitely expandable steel frame clad in stove-enamelled steel panels with a polyurethane core (made in Italy, used here for the first time in England). Outside just a large white shed, but inside the structure and machinery is picked out in vivid contrasting colours.)

TICKNALL

3020

ST GEORGE. 1842 by *Stevens*. Good honest simple Gothic Revival. W tower with the recessed spire usual in the Perp style of this part of the county. Aisle arcades with octagonal piers. – STAINED GLASS. Two windows by *Morris & Co.* N aisle centre, 1922, with angels on l. and r. by *Morris*, central angel by *J. Henry Dearle*; S aisle E, 1923, the Feeding of the Five Thousand, by *Dearle*. – PLATE. Chalice and two Patens, 1715, Flagon, 1716, and Paten on baluster stem, 1727, all by *Petley Ley*. – MONUMENTS. Effigy of a Civilian holding his heart in his hand. – Incised alabaster slab to John Frances, knight in armour, *c*. 1375.

The previous church stood farther S, and picturesque fragments of the W tower and the E end (three-light window with intersected tracery) survive. S of this the HARPUR ALMSHOUSES, built in 1772, a long, two-storeyed brick building with central pediment and angle quoins.

At the W approach to the village a TRAMWAY BRIDGE of pleasing proportions, part of the Ticknall tramway (*see* Calke Abbey).

(METHODIST CHAPEL, Chapel Street. 1815, brick, with ramped parapet and pediment. C. Stell)

LOCK-UP. Circular with polygonal spire roof.

1 m. N, at KNOWLE HILL, the remains of the Burdetts' mansion before their move to Foremark were demolished in 1976.

TIDESLOW *see* TIDESWELL

TIDESWELL

1070

ST JOHN THE BAPTIST. One of the grandest of Derbyshire parish churches, impressive from far, though lying with the little town in a sheltered dip between the high lands around, and

16

impressive from near, though the churchyard has no old trees, the railings are a rather rigid early C19 cast-iron pattern, and the houses around are low, grey, and not specially attractive.* To the architectural historian the chief interest lies in the fact that Tideswell church was apparently built without major breaks in the course of about seventy-five years during the C14. The chancel may have come first. But of this only the chancel arch remains. Its imposts are exactly like the nave piers halved. The nave and aisles are of five bays with piers taller than usual in Derbyshire and of a section unique in the county: quatrefoil with, in the diagonals, narrow grooves between narrow ridges. The vigorously rising arches also are of unusual section: step, quarter-roll, step, quarter-roll, step. Their labels start from head, leaf, etc., stops. They reach right close to the clerestory. The fifth of the arches on the N and S open into transepts of two bays. To date these earliest parts of the new church one has to study the windows and their tracery. This is flowing throughout, i.e. Dec, i.e. *c.* 1320–50. Nave and aisles and the contemporary two-storeyed S porch (vaulted inside) are embattled.

It cannot now be said for certain whether the chancel had been built *c.* 1325 and was *c.* 1360 no longer regarded as adequate, or whether it had been begun *c.* 1340 and interrupted by the Black Death. The fact remains that the roof-line of the old chancel is still visible, and that about 1360 a new higher chancel was erected, which is one of the three or four finest in the county, of the same type as Sandiacre, Norbury, and Chaddesden (Derby). It has an E window still completely Dec with flowing tracery just like that of the transept windows. But its chief characteristic is its very tall and broad straight-headed three-light windows on the N and S separated by buttresses with pinnacles‡ and with tracery neither Dec nor Perp: namely, simply pierced quatrefoils standing on the trefoiled heads of the individual lights. These are almost archaic motifs, but the straight-headedness is of course a turn towards the new ideals of the Perp style. Inside, the chancel is high as well as wide. The SEDILIA, although each seat is ogee-headed, also have quatrefoil decoration in the spandrels.§ There are two flat ogee

* Except perhaps the GEORGE HOTEL in the square to the SE of the church, which has Venetian windows throughout and was much praised by late C18 travellers.

‡ The S transept also has pinnacles on its buttresses.

§ A PISCINA in the E wall of the S transept has very similar decoration, which also shows how close in date the W and E parts of the church are. Also with similar decoration, the C14 screen at Ilkeston.

recesses in the N wall. In front of one of them is the brass to John Foljambe who died in 1383 and of whom the inscription says 'multa bona fecit circa fabricaciounem huius ecclesiae'. That presumably dates the chancel as *c.* 1360–80. Other notable features are the screen wall to the W of the E wall which divides off a vestry behind the altar (cf. Sawley) and the niches for statuary on this screen wall (with tall canopies) and to the l. and r. of the E window.*

The W tower came last, but the masonry does not look as if it were much later than the rest of the church. Yet it is now fully Perp, in the style which by then had become nationally accepted. The W window is indeed one of the largest in the county, five lights only, but very tall, and with panel tracery of a usual pattern. The tower has angle buttresses, battlements, and eight pinnacles. Of these the four angle ones are developed into proper polygonal angle turrets with pinnacles on: an ambitious but in effect somewhat heavy conception. The tower arch towards the nave is of immense height. Its capitals and moulding are also Perp. The only later work was the restoration of the church by *J. D. Sedding* in the early 1870s.

ROOFS. Nave with heavy tie-beams and broad cusped trefoil tracery above. No doubt original. – N aisle 1632–5. – FONT. Perp, octagonal, with shields and simple panels. – CHANCEL SEATS. Now in the N transept. Of no special ornamental merit. Two have carved misericords. – PEWS. Perp pew fronts now in the N aisle. They may originally have served another purpose. The present pews date from 1824–7. – TOWER SCREEN. Designed by *Oldrid Scott*, 1904. – PANELLING. S porch, upper chamber, made of parts of C17 pews. The date 1632 occurs (cf. Castleton, Hope). – STAINED GLASS. E window, Tree of Jesse, unusually sensitive, given by Mr C. G. S. Foljambe (cf. Bakewell, S aisle window, p. 73) and made in 1875 by *Heaton, Butler & Bayne*. – W window by *Hardman & Powell*, 1907. – PLATE. Chalice given 1683; Paten dated 1724; Flagon dated 1738, by *Francis Spilsbury*; Dutch brass Almsdish.

MONUMENTS. The church is rich in pre-Reformation monuments. The oldest are two defaced stone effigies in the N transept, late C13 and C14. – The big brass to John Foljambe † 1383 has been mentioned above (chancel). It is an excellent copy, made in 1875. – Sir Thurstan de Bower † 1423, good alabaster effigy on a modern tomb-chest (S transept). The naming is more than doubtful, for the man is in armour and Thur-

* Again a similar niche in the SE corner of the S transept.

stan de Bower was a yeoman who had made much money out of lead-mining. He was one of the founders of the Guild of St Mary at Tideswell (foundation charters 1384 and 1392) which held the present Lady Chapel as its Guild Chapel. – Brass with figure of God holding Christ Crucified and divers shields, on the lid of a modern tomb-chest whose openings reveal a stone cadaver underneath: Sampson Meverill † 1462 (chancel). – Brass to Sir Robert Lytton † 1483 and wife, the figures about 28in. long (S aisle). – Brass to Bishop Pursglove † 1579, still entirely in the pre-Reformation tradition of the composition of brasses (chancel). Pursglove was a well-known 'Popish' conservative.

TIDESLOW, 2 m. N. Neolithic round barrow, 132 ft in diameter. This is one of the largest Neolithic round barrows in England.

LONG LOW, 2 m. NE. Round barrow.

TUP LOW, 2 m. NE. Round barrow.

1050

TISSINGTON

From the triangular green one enjoys a picture of exquisite beauty: a few quiet stone houses on two sides (one Georgian of three bays), on the third, raised, well up a green slope, the church, and a little back to the S the Hall, which reveals its extent and character as one approaches it.

ST MARY. Sadly Normanized in 1854 (N aisle added) to match the broad square unbuttressed Norman W tower. It is this tower, fortunately, which is chiefly visible from the green. In its N wall is one slim window with a roll-moulding. The S doorway is Norman too; one order of colonnettes with one scallop and one primitive volute capital, billet frieze in the label, and a tympanum with two little standing figures to the l. and r., a double diaper frieze between them, and the main field decorated by a plain chequerboard pattern and a cross distinguished by diapers in its five chequerboard fields. The tower arch to the nave is large (renewed?). The chancel arch is also Norman, single-stepped, with one order of zigzag in the voussoirs of the arch. – FONT. Norman, tub-shaped, with incised animals, also a snake; very barbaric. – Two-decker PULPIT. – COMMUNION RAIL. Of *c.* 1600, very finely turned, not at all a usual English pattern. – PLATE. Chalice and Paten, 1657; Paten Cover on knob foot, *c.* 1657; Paten, 1747. – MONUMENTS. Francis † 1619 and Sir John Fitzherbert † 1643, with their wives. Standing wall-monument with kneeling figures in two tiers, the father and his two wives facing each other below, the son and his wife above. Outer columns, below intermittently rusticated Ionic, above black Corinthian; top with achievement and obelisks. – In the chancel various Fitzherbert wall-monuments, e.g. Mary † 1677 and Martha † 1699, the latter by *Francis Bird*. – Thomasine Buxton † 1809 by *James Sherwood* of Derby.

TISSINGTON HALL. Plain, square, medium-sized Jacobean house with an E porch, walled garden in front of it, and squat garden gate. The façade is plain with upright mullion-and-transom-cross windows and a parapet. No gables, no visible roof. To the N of the house a little away and not in axis with it a contemporary outbuilding, much restored. In the C18 the W front towards the terraced back garden was remodelled in the classical style with a bay-window in the centre and a loggia open on the ground floor.* A library wing was added on that side *c.* 1910 by *Arnold Mitchell*. The largest room is the hall on the ground floor, placed centrally and at r. angles to the façade, that is in the new position first established a little earlier at Hardwick. In the hall contemporary panelling (with intersected arches) and an elaborate fireplace and plasterwork in the new Gothic taste of *c.* 1750. In the drawing room on the upper floor specially handsome panelling with fluted pilasters. (Fitted into a Jacobean gateway, hence an odd shape, a fine Bakewell-type gate. ES)

92

BOAR'S LOW, ¼ m. NW. Large cairn containing a crouched inhumation and a cremation. An Anglo-Saxon secondary burial was also present.

CRAKE LOW. Round barrow 1 m. to the N.

SHARP LOW, ½ m. W. Low cairn containing crouched inhumation. Under the central slab, a votive offering of a bull's horn. The cairn also included an Anglo-Saxon secondary burial.

HOLLINGTON BARN, 1 m, W. Cairn over a rock-cut grave.

TOADHOLE FURNACE *see* SHIRLAND

TOTLEY MOOR *see* HOLMESFIELD

TRUSLEY

2030

ALL SAINTS. 1713. Small, of brick, with short nave, lower

* If executed, alterations designed by *Wyatville* in 1821 would have swamped the house.

chancel, and W tower. The windows are arched, with stone surrounds. The W front has a straight top to the aisles and the tower rising equally straight from it. The entrance with a scrolly pediment as at Barton Blount near by. – BOX PEWS, three-decker PULPIT, COMMUNION RAILS, and baluster-shaped FONT: all original. – Just inside the S door a successful C20 addition to the C18 furnishings: an engraved glass SCREEN commemorating R. Coke-Street † 1963. – PLATE. Elizabethan Chalice; Paten, 1633. – MONUMENT. Bridget Curzon † 1628, incised slab in the chancel.

HALL. Of the Tudor house one part still stands, the brickwork mainly in stretcher courses, flat stone quoins, the windows converted into sash. Also a separate Elizabethan summer house on its own, with pyramidal roof. Much adding and restoration in 1902, when a new house, now mostly demolished, was built 100 yds away. The neo-Georgian tidying up was done in 1945–7. In the coach house (now village hall) C17 panelling from Kirkby Hall, Notts.

TUP LOW *see* TIDESWELL

3060

TUPTON

(EGSTOW HALL. Three-storey T-plan gabled house with a stair-turret in the N angle. Dated 1671 but part may be earlier. Mullioned windows, continuous hoods making string-courses on the front. Barn with three cruck frames.)

TUPTON HALL (COMPREHENSIVE) SCHOOL. One of the best uses of the CLASP system for school buildings in the county. The thirteen houses on a sloping site are linked by bridges and covered ways with landscaped courtyards between, creating a village-like atmosphere. At the centre of the complex the theatre, music room, and library, the latter with oriel windows.

100

Most imaginative perhaps is the craft centre, where two storeys of workshops surround an open exhibition court covered with a space deck from which two gantries are suspended. The old buildings of 1936 by *G. H. Widdows* (then County Architect and a pioneer of open access) have been retained and another floor has been inserted under the roofs. The teaching blocks are clad in grey-brown aggregate, the administration buildings in ceramic. Architects: *George Grey & Partners* in association with *D. S. Davies* (County Architect), 1965–9.

TURNDITCH

2040

(ALL SAINTS. Long, low building with the date 1630 over the S door. Enlarged and given a new chancel in 1882–4 by *Giles & Brookhouse*. Aisleless; open timber roof. J. B. Wright)

TWO DALES *see* DARLEY DALE

TWYFORD

3020

ST ANDREW. Norman chancel arch, narrow, with zigzag ornament. W tower unbuttressed, with lancet window below, Perp above, with spire recessed behind battlements. Chancel with Dec windows. Nave remodelled in brick in the C18 and now prettily overgrown with ivy. May no purist insist on its removal. – PLATE. Elizabethan Chalice.

(OLD HALL COTTAGE. C19, brick, but at the back stone with two huge chimneystacks and corresponding fireplaces inside. Apparently the remains of the C16 Twyford Hall, belonging to the Harpurs of Swarkestone. Stone cross-wing at the W end. RE)

Large, conical BARROW, 15 ft high and 33 ft in diameter. A barrow of these dimensions is a rare survival in the Trent valley. The mound appears to lie over a large ring-ditch of earlier date, possibly a henge monument.

UNSTONE

3070

MANOR FARM. Just NW of the railway bridge at the Dronfield end of Unstone: L-shaped gabled manor house of 1663. The windows are mullioned, also mullioned and transomed, and under hood-moulds. The door surround was apparently altered in the C18. The inscription above the door is quite legible but also quite incomprehensible.

WEST HANDLEY OLD HALL, 1½ m. ENE. Small Jacobean or later C17 house. (Good staircase.)

(ASH LANE FARMHOUSE, West Handley. Remarkable thatched cruck house, almost concealed by corrugated iron protection. RE)

(SUMMERLEY HALL and SUMMERLEY FARM. Both C17, the hall with evidence of C16 work (rounded stair projection at the back). RE)

5060

UPPER LANGWITH

HOLY CROSS, Upper Langwith (the rest of Langwith is in Notts). Nave and chancel; no tower. Chancel C13, see one long lancet window. S porch with big pinnacles, vaulted inside with transverse arches (cf. Ault Hucknall, etc.). Most of the windows Perp. (Bellcote 1877 by *Norman Shaw*, who restored the church. – FONT and PULPIT by *Shaw*, the latter with unusual fruit patterns in gilt leather-paper. A. Saint) – PLATE. Small simple bronze Censer, C15.

VIATOR'S BRIDGE *see* ALSOP-EN-LE-DALE

3060

WALTON

Near Chesterfield

(HIPPER HALL, Holymoorside. C17, probably early. Square plan with two gables. Late C17 porch with oval gable opening with voussoir surround. Gabled projection to the garden with five-light mullioned-and-transomed windows. Interesting internal features, oak partition, etc. Two barns, both with crucks, the larger one partly timber-framed. RE)

(BELMONT, Chatsworth Road. Big, ugly house with a C19 tower, but some pretty neo-Greek interiors by *Sir Charles Reilly*. RE)

PARK HALL. *See* Chesterfield, p. 151.

2010

WALTON-UPON-TRENT

ST LAURENCE. Perp W tower with diagonal buttresses overlooking the river. The interior has a Late Norman arcade of some interest. The two circular piers and the two responds have capitals all with very stylized small upright leaves and all different. The arches are of two steps, the big inner one unmoulded, the outer one slightly chamfered. Above the arcade at the W end some earlier masonry, possibly the remains of a window head. The chancel is C13 with one lancet window on the S side and trefoiled SEDILIA. (Windows renewed by *Street* in 1868. P. Joyce) The S transept (large squint to the chancel) was the Waley Chantry, founded in 1334. It has a low S recess with a defaced effigy. The windows on the E side of a big, rather coarse Dec variety. – (There is much elaborate early C20 woodwork, carved by the then rector, the Rev. *F. Fisher*. P. Joyce) –

PLATE. Elizabethan Chalice. – MONUMENTS. Brass of Robert Morley, rector, † 1492. – Also in the chancel three small C17 incised alabaster slabs. – Thomas Bearcroft † 1680, demi-figure of a divine between twisted columns.

WALTON HALL. Brick house of *c.* 1720. Seven bays and two and a half storeys with top parapet. The garden side has giant angle pilasters, the river side angle pilasters and additional pilasters between the second and third and fifth and sixth bays. On the garden side a simple central doorway with segmental pediment and much decayed wrought-iron balustrade (perhaps by *Bakewell*: ES). Inside a two-storey staircase hall with contemporary staircase (three different balusters to each tread and richly carved tread ends). It is really spectacular, filling the whole centre of the house. Evidently all the money was spent on it, for the other rooms are quite bare of decoration.*

WASH GREEN *see* WIRKSWORTH

WENSLEY

2060

ST MARY. Neo-Norman. 1841–3, by *Weightman & Hadfield* (GR).‡ Chancel added 1866.

WEST HALLAM

4040

ST WILFRID. Nave and two aisles. The N arcade has octagonal piers and the most elementary moulded capitals; hard to date. The S arcade more usual C14. The chancel arch with semicircular responds clearly early C14. The chancel E window is renewed, but its flowing tracery (three lights) would go well with the arch. The S aisle windows (renewed) of two lights, flowing but straight-headed, later C14, if a copy of the original. The other windows Perp. Perp W tower. – Elizabethan COMMUNION RAIL. – PLATE. Chalice and Paten Cover, *c.* 1660; two brass Almsdishes, probably Dutch C17. – MONUMENTS. Thomas Powtrell † 1484, incised slab. – Walter Powtrell † 1598 and wife, recumbent alabaster effigies on a tomb-chest with two panels in the front wall containing the children standing upright.

* According to Dr Gomme.

‡ (The attribution has been questioned. According to Professor Steven Welsh, the architect may be *Joseph Mitchell* of Sheffield, and the chancel by his son *J. B. Mitchell-Withers*. RE)

WEST HANDLEY *see* UNSTONE

4020

WESTON-UPON-TRENT

ST MARY. Essentially a C13 church, prettily placed near the river. W tower with recessed spire and Perp windows. The interior exceptionally impressive for a church of its size, thanks to the surprisingly tall circular piers with moulded capitals and double-chamfered arches. They give a noble uprightness to the whole. The nave is not long (three bays), the chancel lower than the nave. The chancel windows are small lancets with inner chamfered arches. The S doorway to the chancel is contemporary; the E window is new. The S aisle has windows of three stepped lancet lights uncusped, an E window also of three lancet lights but with an unfoiled circle above the lower middle lancet, and a PISCINA with a trefoiled head. The N aisle windows are C14 (with ogee details). Special features are the dogtooth course below the battlements and the pretty timber-framed S porch, added early in the C17. – FONT. Dated 1661; of the type with elementary decorated panels as usual in Notts around Southwell. – PULPIT. Jacobean, dated 1611. – PARISH BIER. 1653. – CHEST. 1662. – PLATE. Elizabethan Chalice and Paten Cover. – MONUMENT. Fragments of a large monument to Richard Sale † 1615 with kneeling figures. Above this in an oval a skele-
45 ton with pick and shovel and the inscription: 'Ecce nosce te ipsum. Ut sum tu eris.'

(WESTON HALL, a landmark for miles on its hill. It is rather less than half of a great H-plan mansion begun by the Roper family soon after 1633, and left unfinished because of their impoverishment and the Civil War. On one side the brick toothing is still exposed where the central hall section would have been. The house would have rivalled Hardwick, Wollaton, and Bolsover in size, but its design is conservative by comparison. Like these Smythson buildings, however, it is very tall, of five storeys altogether, and its huge semi-basement contained kitchens.

What was built was a large brick and stone wing, of double thickness, with two gables. At the back a curious angle turret with circular niches. On the side elevation a projecting gabled staircase tower containing the original well staircase. Mullioned and transomed windows, some with stonework removed, others blocked. Two rooms on the ground floor have original panelling. The second-floor rooms were evidently never used. Restored and strengthened in 1973. RE)

WET WITHENS MOOR *see* EYAM

WHALEY BRIDGE

0080

The typical small industrial North Country town in a rural setting. It is missed out in practically all guide-books because of no artistic, historical, or architectural interest. Yet, as one walks through, there are a few eminently characteristic, if not beautiful buildings.

JODRELL ARMS HOTEL, along the main road. Built *c.* 1800 with additions of *c.* 1850 in conjunction with the situation close to the new railway. The additions comprise a heavy Tuscan porch and minimum-Elizabethan gables. – METHODIST SUNDAY SCHOOL, 1821, simple and friendly, with arched windows, and next to it the WESLEYAN CHAPEL, rebuilt 1867, still classical, but debased (see the pediment which has become a low-pitched gable and the overdone rustication). – (TOWN HALL (now Area Office), Spring Bank. 1871, enlarged 1887. Free Italianate style with block rustication to the porch, Venetian windows, and a clock tower. T. Cocke) – MECHANICS INSTITUTE, 1876, preposterous Frenchy style with bits of incised ornament. – (CARNEGIE LIBRARY, Hall Street. 1909. Classical, of an ingenious composition to suit the steep hill. T. Cocke)

PEAK FOREST CANAL BASIN. Large basin with covered dock. The dock building is on three piles, allowing barges to enter centrally and wagons from the High Peak railway to enter alongside. Completed in 1832, extended to the N in 1916.

TAXAL. *See* p. 339.

WHESTON

1070

WHESTON HALL. The front Mid Georgian. It had a recessed centre and two-bay side wings projecting from the centre in two steps (a type of plan which may easily be much earlier: cf., for example, Ham House, Surrey) but the l. wing has been demolished. The first step of the remaining wing has arched windows, the centre of the recessed part a pedimented doorway. Above it an upright oval window. The back is like a complete five-bay Georgian house with central doorway. Pineapple-topped gatepiers and the remains of an avenue opposite.

VILLAGE CROSS, to the W of Wheston Hall. C15. Preserved complete with its cusped head with clumsy renderings of Christ

Crucified and the Virgin. The shaft stands on four steps: the whole is *c.* 11½ ft high.

E of the Hall the remains of another CROSS, and VICARAGE FARM, dated 1637 on the door lintel. L-shaped, with long, low mullioned windows with hood-moulds. Door in an odd position in the cross wing. Long C17 and C18 BARN attached.

0080

WHITEHOUGH

1¼ m. NW of Chapel-en-le-Frith

OLD HALL. Gabled, with hood-moulded low mullioned windows. Above the entrance a C20 inscription *A.K.* 1559, not reliable.

WHITFIELD *see* GLOSSOP

WHITTINGTON *see* CHESTERFIELD, pp. 148, 149, 151

5070

WHITWELL

ST LAWRENCE. The church is important equally for its contribution to the Norman and to the Dec styles in Derbyshire. As to the former we see a W tower, originally unbuttressed, with an original W doorway (one order of colonnettes, leaf capitals, zigzag in the arch), a window above, and the blocked bell-openings, replaced by higher Perp ones when the battlements and pinnacles were added. Also Norman is the masonry of the whole nave (see the fully preserved clerestory, a rarity, and the corbel table above), the masonry of the whole chancel also revealed by the corbel table, the plain S doorway, and the interior of the nave in its predominant features, i.e. the circular piers, very simply moulded capitals, and round arches with single-stepped profiles. The E responds are keeled, a usual late C12 feature in this part of the county. The tower arch looks earlier (unmoulded arch on the simplest responds), and that goes well with the evidence of the W doorway. The chancel arch on the other hand, with keeled shafts, waterleaf side by side with scalloped capitals, and finely detailed arch mouldings, is clearly on the way towards the E.E., although the arch is still round.

The second great building period of the church was the time from *c.* 1300 to *c.* 1350. To this belong the chancel and the two transepts: see the geometrical tracery of the chancel with such no longer quite classical motifs as unencircled quatrefoils, encircled trefoils (exactly as at North Wingfield), and sharply pointed trefoils and quatrefoils (i.e. *c.* 1300), the SEDILIA and the niche opposite (aumbry? miniature Easter Sepulchre?) with delightful openwork cusping, ogee elements, steep gables, and much crocketing (an offshoot probably of the Notts–Lincs workshops of Hawton, etc.), the flowing tracery in the N transept N and S transept S windows, and the ogee recess in the N transept with its openwork double-cusping.* – FONT. Norman, plain tub-shape. – PANELLING in the chancel, Jacobean. – MONUMENTS. Sir Roger Manners † 1632, standing wall-monument, recumbent effigy in armour under shallow arch between two black columns.

N of the church WHITWELL HALL (MANOR HOUSE), seat of the Manners. The hall of the manor house is now the N end of the school hall. (The other half of it was originally two-storey. NW in Manor Cottage a barrel-vaulted long gallery, divided into two. DOE) Three-light and six-light mullioned and transomed windows. On the E side a porch very close in detail to a drawing by *John Smythson* of 'a porch at Welbeck' (RIBA III/15). As Whitwell is on the Welbeck estate it no doubt came from there. Fairly unambitious, with a quatrefoil parapet, but with corbelled angle pieces reminiscent of the Gallery parapet at Bolsover.

(OLD PARSONAGE. 1885 by *J. L. Pearson* for the Rev. George Mason, for whom he restored Steetley chapel and Whitwell church. Of local stone with a brown tile roof, and tile-hanging in the E gable. Prominent chimneystacks, Gothic doorways, mullioned windows. A. Quiney)

(The OLD MANOR HOUSE is L-shaped and old but with all features C18. Also C18 the former GEORGE INN with a nice classical doorcase. RE)

WILLERSLEY CASTLE *see* CROMFORD

WILLIAMTHORPE COLLIERY *see* NORTH WINGFIELD

* It should, however, be said that the chancel E and S windows are not in their present form in the Rawlins manuscript. (*J. L. Pearson* restored the whole church except for the chancel in 1885–6. A. Quiney)

2020

WILLINGTON

ST MICHAEL. Pretty, modest W tower of 1824 with quoins and no pinnacles. S doorway Norman with defaced tympanum. The lancet windows in the chancel and the coupled lancets in the S wall are C19. The interior is aisleless and has white plaster ceilings in nave and chancel, no doubt of *c.* 1824. Also of that date the addition of a N transept. – FONT. C18, baluster, richly acanthus-ornamented. – PLATE. Elizabethan Chalice and Paten Cover; Cup and Cover, 1678; Paten on foot, 1694.

(WILLINGTON HALL, Hall Lane. Stucco villa of *c.* 1840 with a big columned porch. RE)

To the E the five huge cooling towers of Willington POWER STATION (*Farmer & Dark*, 1959–62).

On the river terrace, a settlement site of the Beaker period has been excavated, the houses being of timber on a trapezoidal plan. In the same area, Roman and Saxon settlements have also been identified.

4030

WILNE

ST CHAD. Outside the village, fairly close to the river Derwent. W tower, the lower part C13 with rectangular stair turret, the upper part later. Embattled, but no pinnacles. Nave and S aisle separated by octagonal piers with double-chamfered arches. The aisle windows of three lancet lights of which the centre one is higher than the others, i.e. *c.* 1300. S porch Perp with very pointed stone tunnel-vault with transverse arches (cf. Ault Hucknall, etc.). S aisle and chancel embattled. The windows on the N side of the nave Dec. Small C15 clerestory. The church was gutted by fire in 1917, but accurately restored by *Currey & Thompson*, 1917–23, and given their characteristic Arts and Crafts furnishings (cf. Buxton, St Mary). – FONT. Part of a circular Saxon cross with carvings of dragons and birds. – CHEST. With chip-carved roundels on the front. – PLATE. Chalice and Paten Cover, 1568. – MONUMENTS. Hugh Willoughby † 1491 and wife, incised alabaster slab, nave floor, large figures, badly preserved. – Hugh Willoughby † 1513 and wife, brass with kneeling figures.

The main interest of the church is the WILLOUGHBY CHAPEL at the E end of the S aisle. This was established in 1622. 30 It has its original STAINED GLASS, with large figures in strong colours, probably by the *Van Linges*, who worked at Oxford and at Lincoln's Inn Chapel.* It also has very pretty floor TILES. The MONUMENT for which the chapel was founded is that of Sir John Willoughby † 1622, a big standing wall-monument of alabaster with small kneeling figures against the tomb-chest, two recumbent effigies, a big coffered arch between coupled columns, plenty of strapwork decoration of the back wall, and a top achievement. The workmanship is not good. – To its l. Ann Grey *née* Willoughby † 1688, also a standing wall-monument, black pedestal, large white urn with white putti to the l. and r.

Earthworks of the medieval village about the church, where Saxon pottery has been found. The church now stands all alone. The village is at Draycott p. 199).

WIND LOW *see* WORMHILL

WINGERWORTH

3060

ALL SAINTS. The interest of the church lies in its Norman remains, the low, completely plain, small, unmoulded early chancel arch on the plainest imposts, three-bay N arcade, higher, with circular piers, simply moulded capitals, and round single-chamfered arches, and the S doorway, of rather narrow proportions, with one order of colonnettes and no ornamentation. There are in the outer S wall also the remains of another round arch. The chancel has C13 lancet windows. The rest, including the W tower (diagonal buttresses, embattled), the clerestory, and all the battlements, is Perp. In 1783 the Hunloke family added on the N side a family MAUSOLEUM, an entirely plain parallelogram without decoration. The medieval nave is now a vestibule, the chancel the Lady Chapel, and the Hunloke Mausoleum a vestry of the church built in 1963–4 by *Naylor, Sale & Widdows*. The nave, at r. angles to the old nave, is entered through the Norman N arcade. Light simple interior, constructed with precast concrete arches. Semicircular apse and long mullioned windows with abstract glazing by *Pope & Parr*.‡ – FONT. Norman, plain big tub. – ROOD LOFT. A rare survival. It does not stand on a rood screen but is affixed to the wall above the low Norman chancel arch. The underside projects in a straight diagonal, not coved. It is decorated with ribs and bosses at wide intervals. The beam at the foot is

* Information kindly given by Mr J. T. Brighton.

‡ Details of the C20 extension from Mr D. G. Edwards.

moulded; crenellation at the top – WALL PAINTING. On the inner face of the Norman chancel arch, the Head of Christ and four Saints in roundels, late C12. – PLATE. Chalice, *c.* 1640. – MONUMENT. Effigy of a Priest, C13, a chalice lying below his folded hands.

Of WINGERWORTH HALL only two earlier (?) service wings and outbuildings are preserved. Note the lodges of 1794, which in conception were part of Repton's landscaping for Sir Henry Hunloke. The Hall itself, completed in 1729, was pulled down in 1924–7. Mr Colvin attributes it to *Francis Smith* of Warwick.*

BRITISH CARBONIZATION RESEARCH ASSOCIATION LABORATORIES. By *Westwood, Sons & Partners*, 1956–8. T-shaped; the three wings are laboratories, offices, and canteens differentiated by use of contrasting materials. Glass and steel curtain walling for the labs, exposed aggregate and brick for the offices, the library cantilevered out over the main entrance.

STUBBING COURT. *See* p. 330.

WINGFIELD MANOR HOUSE *see* SOUTH WINGFIELD

WINSTER

2060

ST JOHN THE BAPTIST. Plain W tower of 1721 with segment-headed windows. The rest 1840–2 by *Habershon* and again altered in 1883. The latter alteration (by *A. Roland Barker*) is quite remarkable. It made the church two-aisled with tall slim quatrefoil shafts along the middle. The easternmost of these is connected with the chancel arch by two arches thrown diagonally across to the NE and SE; a surprising and successful effect. – FONT. A puzzling piece; circular, tub-shaped bowl on a conical foot. The carvings of a style that could be a Tudor imitation of Norman. – STAINED GLASS. Chancel S window by *Burne-Jones* (*Morris & Co.*), 1887. – PLATE. Chalice and Flagon, C18, Lincoln-made; Paten on foot, 1729.

The village has an urban character: good houses, both above the church in WEST BANK (WESLEYAN CHAPEL of 1837 with Venetian windows l. and r. of the door and contemporary stables opposite), and along MAIN STREET. Set back behind

* *See Warwickshire History*, II, No. 2 (1972–3), p. 3. (It was somewhat blockish outside but had an interior of great grandeur. The Saloon was of particular note, with giant Corinthian pilasters. A. Gomme)

rusticated gatepiers is WINSTER HALL, an Early Georgian five-bay stone house with giant pilasters to single out the centre bay, and top balustrade; the doorway with Doric half-columns and a pediment. The chief building of Winster is the MARKET HALL with an originally open ground floor on pointed arches, C15 or C16, and an upper floor of brick with gabled ends and windows of one mullion and one transom, evidently late C17 or early C18. (It may have replaced a timber-framed upper storey. RE)* Past the Market Hall several more houses worth noticing, e.g. THE ARCHWAY dated 1754 which still has the traditional low two-light windows, but now systematized by being placed between horizontal string-courses running all along the front. Also a pair of Palladian houses (STANLEY and NEWHOLME) with two Tuscan porches and between them on the ground floor and the upper floor a Venetian window. The date no doubt mid C18. Closing the vista back along main street the C17 DOWER HOUSE, with two gables to the front.

WHITE LOW. On Winster Moor, ½ m. to the S, a richly furnished Anglo-Saxon barrow.

WIRKSWORTH

2050

ST MARY. An impressive church of the ambitious type of Ashbourne, 152 ft long, with a crossing tower and spire and transepts. The chancel with aisles. Nothing survives necessarily older than 1272, the date when the Dean and Chapter of Lincoln, to which Wirksworth belonged, appointed the first special vicar for the church. Of that time the tall N and S windows of the chancel and the less tall lancets in the W wall of the N transept. They look influenced by Ashbourne.‡ The other windows have to be examined with caution. In their present appearance they all belong to *Sir George Gilbert Scott*'s restoration of 1870–6. The restoration also added the clerestory and kept and made historically probable-looking the E transept aisles enlarged in 1820 to house galleries for a fast-growing congregation. They confused the appearance of the E parts of the church considerably. The chancel E window incidentally dates from 1855, i.e. before Scott. The other windows and their tracery are Dec (S aisle; probably by *Scott*) or Perp (W rebuilt by *William Maskrey* in 1813; N aisle, N transept N, S transept S). The S porch is roofed with pitched stone slabs. The crossing tower is C13 below, and

* The upper storey was taken down in the 1880s and rebuilt in 1905.

‡ Also the large chancel PISCINA.

early C14 above. It has a quatrefoil frieze instead of battlements and the exceptional feature of a lead-covered 'spike' instead of a spire proper. The interior tells of the late C13. There are first all the four arches of the crossing tower with their massive supports (see for example the occasional use of nailhead ornamentation and the keeling or filleting of shafts). The arcades between nave and aisles belong to a slightly later building phase: three bays, quatrefoil shafts with fillets, double-chamfered arches; E responds slimmer and with shaft-rings. The nave is wider than the chancel.

The furnishings of the church take us back much further than the present building. In Anglo-Saxon times Wirksworth was dependent on Repton. The Anglo-Saxon COFFIN LID of *c.* 800 (N wall) found in 1820 must have been from the sarcophagus of an important saint buried here. It is one of the most interesting sculptural remains of its date, embellished with stories from the life of Christ, in short, stumpy figures coarsely carved with schematic parallel reeding of the draperies. The most recent interpretation of the iconography relates it to Byzantine cycles.* Upper tier: Washing the Disciples' Feet; Crucifixion with the Lamb on a Greek cross, no doubt the centre of the slab; Burial of the Virgin; Presentation in the Temple. Lower tier: Descent into Hell; Ascension; Annunciation; Mission (i.e. St. Peter receiving a scroll from the Virgin and Child). Sir Thomas Kendrick compares the style of the figures with that of the Rothbury Cross. – Next in time is a large number of NORMAN ARCHITECTURAL FRAGMENTS in the N transept N wall, S transept S wall, and S transept W wall, also one in the N aisle wall. They deserve close study and might yield quite some information on the lavish appointment of the predecessor of the C13 church.

FONTS. One Norman, a large, plain, impressive cauldron, the other of 1662 by *John Ashmore*, octagonal, with the usual style of carving of the 1662 fonts, and a series of florid initials. – STAINED GLASS. N transept window 1909 by *Morris & Co.*, with Christ, saints, and prophets by *Burne-Jones* and angels by *Morris*. – PLATE. Chalice, Paten Cover on knob foot, and Flagon, 1777 by *William Grundy*. – MONUMENTS. Foliated cross with sword and forester's horn (N transept). – Brasses to Thomas Blackwell † 1525 and wife. On the same panel the figures from another Blackwell brass (N transept). – Anthony Lowe † 1555, the best monument in the church, already com-

* *See* R. W. P. Cockerton's article in *Archaeological Journal*, CXVIII, 1961, p. 230.

pletely in the new Renaissance style. Tomb-chest with putti and fine panel of kneeling children on the W side, effigy, in armour (does it belong?), and back plate against the wall with short fluted Corinthian pilasters and cornice (chancel). – Incised alabaster slab to Ralph Gell † 1564 with two wives and children, attributed by Jeavons to the *Royleys* of Burton-on-Trent (N chancel aisle). – Tomb-chest of Anthony Gell † 1583, with good alabaster effigy, inscription on a plate against the wall, and copious strapwork decoration of the chest (N chapel).

Wirksworth is attractive as an *ensemble* rather than by means of individual houses (as, for example, Ashbourne is.) The visual effect which one remembers is of the differences of levels, the curved course of the two main streets and their ascent towards the crown of the Market Place, but more fascinating and possibly unique is the network of tiny lanes lined with cottages of varying shapes and sizes high up on the hillside NW of the Market Place.

THE TOWN. Around the churchyard to the S of the church two stone GATEPIERS of 1721. To the E the foundations of the C15 and C16 PRIESTS' HOUSE, demolished 1956; GELL'S BEDE-HOUSES, *c.* 1584, of two storeys, with three-light mullioned windows and gabled ends; and the GRAMMAR SCHOOL, also founded (1576) by Anthony Gell, but rebuilt in 1828 in a pretty neo-Gothic style with battlements and crocketed pinnacles, and small-paned window casements, by a local mason, *William Maskrey*. More substantial C18 stone houses (e.g. the VICARAGE) N of the church. Church Street, N of the church, leads to COLDWELL STREET. Turning to the E down the hill on the l. the OLD MANOR HOUSE, early C17 with Georgianized gabled side projections (inside an early C17 plaster ceiling). Opposite is the MANSE, an C18 brick house with a one-bay pediment, built on to a stone range (Nos. 1–3 BLIND LANE) with three Venetian windows to the ground floor and mullioned windows in the two upper storeys. Lower down Coldwell Street the remaining wing of the late C18 stables of Wirksworth Hall. Up Coldwell Street to the W one should first turn into Chapel Lane to the MOOT HALL, rebuilt one-storeyed in plain ashlar work in 1814. It is the place in which the Barmote Courts are held, the prerogative of Wirksworth, which was the centre of English lead-mining. It is known from literature that the Romans and Saxons mined here. In the Hall is the 14-pint oblong measuring vessel for the lead. It has an inscription referring to the third year of Henry VIII's reign. Further on the former EBENEZER CHAPEL, 1810, small, the façade rendered, with a deep segmental hood over the door.

Back into Coldwell Street and up to the COMPLEAT ANGLER (formerly The Vaults), a picturesque but partly demolished early C19 group, then a late C18 brick house and the RED LION (Mid Georgian, brick, painted white, with archway, Venetian window above and semicircular tripartite window above that) facing into the MARKET PLACE. Next to the Red Lion across the road to Middleton, SYMONDS HOUSE (No. 15), a fine Mid Georgian five-bay stone house, doorway with steep pediment. To the l. of this a one-bay brick addition with stone dressings. Venetian windows on both main floors and flanking giant pilasters supporting a moulded eaves cornice with inset open pediment. (Inside, the original staircase lighted by a full-length mullioned window characteristic of the region. RE) Round the corner, DALE HOUSE (No. 13) is late C18, with an elaborate doorcase between modern shop-fronts. Opposite, in DALE END, a broad gabled C17 house with mullioned windows (derelict). Farther up the hill in GREENHILL, BABINGTON HOUSE, gabled and apparently early C17, although on the modern porch the date 1588. The Market Place spreads down the hill and opens to the W into the wide WEST END (No. 1, late C18 three-bay brick house). Down the hill St John's Street leads to the S. On the corner of CAUSEWAY, LLOYDS BANK, early C19, painted stucco, and at the end of Causeway the GATE HOUSE, an independent house in its garden: C17 (mullioned windows at the back), with a late C18 brick front (three storeys, three bays, the slightly projecting centre bay defined by pilasters). Back to ST JOHN'S STREET and on the W side No. 6, a fine C19 stone *palazzo* with rusticated ground floor and ashlar *piano nobile* with cornice hoods on brackets over the windows. Opposite, an exposed cruck frame. Further S, the MATERNITY HOME, also C19, stone and classical.

(At WASH GREEN, at the E edge of the town, Nos. 47–50 are the late C18 HOUSE OF CORRECTION. Four massive rusticated doorways with similar semicircular windows above. RE)

1 m. S, at MILLER'S GREEN, HAARLEM MILL, a complex of mill buildings, originally water-powered. Arkwright built the four-storey, L-shaped mill (brick on stone plinth) between 1777 and 1780. To the S, an engine house and chimney; in front, a mid-C19 stone manager's house; to the E, a silk mill of 1825.

At GORSEY BANK (SE) another attractive group of industrial

buildings: PROVIDENCE MILL, *c.* 1880, and, above it, a terrace of stone cottages. The introduction of mechanized industry in the late C18 apparently changed the town from Defoe's large, well frequented market town (see C18 houses in and around the Market Place) into George Eliot's industrialized, inhospitable Snowfield.

WOLFSCOTE GRANGE *see* HARTINGTON

WOODTHORPE HALL *see* CLAY CROSS *and* HOLMESFIELD

WOODVILLE

3010

ST STEPHEN. 1846 by *Stevens*, stone, in the Norman style, with SW turret and apsed E end. – PLATE. Chalice, 1790 by *James Young*.

On the road to Swadlincote, the showroom of the BRETBY ART POTTERY with a moulded brick façade with Art Nouveau style lettering. Inside, original fittings, including ceiling panels showing the decoration of pottery.

WORMHILL

1070

ST MARGARET. Almost rebuilt in 1864 by *T. H. Rushforth*. Transept added in 1904–10. Only the base of the narrow unbuttressed W tower is medieval. The top is inspired by the Rhineland Romanesque style (or by Sompting, Sussex).

OLD HALL FARM. C16–17, with mullioned windows under hood-moulds, probably the old Manor House, before Wormhill Hall was built. (The cross-wing seems the oldest part. RE)

WORMHILL HALL. Dated 1697 on a rainwater-head, and a good example of the style of its date in Derbyshire. H-shaped, with quoins and a segmental pediment above the doorway. The windows with mullion-and-transom-crosses under straight hoods. In the projecting wings of the front the window hoods are connected by flat string-courses.

WIND LOW, ½ m. NW. Round barrow with kerb. Medieval cross base on the summit.

BOLE HILL, 1 m. NW. Large, flat-topped cairn.

1040

YEAVELEY

HOLY TRINITY. 1840. Small brick church with lancet windows and a pretty little embattled brick W tower.

STYDD HALL, 1 m. W. Interesting remains of a preceptory of the Knights Hospitallers, founded *c.* 1190. One wall of the C13 chapel with lancet windows, their labels on head-stops. Shafts between the windows. The present house stands on medieval stone foundations, but is Elizabethan or Jacobean, brick and stone, tall and square, almost tower-like, with mullioned windows and battlements. Gothic bay-windows added in 1840.

2060

YOULGREAVE

ALL SAINTS. One of the most impressive churches of Derbyshire. Externally the impression is dominated by the broad, big and tall Perp W tower (angle buttresses with many set-offs, big W door, big W window, two tall two-light bell-openings on each side, battlements and eight pinnacles, tall and wide arch towards the nave) and by the crenellation of the rest of the church. Internally the capital quality of the church is its very wide nave with its interesting three-bay arcades. The S arcade is Late Norman at its sturdiest: circular piers, capitals many-scalloped or even scalloped in two tiers, double-chamfered round arches. The N arcade is a little later, also circular piers, also Norman capitals, but with volutes and heads in various combinations, and pointed double-chamfered arches and head label-stops. The W respond is even keeled.* The S doorway can hardly be as early as the S arcade. When the W tower was built, it was placed considerably farther W than the W end of the Norman nave. The two were connected by an aisleless part. The windows are mostly Perp, especially the chancel E (five lights). The S aisle windows are of typical designs of *c.* 1300. The plain clerestory windows are dated C17 by Cox, but may well be Early Tudor, i.e. of the time of the well-preserved nave roof. The restoration of 1869–70 (by *Norman Shaw*) was on the whole satisfactorily done. By *Shaw* the interesting reredos and tiles round the sanctuary and the chancel stalls.‡ – FONT. Big, circular, with a few motifs (animals, fleurs-de-lis) pointing to *c.* 1200. Its remarkable feature is the addition of a separate projecting side stoup. It was brought from Elton church in 1838. –

24

* The blocked N doorway belongs to the date of the N arcade.

‡ Information from Mr Andrew Saint.

SCULPTURE. Fine small arched panel with figure of a man in a long frock, Norman (N nave wall). – STAINED GLASS. E window by *Burne-Jones* (*Morris & Co.*), 1876. – Chancel S window by *Burne-Jones*, 1897. – N aisle E window and nave S window by *Kempe*, 1893, the former a specially good example of his manner. – PLATE. Paten, 1724; two Chalices and Paten, 1730, Flagon and Almsdish, 1731, all by *Gabriel Sleath*; Almsdish, 1733 by *Thomas Parr*; Paten, 1751 by *William Hunter*. – MONUMENTS. Cross-legged bearded Knight holding his heart in his hands (cf. Darley Dale), *c.* 1325 (chancel N wall). – Alabaster effigy of Thomas Cokayne † 1488, on tomb-chest, of exceptionally good quality, but also exceptionally small size (Thomas Cokayne was young when he died, cf. a similar small effigy of *c.* 1400 at Hacombe, Devon). The tomb-chest on the long sides with two standing angels separated by a tracery panel (instead of the more usual two panels and three angels). – Exquisite oblong alabaster panel to Robert Gylbert † 1492, his wife and children. In the centre seated Virgin, r. and l. the kneeling figures first of husband and wife, then of the seventeen children. It probably formed the reredos panel of the Lady Chapel chantry altar at the E end of the S aisle, round which Gylbert erected the parclose screen referred to in the inscription. – Frideswide Gilbert † 1604, small brass figure. – Roger Rowe † 1613, fairly large, one of the usual wall-monuments with kneelers, the children below the parents in the predella.

38

(CONGREGATIONAL CHAPEL (now British Legion). 1853, Romanesque, by *Thomas Bateman*, the antiquarian, *see* Middleton-by-Youlgreave. C. Stell)

In the Market Place a big plain lumpy circular CONDUIT HEAD of 1829. To the NW OLD HALL FARM, 1630, gabled and with mullioned windows, and below the OLD HALL of 1650 or 1656 (date on panelling inside). The Old Hall has somewhat projecting symmetrical wings with five- and six-light mullioned windows and gables. (Its core may be earlier. DOE)

HERMITS CAVE, 1 m. SE. At the end of a footpath branching off the path whch runs between Gratcliffe Rocks and Woods and Robin Hood's Stride. Rudely carved Crucifixus in the cave.

BEE LOW, 1¼ m. NW of the village. Beaker barrow, containing several later burials also. Twenty-three inhumations and five cremations in all have been recovered from the mound.

ARBOR LOW, 2¾ m. W. Well preserved Bronze Age henge monument. The rock-cut ditch and accompanying outer bank surrounding the circular monument are particularly imposing.

The whole work measures 250 ft in diameter and has two opposed entrances. Within the ditch lies a stone circle in which forty-seven stones, all now recumbent, still survive. A further three stones lie in the centre: originally there were probably several more. On the edge of the outer bank stands a later Bronze Age barrow containing a stone cist. Running up to Arbor Low from the S is a linear earthwork, which can still be traced for about 600 ft. It may represent a later property or territorial boundary.

GIB HILL, close to Arbor Low. Large, round barrow, still standing 15 ft in height. It probably dates from the Early Bronze Age, but it appears to cover earlier burials.

END LOW, 2 m. S of Gib Hill. Round barrow.

MIDDLETON-BY-YOULGREAVE. *See* p. 281.

GLOSSARY

ABACUS: flat slab on the top of a capital (q.v.).

ABUTMENT: solid masonry placed to resist the lateral pressure of a vault.

ACANTHUS: plant with thick fleshy and scalloped leaves used as part of the decoration of a Corinthian capital (q.v.) and in some types of leaf carving.

ACHIEVEMENT OF ARMS: in heraldry, a complete display of armorial bearings.

ACROTERION: foliage-carved block on the end or top of a classical pediment (q.v.).

ADDORSED: two human figures, animals, or birds, etc., placed symmetrically so that they turn their backs to each other.

AEDICULE, AEDICULA: framing of a window or door by columns and a pediment (q.v.).

AFFRONTED: two human figures, animals, or birds, etc., placed symmetrically so that they face each other.

AGGER: Latin term for the built-up foundations of Roman roads; also sometimes applied to the banks of hill-forts or other earthworks.

AMBULATORY: semicircular or polygonal aisle enclosing an apse (q.v.).

ANNULET: *see* Shaft-ring.

ANSE DE PANIER: *see* Arch, Basket.

ANTEPENDIUM: covering of the front of an altar, usually by textiles or metalwork.

ANTIS, IN: *see* Portico.

APSE: vaulted semicircular or polygonal end of a chancel or a chapel.

ARABESQUE: light and fanciful surface decoration using combinations of flowing lines, tendrils, etc., interspersed with vases, animals, etc.

ARCADE: range of arches supported on piers or columns, free-standing: or, BLIND ARCADE, the same attached to a wall.

ARCH: round-headed, i.e. semicircular; pointed, i.e. consisting of two curves, each drawn from one centre, and meeting in a point at the top; segmental, i.e. in the form of a segment; pointed; four-centred (a late medieval form), *see* Fig. 1(*a*);

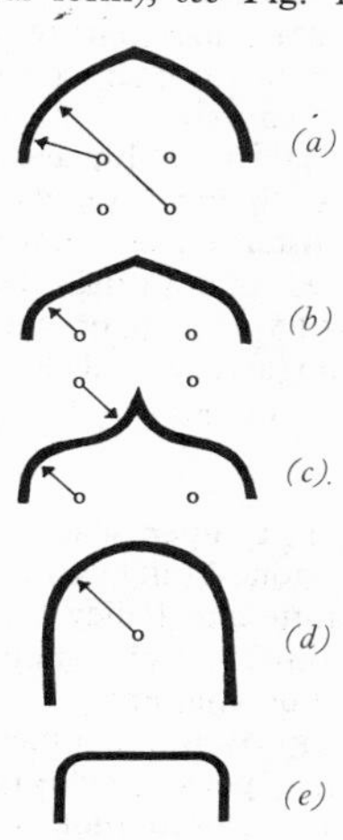

Fig. 1. Arches

Tudor (also a late medieval form), *see* Fig. 1(*b*); Ogee (introduced *c.* 1300 and specially popular in the C14), *see* Fig. 1(*c*); Stilted, *see* Fig. 1(*d*); Basket, with lintel connected to the jambs by concave quadrant curves, *see* Fig. 1(*e*) for one example; Diaphragm, a transverse arch with solid spandrels carrying not a vault but a principal beam of a timber roof. *See also* Strainer Arch.

ARCHITRAVE: lowest of the three main parts of the entablature (q.v.) of an order (q.v.) (*see* Fig. 12).

ARCHIVOLT: a continuous moulding on the face of an arch and following its contour.

ARRIS: sharp edge at the meeting of two surfaces.

ASHLAR: masonry of large blocks wrought to even faces and square edges.

ATLANTES: male counterparts of caryatids (q.v.).

ATRIUM: inner court of a Roman house, also open court in front of a church.

ATTACHED: *see* Engaged.

ATTIC: topmost storey of a house, if distance from floor to ceiling is less than in the others.

AUMBRY: recess or cupboard to hold sacred vessels for Mass and Communion.

BAILEY: open space or court of a stone-built castle; *see also* Motte-and-Bailey.

BALDACCHINO: canopy supported on columns.

BALLFLOWER: globular flower of three petals enclosing a small ball. A decoration used in the first quarter of the C14.

BALUSTER: small pillar or column of fanciful outline.

BALUSTRADE: series of balusters supporting a handrail or coping (q.v.).

BARBICAN: outwork defending the entrance to a castle.

BARGEBOARDS: projecting decorated boards placed against the incline of the gable of a building and hiding the horizontal roof timbers.

BARREL-VAULT: *see* Vault.

BARROW: *see* Bell, Bowl, Disc, Long, *and* Pond Barrow.

BASILICA: in medieval architecture an aisled church with a clerestory.

BASKET ARCH: *see* Arch (Fig. 1*e*).

BASTION: projection at the angle of a fortification.

BATTER: inclined face of a wall.

BATTLEMENT: parapet with a series of indentations or embrasures with raised portions or merlons between. Also called Crenellation.

BAYS: internal compartments of a building; each divided from the other not by solid walls but by divisions only marked in the side walls (columns, pilasters, etc.) or the ceiling (beams, etc.). Also external divisions of a building by fenestration.

BAY-WINDOW: angular or curved projection of a house front with ample fenestration. If curved, also called bow-window: if on an upper floor only, also called oriel or oriel window.

BEAKER FOLK: Late New Stone Age warrior invaders from the Continent who buried their dead in round barrows and introduced the first metal tools and weapons to Britain.

BEAKHEAD: Norman ornamental motif consisting of a row of bird or beast heads with beaks biting usually into a roll moulding (q.v.).

BELFRY: turret on a roof to hang bells in.

BELGAE: aristocratic warrior bands who settled in Britain in two main waves in the C1 B.C. In Britain their culture is termed Iron Age C.

BELL BARROW: Early Bronze Age round barrow in which the mound is separated from its encircling ditch by a flat platform or berm (q.v.).

BELLCOTE: framework on a roof to hang bells from.

BERM: level area separating ditch from bank on a hill-fort or barrow.

BILLET FRIEZE: Norman ornamental motif made up of short raised rectangles placed at regular intervals.

BIVALLATE: of a hill-fort: defended by two concentric banks and ditches.

BLIND ARCADE: *see* Arcade.

BLOCK CAPITAL: Romanesque capital cut from a cube by having the lower angles rounded off to the circular shaft below. Also called Cushion Capital (Fig. 2).

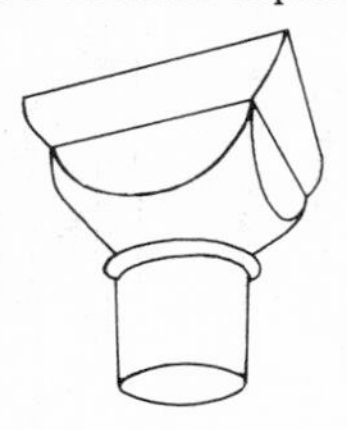

Fig. 2. Block capital

BOND, ENGLISH or FLEMISH: *see* Brickwork.

BOSS: knob or projection usually placed to cover the intersection of ribs in a vault.

BOWL BARROW: round barrow surrounded by a quarry ditch. Introduced in Late Neolithic times, the form continued until the Saxon period.

BOW-WINDOW: *see* Bay-Window.

BOX: small country house, e.g. a shooting box. A convenient term to describe a compact minor dwelling, e.g. a rectory.

BOX PEW: pew with a high wooden enclosure.

BRACES: *see* Roof.

BRACKET: small supporting piece of stone, etc., to carry a projecting horizontal.

BRESSUMER: beam in a timber-framed building to support the, usually projecting, superstructure.

BRICKWORK: *Header:* brick laid so that the end only appears on the face of the wall. *Stretcher:* brick laid so that the side only appears on the face of the wall. *English Bond:* method of laying bricks so that alternate courses or layers on the face of the wall are composed of headers or stretchers only (Fig. 3*a*). *Flemish Bond:* method of laying bricks so that alternate headers and

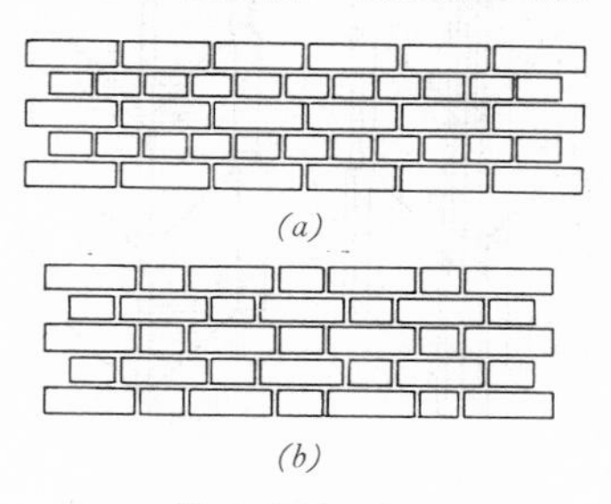

Fig. 3. Brickwork

stretchers appear in each course on the face of the wall (Fig. 3*b*). *See also* Herringbone Work, Oversailing Courses.

BROACH: *see* Spire.

BROKEN PEDIMENT: *see* Pediment.

BRONZE AGE: in Britain, the period from *c.* 1600 to 600 B.C.

BUCRANIUM: ox skull.

BUTTRESS: mass of brickwork or masonry projecting from or built against a wall to give additional strength. *Angle Buttresses:* two meeting at an angle of 90° at the angle of a building (Fig. 4*a*). *Clasping Buttress:* one which encases the angle (Fig. 4*d*). *Diagonal Buttress:* one placed against the right angle formed by two walls, and more or less equiangular with both (Fig. 4*b*). *Flying Buttress:* arch or half arch transmitting the thrust of a vault or roof from the upper part of a wall to an outer support or buttress. *Setback Buttress:* angle buttress set slightly back from the angle (Fig. 4*c*).

CABLE MOULDING: Norman moulding imitating a twisted cord.

CAIRN: a mound of stones usually covering a burial.

CAMBER: slight rise or upward curve of an otherwise horizontal structure.

CAMPANILE: isolated bell tower.

CANOPY: projection or hood over

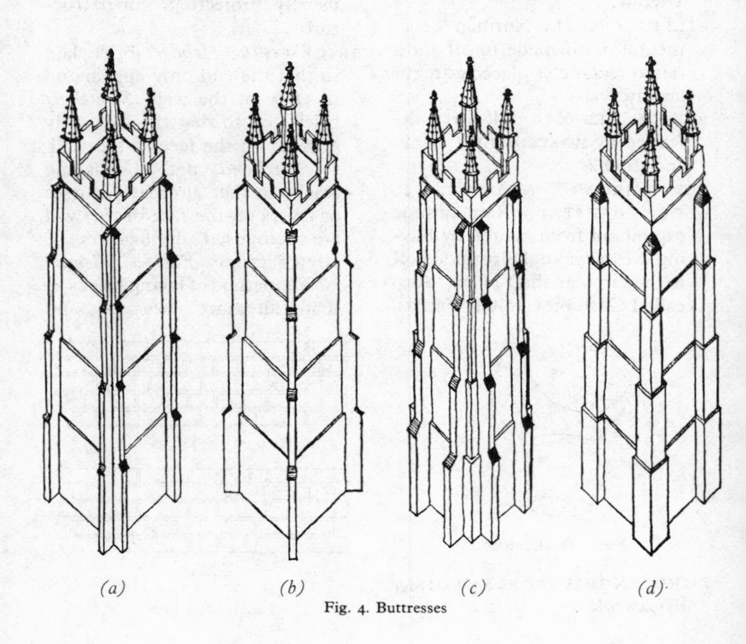

Fig. 4. Buttresses

an altar, pulpit, niche, statue, etc.

CAP: in a windmill the crowning feature.

CAPITAL: head or top part of a column. *See also* Block Capital, Crocket Capital, Order, Scalloped Capital, Stiff-leaf, *and* Waterleaf.

CARTOUCHE: tablet with an ornate frame, usually enclosing an inscription.

CARYATID: whole female figure supporting an entablature or other similar member. *Termini Caryatids:* female busts or demi-figures or three-quarter figures supporting an entablature or other similar member and placed at the top of termini pilasters (q.v.). Cf. Atlantes.

CASTELLATED: decorated with battlements (q.v.).

CELURE: panelled and adorned part of a wagon roof above the rood or the altar.

CENSER: vessel for the burning of incense.

CENTERING: wooden framework used in arch and vault construction and removed when the mortar has set.

CHALICE: cup used in the Communion service or at Mass. *See also* Recusant Chalice.

CHAMBERED TOMB: burial mound of the New Stone Age having a stone-built chamber and entrance passage covered by an earthen barrow or stone cairn. The form was introduced to Britain from the Mediterranean.

CHAMFER: surface made by cutting across the square angle of a stone block, piece of wood, etc., usually at an angle of 45° to the other two surfaces.

CHANCEL: that part of the E end of a church in which the altar is placed, usually applied to the whole continuation of the nave E of the crossing.

CHANCEL ARCH: arch at the W end of the chancel.

CHANTRY CHAPEL: chapel attached to, or inside, a church, endowed for the saying of Masses for the soul of the founder or some other individual.

CHEVET: French term for the E end of a church (chancel, ambulatory, and radiating chapels).

CHEVRON: Norman moulding forming a zigzag.

CHOIR: that part of the church where divine service is sung.

CIBORIUM: a baldacchino (q.v.).

CINQUEFOIL: *see* Foil.

CIST: stone-lined or slab-built grave. First appears in Late Neolithic times. It continued to be used in the Early Christian period.

CLAPPER BRIDGE: bridge made of large slabs of stone, some built up to make rough piers and other longer ones laid on top to make the roadway.

CLASSIC: here used to mean the moment of highest achievement of a style.

CLASSICAL: here used as the term for Greek and Roman architecture and any subsequent styles inspired by it.

CLERESTORY: upper storey of the nave walls of a church, pierced by windows.

COADE STONE: artificial (cast) stone made in the late C18 and the early C19 by Coade and Sealy in London.

COB: walling material made of mixed clay and straw.

COFFERING: decorating a ceiling

with sunk square or polygonal ornamental panels.

COLLAR-BEAM: *see* Roof.

COLONNADE: range of columns.

COLONNETTE: small column.

COLUMNA ROSTRATA: column decorated with carved prows of ships to celebrate a naval victory.

COMPOSITE: *see* Order.

CONSOLE: bracket (q.v.) with a compound curved outline.

COPING: capping or covering to a wall.

CORBEL: block of stone projecting from a wall, supporting some feature on its horizontal top surface.

CORBEL TABLE: series of corbels, occurring just below the roof eaves externally or internally, often seen in Norman buildings.

CORINTHIAN: *see* Order.

CORNICE: in classical architecture the top section of the entablature (q.v.). Also the term for a projecting decorative feature along the top of a wall, arch, etc.

CORRIDOR VILLA: *see* Villa.

COUNTERSCARP BANK: small bank on the down-hill or outer side of a hill-fort ditch.

COURTYARD VILLA: *see* Villa.

COVE, COVING: concave undersurface in the nature of a hollow moulding but on a larger scale.

COVER PATEN: cover to a Communion cup, suitable for use as a paten or plate for the consecrated bread.

CRADLE ROOF: *see* Wagon Roof.

CRENELLATION: *see* Battlement.

CREST, CRESTING: ornamental finish along the top of a screen, etc.

CRINKLE-CRANKLE WALL: undulating wall.

CROCKET, CROCKETING: decorative features placed on the sloping sides of spires, pinnacles, gables, etc., in Gothic architecture, carved in various leaf shapes and placed at regular intervals.

CROCKET CAPITAL: *see* Fig. 5. An Early Gothic form.

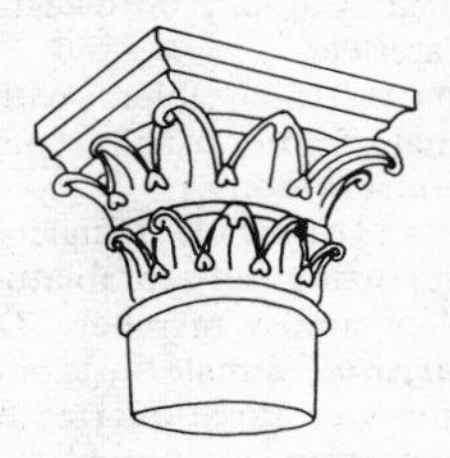

Fig. 5. Crocket capital

CROMLECH: word of Celtic origin still occasionally used of single free-standing stones ascribed to the Neolithic or Bronze Age periods.

CROSSING: space at the intersection of nave, chancel, and transepts.

CROSS-VAULT: *see* Vault.

CROSS-WINDOWS: windows with one mullion and one transom.

CROWN-POST: *see* Roof (Fig. 15).

CRUCK: cruck construction is a method of timber framing by which the ridge beam is supported by pairs of curved timbers extending from floor to ridge.

CRYPT: underground room usually below the E end of a church.

CUPOLA: small polygonal or circular domed turret crowning a roof.

CURTAIN WALL: connecting wall between the towers of a castle. In C20 architecture, a non-load-bearing wall which can be applied in front of a framed structure to keep out the weather; sections may include windows and the spans between.

CUSHION CAPITAL: *see* Block Capital.

CUSP: projecting point between the foils (q.v.) in a foiled Gothic arch.

DADO: decorative covering of the lower part of a wall.

DAGGER: tracery motif of the Dec style. It is a lancet shape rounded or pointed at the head, pointed at the foot, and cusped inside (Fig. 6).

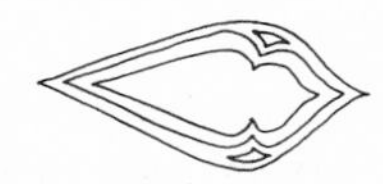

Fig. 6. Dagger

DAIS: raised platform at one end of a room.

DEC ('DECORATED'): historical division of English Gothic architecture covering the period from *c.* 1290 to *c.* 1350.

DEMI-COLUMNS: columns half sunk into a wall.

DIAPER WORK: surface decoration composed of square or lozenge shapes.

DIAPHRAGM ARCH: *see* Arch.

DIOCLETIAN WINDOW: semicircular, with two mullions.

DISC BARROW: Bronze Age round barrow with inconspicuous central mound surrounded by bank and ditch.

DOGTOOTH: typical E.E. ornament consisting of a series of four-cornered stars placed diagonally and raised pyramidally (Fig. 7).

DOMICAL VAULT: *see* Vault.

DONJON: *see* Keep.

Fig. 7. Dogtooth

DORIC: *see* Order.

DORMER (WINDOW): window placed vertically in the sloping plane of a roof.

DRIPSTONE: *see* Hoodmould.

DRUM: circular or polygonal vertical wall of a dome or cupola.

DUTCH GABLE: *see* Gable.

E.E. ('EARLY ENGLISH'): historical division of English Gothic architecture roughly covering the C13.

EASTER SEPULCHRE: recess with tomb-chest (q.v.), usually in the wall of a chancel, the tomb-chest to receive an effigy of Christ for Easter celebrations.

EAVES: overhanging edge of a roof.

EAVES CORNICE: cornice below the eaves of a roof.

ECHINUS: convex or projecting moulding supporting the abacus of a Greek Doric capital, sometimes bearing an egg and dart pattern.

EMBATTLED: *see* Battlement.

EMBRASURE: small opening in the wall or parapet of a fortified building, usually splayed on the inside.

ENCAUSTIC TILES: earthenware glazed and decorated tiles used for paving.

ENGAGED COLUMNS: columns attached to, or partly sunk into, a wall.

ENGLISH BOND: *see* Brickwork.

ENTABLATURE: in classical architecture the whole of the horizontal members above a column (that is architrave, frieze, and cornice) (*see* Fig. 12).

ENTASIS: very slight convex deviation from a straight line; used on Greek columns and sometimes on spires to prevent an optical illusion of concavity.

ENTRESOL: *see* Mezzanine.

ESCUTCHEON: shield for armorial bearings.

EXEDRA: the apsidal end of a room. *See* Apse.

FAN-VAULT: *see* Vault.

FERETORY: place behind the high altar where the chief shrine of a church is kept.

FESTOON: carved garland of flowers and fruit suspended at both ends. *See also* Swag.

FILLET: narrow flat band running down a shaft or along a roll moulding.

FINIAL: top of a canopy, gable, pinnacle.

FIRRED: *see* Roof.

FLAGON: vessel for the wine used in the Communion service.

FLAMBOYANT: properly the latest phase of French Gothic architecture where the window tracery takes on wavy undulating lines.

FLÈCHE: slender spire on the centre of a roof. Also called Spirelet.

FLEMISH BOND: *see* Brickwork.

FLEURON: decorative carved flower or leaf.

FLUSHWORK: decorative use of flint in conjunction with dressed stone so as to form patterns: tracery, initials, etc.

FLUTING: vertical channelling in the shaft of a column.

FLYING BUTTRESS: *see* Buttress.

FOIL: lobe formed by the cusping (q.v.) of a circle or an arch. Trefoil, quatrefoil, cinquefoil, multifoil, express the number of leaf shapes to be seen.

FOLIATED: carved with leaf shapes.

FOSSE: ditch.

FOUR-CENTRED ARCH: *see* Arch (Fig. 1*a*).

FRATER: refectory or dining hall of a monastery.

FRESCO: wall painting on wet plaster.

FRIEZE: middle division of a classical entablature (q.v.) (*see* Fig. 12).

FRONTAL: covering for the front of an altar.

GABLE: *Dutch gable:* a gable with curved sides crowned by a pediment, characteristic of *c.* 1630–50 (Fig. 8*a*). *Shaped gable:* a gable with multi-curved sides characteristic of *c.* 1600–50 (Fig. 8*b*).

GADROONED: enriched with a series of convex ridges, the opposite of fluting (q.v.).

GALILEE: chapel or vestibule usually at the W end of a church

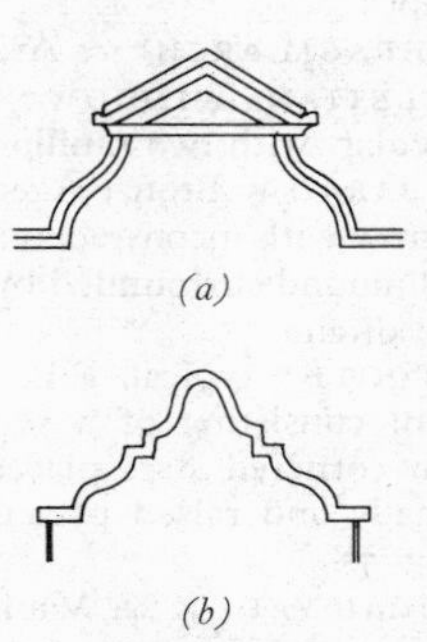

Fig. 8. Gables

enclosing the porch. Also called Narthex (q.v.).

GALLERY: in church architecture upper storey above an aisle, opened in arches to the nave. Also called Tribune and often erroneously Triforium (q.v.).

GALLERY GRAVE: chambered tomb (q.v.) in which there is little or no differentiation between the entrance passage and the actual burial chamber(s).

GARDEROBE: lavatory or privy in a medieval building.

GARGOYLE: water spout projecting from the parapet of a wall or tower; carved into a human or animal shape.

GAZEBO: lookout tower or raised summer house in a picturesque garden.

'GEOMETRICAL': *see* Tracery.

'GIBBS SURROUND': of a doorway or window. An C18 motif consisting of a surround with alternating larger and smaller blocks of stone, quoin-wise, or intermittent large blocks, sometimes with a narrow raised band connecting them up the verticals and along the face of the arch (Fig. 9).

GROIN: sharp edge at the meeting of two cells of a cross-vault.

GROIN-VAULT: *see* Vault.

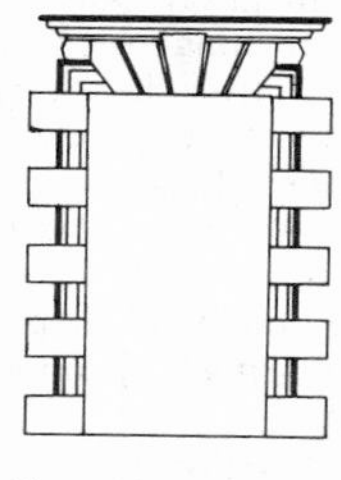

Fig. 9. 'Gibbs surround'

GROTESQUE: fanciful ornamental decoration: *see also* Arabesque.

HAGIOSCOPE: *see* Squint.

HALF-TIMBERING: *see* Timber-Framing.

HALL CHURCH: church in which nave and aisles are of equal height or approximately so.

HAMMERBEAM: *see* Roof (Fig. 18).

HANAP: large metal cup, generally made for domestic use, standing on an elaborate base and stem; with a very ornate cover frequently crowned with a little steeple.

HEADER: *see* Brickwork.

HERRINGBONE WORK: brick, stone, or tile construction where the component blocks are laid diagonally instead of flat. Alternate courses lie in opposing directions to make a zigzag pattern up the face of the wall.

HEXASTYLE: having six detached columns.

HILL-FORT: Iron Age earthwork enclosed by a ditch and bank system; in the later part of the period the defences multiplied in size and complexity. They vary from about an acre to over 30 acres in area, and are usually built with careful regard to natural elevations or promontories.

HIPPED ROOF: *see* Roof.

HOODMOULD: projecting moulding above an arch or a lintel to throw off water. Also called Dripstone or Label.

ICONOGRAPHY: the science of the subject matter of works of the visual arts.

IMPOST: bracket (q.v.) in a wall, usually formed of mouldings, on which the ends of an arch rest.

INDENT: shape chiselled out in a stone slab to receive a brass.

INGLENOOK: bench or seat built in beside a fireplace, sometimes covered by the chimneybreast, occasionally lit by small windows on each side of the fire.

INTERCOLUMNIATION: the space between columns.

IONIC: *see* Order (Fig. 12).

IRON AGE: in Britain the period from *c.* 600 B.C. to the coming of the Romans. The term is also used for those un-Romanized native communities which survived until the Saxon incursions.

JAMB: straight side of an archway, doorway, or window.

KEEL MOULDING: moulding whose outline is in section like that of the keel of a ship.

KEEP: massive tower of a Norman castle. Also called Donjon.

KEYSTONE: middle stone in an arch or a rib-vault.

KINGPOST: *see* Roof (Fig. 14).

KNEELER: horizontal decorative projection at the base of a gable.

KNOP: a knob-like thickening in the stem of a chalice.

LABEL: *see* Hoodmould.

LABEL STOP: ornamental boss at the end of a hoodmould (q.v.).

LACED WINDOWS: windows pulled visually together by strips, usually in brick of a different colour, which continue vertically the lines of the vertical parts of the window surrounds. The motif is typical of *c.* 1720.

LANCET WINDOW: slender pointed-arched window.

LANTERN: in architecture, a small circular or polygonal turret with windows all round crowning a roof (*see* Cupola) or a dome.

LANTERN CROSS: churchyard cross with lantern-shaped top usually with sculptured representations on the sides of the top.

LEAN-TO ROOF: roof with one slope only, built against a higher wall.

LESENE or PILASTER STRIP: pilaster (q.v.) without base or capital.

LIERNE: *see* Vault (Fig. 23).

LINENFOLD: Tudor panelling ornamented with a conventional representation of a piece of linen laid in vertical folds. The piece is repeated in each panel.

LINTEL: horizontal beam or stone bridging an opening.

LOGGIA: recessed colonnade (q.v.).

LONG AND SHORT WORK: Saxon quoins (q.v.) consisting of stones placed with the long sides alternately upright and horizontal.

LONG BARROW: unchambered Neolithic communal burial mound, wedge-shaped in plan, with the burial and occasional other structures massed at the broader end, from which the mound itself tapers in height; quarry ditches flank the mound.

LOUVRE: opening, often with lantern (q.v.) over, in the roof of a room to let the smoke from a central hearth escape.

LOWER PALAEOLITHIC: *see* Palaeolithic.

LOZENGE: diamond shape.

LUCARNE: small opening to let light in.

LUNETTE: tympanum (q.v.) or semicircular opening.

LYCH GATE: wooden gate structure with a roof and open sides placed at the entrance to a churchyard to provide space for the reception of a coffin. The word *lych* is Saxon and means a corpse.

LYNCHET: long terraced strip of soil accumulating on the downward side of prehistoric and medieval fields due to soil creep from continuous ploughing along the contours.

MACHICOLATION: projecting gallery on brackets (q.v.) constructed on the outside of castle towers or walls. The gallery has holes in the floor to drop missiles through.

MAJOLICA: ornamented glazed earthenware.

MANSARD: *see* Roof.

MATHEMATICAL TILES: small facing tiles the size of brick headers, most often applied to timber-framed walls to make them appear brick-built.

MEGALITHIC TOMB: stone-built burial chamber of the New Stone Age covered by an earth or stone mound. The form was introduced to Britain from the Mediterranean area.

MERLON: *see* Battlement.

MESOLITHIC: 'Middle Stone' Age; the post-glacial period of hunting and fishing communities dating in Britain from *c.* 8000 B.C. to the arrival of Neolithic communities, with which they must have considerably overlapped.

METOPE: in classical architecture of the Doric order (q.v.) the space in the frieze between the triglyphs (Fig. 12).

MEZZANINE: low storey placed between two higher ones. Also called Entresol.

MISERERE: *see* Misericord.

MISERICORD: bracket placed on the underside of a hinged choir stall seat which, when turned up, provided the occupant of the seat with a support during long periods of standing. Also called Miserere.

MODILLION: small bracket of which large numbers (modillion frieze) are often placed below a cornice (q.v.) in classical architecture.

MOTTE: steep mound forming the main feature of C11 and C12 castles.

MOTTE-AND-BAILEY: post-Roman and Norman defence system consisting of an earthen mound (the motte) topped with a wooden tower eccentrically placed within a bailey (q.v.), with enclosure ditch and palisade, and with the rare addition of an internal bank.

MOUCHETTE: tracery motif in curvilinear tracery, a curved dagger (q.v.), specially popular in the early C14 (Fig. 10).

Fig. 10. Mouchette

MOURNERS: *see* Weepers.

MULLIONS: vertical posts or uprights dividing a window into 'lights'.

MULTIVALLATE: of a hill-fort: defended by three or more concentric banks and ditches.

MUNTIN: post as a rule moulded and part of a screen.

NAIL-HEAD: E.E. ornamental motif, consisting of small pyramids regularly repeated (Fig. 11).

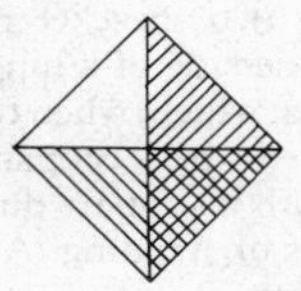

Fig. 11. Nail-head

NARTHEX: enclosed vestibule or covered porch at the main entrance to a church (*see* Galilee).

NEOLITHIC: 'New Stone' Age, dating in Britain from the appearance from the Continent of the first settled farming communities *c.* 3500 B.C. until the introduction of the Bronze Age.

NEWEL: central post in a circular or winding staircase; also the principal post when a flight of stairs meets a landing.

NOOK-SHAFT: shaft set in the angle of a pier or respond or wall, or the angle of the jamb of a window or doorway.

NUTMEG MOULDING: consisting of a chain of tiny triangles placed obliquely.

OBELISK: lofty pillar of square section tapering at the top and ending pyramidally.

OGEE: *see* Arch (Fig. 1*c*).

OPEN PEDIMENT: *see* Pediment.

ORATORY: small private chapel in a house.

ORDER: *see* Fig. 12. (1) *of a doorway or window:* series of concentric steps receding towards the opening; (2) *in classical architecture:* column with base, shaft, capital and entablature (q.v.) according to one of the following styles: Greek Doric, Roman Doric, Tuscan Doric, Ionic, Corinthian,

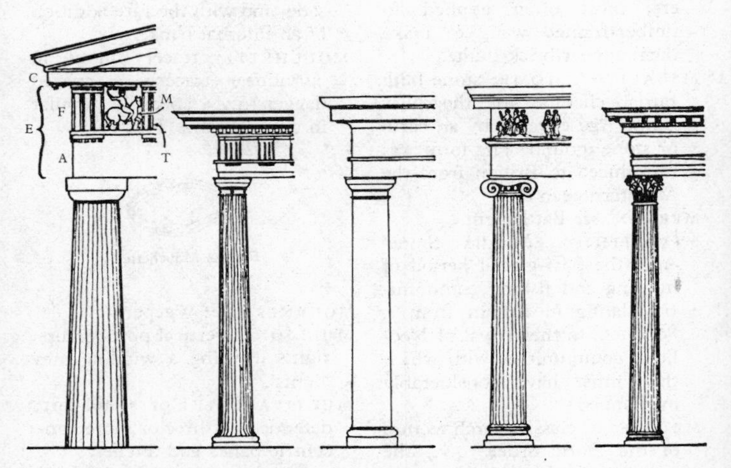

Fig. 12. Orders of columns (Greek Doric, Roman Doric, Tuscan Doric, Ionic, Corinthian)
E, Entablature; C, Cornice; F, Frieze; A, Architrave; M, Metope; T, Triglyph

Composite. The established details are very elaborate, and some specialist architectural work should be consulted for further guidance.

ORIEL: *see* Bay-Window.

OVERHANG: projection of the upper storey of a house.

OVERSAILING COURSES: series of stone or brick courses, each one projecting beyond the one below it.

OVOLO: convex moulding.

PALAEOLITHIC: 'Old Stone' Age; the first period of human culture, commencing in the Ice Age and immediately prior to the Mesolithic; the Lower Palaeolithic is the older phase, the Upper Palaeolithic the later.

PALIMPSEST: (1) *of a brass:* where a metal plate has been re-used by turning over and engraving on the back; (2) *of a wall painting:* where one overlaps and partly obscures an earlier one.

PALLADIAN: architecture following the ideas and principles of Andrea Palladio, 1508–80.

PANTILE: tile of curved S-shaped section.

PARAPET: low wall placed to protect any spot where there is a sudden drop, for example on a bridge, quay, hillside, housetop, etc.

PARCLOSE SCREEN: *see* Screen.

PARGETTING: plaster work with patterns and ornaments either in relief or engraved on it.

PARVIS: term wrongly applied to a room over a church porch. These rooms were often used as a schoolroom or as a store room.

PASSING-BRACE: *see* Roof (Fig. 16).

PATEN: plate to hold the bread at Communion or Mass.

PATERA: small flat circular or oval ornament in classical architecture.

PEDIMENT: low-pitched gable used in classical, Renaissance, and neo-classical architecture above a portico and above doors, windows, etc. It may be straight-sided or curved segmentally. *Broken Pediment:* one where the centre portion of the base is left open. *Open Pediment:* one where the centre portion of the sloping sides is left out.

PENDANT: boss (q.v.) elongated so that it seems to hang down.

PENDENTIVE: concave triangular spandrel used to lead from the angle of two walls to the base of a circular dome. It is constructed as part of the hemisphere over a diameter the size of the diagonal of the basic square (Fig. 13).

PERP (PERPENDICULAR): historical division of English Gothic architecture covering the period from *c.* 1335–50 to *c.* 1530.

PIANO NOBILE: principal storey of a house with the reception rooms; usually the first floor.

PIAZZA: open space surrounded by

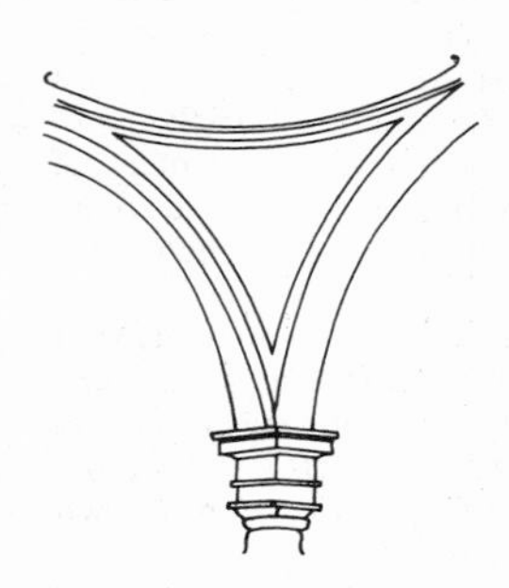

Fig. 13. Pendentive

buildings; in C17 and C18 England sometimes used to mean a long colonnade or loggia.

PIER: strong, solid support, frequently square in section or of composite section (compound pier).

PIETRA DURA: ornamental or scenic inlay by means of thin slabs of stone.

PILASTER: shallow pier attached to a wall. *Pilaster Strip: see* Lesene. *Termini Pilasters:* pilasters with sides tapering downwards.

PILLAR PISCINA: free-standing piscina (q.v.) on a pillar.

PINNACLE: ornamental form crowning a spire, tower, buttress, etc., usually of steep pyramidal, conical, or some similar shape.

PISCINA: basin for washing the Communion or Mass vessels, provided with a drain. Generally set in or against the wall to the S of an altar.

PLAISANCE: summer house, pleasure house near a mansion.

PLATE TRACERY: *see* Tracery.

PLINTH: projecting base of a wall or column, generally chamfered (q.v.) or moulded at the top.

POND BARROW: rare type of Bronze Age barrow consisting of a circular depression, usually paved, and containing a number of cremation burials.

POPPYHEAD: ornament of leaf and flower type used to decorate the tops of bench- or stall-ends.

PORTCULLIS: gate constructed to rise and fall in vertical grooves; used in gateways of castles.

PORTE COCHÈRE: porch large enough to admit wheeled vehicles.

PORTICO: centrepiece of a house or of a church, with classical detached or attached columns and a pediment. A portico is called *prostyle* or *in antis* according to whether it projects from or recedes into a building. In a portico *in antis* the columns range with the side walls.

POSTERN: small gateway at the back of a building.

PREDELLA: in an altarpiece the horizontal strip below the main representation, often used for a number of subsidiary representations in a row.

PRESBYTERY: the part of the church lying E of the choir. It is the part where the altar is placed.

PRINCIPAL: *see* Roof (Figs. 14, 17).

PRIORY: monastic house whose head is a prior or prioress, not an abbot or abbess.

PROSTYLE: with free-standing columns in a row.

PULPITUM: stone screen in a major church provided to shut off the choir from the nave and also as a backing for the return choir stalls.

PULVINATED FRIEZE: frieze (q.v.) with a bold convex moulding.

PURLINS: *see* Roof (Figs. 14–17).

PUTHOLE or PUTLOCK HOLE: putlocks are the short horizontal timbers on which during construction the boards of scaffolding rest. Putholes or putlock holes are the holes in the wall for putlocks, which often are not filled in after construction is complete.

PUTTO: small naked boy.

QUADRANGLE: inner courtyard in a large building.

QUARRY: in stained-glass work, a small diamond- or square-shaped piece of glass set diagonally.

QUATREFOIL: *see* Foil.

QUEENPOSTS: *see* Roof (Fig. 16).

QUEEN-STRUTS: *see* Roof (Fig. 17).

QUOINS: dressed stones at the angles of a building. Sometimes all the stones are of the same size; more often they are alternately large and small.

RADIATING CHAPELS: chapels projecting radially from an ambulatory or an apse.

RAFTER: *see* Roof.

RAMPART: stone wall or wall of earth surrounding a castle, fortress, or fortified city.

RAMPART-WALK: path along the inner face of a rampart.

REBATE: continuous rectangular notch cut on an edge.

REBUS: pun, a play on words. The literal translation and illustration of a name for artistic and heraldic purposes (Belton = bell, tun).

RECUSANT CHALICE: chalice made after the Reformation and before Catholic Emancipation for Roman Catholic use.

REEDING: decoration with parallel convex mouldings touching one another.

REFECTORY: dining hall; *see also* Frater.

RENDERING: plastering of an outer wall.

REPOUSSÉ: decoration of metal work by relief designs, formed by beating the metal from the back.

REREDOS: structure behind and above an altar.

RESPOND: half-pier bonded into a wall and carrying one end of an arch.

RETABLE: altarpiece, a picture or piece of carving, standing behind and attached to an altar.

RETICULATION: *see* Tracery (Fig. 22*e*).

REVEAL: that part of a jamb (q.v.) which lies between the glass or door and the outer surface of the wall.

RIB-VAULT: *see* Vault.

ROCOCO: latest phase of the Baroque style, current in most Continental countries between *c.* 1720 and *c.* 1760.

ROLL MOULDING: moulding of semicircular or more than semicircular section.

ROMANESQUE: that style in architecture which was current in the C11 and C12 and preceded the Gothic style (in England often called Norman). (Some scholars extend the use of the term Romanesque back to the C10 or C9.)

ROMANO-BRITISH: a somewhat vague term applied to the period and cultural features of Britain affected by the Roman occupation of the C1–5 A.D.

ROOD: cross or crucifix.

ROOD LOFT: singing gallery on the top of the rood screen, often supported by a coving (q.v.).

ROOD SCREEN: *see* Screen.

ROOD STAIRS: stairs to give access to the rood loft.

ROOF: *see* Figs. 14–18. *Single-framed:* if consisting entirely of transverse members (such as rafters with or without braces, collars, tie-beams, etc.) not tied together longitudinally. *Double-framed:* if longitudinal members (such as a ridge beam and purlins) are employed. As a rule in such cases the rafters are divided into stronger principals and weaker subsidiary rafters. *Hipped:* roof with sloped instead of vertical ends *Mansard:* roof with a double slope, the lower slope being larger and steeper than the upper. *Saddleback:* tower roof shaped like an ordinary gabled timber roof. The following members have special names: *Rafter:* roof-timber sloping up from the wall-plate to the ridge. *Principal:* principal rafter, usually corresponding to the main bay divisions of the nave or chancel below. *Wall-plate:* timber laid longitudinally on the top of a wall. *Purlins:* longitudinal members laid parallel with wall-plate and apex some way up the slope of the roof. These are side purlins and may be *tenoned* into the principal rafter, or they may be *through purlins*, i.e. resting in slots cut into the back of the principals. *Clasped purlins:* purlins held between collar-beam and principal rafter. *Collar purlin:* a lengthwise beam supporting the collar-beams, found in the context of crown-post roofs, which do not have a ridge-piece. *Tie-beam:* beam connecting the two slopes of a roof at the height of the wall-plate, to prevent the roof from spreading. *Cambered tie-beam roof:* one in which the ridge and purlins are laid directly on a cambered tie-beam; in a *firred tie-beam roof* a solid blocking piece (firring piece) is interposed between the cambered tie-beam and the purlins. *Collar-beam:* tie-beam applied higher up the slope of the roof. *Strut:* an upright or sloping timber supporting a transverse member, e.g. connecting tie-beam with rafter. *Post:* an upright timber supporting a lengthwise beam. *Kingpost:* an upright timber carried on a tie-beam and supporting the ridge-beam (*see* Fig. 14). *Crown-post:* an upright timber carried on a tie-beam and supporting a collar purlin, and usually braced to it and the collar-beam with four-way struts (*see* Fig. 15). *Queenposts:* two upright timbers placed symmetrically on a tie-beam and supporting purlins (*see* Fig. 16); if such timbers support a collar-beam or rafters they are *queen-struts* (*see* Fig. 17). *Braces:* inclined timbers inserted to strengthen others. Usually

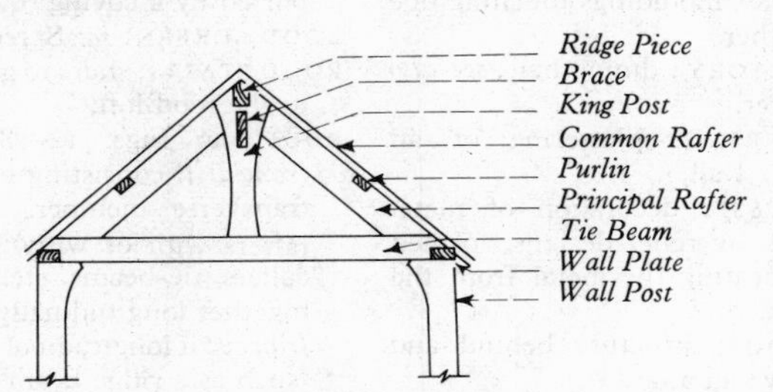

Fig. 14. Kingpost roof

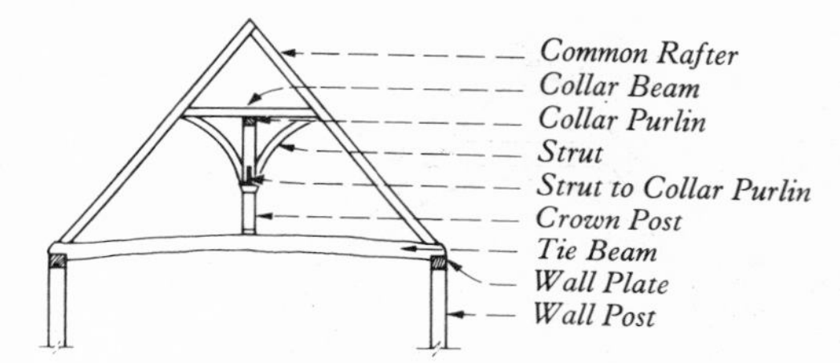

Fig. 15. Crown-post roof

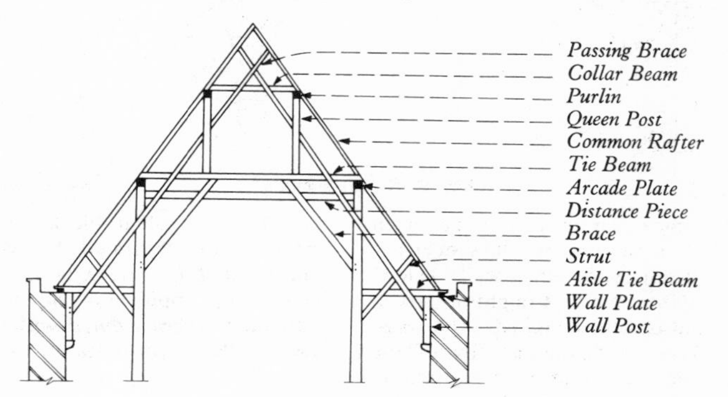

Fig. 16. Queen post roof

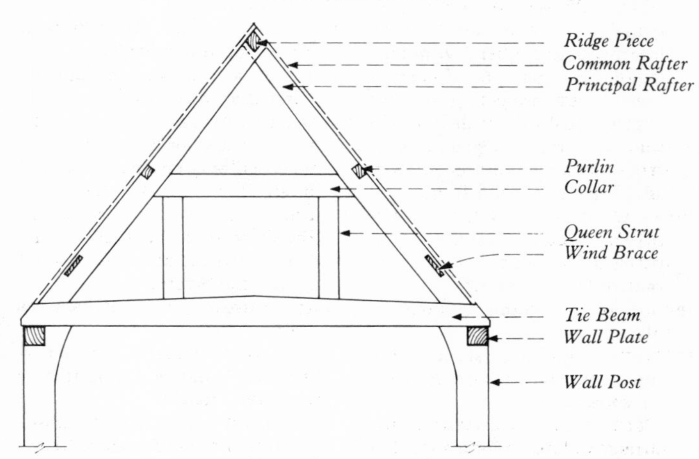

Fig. 17. Queen-strut roof

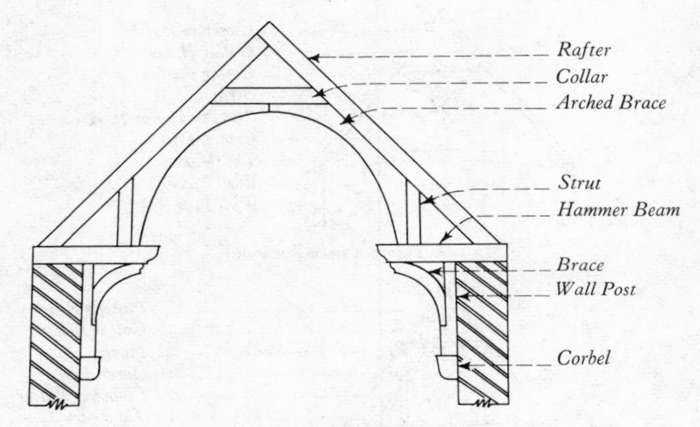

Fig. 18. Hammerbeam roof

braces connect a collar-beam with the rafters below or a tie-beam with the wall below. Braces can be straight or curved (also called arched). *Passing-brace:* a brace, usually of the same scantling as the common rafters and parallel to them, which stiffens a roof laterally by being halved across one or more intermediate timbers within its length (*see* Fig. 16). *Hammer-beam:* beam projecting at right angles, usually from the top of a wall, to carry arched braces or struts and arched braces (*see* Fig. 18). *See also* Wagon Roof.

ROSE WINDOW (or WHEEL WINDOW): circular window with patterned tracery arranged to radiate from the centre.

ROTUNDA: building circular in plan.

RUBBLE: building stones, not square or hewn, nor laid in regular courses.

RUSTICATION: *rock-faced* if the surfaces of large blocks of ashlar stone are left rough like rock; *smooth* if the ashlar blocks are smooth and separated by V-joints; *banded* if the separation by V-joints applies only to the horizontals; *vermiculated*, with a texture like worm-holes.

SADDLEBACK: *see* Roof.

SALTIRE CROSS: equal-limbed cross placed diagonally.

SANCTUARY: (1) area around the main altar of a church (*see* Presbytery); (2) sacred site consisting of wood or stone uprights enclosed by a circular bank and ditch. Beginning in the Neolithic, they were elaborated in the succeeding Bronze Age. The best known examples are Stonehenge and Avebury.

SARCOPHAGUS: elaborately carved coffin.

SCAGLIOLA: material composed of cement and colouring matter to imitate marble.

SCALLOPED CAPITAL: development of the block capital (q.v.) in which the single semicircular

Fig. 19. Scalloped capital

surface is elaborated into a series of truncated cones (Fig. 19).

SCARP: artificial cutting away of the ground to form a steep slope.

SCREEN: *Parclose screen:* screen separating a chapel from the rest of a church. *Rood screen:* screen below the rood (q.v.), usually at the W end of a chancel.

SCREENS PASSAGE: passage between the entrances to kitchen, buttery, etc., and the screen behind which lies the hall of a medieval house.

SEDILIA: seats for the priests (usually three) on the S side of the chancel of a church.

SEGMENTAL ARCH: *see* Arch.

SET-OFF: *see* Weathering.

SEXPARTITE: *see* Vault.

SGRAFFITO: pattern incised into plaster so as to expose a dark surface underneath.

SHAFT-RING: motif of the C12 and C13 consisting of a ring round a circular pier or a shaft attached to a pier. Also called Annulet.

SHAPED GABLE: *see* Gable.

SHEILA-NA-GIG: fertility figure, usually with legs wide open.

SILL: lower horizontal part of the frame of a window.

SLATEHANGING: the covering of walls by overlapping rows of slates, on a timber substructure. Tilehanging is similar.

SOFFIT: underside of an arch, lintel, etc. Also called Archivolt.

SOLAR: upper living-room of a medieval house.

SOPRAPORTA: painting above the door of a room, usual in the C17 and C18.

SOUNDING BOARD: horizontal board or canopy over a pulpit. Also called Tester.

SPANDREL: triangular surface between one side of an arch, the horizontal drawn from its apex, and the vertical drawn from its springer; also the surface between two arches.

SPERE-TRUSS: roof truss on two free-standing posts to mask the division between screens passage and hall. The screen itself, where a spere-truss exists, was originally movable.

SPIRE: tall pyramidal or conical pointed erection often built on top of a tower, turret, etc. *Broach Spire:* a broach is a sloping half-pyramid of masonry or wood introduced at the base of each of the four oblique faces of a tapering octagonal spire with the object of effecting the transition from the square to the octagon. The *splayed foot spire* is a variation of the broach form found principally in the south-eastern counties. In this form the four cardinal faces are splayed out near their base, to cover the corners, while oblique (or intermediate) faces taper away to a point. *Needle Spire:* thin spire rising from the centre of a tower roof, well inside the parapet.

SPIRELET: *see* Flèche.

SPLAY: chamfer, usually of the jamb of a window.

SPRINGING: level at which an arch rises from its supports.

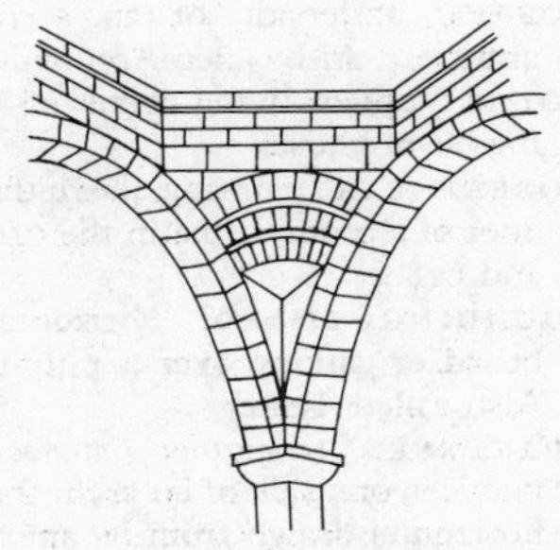

Fig. 20. Squinch

SQUINCH: arch or system of concentric arches thrown across the angle between two walls to support a superstructure, for example a dome (Fig. 20).

SQUINT: a hole cut in a wall or through a pier to allow a view of the main altar of a church from places whence it could not otherwise be seen. Also called Hagioscope.

STALL: carved seat, one of a row, made of wood or stone.

STAUNCHION: upright iron or steel member.

STEEPLE: the tower of a church together with a spire.

STIFF-LEAF: E.E. type of foliage of many-lobed shapes (Fig. 21).

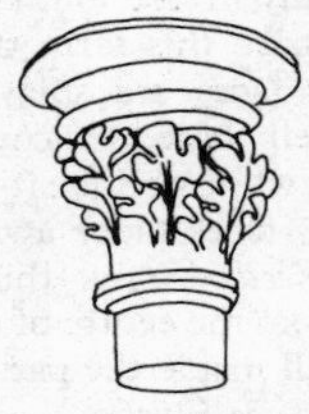

Fig. 21. Stiff-leaf capital

STILTED: *see* Arch (Fig. 1*d*).

STOREY-POSTS: the principal posts of a timber-framed wall.

STOUP: vessel for the reception of holy water, usually placed near a door.

STRAINER ARCH: arch inserted across a room to prevent the walls from leaning.

STRAPWORK: C16 decoration consisting of interlaced bands, and forms similar to fretwork or cut and bent leather.

STRETCHER: *see* Brickwork.

STRING COURSE: projecting horizontal band or moulding set in the surface of a wall.

STRUT: *see* Roof.

STUCCO: plaster work.

STUDS: the subsidiary vertical timber members of a timber-framed wall.

SWAG: festoon (q.v.) formed by a carved piece of cloth suspended from both ends.

TABERNACLE: richly ornamented niche or free-standing canopy. Usually contains the Holy Sacrament.

TARSIA: inlay in various woods.

TAZZA: shallow bowl on a foot.

TERMINAL FIGURES (TERMS, TERMINI): upper part of a human figure growing out of a pier, pilaster, etc., which tapers towards the base. *See also* Atlantes, Caryatid, Pilaster.

TERRACOTTA: burnt clay, unglazed.

TESSELLATED PAVEMENT: mosaic flooring, particularly Roman, consisting of small 'tesserae' or cubes of glass, stone, or brick.

TESSERAE: *see* Tessellated Pavement.

TESTER: *see* Sounding Board.

TETRASTYLE: having four detached columns.

THREE-DECKER PULPIT: pulpit with clerk's stall below and reading desk below the clerk's stall.

TIE-BEAM: *see* Roof (Figs. 14–17).

TIERCERON: *see* Vault (Fig. 23).

TILEHANGING: *see* Slatehanging.

TIMBER-FRAMING: method of construction where walls are built of timber framework with the spaces filled in by plaster or brickwork. Sometimes the timber is covered over with plaster or boarding laid horizontally.

TOMB-CHEST: a chest-shaped stone coffin, the most usual medieval form of funeral monument.

TOUCH: soft black marble quarried near Tournai.

TOURELLE: turret corbelled out from the wall.

TRACERY: intersecting ribwork in the upper part of a window, or used decoratively in blank arches, on vaults, etc. *Plate tracery: see* Fig. 22(*a*). Early form of tracery where decoratively shaped openings are cut through the solid stone infilling in a window head. *Bar tracery:* a form introduced into England *c.* 1250. Intersecting ribwork made up of slender shafts, continuing the lines of the mullions of windows up to a decorative mesh in the head of the window. *Geometrical tracery: see* Fig. 22(*b*). Tracery characteristic of *c.* 1250–1310 consisting chiefly of circles or foiled circles. *Y-tracery: see* Fig. 22(*c*). Tracery consisting of a mullion which branches into two forming a Y shape; typical of *c.* 1300. *Intersecting tracery: see* Fig. 22(*d*). Tracery in which each mullion of a window branches out into two curved bars in such a way that every one of them is drawn with the same radius from a different centre. The result is that every light of the window is a lancet and every two, three, four, etc., lights together form a pointed arch. This treatment also is typical of *c.* 1300. *Reticulated tracery: see* Fig. 22(*e*). Tracery typical of the early C14 consisting entirely of circles drawn at top and bottom into ogee shapes so that a net-like appearance results. *Panel tracery: see* Fig. 22(*f*) and (*g*). Perp tracery, which is formed of upright straight-sided panels above lights of a window.

TRANSEPT: transverse portion of a cross-shaped church.

TRANSOM: horizontal bar across the openings of a window.

TRANSVERSE ARCH: *see* Vault.

TREFOIL: *see* Foil.

TRIBUNE: *see* Gallery.

TRICIPUT, SIGNUM TRICIPUT: sign of the Trinity expressed by

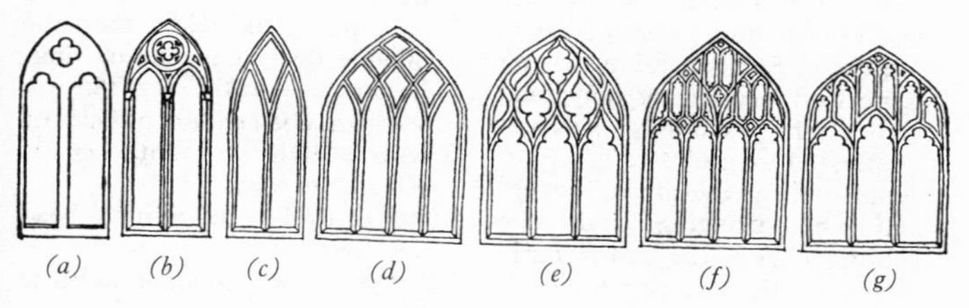

Fig. 22. Tracery

three faces belonging to one head.

TRIFORIUM: arcaded wall passage or blank arcading facing the nave at the height of the aisle roof and below the clerestory (q.v.) windows. (*See also* Gallery.)

TRIGLYPHS: blocks with vertical grooves separating the metopes (q.v.) in the Doric frieze (Fig. 12).

TROPHY: sculptured group of arms or armour, used as a memorial of victory.

TRUMEAU: stone mullion (q.v.) supporting the tympanum (q.v.) of a wide doorway.

TUMULUS: *see* Barrow.

TURRET: very small tower, round or polygonal in plan.

TUSCAN: *see* Order.

TYMPANUM: space between the lintel of a doorway and the arch above it.

UNDERCROFT: vaulted room, sometimes underground, below a church or chapel.

UNIVALLATE: of a hill-fort: defended by a single bank and ditch.

UPPER PALAEOLITHIC: *see* Palaeolithic.

VAULT: *see* Fig. 23. *Barrel-vault:* *see* Tunnel-vault. *Cross-vault:* *see* Groin-vault. *Domical vault:* square or polygonal dome rising direct on a square or polygonal bay, the curved surfaces separated by groins (q.v.). *Fan-vault:* late medieval vault where all ribs springing from one springer are of the same length, the same distance from the next, and the same curvature. *Groin-vault* or *Cross-vault:* vault of two tunnel-vaults of identical shape intersecting each other at r. angles. Chiefly Norman and Renaissance. *Lierne:* tertiary rib, that is, rib which does not spring either from one of the main springers or from the central boss. Introduced in the C14, continues to the C16. *Quadripartite vault:* one wherein one bay of vaulting is divided into four parts. *Rib-vault:* vault with diagonal ribs projecting along the groins. *Ridge-rib:* rib along the longitudinal or transverse ridge of a vault. Introduced in the early C13. *Sexpartite vault:* one wherein one bay of quadripartite vaulting is divided into two parts transversely so that each bay of vaulting has six parts. *Tierceron:* secondary rib, that is, rib which issues from one of the main springers or the central boss and leads to a place on a ridge-rib. Introduced in the early C13. *Transverse arch:* arch separating one bay of a vault from the next. *Tunnel-vault* or *Barrel-vault:* vault of semicircular or pointed section. Chiefly Norman and Renaissance.

VAULTING SHAFT: vertical member leading to the springer of a vault.

VENETIAN WINDOW: window with three openings, the central one arched and wider than the outside ones. Current in England chiefly in the C17–18.

VERANDA: open gallery or balcony with a roof on light, usually metal, supports.

VESICA: oval with pointed head and foot.

VESTIBULE: anteroom or entrance hall.

VILLA: (1) according to Gwilt (1842) 'a country house for the residence of opulent persons'; (2) Romano-British country houses cum farms, to which the description given in (1) more or less applies. They developed with the growth of urbanization. The basic type is the simple corridor pattern with rooms opening off a single passage; the next stage is the addition of wings. The courtyard villa fills a square plan with subsidiary buildings and an enclosure wall with a gate facing the main corridor block.

VITRIFIED: made similar to glass.

VITRUVIAN OPENING: a door or window which diminishes towards the top, as advocated by Vitruvius, bk. IV, chapter VI.

VOLUTE: spiral scroll, one of the component parts of an Ionic column (*see* Order).

VOUSSOIR: wedge-shaped stone used in arch construction.

WAGON ROOF: roof in which by closely set rafters with arched braces the appearance of the inside of a canvas tilt over a wagon is achieved. Wagon roofs can be panelled or plastered (ceiled) or left uncovered. Also called Cradle Roof.

WAINSCOT: timber lining to walls.

WALL-PLATE: *see* Roof.

WATERLEAF: leaf shape used in later C12 capitals. The waterleaf is a broad, unribbed, tapering leaf curving up towards the angle of the abacus and turned in at the top (Fig. 24).

WEALDEN HOUSE: timber-framed house with the hall in the centre and wings projecting only slightly and only on the jutting upper floor. The roof, however, runs through without a break between wings and hall, and the eaves of the hall part are therefore exceptionally deep. They are supported by diagonal, usu-

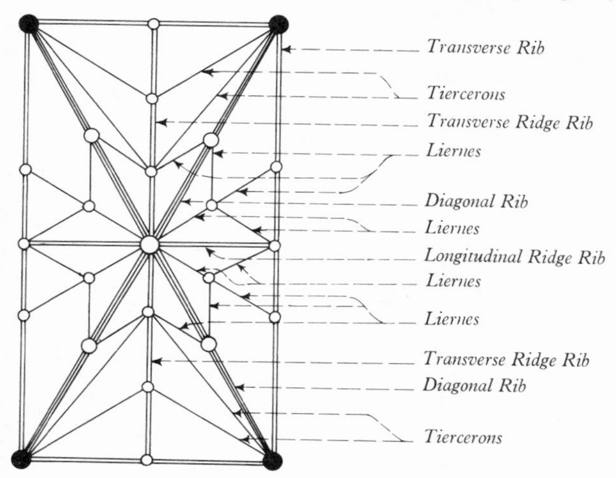

Fig. 23. Vault

ally curved, braces starting from the short inner sides of the overhanging wings and rising parallel with the front wall of the hall towards the centre of the eaves.

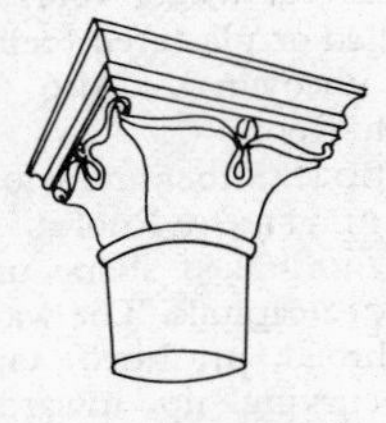

Fig. 24. Waterleaf capital

WEATHERBOARDING: overlapping horizontal boards, covering a timber-framed wall.

WEATHERING: sloped horizontal surface on sills, buttresses, etc., to throw off water. Also called Set-off.

WEEPERS: small figures placed in niches along the sides of some medieval tombs. Also called Mourners.

WHEEL WINDOW: *see* Rose Window.

INDEX OF PLATES

INDEX OF ARTISTS

INDEX OF PLACES

ADDENDA

AUGUST 1977

p. 106 [Brampton.] BIRLEY GRANGE, ½ m. NW. Dated 1689. With a rusticated architrave door surround, a Baroque scroll over, and a ball finial (DOE).

p. 110 [Brizlincote Hall.] According to Knyff's view of Bretby Hall of *c.* 1700, there were similar pediments on the ends of the wings, added as part of the second Earl's extensive post-Restoration improvements (RE).

p. 122 [Carnfield Hall.] There is evidence in the S wing for a previous timber-framed house. The present house is probably of *c.* 1630, remodelled between 1693 and 1699 (RCHM).

p. 125 [Chapel-en-le-Frith.] SCHOOL, High Street. Elizabethan-style, 1839 by *Robert Potter* of Lichfield.

p. 125 [Chapel-en-le-Frith, Bank Hall, lodge.] This was *Unwin*'s home from 1896 to 1904, during his partnership with Parker in Buxton.

p. 151 [Chesterfield.] BROOKSIDE, New Brampton. *Percy Houfton*'s own house, built before 1922 and influenced by the local vernacular.

p. 168 [Derby, Cathedral.] The old tower was demolished *c.* 1475. The new one had been begun by 1520 and was finished in 1532. The mason *John Otes*, first mentioned in 1527, worked under Wastell at King's College, Cambridge.

p. 202 [Duffield.] MOSCOW FARM. One of the farms built by the Strutts to supply their workers (cf. Crossroads Farm, Belper). Brick arches were used in the construction according to Glover. (Were they supported by iron framing as in the Strutt mills?)

p. 259 [Kedleston, Home or Ireton Farm.] Is this by *Adam* and *Wyatt*? According to correspondence at Kedleston and drawings in the Soane Museum they designed the poultry yard.

p. 259 [Kingsterndale.] CHURCH. By *Bonomi*. Small, E. E.